THE ESTABLISHMENT
IN TEXAS POLITICS

Contributions in Political Science
Series Editor: BERNARD K. JOHNPOLL

THE ESTABLISHMENT IN TEXAS POLITICS

THE PRIMITIVE YEARS, 1938–1957

GEORGE NORRIS GREEN

Contributions in Political Science, Number 21

Greenwood Press

Westport, Connecticut • London, England

Library of Congress Cataloging in Publication Data

Green, George Norris.
  The establishment in Texas politics.

  (Contributions in political science ; no. 21 ISSN 0147-1066)
  Bibliography: p.
  Includes index.
  1. Texas—Politics and government—1865-1950.
  2. Texas—Politics and government—1951-   I. Title.
  II. Series.
  F391.G76   320.9′764′06   ~~78-55340~~
  ISBN 0-313-20525-6   78-55339

Library of Congress Catalog Card Number: 78-55340
ISBN: 0-313-20525-6
ISSN: 0147-1066

First published in 1979

Greenwood Press, Inc.
51 Riverside Avenue, Westport, Connecticut 06880

Printed in the United States of America

10 9 8 7 6 5 4 3 2 1

For My Parents

MALCOLM AND ELIZABETH GREEN

Contents

Illustrations

Preface

State political histories about recent times have not received much attention from professional historians. Most historians are not very interested in state history, and, perhaps, the political histories of many states are not very interesting. Necessary primary records are also doubtless unavailable in some states. Texas, however, with its history of producing nationally prominent leaders and with its burgeoning population and natural resources, is important as states go, and few would argue that its politics are not fascinating. Also a wealth of primary resource materials has been opened in the state during the past several years.

Since some of the forces that enmesh to create Texas's political history are unique, this work probably cannot be considered a case study. Yet the Texas political scene from 1938 to 1957 was similar to that of several of its smaller southern brethren. The Lone Star state's political performance during those crucial years appears to constitute one of the more monumental failures of states' rights in the twentieth-century South. By the end of the period Texas was drifting out of the southern orbit.

During an earlier time, roughly between Reconstruction and World War II, corporate interest groups were forced to share the Texas political limelight with reform movements and a few colorful politicians. In the late 1930s, however, the corporations got a grip on the state that they have yet to relinquish. Texans have voted for an unbroken line of conservative governors and legislatures since 1939, a political history probably unparalleled in the nation. The 1938 to 1957 period marked the most primitive phase of this Establishment rule, reflected in numerous and harsh antilabor laws, the suppression of academic freedom, a segregationist philosophy, elections marred by demagoguery and corruption, the devolution of the daily press, and a state government that offered its citizens, especially the minorities, very few services. The Establishment, a loosely knit plutocracy of the Anglo upper classes, were induced to modify the harsher features of their control after the elections of 1956 and 1957. Since then conservative hegemony has been more relaxed and mature than in the earlier epoch.

The effects of the earlier period linger on, of course. Important elements in the state's political structure originated during the primitive years, including the three-way competition among conservative Democrats, liberal Democrats, and Republicans. It became the trend for a liberal to muster enough strength in a field of generally conservative candidates to force a runoff in the Democratic gubernatorial primary, but then to lose as the conservative vote, money, and press coalesced around the conservative survivor of the first primary. Republicans were trounced in general elections, except for the two presidential contests in the 1950s, but by 1957 they showed signs of offering genuine competition against the reigning Democrats on the state level and have occasionally continued to do so. Finally Democratic party bolting and indifferent support for party nominees, although not unknown before the late 1930s, became commonplace in the primitive years and have been constantly practiced and threatened since then.

The mature Establishment of the 1960s and 1970s seldom engages in demagoguery and no longer actively attacks labor and minority groups, but it still does not deliver many services to its citizenry. This is particularly tragic since wise taxation on Texas's abundant natural resources once would have allowed, say, the building of a first-rate network of schools around the state, and may still do so, but it will require a different leadership than prevails in 1978.

Some readers will find this book depressing, and the political leaders described in it have plainly achieved what H. L. Mencken called "natural instinct for the low, disingenuous, fradulent manipulations that constitute the art and mystery of politics under democracy."[1] The wonder is that the state has survived at all, and perhaps it is actually under the special protection of God, as many of the state's clergymen used to allege on Texas Independence Day. At any rate, through the years, I nevertheless continue to be strangely exhilarated by watching and practicing Texas politics. I hope readers can stave off the feelings of depression and allow themselves to be infected, however temporarily, by the uniqueness and excitation of Texas' own "carnival of buncombe."

During the research and writing of this book, I became obliged to the librarians and archivists at the following institutions: the University of Texas at Austin, Texas Tech University, Texas A & M University, the University of Missouri, Sam Rayburn Library, the Library of Congress Manuscripts Division, the Dallas Historical Society, Lyndon B. Johnson Library, Dwight Eisenhower Library, Harry S. Truman Library, and Franklin D. Roosevelt Library. I am particularly indebted to Chris LaPlante and the rest of the courteous staff at the Texas State Archives and to Marian Orgain, director of Special Collections at the University of Houston. I owe special thanks to J. C. Martin, Jan Hart, and all the excellent and patient staff at the University of Texas at Arlington Archives, who have tolerated me for many years now.

I am exceedingly grateful to University of Texas at Arlington head librarian John Hudson, *Texas Observer* publisher Ronnie Dugger, and the late columnist Stuart Long for reading earlier versions of this manuscript and offering constructive criticism. Political veteran Creekmore Fath was also kind enough to read several chapters. Congressman Bob Eckhardt and *Austin American-Statesman* cartoonist Ben Sargent graciously allowed me to use some of their cartoons. It is a pleasure to note that my mentors at Florida State University, Richard Bartlett and Bill Hair, played a role in inspiring this work. Any imperfections in the book, as well as the political interpretations, are my sole responsibility.

Much of the labor-related research was carried out years ago under a National Endowment for the Humanities Fellowship, and the out-of-state research was partially funded by a grant from the organized research fund at the University of Texas at Arlington. I appreciate the assistance of several typists who helped put together the final manuscript: Sue Williamson, Charlotte Sanders, Kay May, and Claire Lawrence. I gratefully acknowledge permission to publish copyrighted material from my articles, "W. Lee O'Daniel and Texas Politics: The 1942 Campaign," *McNeese Review* 23 (Summer 1977):3-10, and "McCarthyism in Texas: The 1954 Campaign," *Southern Quarterly* 16 (April 1978):255-276, where portions of this book appeared in somewhat different form.

Finally, my wife Kathryn read innumerable gubernatorial letters, took notes, typed and edited, and sustained the project at every juncture. Without her help this book would never have come about, and I owe her more than words can express.

THE ESTABLISHMENT
IN TEXAS POLITICS

1

Texas, Our Texas

*I find over here that most of the French and English
believe that Texas IS an independent nation NOW. I
have talked with a lot of people who have heard
of Texas, but who didn't know that it was supposed
to be part of the U.S. I preach Texas day and night.*

Major Homer Fry to Beauford Jester,
January 23, 1947, advocating Texas's
secession from the Union

*Any man born in the United States is twice-blessed.
And he is thrice-blessed if born in Texas.*
H. Ross Perot

During the past two generations—about since 1939—Texas has been governed by conservatives, collectively dubbed the Establishment. There are other states, of course, that have long been dominated by standpat politicians, but the Texas type of conservatism seems more virulent and entrenched than most other strains. One factor that exacerbates the state's conservatism is "Texanism" or "super-Americanism." We Americans have enjoyed a history of security and success that has made us conscious of our strength, a history that has given us what Sir Denis Brogan calls "the illusion of American omnipotence." The illusion is magnified in Texas, the only state that ever stood as a viable republic and long the largest state in the Union. Of all the states, only Texas won its own independence by shedding its own blood on its own soil, by hurling back a "foreign invader." Texans believe that there is a difference politically between their state and other states, and that the federal government is almost a foreign menace to Texas rights and privileges. Texas history is treated in the state's public schools as if it were about as important as United States history; state law even allows college students to substitute three hours of Texas history for one half of the required six hours of American history. The state's history and legends are taught to its children with far greater intensity than a Boston child is taught about the battle of Bunker Hill. Not many years ago the Texas constitution, a documental derelict famous for its verbosity and lack of clarity, was defended against revisionists on the grounds that it was sacred.[1]

"Texanism" may arise on any occasion. When gasoline rationing was decreed during World War II, Texans fought to be exempted because they had plenty of gas in their own backyard. Another wartime conservation measure cut the length of coffins from six feet six inches to six feet three inches. The state's undertakers protested, apparently endorsing the tribal myth that Texans are taller than other Americans. During the legal tussle between Texas and the federal government over the ownership of the offshore oil lands, Governor Price Daniel announced that he was combating the United States by reactivating the Texas navy. All Texans knew that the fleet had become a mythical body whose best-known admiral was Ginger Rogers, but Daniel went on to request solemnly the owners of 286,000 pleasure boats to "register their craft as ready for emergency service at any time." Even as a jest, the order implies that Texans will fight to prove that they are not subject to the same laws as other Americans. The old Ford assembly plant in Dallas advertised its cars as "Made in Texas by Texans," and decals were available with this slogan.[2]

Anglo-Texas nationalism retains what has been labeled a complementarity of social communication—a feeling that Texans can communicate more effectively with other Texans, even with those hundreds of miles across the state when Oklahoma, New Mexico, or Louisiana neighbors are only a few miles across the border. The feeling may be an illusion, but it is nonetheless real. This solidarity is fading somewhat before the onslaught of emigration, instant communciations, rapid transportation, and high mobility. The Mexican-American and black minorities, which were powerless and unassimilated, rarely felt any fierce loyalty to the state or desire to enhance its power and prestige. Their social and economic gains of the past two generations have probably also helped undermine Texas nationalism. Although no state or region is immune to America's assimilation process, one historian in the 1970s concluded—just as John Gunther did in the 1940s and Theodore White in the 1950s—that Texas's "demonstrative display of excessive pride" was recognized by all Americans and that "there is nothing comparable in any of the other states."[3] Such insular pride discourages any feeling that some changes might be desirable.

Another factor promoting extreme conservatism in Texas is the unique convergence of southern, western, and Mexican traditions. While this amalgam produces a cosmopolitanism unusual in the South and Southwest, it does not always operate for the public good. The bulk of the 1.5 million to 2 million Mexican-Americans, with notable exceptions, live in ignorance and political inertia. They are more poorly educated, have a lower income, and are probably more culturally isolated than Texas blacks are. Bound by a heritage of poverty, illiteracy, and allegiance to one-man-rule—in their institutions and communities—tens of thousands of them historically have been manipulated by patróns who take advantage of these feudal traditions. These unscrupulous political bosses have not only been contemptuous of the democratic process but also have been expert in plundering the public till. Since the early 1960s, considerable Anglo tension has arisen over the latent political power of the Mexican-American majority in south Texas. The feudal baronies behind the "cactus curtain" may be giving way—though gradually— to the rising expectations of the Chicanos. Brown power is most dramatically symbolized by the la raza movement that captured a few towns (by majority rule) in the 1960s and 1970s and the Valley Farm Workers organizing drive that was crushed in 1967.[4]

The story of the Parr family in Duval County illustrates Establishment adaptations to the worst aspects of Mexican political customs. In the early part of this century, Archie Parr was a cowboy county commissioner who cultivated strong ties with the Mexican-American majority of the population. He sided with them in an election day shoot-out in 1912 against the Anglo Republicans. Since that time the reigning member of the Parr family— always a Democrat—has ruled as the duke of Duval. Archie and his son George, who succeeded as jefe or patrón in the 1930s, treated the county budget virtually as their own personal bank account, but they saw to it that a good deal of money, food, clothing, and lesser political offices trickled down to the loyal subjects. Just to ensure voter regularity, pistoleros accompanied many illiterate peons into the voting booths. Parr-endorsed candidates, usually Establishment conservatives, racked up majorities as large as a hundred to one. Archie was hauled into court a couple of times, and George was actually convicted three times (mail fraud, 1956, and income tax evasion, 1934 and 1974). With his empire and personal fortunes crumbling, George committed suicide in 1975. His nephew Archer briefly attempted to perpetuate the Parr reign but soon went to prison for perjury.

The Parr machine is evidently finished, but that does not necessarily mean that machine politics have disappeared from Duval County. Rival factions have picked up the cudgels. Over the years the Parrs dominated Duval County and exerted heavy influence over petty despots in Zapata, Jim Hogg, Jim Wells, and Starr counties, among others. The Guerras, who have been in the area since 1767, have run Starr County since about 1911; the Guerra family has also long been prominent in Jim Hogg County. Judge Manuel J. Raymond's long reign in Webb County was eventually replaced by the more refined Martins and Kazens, but the entrenched Old Party was buried under a wave of court indictments in 1977, and Laredo mayor J. C. Martin, Jr., announced he would not seek reelection. The Klebergs (of the King Ranch) in Kleberg and Kenedy counties have been in the saddle for a century. Nearly all of the deep South Texas counties are run by these rich, conservative sheriffs and judges, distrustful of democracy, who dominate their areas

politically, economically, and socially. The patron system is more openly
dictatorial and paternalistic than Establishment rule in other Texas cities
and counties, but there are more similarities than differences. The patrons
are usually tied into the Texas power structure of oil, gas, banking, and
ranching.[5]

A more common ingredient in fostering reactionary politics is the traditional Old South legacy of ignorance, racism, fundamentalism, states' rights
at all costs, and a streak of violence. East Texas is the seat of this inheritance,
and there the Ku Klux Klan still rides, especially in the South's largest city,
Houston. In 1973—to cite a recent example of this heritage—one reporter
was allowed to interview and photograph Klan leaders in a secret nocturnal
meeting. He wrote: "A powerful flashlight was turned on me and a City of
Houston police officer removed my blindfold. Silently he searched me in
case I was concealing a tape recorder. He was the most frightening policeman
I had ever seen in the United States, for across his face and over his head he
wore the mask and hood of the Ku Klux Klan."[6] The Klansmen claimed
that they were giving up their long battle against integration and were now
locked in a death grip with a far more dangerous enemy, communism. Communism, in Klan eyes, embraces socialists, liberals, members of the American Civil Liberties Union, militant minority leaders, hippies, and sex films.
In the late 1960s and early 1970s Houston was plagued with hundreds of
bombings, burnings, shootings, and tire slashings. The mayor, a follower of
George Wallace, refused to investigate the local Klan, and the police chief,
another Wallace follower, could not boast of a single arrest. In 1974, after
these two officials departed, several purported Klan members were fired
from the police force. Even in the late 1970s, however, the Houston police
were widely regarded as the most violent law officers in the nation.[7]

The Klan has not been an important election force since the 1920s, but
too many local Establishment leaders in East Texas (especially since the
integration struggles of the mid-1950s) have been Klan sympathizers. By
winking at the activities and attitudes of this native American underground,
local leaders have allowed the entrenchment of reactionary political thought
and the erosion of democratic government. As one east Texan succinctly
put it: "There are two things that every genuine, true American should
have at his fingertips at all times: a gun and Bible."[8]

Certainly Texas's political behavior has been essentially southern in that
most of its battles have been fought within the Democratic party—primarily
because in 1860 a substantial part of its population consisted of black slaves.
The virulence of the state's politics has been exacerbated since the early
1940s by the existence of two powerful, organized factions within the one-
party system. Indeed as political scientist V. O. Key put it in 1949, "Texas
has developed the most bitter intra-Democratic fight along New Deal and
anti-New Deal lines in the South." With only one party, considerable dis-
sidence is inevitable within it—there is no other place to go. Even after the

frustrations and frayed nerves of internecine warfare, the Democrats find themselves in the same ring. Thus Texas's two Democratic senators in the 1940s—Tom Connally, who was hardly liberal but was a party loyalist, and W. Lee O'Daniel, whose voting record was "more Republican than most Republicans"—rarely conversed and even refused to allow their secretaries to deal with each other on state matters. Everyone felt the tension when Connally and O'Daniel walked into the same room. In the 1960s no other state could boast of a governor (conservative John Connally) and a senator (liberal Ralph Yarborough) in the same party who hardly spoke to each other and who took every opportunity to undermine each other for six years. It must be added that although other states have one-party systems, Texas is by far the richest of them; consequently the vested interests and their opponents have more to win or lose in the Lone Star state.[9]

There has been considerable debate among historians as to just what constitutes our western heritage. Logrollings, the building of forts, neighbors caring for the sick, and other collectivist endeavors have been cited to demonstrate that the idea of the frontier as a haven for individualism is a myth. This thesis may be correct, frontier individualism may be a historical myth, but today's west Texans are individualistic, and they think that quality is a frontier heritage. West Texas and the west-central Texas hill country are arid, sparse regions with monotonous beige prairies and extremes of heat, cold, droughts, winds, and floods. Such an environment, bound to leave an imprint on its people, has helped produce a self-sufficient, lonely, suspicious citizenry, slow to change. The ultraconservatism spawned, at least in part, by the west Texas environment and the frontier and vigilante memories have had serious material consequences in the region. Parts of west Texas, including the Midland-Odessa area, are critically short of water. Yet no sensible water program is being carried out because the people are too fearful of federal control and because the local Establishments are too provincial. Once the oil finally plays out, as one close observer noted, these people may actually prefer to create "ghost towns on the prairies."[10]

Candidates all over the state, but especially in west Texas, wear cowboy hats and identify themselves as cattlemen and ranchers, or at least as men of the soil. Terms that the frontier found objectionable are sometimes used by vindictive candidates, who may liken their opponents to rattlesnakes, coyotes, or gophers. Frontier symbols may divert attention from real issues. Upon signing an open-shop bill, for instance, Governor Beauford Jester announced that Texans had always supported the economic independence of an open range. Governor Coke Stevenson used his "hot coffee pot" phrase to gloss over his noninvolvement in important matters of state. Governor W. Lee O'Daniel, an urbanite, campaigned against Johnson grass, the bane of many farmers and ranchers because it saps moisture from row crops and is difficult to exterminate. West Texas's own conservative politics are often couched in frontier rhetoric. A Midland dentist wrote in

1961, ". . . if our grandfathers had fought the Indians and Red Coats like we are fighting the Communists, we wouldn't be alive today." This phraseology perhaps encourages voters to look backward, not the healthiest approach toward state affairs.[11]

Another view of Texas regionalism is afforded in a political scientist's study of the United States. American political culture, according to one analysis, is a mixture of three major political subcultures: the traditionalistic, the individualistic, and the moralistic. In an area dominated by traditionalistic politics, such as east and south Texas, government is in the hands of a small, paternalistic elite (the local Establishment) dedicated to preserving the status quo. They govern because of their family or social position, and they do not expect average citizens to participate in politics. In an individualistic political region, such as the Panhandle and west Texas, government does little more than protect the self-interest of the more aggressive individuals and groups. Such governments, largely in the hands of professional politicians, will not intervene in business activities, which they regard as private. Generally Texas combines traditionalism with strains of individualism, though it is the reverse in the western reaches. In a moralistic political culture, people believe that government exists to promote the shared interests of all citizens. Everyone is encouraged to participate. A moralistic government will intervene in private matters to advance the public good. But this philosophy did not seep into Texas. In 1969 still another political scientist seemed to be measuring traditionalism when he clocked each state's speed of adaptation to new policy ideas in solving problems. In the adoption of eighty-eight programs—a merit system for state employees, pollution controls, and child labor standards among them—Texas wallowed in forty-second place.[12]

One aspect of traditionalistic-individualistic Texas politics observed by journalist David Nevin among others is the tendency of Texas to emphasize material self-interest above notions of the public good. This fast-buck philosophy stresses movement and accomplishment, action rather than reflection, building rather than thinking. Two political scientists, Dan Nimmo and William Oden, have observed other Texas characteristics that deserve the designation of traditionalistic-individualistic. Both these political cultures, for instance, depend on an indifferent citizenry, and the polls taken over the years reveal that Texans are not very knowledgeable or concerned about state issues. Politicians are free to make policies without much public assistance or hindrance. Also keeping with the pattern are the one-party system, the consistently low level of electoral participation, and the extreme power of interest groups.[13]

Texas's brand of conservatism also feeds upon the enormous changes in the state in the past thirty years. Two generations ago cotton was still king; the sixteen million acres once devoted to it have now shrunk to four million. Odessa claimed only twenty-four hundred people in 1930 and over eighty thousand by 1960. In the same period greater Houston climbed from about three hundred thousand to over a million and easily led the nation's cities in postwar construction and capital investment. In 1930 Dallas was a wholesaling and cotton trading center; today it is the financial capital of the Southwest, with two of the nation's top twenty-five banks and a host of insurance companies. Such new wealth, according to a trio of Texas political scientists, is "fretful, suspicious, and uneasy, especially when it rests on an economically volatile petroleum base." In the 1930s and 1940s many of the newly urbanized financiers of militantly conservative causes, such as Hugh Roy Cullen, H. L. Hunt, Sid Richardson, and Clint Murchison, were preoccupied with making their first ten or twenty million dollars. Then, as one millionaire phrased it in the 1950s. "We all made money fast. We were interested in nothing else. Then this Communist business burst upon us. Were we going to lose what we had gained?" Cullen, Hunt, Richardson, and Murchison were throwbacks to the robber baron era.[14] As the leading chronicler of oil politics put it: "Their simple image of the boundless opportunity for all who would reach out for it has been reinforced by their own experiences and unchallenged by continuous direct dealings with stockholders, unions, welfare problems, and social responsibility. Interference with profits and regulation by government easily became equated with socialism."[15]

Corporate influence in Texas, whether based on oil, banking, insurance, or other lesser but burgeoning industries, hails from within the state and from without. No attempt is made to distinguish between the two, since it does not appear to matter. In any case the economic power of the Texas conservatives gives political meaning to their reaction against social change. As Theodore White wrote:

> These elements—the common national struggle, the unsettling effect of rapid change, the myths of Texanism—are in themselves almost enough to explain why Texas politics has taken on such a peculiar cast. But when all these elements are manipulated by clever men and by the kind of money the Little Rich—the prosperous car dealers, the contractors, the bottling concessionaires, the little oil men, the real estate men—can make available to state candidates of their choice, these emotions can be made to stand up and march.[16]

Some of the blame for political tensions must devolve on unscrupulous public relations men, those who use the most sordid tactics to propel their clients to victory. They can be found everywhere, of course, but as one former public relations man admitted to *Texas Observer* writer Bill Brammer, Texas is so big that it takes a great deal of propagandizing over the whole state for an idea to sink in with the people, so issues are always oversimplified and given an emotional twist. If no simple issues arise, he noted, the real ones are tossed aside, and "nice new primitive ones are fabricated." In Texas this strategy was long known as "the glandular technique" and was credited for the election of several conservative and reactionary politicians.[17]

Corporate PR had a hand in converting Texas newspapers into something of a plaything for the propertied class, beginning around 1945. Indeed public relations and the press became intertwined. One Texas editor conceded in 1953:

> The fact remains . . . that any editor worth his salt knows that he is just about as dependent upon the public relations man as they are about him.
> The task of covering the news . . . has become a job of such magnitude and of such complexity that it cannot be done without help.
> No newspaper could afford the staff it would take to turn out the vast amount of news that fills the papers every day.[18]

In 1939 the Austin newspapers helped destroy the sales tax lobby, and during the war the Scripps-Howard papers in Texas criticized some of the more corrosive lobbyists. Much of the urban press exposed the W. Lee O'Daniel smokescreeens in 1941 and 1942, but the war years seemed to drain the papers of what little crusading zeal they had. Shortly after the war, columnist Lynn Landrum suggested, "If you don't like what the newspaper says or does, you can always go out and start your own newspaper." Landrum may have even believed what he wrote, but in fact even such multimillionaires as Jim West and Karl Hoblitzelle had already failed in the publishing business. The columnist may have been responding to criticism of his own paper, the *Dallas Morning News*, a supposedly respectable family organ. In the postwar years the *News* and most other Texas dailies provided a creditable platform for some of the baser political convictions of the day. The *News*, for instance, opined that the presidency of Franklin Roosevelt was actually destructive of the Republic, the Senate's censure of Joe McCarthy "a happy day for Communists," and the Supreme Court "a threat to state sovereignty second only to Communism itself." Radio and television stations echoed the ultraconservative drumbeat of conformity, not because they took a stand on anything themselves, but because it was the conservatives who had the monetary resources to buy political advertising time. The effects of the mass media upon deeds and votes cannot readily be measured, but as was noted long ago, "Whatsoever a man soweth, that shall he also reap."[19]

The interaction of all these factors—Texanism, the politically unhealthy convergence of the Old South, Wild West, and Mexican cultures, the rapid and turbulent economic changes, and the rise of reactionary newspapers, and unprincipled public relations men—help explain Texas's persistent and unyielding conservatism of the 1940s and 1950s. Even before the tumultuous decades between 1938 and 1957, when the conservative grip was strongest, the state's political history revealed that it was a happy hunting ground for predatory interest groups.

2

The Rise
of Conservatism

> *We have only two or three laws [in Texas], such as*
> *against murder before witnesses and being caught*
> *stealing horses, and voting the Republican ticket.*
> O. Henry as a Texas newspaperman
> in the 1890s

> *I saw too many utility, gas, and oil officials and*
> *executives milling about the convention and heading*
> *committees to make me an enthusiastic member of the*
> *Democratic party.*
> Letter to the editor of *Emancipator*,
> September 1940

> *I don't know anywhere else where the people of*
> *substance have this type of working political relation-*
> *ship to each other. You know, not like it's schemed*
> *out, but everybody just gets the idea and they go the*
> *same way.*
> Texas lobbyist Ed Clark, 1960

Texas politics took on a breezy, free-for-all style as soon as the Anglo-Americans arrived in the state. In the quarter century before the Civil War, many of the issues of the day whirled around Sam Houston. As president of the Republic of Texas, Houston evoked controversy with his economizing and his peaceable policies toward Mexicans and Indians. Then, after Texas was annexed, as senator and later as governor, he antagonized an eventual majority of Texans with his unionist positions in the face of the secession movement and secession itself. Not all of these battles were fought within the Democratic party, but since Reconstruction, the Democrats have absorbed most of the partisan political activity in the state. The despised carpetbaggers were Republicans, and not until 1979 has a Republican served as governor since Edmund J. Davis was defeated for reelection in 1873.

During much of the time between Reconstruction and World War II, powerful interest groups seemed to dominate Texas. Many of the cotton fortunes were destroyed in the Civil War, but the vacuum was quickly filled by ranching, railroad, and lumber fortunes. Then along came the oil, gas, and sulfur interests, as well as the banks, insurance companies, and utilities, all of them adept at protecting their activities from undue state interference by state regulations. As one observer put it, they "exerted enough influence on state government to protect the interests of the national and international business combinations of which their Texas operations are a profitable part, at the expense of organized political development among residents of the state."[1]

Occasional popular outbreaks, however, obstructed the corporations. For two decades after the Civil War, Texans were well disposed toward business and conservatism, but by 1890 the plight of the majority of the people—the farmers—became so acute that they were spurred into political rebellion against the conservative state government. The Southern Farmers Alliance, which originated in Texas, and the People's party demanded better breaks for farmers—especially curbs on the railroads and their high freight rates, on the great banking houses of the East, which held farm mortgages, and on such holding companies as the cotton bagging trust, which fixed the prices of farm supplies. The irate farmers were strong enough in 1890 to force the nomination of James Stephen Hogg as the Democratic candidate for governor. Hogg was pledged to uproot these business abuses. As attorney general he had already helped frame a state antitrust law. After his election as governor, he established the Texas Railroad Commission, one of the first such regulatory bodies in the country and a model for many similar agencies in state and national government. Hogg's political philosophy was carried on by his successor, Charles Culberson, although both displeased the People's party by failing to enact their favorite measure, the subtreasury plan.[2]

Conservatism again held sway from 1899 to 1907 as Texas's last ex-Confederate governors, Joseph Sayers and S. W. T. Lanham, occupied the executive mansion in Austin. Neither made a move against the increasing colonialization of the Texas economy by out-of-state corporations, especially in the oil industry. Lanham presided over the adoption of the poll tax and the Terrell election law, which together drastically reduced the Texas electorate (effectively eliminating blacks and many poor whites from the voting population). In 1907, however, Governor Thomas Campbell, supported by Hogg, renewed the progressive movement. His administration instituted antitrust and antilobby legislation, adopted a pure food act and a maximum-working-hours law for railroad employees, and reformed the tax structure. In the 1910 election conservatism returned under Oscar Colquitt, only to be ousted in the 1914 race by James "Pa" Ferguson, the "farmer's friend."[3]

Ferguson was reelected in 1916 and soon persuaded the legislature to enact his famous rental plank into law. It provided that landlords could take a rental of no more than one-fourth of the cotton and one-third of most other crops. The law was never rigidly enforced and was declared unconstitutional in 1921, which Ferguson probably anticipated. The governor was impeached in 1917 and convicted on ten charges of misusing state funds and of other irregularities in office. His wife, Miriam A. "Ma" Ferguson, was elected governor in 1924 and in 1932, parading the slogan, "Two Governors for the price of one." Although "Ma" was the titular governor, "Pa" usually made the decisions. In the 1920s the Fergusons opposed the Ku Klux Klan and prohibition, but "Pa" roused poor whites with his speeches, which were just as racist as those of the Klansmen. Such was his ability to twist the language, Ferguson could make simple homilies sound significant. He concluded one speech with the astonishing pronouncement, "I'm for the HOME. If that be treason, make the most of it."[4]

According to V. O. Key, the author of the most original treatise on modern Texas politics, the Fergusons engaged in very little government action to justify their strong rural support. Instead they became an issue unto themselves. They reputedly distracted the voters' attention from social and economic concerns and induced the citizenry to think of politics in terms of like or dislike for "Farmer Jim." Key believed that elections before Ferguson's time revolved around such meaningful issues as public services, taxes, and the growth of monopolistic corporations. But during the two decades when Fergusonism was a subject for debate in almost every election, less meaningful and more melodramatic questions were in the forefront, such as "Pa's" alleged acceptance of bribes from breweries and contractors and "Ma's" pardons for thousands of state prisoners.[5]

The other governors of the period were Will Hobby, 1917-1921; Pat Neff, 1921-1925; Dan Moody, 1927-1931; Ross Sterling, 1931-1933; and James Allred, 1935-1939. These men, according to Key's treatise, did not champion any great cause or accomplish anything that touched the hearts and minds of men; but it seems unfair to assert that the Fergusons always obscured real issues or that James Allred did nothing "that touched the hearts and minds of men." In fact both the Fergusons and Allred, like Hogg and Campbell before them, often fought the state's powerful interest groups. By defeating the Klan and denouncing prohibition, the Fergusons were at least dealing with two of the important issues of the 1920s. That was as much as most other American politicans were doing. Moreover the Fergusons and Allred met the challenges of the depression in a progressive manner. The Fergusons approved a statewide "bread bond" issue of $20 million, which was used to buy food and clothing for the destitute, and they secured federal public works projects, which were financed directly by the federal government or through matching grants. Governor Allred also cooperated with the relief and recovery programs of the New Deal. He helped set up assistance programs for the aged, the needy blind, and indigent children but could not persuade the legislature to fund them. He successfully taxed the chain stores and opposed a sales tax and, facing a hostile senate, unsuccessfully attempted to install a state income tax, to raise the tax on crude oil, natural gas, and sulfur, and to reduce rates on public utilities. Allred earned the hatred of the corporate lobby after trying to subject lobbyists to registration and regulation. No subsequent governor of Texas has endorsed such a liberal program. Indeed veteran liberals such as Senator Ralph Yarborough, labor leaders John Crossland and Harry Acreman, and editor Paul Holcomb regarded Allred as the last of the "people's governors."[6]

Liberalism had not completely disappeared in the Lone Star state in the 1930s. Senator Morris Sheppard was a popular old Wilsonian who benefited from an adjustment lag in the attitude of his constituency. The veteran incumbent had built up a following and an organization and "in the never-never land of one-party politics where everyone is alike but different," he could go down the line for the New Deal without worrying about reelection. Texas votes in the House still embraced traditional southern internationalism. Most Texas congressmen still supported rural electrification, conservation, and tax relief for the lower classes. New Deal labor laws were not always opposed, since they had little impact on rural Texas. In Austin in 1937, young Lyndon B. Johnson defeated eight opponents while running on a New Deal platform in a special election for congress. Johnson and his campaign strategist, former Under Secretary of Interior Alvin Wirtz, were able to convince the voters and the Roosevelt administration that he was the only pro-New Deal candidate and more especially the only one who favored the president's court reform bill, though in fact he was not. Johnson billboards proclaimed "Franklin D. and Lyndon B." while the irreverent pressroom version was "Franklin D., Lyndon B. and Jesus C." Not content merely to ride the president's coattails, Johnson also vigorously attacked each opponent's weak points, despite Lady Bird Johnson's fears that it was mudslinging. Johnson's peripatetic campaigning from dawn to midnight was also crucial to the outcome. Johnson's election seemed exceptional, since Roosevelt's court packing bill was oppugned by most of Texas's attorneys, businessmen, and newspapers; and alone among southern legislatures, the Texas senate resolved against the measure, 22 to 3. But Texas's political leaders did not speak for the citizenry, who continuously sustained the court bill in the polls.[7]

Johnson and some of the other Texas congressmen could afford to be liberal because the oil, gas, and other corporate interests had not yet fully asserted their political power. The oil industry was plagued by overproduction and consequent low prices. There was virtually no natural gas industry at the time, since gas was regarded as hardly more than a waste product. Indeed Texas still had a colonial economy; its livelihood came from crops, livestock products, minerals, and other raw materials, the surpluses of which it traded to the outside business world for most of its consumer goods. Texas, moreover, was still an agrarian state with the traditional agrarian distrust of Wall Street capitalism. Urban Texans, those living in towns of twenty-five hundred or more, were 32 percent of the population in 1920 and 41 percent in 1930 and virtually throughout the decade.[8]

New Deal legislation fostered liberalism, in fact, but in Texas and the rest of the South, it also generated a tremendous counterreaction among the monied interests. Home owners were saved from mortgage foreclosures, and many small businessmen benefited from alternate sources of credit, but in the process, the power of the local banker was undermined. Economically deprived families could depend on Works Progress Administration jobs, thus bypassing and alienating the local dispensers of charity and employment. New labor standards and some union activities caused wages to rise for most workers, despite the invariable opposition of employers. Farm programs helped thousands but also upset landlord-tenant relationships. Various new federal programs skirted county commissioners and even state agencies.[9]

Perhaps the relative stability of Texas's underlying economic situation also aided Texas conservatives' ascent to power. Economic suffering may not have been as severe in Texas as in the industrial North or in the rest of the South. During the recession of 1937-1938, for instance, factory payrolls dropped only 5 percent in Texas compared with 27 percent in the rest of the country. Texas's per-capita farm income stood at 76 percent of the 1929 index, the rest of the nation's at 69 percent. Total manufacturing establishments in Texas between 1929 and 1939 declined only 2.2 percent, which was far less precipitous than in any other southern state.[10]

More important, the sweeping Democratic victory in 1936 had given the party an overwhelming preponderance in both houses of Congress and had placed the liberal northern Democrats in a more influential position. The old-line southern conservatives, led by Texans, had already grown restive at the drift of New Deal legislation. Conflict became more intense when President Roosevelt proposed to enlarge the Supreme Court; Roosevelt's appointments to a larger court could prevent it from blocking New Deal reforms. Vice-President John Nance Garner, from Uvalde, Texas, reacted to the reading of the bill by striding from the rostrum holding his nose, making the thumbs down gesture of the Roman arena. Garner was accurately described by one contemporary observer as "a small town banker, a thick-skinned politician, an invincible poker player, the breadth of whose horizons were indicated by his willingness to sponsor a national sales tax proposal."[11] But even the junior senator from Texas, Tom Connally, previously a New Deal stalwart, split with the president on the court reform bill.[12]

Despite anticipated opposition in the Senate, the administration was confident of easy passage in the House. This confidence was shattered when Hatton Sumners, congressman from Dallas and chairman of the House Judiciary Committee, publicly urged Roosevelt to withdraw the court bill for the sake of the country. Otherwise, he declared, he would make every effort to prevent a vote on the measure. Bonham Congressman Sam Rayburn, the Democratic floor leader, also doubted the wisdom of the bill, but he worked to salvage part of the president's program. Sumner's stand, however, forced the administration to run with the bill in the Senate first. The Dallas congressman also may have had a hand in persuading one court justice to announce his retirement, which undermined the president's position during a crucial juncture in the clash. As Congress turned against the court bill in the summer of 1937, the White House called upon the vice-president to effect a compromise. Garner, who exiled himself to Texas during the bitter phase of the fight, allowed the bill's opponents to cut the heart out of it.[13]

Texas liberalism was also stung by a bitter congressional session on an antilynching bill, widely disliked in Texas, and a long, drawn-out congressional struggle over the wages and hours bill. With almost all Texas leaders opposed to these controversial measures, the New Deal's prestige in the state inevitably waned, hastening the decline of progressivism itself.[14]

Two of Texas's progressive congressmen were beaten in the 1938 elections. Conservatism won its most stunning electoral victory in the Democratic primary in San Antonio, with the defeat of the fiery liberal, Maury Maverick, who was endorsed by President Roosevelt. Maverick was the only southern congressman who favored the antilynching bill and was also a strong supporter of the wages and hours measure. Chieftain of the liberal bloc in the House, singled out by the *New York Times* as one of the eighteen outstanding leaders of Congress, Maverick still had to face reelection in a city run by an old, vice-ridden political machine along with the usual clique of wealthy bankers and businessmen, all of whom opposed him from the time of his first election in 1934. Every businessman in San Antonio knew that Vice-President Garner wanted Maverick crushed. The congressman's rousing support from the Congress of Industrial Organizations also prompted a heavy antilabor turnout, much of it from surrounding rural precincts. The national office of the American Federation of Labor opposed Maverick too. The tone of the campaign was set by his opponent, Paul Kilday, who stated that his goal was "the elimination from Congress of one overwhelmingly shown to be the friend and ally of Communism."[15]

Title to the statehouse, however, is the grand prize in Texas. The deterioration of liberalism in the state was most spectacularly illustrated in the Democratic gubernatorial primary in 1938 when conservative, corporate interests took over the state, once and for all, perhaps permanently. They launched the Establishment, a loosely knit plutocracy comprised mostly of Anglo businessmen, oilmen, bankers, and lawyers. These leaders—especially in the 1940s and 1950s—were dedicated to a regressive tax structure, low corporate taxes, antilabor laws, political, social, and economic oppression of blacks and Mexican-Americans, alleged states' rights, and extreme reluctance to expand state services. On federal matters they demanded tax reduction, a balanced budget, and the relaxation of federal controls over oil, gas, water, and other resources.[16]

The concept of an Establishment may seem anomalous since Texas politics retain the old, spirited, free-for-all appearance. Factionalism within the state's one-party system has been compared with the complexity of multi-party politics in France. Texans like to boast that their state has no machine. True, there is no machine in the eastern form of patronage, spoils, and bloc-delivered votes (except in a few south Texas counties). Informality prevails, whereby the governing elite, in a "subrosa accord," set the ideas and the mood, and "the little fish then swim along—the contractors, the car dealers, the real estate men, the small oil operators."[17]

Governors have always been the political focus of the state. Three of the four chief executives during these politically stormy years—W. Lee O'Daniel, 1939-1941, Coke Stevenson, 1941-1947, and Allan Shivers, 1949-1957—were distinguishable from their predecessors and successors by their ideological vigor. O'Daniel and Shivers were also very active leaders compared to most of the governors who preceded and followed them. All three governors indulged in primitive and controversial actions that went beyond the ordinary demands of the interest groups. Moreover O'Daniel and Shivers as well as the fourth governor in this period—Beauford Jester, 1947-1949—were even strong enough and capable enough to defy the corporations, though they did not often do so. Establishment sovereignty has been made easier by the fact that since 1939, Texas, alone among industrial states (perhaps all states), has been subjected to an unbroken series of conservative governors.

There is no particular Establishment organization, and it would be well to heed the words of Howard Zinn, who observed that those "who postulate 'power elites' are right for the most part, I think, but they often overestimate self-consciousness and confidence as characteristics of those elites." Class consciousness is not a criterion for the existence of a ruling class. Nor is there necessarily a central clique. There was talk in Texas in the 1940s and 1950s that state affairs were handled by the card-playing multimillionaires who convened in Herman Brown's suite in the Lamar Hotel in Houston, the "8-F Crowd." The group may, in fact, have been very powerful, but it did not leave much of a trail for the historian to follow. Many transactions, of course, occurred on the telephone. It should also be borne in mind that political antagonisms may exist within a power elite, as during an election

that features more than one major conservative candidate or during a legislative session. Generally corporate interests from inside and outside of
Texas exude enormous influence over the state by successfully financing
campaigns for conservative candidates, lobbying, and controlling the press.
The ruling elite of Texas politics, however, not only includes the business
and corporate upper class but also the governors and, to a much lesser
extent, the community aristocracies.[18]

Interest groups were well entrenched long before the conservative governors were continuously elected, but the classic superpower among corporate
lobbies, the oil industry, came of age simultaneously with the Establishment. More than any other single lobby, it has kept the conservatives and
their philosophy in power. Oil companies became seriously concerned
about Texas politics in 1930, when the great east Texas field was discovered.
A deluge of oil glutted the world market; hundreds of independent operators
forced the price down from a dollar to as low as ten cents a barrel. The
major companies, already pushing for production limitation, redoubled
their efforts. A Humble Oil executive noted, "We had to let a president of
Humble quit to become governor to establish proration [production con-
trol]." It was Governor Ross Sterling who sent in the National Guard to
stop all that wasteful free enterprise. The guard was headed by General Jake
Wolters, lobbyist and chief counsel for the Texas Oil Company (Texaco);
one of his aides was a Gulf official.[19]

At first the majors did not entirely succeed, since the proration that was
tentatively agreed upon still allowed a good deal of pumping and since every
day thousands of barrels of so-called hot oil were brought up secretly and
illegally. The administration introduced a bill directly regulating the industry, but the federal conservationist attempt was effectively blocked by
Texas's states' rights champions—Garner, Rayburn, and Connally. The
Texans then aligned themselves with the administration in pushing through the
Connally Hot Oil Act, which outlawed the interstate shipment of oil produced
in violation of state quotas. This measure ensured that the Texas Railroad
Commission would "stabilize" the industry. The commission allowed the
majors to drive the independents out of the processing end of the business,
but it also protected the independents from the price-cutting practices of
the majors. The commission soon became the creature of the industry it
purported to regulate. During World War II Fort Worth political boss
and publisher, Amon Carter, who was an independent oilman, was so
alarmed at the depredations of the majors that he wrote to Governor Coke
Stevenson, Speaker Rayburn, and Secretary of Interior Harold Ickes. The
big companies, he claimed, were trying to kill off and absorb all the little
fellows. He noted that the majors controlled less than 53 percent of the
nation's reserves in 1939 but 70 percent by 1942. The independents, however, managed to hang on. In 1947 Carter sold part of his oil holdings for
$16.5 million.[20]

1. Railroad Commission, Gas Industry, and Consumer. *Cartoon by Ben Sargent, copyright © 1976* Austin American Statesman, *reprinted by permission.*

Texas oil operators—both independents and majors—began flexing their political muscles again by 1938, not only in the governor's race but also in at least one congressional district. A liberal fifteen-year veteran of the state legislature and Congress, W. D. McFarlane, had angered the oilmen with his record against tax loopholes and his proposal to tax industrial motors. Despite the personal appearance of President Roosevelt on his behalf, McFarlane was defeated in the 1938 Democratic primary by Ed Gossett, who went on to serve the oil and gas industries as congressman from the Wichita Falls district and later was sought by the American Petroleum Institute to become its official spokesman in Washington, D.C.[21]

Oilmen became particularly adept at avoiding taxation, and it has hardly been unusual for oil and gas lobbyists to outnumber state senators at tax hearings. In 1936 the legislature lifted the tax on the wellhead production of crude oil to 2.75 percent of the market value; the oil lobby hollered "confiscation." Yet the increased efficiency of proration—deliberate price fixing by the state government—had just added half a billion dollars per year to the income of the oil industry. Oklahoma already had a 5 percent levy and Louisiana approximately 8 percent. One keen observer, journalist A. Hope Wheeler, noted in his Arlington newspaper, the *Texas Citizen*, that Louisiana oil taxation "is being kept remarkably quiet in Texas, as certain influential interests prefer that the people of this state do not learn about the situation." Texas's 1936 percentage was raised only once in the next fifteen years. It was in 1947 that Robert Calvert, chairman of the Democratic party of Texas, candidly informed the Hillsboro Lions Club that the oil industry controlled the state and could bring about any program it was united behind.[22]

The third element in the Establishment are the local commercial potentates—bankers, businessmen, lawyers, contractors, oilmen, publishers, and their wives—who dominate their cities and towns as though these communities were their private clubs. This phenomenon is hardly peculiar to the Lone Star state or to the wartime and postwar period, but local aristocracies in Texas since the depression have probably gotten richer than those in other states and at a faster rate. The city elites are not directly related to the governance of the state, however, and I will not discuss them extensively.

It was the corporations—forced to share the Texas political limelight between Reconstruction and World War II with reform movements and self-serving politicians—that transmuted their influence into corporate control in the late 1930s. From the perspective of four decades, this informal reign of the Establishment is far more long-lived than that of any previous reforming crusade or retrenchment or individual power broker. Any narrative dealing with the history of the Establishment governors and interest groups must begin with the incredible Texas election of 1938.

2. Texas's Natural Resource Philosophy. *Courtesy of Bob Eckhardt.*

3

"PASS THE BISCUITS, PAPPY":
The O'Daniel Era

> *No use to have a grouch*
> *Or even have a frown*
> *For everybody's happy*
> *When Pappy comes to town.*
>> Stanza of a song composed
>> for O'Daniel, 1940

> *You promised us pensions,*
> *The earth, and the moon,*
> *And all you've delivered is*
> *A Hill-Billy tune.*
>> Anonymous anti-O'Daniel
>> poem, 1942

> *Had . . . Lee O'Daniel been even slightly less astute,*
> *had he made a slightly less careful analysis of his own*
> *talents and the emotional requirements of his*
> *constituents, he might very well have gone on the*
> *road with a medicine show.*
>> George Sessions Perry,
>> *Texas: A World in Itself,* 1942

Political issues in Texas in 1938 centered around the desire for industrialization, the financial straits of the state government which was over $19 million in debt, and the proposed state social security plan. This plan had been supported by Governor James Allred and had been ratified as a Texas constitutional amendment in 1935, but the legislature still refused to make the necessary appropriations. The state treasury was so depleted that house members sat at their desks with umbrellas hoisted because there were no funds to pay for repairing the capitol roof.[1]

Among the candidates in the primary, the strongest contender early in the campaign was Attorney General William McCraw of Dallas, who had served well since his election in 1934. Ernest Thompson, former mayor of Amarillo and chairman of the Texas Railroad Commission since 1932, was the second leading contender. Wichita Falls oilman Tom Hunter was also a serious candidate. Another hopeful was a lifelong Republican, W. Lee O'Daniel, who was unknown as a politician but well known as a flour merchant operating out of Fort Worth. There were also nine minor candidates, who polled fewer than forty thousand votes out of over one million cast.[2]

O'Daniel was born in Ohio but had spent most of his early life in Kansas, making his living as a flour salesman. He moved to Texas in 1925 and became sales manager and later general manager of the Burrus Mill and Elevator Company of Fort Worth. He was master of ceremonies on a daily radio show featuring a young fiddler and his western band, Bob Wills and the Lightcrust Doughboys. The show invariably opened with a woman's request to O'Daniel: "Please pass the biscuits, Pappy." The program was heard each noon over Texas's three most powerful stations—WBAP, Fort Worth, WOAI, San Antonio, and KPRC, Houston. It probably had more daily listeners than any other show in the history of Texas radio.

O'Daniel organized his own company in 1935 and began to advertise his "Hillbilly Flour" in a regular radio program. (After a dispute with O'Daniel, Wills left and went on to country music stardom.) O'Daniel even composed music for his orchestra, including the tune "The Boy Who Never Gets Too Big to Comb His Mother's Hair." In addition to hillbilly and sacred music, there were religious talks, lectures on morals, stories of Texas heroes, and various crusades that were unlikely to stir political storms. O'Daniel organized a statewide safety association for children and mailed badges to all the members; the only membership requirement was that one walk on the left-hand side of the street, facing the approaching traffic. O'Daniel related that his radio fans had begun to ask him every two years to make the race for governor, but he had thought the idea ridiculous. There were so many requests, however, that he asked the people in a broadcast on Palm Sunday, 1938, to write him if they thought he should make the race. By his own count he received messages from over fifty-four thousand people asking him to run, four advising him not to run. He announced as a candidate on May 1, 1938.[3]

In their platform announcements, Thompson and McCraw promised payment of the state's social security pledges, economy in state government, no new taxes, and the encouragement of industry in Texas. As part of the regular "Hillbilly Flour" program of May 1, O'Daniel set forth a platform his opponents could not surpass or even oppose: the Ten Commandments. He also promised pensions of thirty dollars a month for everyone over sixty-five. He said his motto would be the golden rule. When his listeners hinted that he be a little more specific, he conjured up an additional slogan: "Less Johnson grass and politicians, more smokestacks and businessmen."[4]

By the middle of June, it was apparent that the flour merchant, accompanied by his hillbilly band and the scriptures, was drawing larger and more enthusiastic crowds than any other candidate. O'Daniel stressed industrialization and tax cuts more than his opponents did and pointed to his business experience, which, he said, qualified him to run the state government in a business-like manner. He also went out of his way to berate "professional politicians." His appeal was magnetic. Crowds of twenty thousand to forty thousand would wait for hours along the highways to glimpse the salesman-candidate. These predominant rural audiences sometimes forced him to speak in towns where he was not even scheduled to stop.[5]

Texas, still considered a wellspring of evangelism, was reputedly influenced by cotton and religion until the Civil War, by cattle and religion until the end of the century, and by oil and religion since then. The O'Daniel gatherings did indeed reveal a widespread fundamentalist fervor among the people of the state. (J. Frank Norris, a Detroit Baptist minister, formerly of Fort Worth, compared O'Daniel to Moses and thought that he might lead the nation back to the fundamentals of God and home.) When the candidate's bus rolled into town, he ignored the local potentates, just as the camp-meeting preachers of previous generations had done, and like the camp meetings of old, his rallies were out in the open, "basking in God's sunlight."[6] Texas historian Frank Goodwyn has written:

> The O'Daniel rallies appealed to the same deep human instinct and provided the same emotional outlets which the camp meeting formerly offered. Here again was the chance to enjoy the thrill and glory of a martial movement without risking any physical bloodshed. Christ was still the hero and Satan still the enemy, but both had new mouthpieces now. Christ's good, which had previously radiated from the camp-meeting preacher, was now represented by the flour-salesman. Satan's evil, previously attached to that abhorred aristocracy which had been the pioneer's European superior, was now found to reside in the professional politician. Roles, stage setting, and costumes changed, but the plot of the drama was the same.[7]

Befitting the Texas Establishment's first candidate, O'Daniel, a hustling businessman, discovered that the 1938 primary gave a great boost to Hillbilly Flour sales. He never denied that one of the aims of his campaign was to sell more flour, and he admitted that the campaign was "sure good for business." All his speeches contained endorsements for Hillbilly Flour. Such advertising was free since voluntary contributions (pitched into little flour kegs) more than paid for the campaign.[8]

O'Daniel's country-boy image was merely a pose; he was, in fact, a business college graduate worth half a million dollars. It was not generally known that he acted under the shrewd, professional direction of public relations expert Phil Fox of Dallas, who thought up some of the candidate's folksy, "spontaneous" statements. To maintain the rustic posture, O'Daniel had to be wary of corporate support. The public did not know that some of richest corporate leaders in the state were the people who persuaded him to enter the race. He denied that big business aided him, but by the end of his first campaign, three wealthy businessmen appeared in public as his "closest friends." They were oilman Jesse McKee of Fort Worth; Maco Stewart, Galveston oilman and banker; and Carr P. Collins, Dallas insurance executive and O'Daniel's unofficial manager. Collins, a Republican and a Baptist fundamentalist, made a fortune not only in insurance but also in the peddling of a quack laxative. Sales of Collins's laxative, known as Crazy Crystals, reputedly reached $3 million a year before the Pure Food and Drug Administration exposed it as fraudulent. The product was apparently a mixture of mineral water and Glauber's salts, used in treating horses.[9]

O'Daniel received a majority of the votes cast, eliminating the usual necessity of a runoff. His total was 573,000, Thompson's 231,000, and McCraw's 152,000. The flour salesman led in 231 counties, was second in 14, and third in the other 9. The 23 counties that failed to give him pluralities were hundreds of miles from the radio stations that had carried the O'Daniel programs regularly for ten years.[10]

During and shortly after the campaign, O'Daniel had made several promises that were ordinarily identified with liberals: to block any sales tax and to abolish capital punishment and the poll tax (which he had not paid that year). And at least once, when a union member asked if "Pappy" was a labor supporter, Mrs. O'Daniel wrote back (while he was campaigning) that her husband had always been in favor of organized labor. (Many union members voted for O'Daniel, though most union officers had him pegged as "an open shop champion" who preferred "low wage scales.") In the last week of October 1938, O'Daniel hinted he might favor a levy on natural resources: "We have got to tax those who have it in order to raise money for those pensions we promised. I for one intend to let the chips fall where they may."[11] The governor was spared accusations of liberalism since he made no serious effort to carry out his pledges.

Most of the remainder of O'Daniel's statements and actions exemplify the general stance taken by all subsequent governors, though O'Daniel was the only one who ignored Democratic party machinery and who severely weakened his own administration with unpopular appointments and tax proposals. The governor, for instance, appointed James M. West, oil, cattle, and lumber millionaire from Houston, to the Highway Commission in 1939. His nomination was rejected by the senate when it was revealed that he had been an active member of the Jeffersonian Democrats, an extremist organization bitterly opposed to the reelection of Franklin Roosevelt in 1936. Also, it was feared that West's presence might hinder the flow of highway funds from the Roosevelt administration. Without consulting Texas unions, O'Daniel selected the state labor commissioner from the ranks of the union at Southwestern Bell Telephone. Joe Kunschik was a desk worker who had met O'Daniel after writing him a fan letter following a radio broadcast. Kunschik was not even an officer in the local, and, in any event, the Bell union was pawn of management. AFL and CIO union officials deluged the governor with telegrams of protest, but O'Daniel paid no heed. Even the secretary of the company union wrote O'Daniel that he was surprised at the nomination and that other members were too. The secretary supported the nominee, of course, but implied that anyone else in the local could have filled the position just as well. The selection was praised by a few, such as the company union at the (Howard) Hughes Tool Company, a notorious antilabor bastion, and by Herman Brown, who complimented the governor on his "nerve."[12]

The governor believed that the mere enforcement of the existing tax laws would pay all the state's expenses, especially the higher pensions that he and the legislature were committed to. After it became obvious that such enforcement would not suffice, the governor condemned such legislative proposals as a state income tax and levies on natural resources. He asked instead for a 1.6 percent tax on most business transactions, which he claimed as his own idea, but which he refused to elaborate upon even when pressed for details.

Unknown at the time, this entire tax plan had been presented to O'Daniel in secret sessions at the governor's mansion by C. A. Jay, head of the Texas Industrial Conference, Dallas's counterpart of the Texas Manufacturers Association. This plan was widely and rightly regarded as a multiple sales tax that would place its main burden on the small wage earner and small businessman. The legislature voted the tax down. O'Daniel then called frankly for the adoption of a sales tax constitutional amendment with a proviso freezing the severance taxes on oil, gas, and sulfur at rates just above the low 1939 level. In the state house of representatives, one member referred to the governor as the "crooning corporal of the panoplied forces of financial marauders." O'Daniel was, in fact, bowing to the big lobby, especially oil, gas, and utilities. Slipping a regressive tax bill (or any statute) into the basic framework of government was a violation of representative constitutional government, as Representative S. J. Isaacks, among others, tried to explain to his constituents, but that did not bother O'Daniel or the lobby. Nor were they concerned that a constitutional amendment, assuming it was adopted, would postpone pensions for two years. Led by the "immortal 56," a phalanx of legislators who had sworn to block the sales tax, the house refused to submit the amendment to the voters. The house overwhelmingly passed an omnibus tax bill, mainly on natural resources and utilities, but O'Daniel and the lobby were strong enough to kill it in the senate.[13]

As the 1939 session dragged on, the legislature appropriated $572,000 for new buildings at state hospitals to provide 684 new beds for the insane. O'Daniel vetoed the measure, which meant that the 465 insane persons in jails would have to remain in their cells for another two years. He vetoed $225,500 for 291 new beds for orphans, epileptics, and the feebleminded. He vetoed a bill that would have provided a joint rural school supervisor for two counties because it specified a minimum salary but not a maximum one, which he thought violated sound business principles. The greatest blow was delivered to the State Highway Department, whose biennial appropriation was slashed more than 50 percent. Texas Ranger funds were cut to a point where the men had to borrow ammunition from highway patrolmen. The governor even ordered a cut in state pension checks. The reductions were made, O'Daniel explained, in the interests of economy.[14]

Through it all, the governor continued his radio appeals to the numerous pensioners in the countryside and managed to set up the paralyzed legislature as a whipping boy. He bitterly attacked sales tax opponents and called the "honor roll" of those who supported him. In answer to a number of letters about pensions, the governor replied that the writer should take up the matter with the legislature. Scores of letters, perhaps hundreds, were mailed out of O'Daniel's office with lists naming the legislators who had voted against the sales tax-pension bill.

Judging by the carbon copies sent to the governor's mansion, the legislators were pelted with hostile messages and local resolutions of impeachment. Senator Penrose Metcalfe and Representative Frank Howington were warned by a petition signed by about 170 of the 400 residents of Gustine that they "were watching every move." A hundred or more signed a Baptist minister's warning for the Fannin County representative to join O'Daniel's movement. Hale Center had 63 signers urging their representative and senator to "quit playing politics and support O'Daniel in everything." O'Daniel's browbeating was resented by a number of legislators and probably diminished the chances of the sales tax amendment.[15]

The governor and the legislature could not solve the social security taxation problem during the 1939 session. Afterward there was general demand for a special session, particularly after mid-August, when the major oil companies posted drastic price reductions. This was probably the last occasion when an action of the majors drew a barrage of criticism in Texas. The price cuts threatened to end drilling and eventually wipe out the independent operators. At the instigation of the Texas Railroad Commission, especially Ernest Thompson, the oil states shut down all production for fifteen days. Thompson, looking ahead to his own candidacy in the next gubernatorial election, proposed that O'Daniel call the legislature into special session to adopt a $.05 per barrel oil tax to pay for social security requirements. Thompson thought this was "the opportunity of the age" to levy a "nickle for Grandma" tax. He observed that Texas's oil was not going to last forever and reminded statewide radio audiences that Louisiana got $.11 a barrel while Texas got $.0275 or 2.75 percent when the price was over a dollar. O'Daniel, of course, had no intention of taxing the oil industry and flatly refused to call a special session.[16]

Both during and after the session, many state legislators and bureaucrats laughed at the vaudevillian atmosphere of the O'Daniel administration. They were, perhaps, bemused that even the governor's followers wrote poems and songs emulating O'Daniel's criticism of the legislature. One Hillsboro businessman, for instance, wrote nineteen stanzas describing the legislature, two of which were:

> The legislature that's grinding now
> Is mixing meal and husk
> And kind of smells like a cat
> That carries lots of musk.

> We thought we sent great minds down there
> And still suppose we did
> But if it really is the fact
> They've kept their wisdom hid.[17]

The legislators laughed right up to election day, 1940, when a number of them were vanquished at the polls. Among the "immortal 56," only thirty-three ran for reelection, and about half of them were defeated. During the Democratic primary, one representative who perceived what was happening wrote to liberal editor John C. Granbery; the last legislature, he said, had been a total failure, and "many people think O'Daniel has not been given a chance." O'Daniel himself ran for reelection with much the same platform as in 1938, since little of it had been enacted. The major difference was that in 1938 O'Daniel had proposed that there should be no further taxation, whereas in 1940 he urged the passage of the transactions tax. The Ten Commandments were retained, but the golden rule was dropped from the platform. (One paper commended the governor for recognizing that the golden rule was not congenial with "the resentful vituperation with which he paid his respects to his critics in his announcement.") His leading opponent was Ernest Thompson, who talked mostly about an oil tax. The campaign was similar to that of 1938, except that "Ma" and "Pa" Ferguson attempted a comeback and thereby enlivened the race. "Pa" promised that the "Fergusons Won't Deny Milk to Insane Patients" and described the governor as a "slick-haired banjo-picker" who "attempted to ward off pertinent questions by grinning like a jackass in a thistle patch."[18]

O'Daniel hit upon one new election gambit when he announced that he had wired President Roosevelt that he had confidential information on the activities of fifth columnists in Texas, but he declined to identify them. The public stirred. Hundreds of letters flooded the governor's office, and many of them described alleged communist and Nazi activities in the villages and towns of Texas. Among the messages was a telegram on behalf of the Texas Chamber of Commerce Managers Association offering the services of "trained businessmen" for use in suppressing fifth columnists. An even greater curiosity was a plea from the commander of the American Legion post in Denton that the members "be supplied with necessary arms" for active service in the event of invasion from within or without. The governor declined the opportunity to arm the Legion, but he did say that he was sending officials of the Texas National Guard and the Texas Department of Public Safety to Washington to confer with federal authorities. Homer Garrison, director of public safety, received no information concerning such activities, nor did the adjutant general's department. Presumably, as one of his opponents urged, O'Daniel should have revealed the enemy's activity in order to protect the citizenry and should have made immediate arrests in order to stymie the enemy.[19] Since no action was taken against a fifth column, one can only conclude that it never existed. At a time of crisis for the nation, with France being overrun by Nazis, Governor O'Daniel attempted to frighten the populace into keeping him in office.

O'Daniel was concerned for a time during the campaign about press revelations that Jesse McKee had given him a sound truck worth fifteen thousand dollars even though the law limited first primary expenditures to eight thousand dollars. O'Daniel at first said that the truck was the gift of many friends, then claimed that his flour company had purchased it. Company donations to politicians were also illegal, but the issue did not generate enough criticism to destroy O'Daniel. The governor, solidly backed by big and small business, reported campaign expenditures of $4,035.01, a ridiculously low figure that was far below the reported figures of the other serious contenders. By amazing coincidence, the governor's contributions also totaled $4,035.01. Such was the caliber of the gubernatorial candidates in 1940 that none carried a plurality in his own home county. O'Daniel won without a runoff, and Ernest Thompson ran a distant second. The Fergusons never ran another campaign after "Ma's" fourth-place finish in this election.[20]

Also in the 1940 campaigning, the chairman of the state Democratic party, E. B. Germany, joined Sam Rayburn and Senators Connally and Sheppard in actively seeking the presidential nomination for Vice-President Garner, even though it appeared likely that President Roosevelt would seek renomination. At the state party convention in May, which degenerated into a near riot, the Garnerites overwhelmed the Roosevelt forces (under

Johnson, Maverick, Ferguson, and others) and selected delegates to the national convention who were pledged to Garner. The convention did go on record as endorsing the policies of the Roosevelt administration. After Roosevelt captured the nomination, a number of Texas oilmen and financiers, evidently including Germany, turned against the Democratic party. Rayburn, who became Speaker of the House in September 1940, had been of considerable service to the oil industry and was loyally stumping for the Democratic ticket. He complained, "The one quirk in human nature I can't understand is that the people who were the worst broke when we came into power were the ones who recovered the fastest and got the richest, and they are the ones who hate us the most." It was also bizarre that in one of the nation's strongest Democratic states, neither the governor nor the vice-president of the United States, perhaps the two most powerful Texas Democrats, endorsed the Democratic president's reelection. Garner exiled himself in Texas, "sulking among the goats," as one daily phrased it. While Roosevelt won his third term, the Texas turmoil was the harbinger of the internecine warfare that plagued the state's Democratic presidential politics in future years.[21]

With the elections out of the way, O'Daniel finally offered an explanation of the transaction tax in 1941, but it sank out of sight in the legislative hopper. The governor reluctantly abandoned his sales tax notions during the session, perhaps taking heed of a poll showing that 72 percent of Texas voters were against it. He did propose an immediate appropriation of almost $27 million for pensions and teacher retirement, which had the effect of gulling the old folks, putting the legislature on the spot, and (had it passed) plunging the state ever deeper in debt. After this strategem failed, the governor signed an omnibus tax bill that actually raised the levies on natural resources and utilities but also increased several selective sales taxes. After the frustrations of wrestling with O'Daniel for two years, the Texas house passed a resolution urging the federal government to take over all social security payments.[22]

Once again O'Daniel made a series of appointments that had no chance of being approved. Panhandle rancher and historian J. Evetts Haley was picked for the State Livestock Sanitary Commission. The senate turned him down, knowing that he had been state manager for the Jeffersonian Democrats in 1936. Three consecutive nominees for the Texas Liquor Control Board were rejected, largely because they appeared to be less interested in supervising the legalized liquor business than in destroying it. They were a prohibitionist Methodist minister, the head of the militant United Texas Drys (who was not even consulted about the post), and the president of the Women's Christian Temperance Union.[23]

Lobbyists were as active as ever, and one drawn-out clash between two Establishment business groups reached its turning point. During the 1930s the railroads in Texas launched a last-ditch effort to strangle truck transport by legislative load limits and by other means. Both lobbies amassed considerable funds. One legislator, when heckled on the floor of the house by questions regarding his receipt of campaign funds by truckers, replied, "Hell, yes; they gave me $2,000." On balance, there is little doubt that some truckers, farmers, and businessmen had a legitimate grievance against the railroads. The manager of the McAllen Chamber of Commerce, for instance, wrote Governor O'Daniel that trucking firms were quitting Texas because they could not haul fruit profitably with the seven-thousand-pound limit. Rio Grande Valley farmers' fruit crops, he charged, were rotting in the fields, and various businesses were going bankrupt because the farmers could not sell their fruit. One farmer was allegedly jailed for carrying his own crops in an overloaded truck. Finally in the 1941 session, the load limit was raised to thirty-eight thousand pounds by the legislature and approved by the governor.[24]

By 1941 O'Daniel's pose against "professional politicians" was losing its impact—in part because the governor had surrounded himself with politicians, all ultraconservatives; among them were E. B. Germany of Dallas, Orville Bullington of Wichita Falls, and Mayor C. K. Quin of San Antonio. Feeling the need for another target for his crusades, O'Daniel was soon patriotically denouncing "labor union leader racketeers." Unions had risen to power in the nation in the 1930s, and some union leaders had indeed committed abuses. Yet in Texas, unions were weak, agrarianism predominated, and as of mid-April 1941, not a single man-hour of labor had been lost on any Texas defense job because of strikes or labor disturbances. Moreover many unions were caught up in the patriotic spirit of the hour brought about by the war. In 1940 the Texas State Federation of Labor unanimously resolved that all school libraries be purged of all books "pertaining to any isms other than Americanism."[25] Conjuring menace from the Texas labor movement was truly a task for a professional politician.

An organized antilabor campaign arose. The Texas State Manufacturers Association newsletter charged that the CIO obeyed foreign orders that would cripple the nation. Posters sprang up in Borger proclaiming that "an evil influence is creeping into our community—organized labor." At a legislative hearing, Homer Garrison presented—as factual—some House Un-American Activities Committee testimony to the effect that strikes were revolutionary communist weapons. Under this barrage, the legislature, which had appeared to be amiably disposed toward labor early in the session, shied away from any labor associations. Suddenly O'Daniel asked for an immediate joint session of the legislature to hear him on March 13, 1941. He delivered an emotionally charged speech about "labor leader racketeers" who were threatening to take over Texas and who were crippling Britain's struggle against the Nazis. He called upon the legislature to pass his antiviolence bill before leaving the room. One provision required a cooling-off period of sixty days before strikes could begin, making no distinction between just and unjust causes of strikes. In the house the bill failed by only seven votes, even though no one had even read it. The bill was such a legal monstrosity that the attorney general ruled it unenforceable and unconstitutional on ten different counts, but a new bill passed overwhelmingly in both houses. The final version of the O'Daniel act forbade the use of force or violence or threats of force or violence to prevent anyone from working. Assemblies near any place where a labor dispute existed were also illegal. Violators might serve from one to two years in the state penitentiary. Thus a picket who used violence to prevent a strikebreaker from entring a plant was subject to imprisonment. There was no similar punishment for strike breakers who committed violence.[26]

Perhaps a truer indication of O'Daniel's sensitivity regarding United States defense preparations came later that same year, 1941, when he announced his opposition to the draft. He had also alluded to the war as European howling that had no effect on this country.[27] It appears that the governor simply invented a labor crisis as a justification for an antiunion law that served to boost him politically.

O'Daniel's antiunion efforts in Texas appeared to be orchestrated with Congressman Hatton Sumners's in Washington. The Dallas congressman's famous March 27 speech, delivered the day after the Texas house passed O'Daniel's bill, climaxed an outpouring of protests against defense industry strikes. Sumners suggested that war industry strikers "may have to be sent to the electric chair." On March 29 the State Democratic Executive Committee adopted a resolution commending Sumners and O'Daniel for their patriotic actions. On April 2, the day before O'Daniel signed the antiviolence bill, Sumners conceded that the federal government was not enthusiastic about pressuring labor but that the states ought to do it. The governor sent the congressman a copy of the O'Daniel law and expressed the hope that Congress would pass a similar one. O'Daniel obviously yearned for an opportunity to appear on the national stage himself and play the antiunion issue for all it was worth.[28]

Political succor also came his way when Senator Morris Sheppard, father of the Eighteenth Amendment and staunch New Dealer, died on April 9, 1941. The legislature resolved that O'Daniel ought to run for the post, largely in order to get him out of the state. O'Daniel wanted to become senator but was required by Texas law to appoint a "suitable and qualified" interim senator until a new one could be elected. Thus he had to choose some prominent Texan who would be satisfied with temporary honor and would not oppose the governor in the special senatorial election. On April 21, San Jacinto Day, O'Daniel uttered the usual plaudits for Sam Houston

3. Governor O'Daniel Orchestrates Texas Delegates, 1941. *Courtesy of the* Dallas Times Herald.

and then announced the appointment as senator of the only surviving son of Sam Houston, Andrew Jackson Houston. Houston was so ailing and infirm that he could not receive reporters. O'Daniel explained the appointment in one of his radio pageants. He claimed that he had recently stepped from the hurried world to "a sane and solid world of yesteryear." Out on a muddy road, beyond the San Jacinto battlefield, "we met a sweet and kind little lady trudging along in the mud" and persuaded her to get in the car. She explained that they were just country folks and did not wear fine clothes like the city folks. Pause. They drove to the residence. Pause. "She was Marguerite Houston." Pause. They visited her father and recalled General Sam's days of glory. "It was so refreshing to hear that great man discuss the problems of years ago and the problems of today in a sane and conservative manner." Houston was recovering from the flu and still did not know of his appointment. His daughters now thought that he was strong enough to stand the news, and Houston laughed loudly upon learning of his appointment. It had been cloudy and raining, but suddenly the sun shot through the clouds. God wanted Sam to "see his son's smile." O'Daniel blathered on awhile, then paused for "Rock of Ages" and a poem, "Give Them the Flowers Now."[29]

The governor had definitely stepped into the world of yesteryear. In a long and undistinguished career, Houston had been the Republican candidate for governor in 1892 and the Prohibitionist nominee in 1910 and 1912. In 1941 he was eighty-seven years old, the oldest man to that time ever to enter the Senate. The veteran conservative legislator Claude Gilmer recalled of Andrew Jackson Houston, "Well, that old man probably couldn't tell you whether the sun was up or had gone down. I mean he was in his dotage."[30] Houston's daughters did not even want him to take the risk of making the long trip to the nation's capital. Six weeks after his appointment, he did journey to Washington, attended one committee meeting, and died.

During the June special election, O'Daniel emphasized pensions, professed that he had always been a Democrat, and talked of "twisting the politicians' tails" in Washington just as he had in Austin. Senators who failed to vote for the antistrike bill that he promised to introduce would be subjected to his roll call on national radio hookup. On the issue of the country's defense, he suggested that Texas should have its own army and navy. He began riding the labor issue and claimed that after the passage of his antistrike law, the "labor agitators . . . scurried out of Texas overnight." Yet he simultaneously bemoaned that the "radical, wild-eyed labor leaders" were fighting him and supporting other candidates. O'Daniel sometimes hinted—erroneously—that he had Roosevelt's support. Other noteworthy contenders included east Texas congressman Martin Dies, who hurled spectacular charges of internal communist subversion and made the early mistake of

4. W. Lee O'Daniel and Andrew Jackson Houston, 1941. *Texas State Archives.*

sneering at hillbilly music, and Attorney General Gerald Mann, who was not identified with any special issue. The New Deal candidate, after Sam Rayburn had pressured Texarkana congressman Wright Patman out of the race, was Lyndon Johnson.[31]

For the first time since the abortive 1938 purges, Roosevelt took an active hand in a state election. Lyndon Johnson declared his candidacy on the White House steps and campaigned on his apparent ability to "get things done" in Washington. Supposedly using a considerable amount of Brown Root Construction Company money, along with such smaller donations as three thousand dollars from Sid Richardson, Johnson rented an airplane, hired hundreds of paid campaign workers, bought extensive newspaper and radio spots, and paid for pictures on highway billboards throughout the state showing him and President Roosevelt shaking hands. The congressman had learned from O'Daniel that the voters must be entertained. Most of Johnson's speeches were preceded by a swing band, blackface act, dancing girls, patriotic song singing, comedy acts, a long patriotic pageant, and a cash prize lottery. Assuming the correspondence is accurate, the Johnson managers may have erred in deigning to buy off at least two presidents (with their alleged membership lists) of old-age pension clubs. Most Texans were still New Dealers and, in the cities at least, they rallied to the Austin district's congressman. Most of the labor vote probably went to Johnson, though he took his first antilabor potshots and thereby convinced several unions not to endorse him. Blacks who had paid their poll taxes could vote, since this was a general election rather than the Democratic primary. They too appeared to support Johnson. Another boost came from fiery reverend J. Frank Norris, who dramatically switched from O'Daniel to Johnson because he feared the governor was weak on defense matters. The congressman benefited mightily from former governor Jimmie Allred's political organization, as well as a network of young people whom Johnson had helped when he was the Texas director of the National Youth Administration from 1935 to 1937. Early in the race Johnson seemed to be winning.[32]

But old Jim Ferguson, retired in Austin, still wearing his black string tie and big black hat, reputedly had both a method and a reason for impelling O'Daniel out of Texas. The method was to steal enough votes to reverse the outcome of the election. The reason was to prevent the governor from interfering with the beer and whiskey business in Texas, especially the high profits anticipated around army posts with a war coming on. "Pa," of course, had been very friendly with the liquor interests for close to three decades; but O'Daniel had denounced the "booze debauchery" and lamented that the Liquor Control Board was not enforcing state laws. The governor grumbled that the legislature would not confirm his "good clean honest Christian dry citizens" to the liquor board, but the liquor lobby could not be certain that it could hold him off forever. Other business interests, including gamblers and the ever-hopeful horseracing lobby (which wanted to legalize betting), backed O'Daniel in order to get him out of the state. Lieutenant Governor Coke Stevenson's many friends were also instrumental in the O'Daniel campaign in order to elect their man governor. Some secret assistance may even have emanated from inside the administration in Washington, notably from Houston financier Jesse Jones, long-time director of the Reconstruction Finance Corporation. Despite his position, Jones was not a strong New Dealer.[33]

On election night, with the vote 96 percent counted, Johnson led by over five thousand votes. But for the next several days, a dozen or more east Texas counties kept bringing in "corrected returns." A few managed to vote over 100 percent of their potential voting strength. The Johnson forces tried to counter by appealing to George Parr for more votes, but Parr, who had already delivered and reported 1,506 to Johnson and 65 to O'Daniel in Duval County, refused to do anything more. O'Daniel was certified the winner with 175,590 votes to Johnson's 174,279, with 27 others (who had promised everything from a five-ocean navy to free mattresses) trailing behind. The O'Daniel magic was obviously beginning to fizzle. According to a poll of four categories of income level, O'Daniel received a plurality only among the poorest (41 percent of those who made less than five hundred dollars a year). The only age group in which he registered a plurality was the over sixties, who gave him 44 percent. Even on the farms he received only 31 percent, and in cities over a hundred thousand just 16 percent. Outside the ten German-American counties, which were overwhelmingly Republican in general elections, Johnson led O'Daniel by over 3,600 votes. Pollster Joe Belden regarded O'Daniel's sudden jump in the late returns as "somewhat unnatural" and was concerned enough (or hired) to make a secret postelection survey in two of Ferguson's counties. In one, Angelina, Belden concluded that there was an "amazing change of votes" that "baffles all mathematical laws." O'Daniel ultimately collected 35 percent of the county vote although the postelection poll indicated that only 22 percent had voted for him.[34]

Apparent irregularities in O'Daniel's campaign financing attracted the attention of a Texas senate investigating committee. In hearings held in June 1941, the committee discovered that the various expenses involved in publishing and distributing the *W. Lee O'Daniel News* were somehow not considered to be campaign expenditures by O'Daniel's campaign manager. Some $18,000 of radio time was also unaccounted for in the O'Daniel campaign totals. Much of the air time was granted by station XEAW, owned by a Mexican corporation whose president and sole American stockholder was Carr P. Collins. Knowing that the law forbade both foreign and United States corporations from donating anything of value to office seekers, Collins assured the committee that O'Daniel's speeches were purchased at regular commercial rates and paid for by individual friends. Collins himself gave almost $8,000, and two officials of the Texas Employers Company made contributions, but Collins refused to divulge the names of the donors. He could not remember all of them, he said, and besides all transactions were in cash and no records were kept. Without names, the committee was not inclined to go any further in ferreting out possible corporate donations.[35]

There was some talk in the Johnson camp of appealing the election, but as Jimmie Allred phrased it in a private letter, "I doubt that an investigation would have helped Lyndon on account of some of the indiscreet things which are reputed to have been done by some of his over-enthusiastic supporters." Indeed one of Coke Stevenson's corporate friends, Maston Nixon, warned Tom Connally (who was undoubtedly supposed to pass the information on to the White House) that the investigating committee was Stevenson's creature and that it did not have to confine itself to examining O'Daniel's shenanigans. A week later one of the state senators on the committee warned Connally that "many of our mutual friends would be embarrassed" if the committee were allowed to plunge onward, since "state and federal laws were flagrantly violated" and Hatch Act violations occurred on Johnson's behalf. In fact the Stevenson-O'Daniel combine in the legislature had put across a resolution granting the committee full authority to carry on investigations even after the legislature adjourned. The action was a warning to the Johnson camp that it should not challenge the election results. Moreover John Connally and others in the Johnson high command knew that an election probe might have exposed the Brown and Root "bonuses" to employees and "fees" to lawyers that were used to pay Johnson campaign expenses, which far exceeded the $25,000 limit set by federal law. No election contest was filed, though that was not quite the end of the matter. Supposedly in connection with the Brown and Root election expenses, the company later paid a scaled-down tax assessment and fraud penalty of $372,000. Some accounts have it that the contested tax returns mysteriously burned in 1953.[36]

After taking office in August 1941, O'Daniel submitted his antistrike bill several times but was never able to muster more than four votes out of ninety-six senators. He also urged the Senate to outlaw the union shop, to cancel all draft deferments for "labor racketeers and other privileged classes," to eliminate overtime pay and the forty-hour week, and even to ban picketing. Although every measure failed overwhelmingly, the senator declared that World War II could never have been won if he had not prevented strikes by his efforts to pass antilabor laws. O'Daniel never mentioned business abuses, even though all too many American corporations had held up defense legislation, refused to convert to wartime production, did business with Hitler, and paid executives enormous wartime salaries.[37]

In the regular senatorial contest in 1942, O'Daniel asked for reelection on the basis of his record as senator. During this second campaign for the Senate, "Pappy" O'Daniel suddenly became more aware of the communist menace in Texas. He declared that communistic labor racketeers had a slush fund of one billion dollars for political campaigns and that they had allotted from one million to five million dollars to defeat him. He added that the "Communistic labor leader racketeers" were trying, under cover of war, to steal the American form of government and that two of the state's leading newspapers, the *Dallas News* and the *Fort Worth Star-Telegram*, were aiding them. O'Daniel charged that his opponents in the primary, former governors Dan Moody and James Allred, were financed by the "Communistic labor leader racketeers," a phrase he used as often as sixteen times in one speech. Finally O'Daniel charged that there was a conspiracy among Moody, Allred, the professional politicians, the politically controlled newspapers, and, of course, the "Communistic labor leader racketeers"; they joined forces, he said, in the dirtiest campaign of misrepresentation in Texas history. None of these allegations were documented, and it was as ludicrous to place the conservative Texas press in the communist conspiracy as it was to lump Allred and Moody in a cabal when they were running against each other. Writer J. Frank Dobie later noted, as evidence of the "menace," that in the 1940 election the communists polled 260 votes out of over a million votes cast in Texas.[38]

James Allred was subjected to particularly withering fire on the part of Senator O'Daniel. In almost every speech in late July 1942, the senator implied that Allred had been offered $200,000 by the communists to make the race for the Senate and an additional 200,000 if he won. At Corsicana O'Daniel alleged:

> People are constantly asking me why a man with a $10,000 lifetime job would quit a federal bench to run for an office he has no chance of winning. Well, suppose you had a $10,000-a-year job and I came along and wanted to hire you. Let us suppose you hesitated and I would say, "Here's $200,000 in cash—it's yours whether you win or not. On top of that you can spend a million dollars on your campaign, hiring the best speakers you can get. And if you win the race, you'll get $400,000." Of course I'm not going to positively say that the Communistic labor racketeers made such a deal. They didn't call me in on their meeting. But I'll let you form your own conclusions.[39]

During his first year as governor in 1939, O'Daniel had announced that the United States should stay out of the European conflict and that the war would not harm this country. After being elected to Congress, O'Daniel gave his maiden speech in the Senate on the second day of his membership, August 6, 1941, thus breaking the record of Huey Long, who had shocked the chamber by speaking on his third day of service. In his speech, O'Daniel pledged to support the president, praised hillbilly music, and proclaimed his opposition to the bill that would have extended the time of the Selective Service Act, which the president favored. The extension of the draft, he said, meant the abandonment of democracy and the beginning of dictatorship. At this time the Japanese army was marching into Thailand and the Germans were at the gates of Moscow, promising conquest by September.[40]

Thus it came as no surprise that during his 1942 campaign, Senator O'Daniel held that there were no shortages of sugar or gasoline, that the government was restricting production for the sole purpose of rationing it and thereby regimenting the American people. The senator told his audiences that such conservation was the work of crackpots and that there would never be any gasoline rationing in Texas (by the summer of 1942 gasoline rationing was underway in the eastern states but had not yet reached Texas). Yet he supported the administration on most defense matters, knowing that the president was still popular and that the bulk of the citizenry was unified behind the war effort.[41]

By the time of the runoff campaign, after Moody was eliminated in the first primary, O'Daniel was referring to Roosevelt as "the greatest strategist the world has ever seen" and telling radio audiences about his son in the army. This was a desperate effort to shore up his strength among farmers, small-town residents, and pensioners, who were still a bulwark of Roosevelt strength. O'Daniel also appealed to that section of the electorate that voted for FDR, but did believe that the administration was coddling labor and tended to resent Washington's meddling in Texas politics—for example, sending congressmen back home to canvass for Allred. The senator, of course, was already solidly entrenched with the isolationists, Republicans, Roosevelt haters, and most of the corporate Establishment. These interests recognized Lee O'Daniel's true feelings and, in the case of the latter three, were especially fond of his labor program.[42] Dallas political sage Bill Kittrell reported to Democratic boss Ed Flynn that O'Daniel

has the support of the leading figures of business and industry, including the dominant oil industry. They are for him because he hates Roosevelt and labor, and is clever enough to deceive his rural followers (who are for Roosevelt almost to a man) into believing that he is a friend and supporter of the President. During the last few days of the campaign he dwelt on his love of the Commander-in-Chief, but told of his distrust of the professional politicians. He changed his tune from a cheery assertion that there won't be a long war to a tearful appeal as the father of Paddy Boy who had gone to the war. Paddy Boy, by the way, didn't go until they sent for him and the other son, Mickey Boy, is banging a guitar in Pappy's band.[43]

The O'Daniel image was tarnished in both primaries after Allred and Moody investigators found that O'Daniel's marriage, which he described as taking place in 1916, actually occurred after America's entry into World War I in 1917. Though twenty-seven years old at the time, O'Daniel did not serve in the war. The flour salesman was also involved in the operations of a Kansas milling company that had gone bankrupt and whose irate stockholders were alleging fraud. Also the Kansan evidently had not paid his 1934 Tarrant County property taxes on 460 acres. Some or all of this information was allowed to leak out, but its effect was imponderable. O'Daniel's efforts were hurt more by his own inability to revive the folksy fire of his earlier campaigns. There was little cheering of his dry performances, and some crowds melted away.[44]

Jimmie Allred's candidacy was clutched by the Roosevelt administration, labor and other urban New Dealers, the urban press, most servicemen and young people, the liquor interests, and the border bosses. The first two flavored him because of his known progressive views. The second two interests plugged the former governor in part because he was not regarded as an isolationist or shrill obstructionist to the war effort. The liquor lobby may have simply preferred a normal dry to a fanatical, demagogic one. The south Texas bosses knew that Allred could deliver dams and other political projects for their region, while O'Daniel was unable to guide much of anything through the Senate.[45]

Given the antilabor climate of the day and a certain amount of anti-New Deal sentiment, Allred could not afford the public embrace of either, especially labor. In a hotel conference with Austin's New Deal mayor, Tom Miller, and with Texas State Federation of Labor secretary, Harry Acreman, Allred informed them that his financiers wanted him to take a couple of shots at labor. He thought he might criticize the CIO since they were going to vote for him anyway. Miller agreed that he had to, but Acreman warned that CIO leaders and members would go fishing on election day. Possibly a few did, angered by Allred's proposals to prohibit compulsory unionism in defense industries and to limit dues to a dollar a month. A trickier problem for Allred was whether to seek Roosevelt's endorsement. The president would certainly have given it, since he, along with Johnson, Tom Connally, and Jesse Jones, had cleared the Allred candidacy in advance. After receiving much conflicting advice, Allred decided that he had to try to avoid the "yes man" rubber stamp image that O'Daniel was tagging him with. There was no endorsement.[46]

The O'Daniel candidacy continued to delay any possible emergence of ideological voting patterns in Texas. Allred was endorsed by the *Dallas Morning News, Dallas Times-Herald, Houston Post, Houston Chronicle, Fort Worth Star-Telegram, Lubbock Avalanche, Amarillo News-Globe,* and *Abilene Reporter-News*, among others. Mayor C. K. Quin of San Antonio joined the cause, as did fundamentalist reverend J. Frank Norris, and the Fort Worth multimillionaire duo, oilman Sid Richardson and publisher Amon Carter. Carter completely agreed with O'Daniel's antilabor rhetoric but regarded the senator as insincere. The publisher informed the White House that the *Star-Telegram* not only endorsed Allred but also that "we have given him every break that we possibly could." Many in the Dallas Establishment cast their lot with Allred, including E. B. Germany, R. L. Thornton, president of the Mercantile Bank, Fred Florence of the Republic National Bank, Clyde Stewart of Southwestern Bell Telephone, John Carpenter of Texas Power and Light, Karl Hoblitzelle, owner of the Interstate Theater chain, and his lobbyist, D. F. Strickland. Roy Coffee, general attorney for Lone Star Gas in Dallas, sent out hundreds of letters for Allred in the posh cluster of precincts north of Turtle Creek Boulevard. These ten precincts had been Moody's best in Dallas County and had given the safe conservative a majority over the combined votes of O'Daniel and Allred, 2,995 to 2,913. These upper-class neighborhoods swung to the New Deal candidate in the runoff, awarding him a better than two to one majority— 3,691 to 1,816. In Houston Allred was assisted by influential corporate attorney Charles I. Francis and banker-lawyer James Elkins, a member of the 8-F crowd. While Allred lost the ritzy River Oaks section of Houston in the runoff (though no precinct returns are available), he had carried at least three of the city's conservative, generally wealthy precincts by a collective margin of 485 to 423 (to Moody's 325) in the first primary.[47] (See appendixes 1 and 2.) With the possible, but unlikely, exception of Coffee, none of these individuals, newspapers, or precincts favored New Dealer Homer Rainey in his gubernatorial campaign four years later. By that time O'Daniel was out of the picture and all the corporate interests had seen the ideological light.

O'Daniel was strong enough under the prevailing conditions of 1942 to defeat Allred, 451,359 to 433,203. Allred carried all fifteen cities with a population of over thirty thousand, probably captured 80 percent of the voters in their twenties, and swept the border counties (Duval checked in with a 2,770 to 115 margin.) But it proved to be more crucial that O'Daniel still had "the country people fooled," as Allred put it, especially the middle-aged and older voters of east and northeast Texas. Also the state's 100,000 or so Republicans freely crossed over and voted for O'Daniel in the Democratic primary. And of the 240,000 Texans in the armed forces, Allred estimated that only about 10,000 were able to vote. Thousands of workers were away from home on construction jobs and took no interest in the race, a factor that hurt the New Deal in elections all across the country. Texans were probably also caught up in a growing southern animosity toward the administration and resentment against the alleged coddling of labor and wartime restrictions and bureaucracy. Perhaps the outcome was most succinctly summarized by Winnsboro banker C. M. Cain, who observed that "nonthinking voters . . . in this section are in the majority and have been . . . since the Ferguson regime."[48]

O'Daniel won a record number of four contested elections in a four-year span. His success depended in part on the camp meeting fervor of his political rallies and the popularity of his hillbilly music radio show. On both these stages he was perceived by his audiences as sincere, honest, and humble, a man who took the people into his confidence. He had communicated with the elderly, rural, and low-income folks for years, telling them things they wanted to hear, making it easier to be poor. During his messianic campaigns he beefed up his humanitarian image with spirited pension promises. And through the simple (but not easily repeated) device of denouncing politicians as a class, he convinced the electorate that he could deal with politicians. Thus he was embraced by voters "just because he is a good Christian man" and "because he's honest, mister, and because he ain't no politician" and because he was an "honest, trustworthy, Christian gentleman" and "He's a good man. He's almost a preacher. He knows how to catch up with them Congressmen and tell us about it."[49]

The image of the sincere, humble, compassionate man was as counterfeit as the country-boy pose. The studio employees who watched him broadcast for years avowed that he was a born actor who turned on laughter or tears with equal ease and the slightest provocation. They agreed that he may not have believed what he was saying but "feels it at the time." The supreme irony of the pension controversy was that O'Daniel cynically used the issue just to win office and had no real sympathy for old people. He would not even visit with any of them when they straggled into Austin, pitifully anxious to talk to the governor about their problems. O'Daniel regarded the rest of the electorate in a similar light. On one occasion, while the orchestra was playing "Nearer My God to Thee," O'Daniel whispered to a visiting senator, "Boy, that's what brings 'em in; that brings the voters in." Years later as senator, O'Daniel attracted headlines when he evicted elderly tenants and servicemen from an apartment house he had purchased in the nation's overcrowded capital. Though the tenants were able and eager to pay rent, O'Daniel sent them into the streets because he wanted the fourteen apartments (with fourteen separate bathrooms) for his own family dwelling.[50]

Business cronies, such as Carr Collins, who was no political expert himself, could not fully rescue O'Daniel from a lifetime of political innocence. In his inexperience, he often attempted to make appointments without first checking with the state senator in the appointee's home town, generally refused to "trade out" with legislators, vetoed bills that he probably did not understand, and avoided the heads of state agencies because he did not fathom their functions or their relationship with the governor. He was overridden a record twelve out of fifty-seven vetoes. The governor was never quite able to explain what he meant by a transactions tax, but, of course, the lobby knew what it meant. Given his image, cultivated by deliberate blasts at lobbyists on radio, O'Daniel could not afford to be seen in public with them. But secret visits to the mansion were made by the men who really had his ear—such lobbyists as Jack Dies (Humble Oil), J. M. Melson (Gulf Oil), and Charles Neville and Bailey Jones (Lone Star Gas). Since he was introverted and unsure of himself with people, he was reluctant to meet with the public, elected representatives, or the press. A few weeks after his inauguration, he abandoned the daily press conferences, then the weekly ones, and took to the radio. The microphone, after all, could not ask embarrassing questions or talk back. He largely negated his ignorance, his seclusion, and his political handicaps with masterful radio showmanship. In his Sunday broadcasts he often listed recalcitrant legislators, and the resulting deluge of hostile mail to the solons sometimes set bills free from their committee logjams. No other governor made such effective use of the air, either in legislative sessions or in elections.[51]

O'Daniel was once described as the poor man's preacher and the rich man's senator, but his political sins ran deeper than that. Sometime during his governorship O'Daniel evolved into a right-wing extremist. He denied the legitimacy of established public policies and challenged the Constitution on the basis of an ultraconservative ideology. He demonstrated little or no regard for truth, documentation, or rational discourse. He also displayed another extremist criterion, "unbounded brazenness," through such antics as conjuring up a mythical fifth column and appointing an unqualified, nearly senile man to the United States Senate. Yet even though O'Daniel did more to "break down confidence in the institution of Government" than anyone since Reconstruction, as one impeccably conservative congressman put it, Texas kept him in high office for a decade.[52]

4

Rebellion Against
the New Deal, 1944

*It's funny about Texans. They have to hate somebody,
a whole lot of them.*
Alla Clary, Sam Rayburn's
secretary, 1969 (reminiscing about 1944)

*The Democratic party has been stolen by an
unscrupulous political machine in the hands of negroes
and communistic radicals. . . . We denounce as Judas
Iscariots the Allreds . . . and Rayburns.*
Brochure of the Texas Regular
party, 1944

*We appreciate our great oil industry, but if it is
harboring an ambition to remold our political character
to fit its own purposes . . . , then it is time for certain
mushroom millionaires to be shown their place.*
J. O. Cullom to Jimmie Allred,
June 11, 1944

As early as July 1941, a few anti-Roosevelt Democrats were formulating plans to defeat the New Dealers in 1944. The American Democratic National Committee was formally organized in February 1944 by Harry Woodring, Roosevelt's former secretary of war. Texas Agricultural Commissioner J. E. McDonald was on hand for the occasion. Spelling out its goals in the Declaration of Chicago, the ADNC pinned most of its hopes on lining up "independent" electors for the Democratic column on the ballot. If they got a majority of the votes, the state's Democratic electors would decline to cast their ballots for the presumed Democratic nominee, Roosevelt. If no presidential candidate received a majority of the electoral votes, the contest would be thrown into the House, where the conservative South would be disproportionately strong under the Constitution's one-vote-per-state requirement. In March Woodring journeyed south with Robert Harriss, a

Texas rancher and cotton broker who had moved to New York. Visiting with Dallas oilman E. B. Germany and twenty other businessmen, Woodring announced that anti-New Dealers in Texas ought to flock to the front seats in the precinct meetings and begin the process of electing uninstructed states' rights delegates to the larger meetings that followed. Fifty oilmen and bankers turned out for the Fort Worth gathering, where Woodring repeated his message. Dallas publicist Ted Ewart, well known to Texas oilmen, was named ADNC campaign manager for Texas. There was some sentiment among these Democrats to draft Virginia senator Harry Byrd for the nomination, as was announced at an April 20 conference in Dallas, but in Texas the southern-based Byrd movement was swallowed up by the independent electors' strategy. The ADNC, in fact, claimed to be nonpolitical since it did not endorse a particular candidate. And as a nonpolitical organization, it accepted corporate donations. Woodring evidently raised some sixty-three thousand dollars in his two-month stint with the committee. The movement went on without Woodring and Ewart, both of whom resigned in the first week of April.[1]

Texas conservatives were depending on the gradual increase of anti-Roosevelt sentiment in the state. The New Dealers seemed too intimate with the labor movement and had saddled the country with too many wartime restrictions and high-handed bureaus. It also rankled many that Roosevelt was serving an unprecedented third term and that the vice-president was controversial left-winger Henry Wallace. Oilmen were upset over the fixed price of their product. Nor did the New Dealers benefit from such wartime incidents as the use of the army to settle the dispute at Montgomery Ward, which refused to recognize its union, or the Supreme Court decision, *Smith* v. *Allwright* (1944), which struck down the Texas law barring blacks from the Democratic primary. Nevertheless, in 1940, the president had polled over four times as many votes as Willkie in Texas, and in the spring of 1944, there was little reason to think that he would not enjoy another easy victory in the traditionally Democratic state. A Washington's birthday fund raiser divulged healthy support for the administration, and Texans enriched the Democratic National Committee by some forty thousand dollars. A Texas poll in March showed that 65 percent favored FDR, 10 percent Tom Dewey (Republican governor of New York), and 25 percent other Democrats and Republicans.[2]

By early May, however, the anti-New Dealers entrenched on the State Democratic Executive Committee dispatched a letter to Texas precinct leaders calling for the election of uninstructed delegates to the county conventions and the state convention. This tactic was passed off as a party program. SDEC chairman George Butler intimated that uninstructed delegates would be in a better position than Roosevelt delegates to bargain for the restoration of the old two-thirds rule, which, until 1936, was the percentage of delegates required for the Democratic party's presidential nomination. Restoration would strengthen the convention position of the conservative South, which could not block a nomination as long as only a majority vote was necessary. But the letter's phraseology, as at least one New Dealer discovered, was similar to that of the Declaration of Chicago. Despite what should have been ample warnings of the conservatives' real intentions, the New Dealers were caught off guard at the conventions. Anti-Roosevelt delegates from the four biggest cities, including prominent attorneys from Sinclair, Socony-Vacuum, Sun, and other oil and gas companies, dominated the state convention in Austin on May 23. At Butler's instigation, the convention selected uninstructed delegates and also nominated presidential electors who were to vote for party nominees only if the national convention restored the two-thirds rule for national nominations and denounced the *Smith* v. *Allwright* decision. Since the Democrats would never adopt these measures, the nominated electors were really uninstructed and could vote for anyone. Their sympathies were anti-New Deal, so they could be expected to vote for the Republican candidate, Thomas Dewey, or for Byrd. Most Texans would then be completely disfranchised in the general election. If they crossed out the names of the Democratic electors, the Republican electors would vote Republican; if they crossed out the names of the Republican electors, the Democratic electors would vote Republican or for Byrd.[3]

The *Smith* v. *Allwright* decision was less than six weeks old, but the delegates were probably less concerned about race than about New Deal economics. Other resolutions passed at the state convention condemned strikes, forbade the establishment of additional federal boards and bureaus, and denounced all alleged efforts to change the form of government by usurpation of power or by bloodless revolution. There was obviously widespread hatred of the New Deal's wartime controls and fear that the Democrats might not lift those controls after the war. Another resolution opposed all governmental attempts to foster social equality. If these planks had been carried out, they would have curtailed the power and future growth of the federal government and put an end to the civil-rights movement. These measures reflected a deep division within the Texas Democratic party, an Establishment-New Dealer split over economic philosophy and party loyalty.[4]

Some three hundred pro-Roosevelt delegates, waving a large picture of the president, marched out the senate exit—with the organist playing "God Be With You Till We Meet Again"—and held a rump convention. The assembly selected presidential electors and delegates to the national convention, all of whom were pledged to vote for the Democratic party's presidential nominee. The New Dealers added:

. . . we could not trifle with the safety of our country by permitting a meeting of the enemies of democracy—republicans masquerading as democrats—to make it possible to throw the election of a president of the United States into a contest before the lower House of Congress, and thus cause confusion and disunity in the midst of this cruel and desperate war.[5]

The Texas threat to Roosevelt awakened the nation with a start and triggered widespread speculation that the president might be denied a fourth term. The notion of a state's withholding its electoral vote became "a flaming issue in every Southern state." Many southerners would have been appeased if fiery Vice-President Wallace had been replaced on the ticket by Texas's Sam Rayburn, but ironically Texans themselves may have scuttled Rayburn. Facing two rival Texas contingents at the national convention in July, the credentials committee seated both of them and divided the state's vote between them. Their uneasy proximity may have prevented Speaker Rayburn from capturing the vice-presidential nomination since he did not have the support of both delegations. Some of the anti-New Dealers tried to persuade the Speaker that they really favored him, but others later bragged that they "got" Rayburn in 1944. Possibly the issue of the split delegation was merely a pretext for the urban party bosses, who did not favor the independent-minded Texan for vice-president. Also Roosevelt probably preferred keeping Rayburn as Speaker in order to get his legislation through congress. Nor was "Mr. Sam's" cause enhanced by the presence of an anti-New Deal congressional opponent, who represented oil, business, and utility interests in Dallas. According to one conservative oilman, Rayburn's opponent was also given ten thousand dollars by Houston oil millionaire, Hugh Roy Cullen. Rayburn was forced to return to his district to campaign.[6]

Later in July the pro-FDR Texans, led by Alvin Wirtz and James Allred among others, set out to elect a September state convention committed to follow the popular vote. The Democratic county conventions on July 29 were the scene of fistfights, walkouts, and chicanery (on both sides) around the state. One New Dealer told of the proceedings in Big Spring and Howard County, where the anti-Roosevelt county chairman twice planted newspaper items stating that there would be no precinct conventions since no one had expressed any interest. He refused to set the time for the conventions. When the town's liberals showed up, the chairman was there "with an army of the Cosden oil crowd." The New Dealers were heavily outnumbered in the larger boxes but went into the smaller precincts where no meetings were held, assembled conventions, and thus rounded up enough votes to beat the anti-Roosevelt Democrats in the county convention. Howard County sent a New Deal delegation to the state convention, joining the clear majority there that favored a Roosevelt ticket.[7]

Texas's anti-New Dealers, meanwhile, had attempted to breathe life into the American Democratic National Committee's southern strategy and to carry it in a different direction than Woodring and some others had envisioned. Six southern states had been represented in a Shreveport, Louisiana, convention on June 18, and E. B. Germany had been elected chairman. Their cause was embarrassed in August when it was revealed that Germany wanted his electors to consider an option other than voting for Dewey or Byrd. A Mississippi elector made public a letter from Germany expressing the hope that Mississippi, Louisiana, and Texas could control the electoral college and sell their votes to the Democrats in exchange for the control of federal patronage in the rebelling states for the next four years. There was a storm of protest in Texas. Many of the more vehement anti-New Dealers opposed the scheme, and one New Dealer proclaimed, "There will be no appeasement of Germany—either Berlin or Eugene."[8] Politicking at the September state convention was furious. Jimmie Allred reported that Superior Oil threatened to strip him of his sizable retainer if he persisted in his political activities, but he informed them that they had bought his services, not his soul. Robert W. Calvert, the only New Dealer allowed on the stage, cursed chairman George Butler for not closing the vote on the contested delegations. Calvert was unaware that he was broadcasting across the state. In a welter of confusion and emotion, the New Dealers edged the rebels, 803 to 774, on the contested delegate vote. They went on to purge most of the May convention's electoral slate and replace them with Democrats who were pledged to support the party's nominees.[9]

The anti-Roosevelt faction united and formed a third party, the Texas Regulars, who hoped to siphon off enough Democratic votes to prevent another Roosevelt victory. Their premier campaigner was Senator O'Daniel, but the movement was spearheaded by other corporate representatives of the Establishment's ultraconservative wing, especially oil lobbyists and lawyers. They included independent oilmen Al Buchanan of San Antonio; Arch Rowan of Fort Worth; E. B. Germany and Hugh Roy Cullen; Hiram King, the chief lobbyist for Sinclair Oil; Clint Small, attorney for Humble Oil; E. E. Townes, former chief counsel for Humble Oil; Socony-Vacuum attorney R. A. Weinert; and George Heyer, president of the Crude Oil Company, a Sun Oil subsidiary. Heyer may have been acting under orders of Joseph Pew, president of Sun Oil and Republican boss of Pennsylvania. Other Texas Regulars were Interstate Theater lobbyist D. F. Strickland of the Rio Grande Valley, the H. H. Weinerts of Seguin, Oveta Culp Hobby, head of the Women's Army Corps and owner of the *Houston Post*, Austin cement lobbyist Charles Simons, and the Dallas attorney for Lone Star Gas and other corporations, Neth Leachman. One Regular sympathizer, who did not openly affiliate, was Maco Stewart, Jr., Galveston title-guaranty millionaire. The Anderson-Clayton Company, the world's largest cotton brokerage firm, was represented by its top executive, Lamar Fleming, and its attorney, John Crooker. Jesse Jones's vast business interests were represented by his attorney, SDEC chairman Butler, Jones's nephew-in-law. Despite their corporate connections to various Regulars, Jones and Will Clayton (of Anderson-Clayton), both of whom held high positions in the Roosevelt administration, denied any involvement with the third-party effort.[10]

The full platform of the Texas Regulars called for:

1. Restoration of the Democratic party to the integrity which has been taken away by Hillman, Browder, and others.
2. Protection of honest labor unions from foreign-born racketeers who have gained control by blackmail.
3. Return of state rights which have been destroyed by the Communist-controlled New Deal.
4. Restoration of the freedom of education.
5. Restoration of the supremacy of the white race, which has been destroyed by the Communist-controlled New Deal.
6. Restoration of the Bill of Rights instead of rule by regimentation.
7. Restoration of government by laws instead of government by bureaus.
8. Restoration of the individual appeal for justice, instead of a politically appointed bureau.[11]

The white-supremacy plank was a relatively new concern for O'Daniel and other ultraconservatives. They were responding to the civil-rights movement, which seemed to be making inroads in politics and education. The senator's newspaper, the *W. Lee O'Daniel News*, was revived for the 1944 presidential race and attempted to exploit the racial prejudices of the poor whites in Texas. The Lubbock daily ran a Regular advertisement proclaiming, "Let's keep the White in Old Glory." One anonymous pamphlet delved into genetic detail, all erroneous, on the dangers of interracial marriage.[12] Another bit of campaign litrature distributed by the Texas Regulars had these lines:

Gallivantin' Gal

Strike up the Band!
Here's our Globe Trotter!

Call off the bombing for today
Wheel out the Army ship
Hold up the war so Eleanor
Can take another trip.

> For 20,000 miles she goes
> To have her weekly fling,
> And rub her nose against the nose
> Of some wild Zulu king!
>
> 'Twas by design and not by luck
> She chose this distant shore;
> The only place she hasn't stuck
> Her nosey nose before
>
> Now, having rubbed the royal nose
> She crossed another sea,
> To scare the natives I suppose
> And watch them plant a tree
>
> The happy thought occurred to me
> As homeward bound she sped;
> Why couldn't they have shipped the tree
> And planted her instead?[13]

Overtones of anti-Semitism also appeared in the campaign, although apparently not in O'Daniel's paper. One Texas Regular poster showed Uncle Sam being thrown over an abyss by a Sidney Hillman wearing a long, thick black beard. As one oilman-contractor phrased it, "We are through with the Jew Deal, and we don't mean maybe."[14]

One unique campaign subterfuge was unveiled by the Regulars. Public relations man Jan Anderson and his associates, allegedly representing "honored" Texas newsmen (who were unnamed), offered substantial prizes in war bonds to reward "courageous" Texas editors who ran columns on why they were voting against the New Deal or why they favored Jeffersonian democracy. Anderson declared that several scores of newspapers responded favorably.[15]

"Pappy" O'Daniel's speeches in behalf of the Regulars lacked the fire and cunning of earlier campaigns, and the crowds were small and prone to loud jeering. At Waco, when asked whom the Texas Regular electors would vote for, O'Daniel snapped that the question was "silly." Then he disclosed the little-known information that "virtually every high officeholder wants to communize America." The height of his tour was his appearance at Houston on November 2, where he was greeted by a small crowd of three thousand. Some five hundred of them rioted and tossed eggs and tomatoes in the speaker's direction. O'Daniel blamed the riot on "Communistic labor leader racketeers" in the pay of the New Deal.[16]

The effectiveness of his speaking tour was also hindered by a Senate committee's investigation of his campaign expenditures. Twice in June 1944, the committee invited O'Daniel to testify about his fund-raising activities but received no reply. Later Mrs. O'Daniel "weepingly" testified. The senators discovered that something called the Common Citizens Radio Committee had been organized by the O'Daniels's friends and relatives to print and distribute copies of his nonpartisan radio speeches. This "people's crusade" was chartered under Texas law as educational yet was collecting funds for the *W. Lee O'Daniel News*, which was used politically in the 1944 campaign. Donors included such common citizens as Hugh Roy Cullen and multimillionaire oilman and Republican senator from Oklahoma, E. H. Moore, who gave twenty-five thousand dollars each. Lamar Fleming, Maco Stewart, Jr., and Marrs McLean contributed twenty-five hundred dollars each. McLean, a wealthy insurance and oil baron, was treasurer of the Republican party of Texas and frankly marked his check as a political donation. H. E. Butt Grocery Company interests chipped in a thousand dollars.[17]

Post Office officials told the Senate Committee that an application by O'Daniel's paper for second-class mailing privileges was still pending. A requirement for this privilege was a bona-fide list of subscribers, with not more than a few issues going to nonsubscribers. A number of requests from the Post Office Department that the *W. Lee O'Daniel News* supply such a list had not been met. Although the newspaper had fewer than twenty-five hundred subscribers, it printed between seventy thousand and a hundred thousand copies of each issue.[18]

The Senate committee also wondered about the educational value of O'Daniel's radio speeches. In one broadcast he clearly claimed that Roosevelt was a greater danger than Hitler and that the New Deal had rationed and regimented the people into almost a complete state of communism. Another of his broadcasts assaulted the "iron-fisted dictatorship" of the "labor leader racketeers, socialists, fellow travelers, and communists."[19]

Meanwhile the supposedly nonpartisan American Democratic National Committee offered its presidential nomination to O'Daniel, who declined the honor. ADNC assistant treasurer Ralph W. Moore spent several thousand dollars of his own and committee money in lining up radio time for the senator and in urging others to contribute. Moore admitted to Congressman Clinton Anderson's House committee (investigating campaign expenditures) that his actions were political but hastened to add that he could not speak for the ADNC.[20]

Another political outfit that reached its anti-New Deal zenith in 1944 was the Committee for Constitutional Government, which was also investigated by Anderson's committee. Founded in 1937 by Frank Gannett, owner of the third largest newspaper chain in the country, the CCG was supposedly designed as a nonpartisan, nonpolitical committee to educate the American people about the Constitution. For the next several years the organization was directed by Gannett, former Congressman Samuel Pettengill of Indiana, famous New York Presbyterian minister Norman Vincent Peale, and the committee's executive secretary, Edward Rumely. During World War I Rumely had accepted over $1.3 million from imperial Germany to purchase the *New York Evening Mail.* His career as an enemy agent was interrupted in 1918 by his indictment for violation of the Trading with the Enemy Act. He was sentenced to a year and a day in prison but was pardoned by President Coolidge after serving only thirty days.[21]

The CCG began its allegedly nonpolitical activity by campaigning against President Roosevelt's court reform bill in 1937. It spent thousands of dollars in an attempt to block Roosevelt's third term, the "road to dictatorship." This activity was not political, Gannett said, because the committee did not come out against any particular candidate. Other stances called nonpolitical included the drive to end the "one party dictatorship" and the organization of "hard-hitting citizens groups" in various congressional districts.[22]

The Texas CCG was directed by Ted Ewart, whose campaign efforts were launched late in 1943 with the assistance of the Dallas public relations firm of Watson and Associates. Ewart, in addition to collecting over $2,400 for one month's work for the ADNC, was rewarded by the CCG with $10,800 in salary, $60 a week expenses, office rent, and, evidently, a 3 percent commission on all money collected—for eight months' work. From May through July 1944, San Antonio oil lease expert J. W. Crenshaw received $2,500 for his nonpartisan, educational endeavors. Rumely told the curious House investigating committee that Crenshaw's organizing just happened to coincide with the Texas primary. Given these high-priced services in Texas, it is little wonder that the CCG raised $112,000 in the Lone Star state compared to $143,000 in the other forty-seven. The committee's financiers included many of the Texas Regulars' contributors: John Crooker, Edgar Townes, Maco Stewart, Jr., and Lamar Fleming. Hugh Roy Cullen and fellow Houston oilman Craig Cullinan contributed at least $1,000 each. Rumely informed the press that the CCG had nothing to hide and would reveal all expenditures, but when he appeared before the House committee, he declined to do so.[23]

Much of the money was spent on literature claimed as educational, for example, the pamphlet that urged a coalition against the "New Deal Nazis in 1944." Another circular listed numerous New Deal agencies that were leading the nation toward totalitarianism. The circular was written by Houston printer E. M. Biggers, whose list included the Joint Chiefs of Staff, more than a score of war bureaus, several duplications, and several agencies that had been out of existence for ten years. He mailed some four million to eight million of his throwaways, many outside the state. Biggers believed this work was sponsored by himself and God. He put himself in second place but said he was proud of his running mate. Rumely denied that Biggers's mailings were political and denied that the CCG had paid for them, though it had purchased the printer's mailing list for an undisclosed sum.[24]

These activities seemed to be needed primarily in the congressional districts of Texas's most progressive congressmen—Wright Patman, Lyndon Johnson, and Sam Rayburn—none of whom was an Establishment man at this juncture in his career (all three were always party loyalists, in any case). The people in the Gulf Coast district of Richard Kleberg, owner of the King Ranch, and in the Dallas district of Hatton Sumners, did not seem to need to be educated on the Constitution. Kleberg and Sumners had fought the New Deal since its inception.[25]

On April 19, 1944, wealthy Texarkana lumber dealer Arthur Temple announced to the citizenry of the First Congressional District that Samuel Pettengill would speak there in ten days and that a CCG chapter would be organized. The dinner speech on the Constitution raised $4,150. Shortly after the dinner, Harold Buck, a friend of Temple's, announced as Democratic candidate for Congress against the incumbent, Wright Patman. Sudsudenly Texarkana was blanketed with CCG circulars titled "Ten Thousand Dollars is a lot of Money." The committee reasoned that $10,000 would be each Texarkana family's share of the national debt at the end of the war, since the city's share of the debt was supposed to come to almost $44 million. The circular added that Wright Patman thought nothing of debt, that he proposed to continue going into debt when the war was over, and that he did not want any limits on the debt. Rumely assured the House committee that the brochure was not designed to affect the congressional election. Arthur Temple admitted that he had never heard Patman say anything about favoring indebtedness. Temple argued that the literature was not political but just an expression of opinion on governmental philosophy. This transparent chicanery might have finished off a less adroit politician than Wright Patman, but the popular incumbent trounced Buck in the Democratic primary, 27,553 to 9,763.[26]

Corporate support of such front groups as the American Democratic National Committee, Common Citizens Radio Committee, the Committee for Constitutional Government, and the Christian Americans appeared to many congressional investigators to be in violation of the Corrupt Practices Act. This law forbids election contributions by corporations, defines "political committee" in a way that rather obviously embraced the above groups, and requires the filing of a complete and accurate account of all receipts and expenditures. None of the front groups had willingly divulged any financial information, and none disclosed very much even to the congressional committees. As the corporate interests knew, the corrupt practices law is rarely enforced. All of the groups escaped prosecution.[27]

With lavish financing, the Texas Regulars and their allies were able to make their views known. The CCG, for instance, paid for dozens of anti-New Deal broadcasts in several Texas cities. On the first page of every day's edition, the *Dallas Morning News* carried the Regulars' scheduled radio broadcasts for the Dallas area from October 27 to November 6. In that period in Dallas the Regulars sponsored thirty broadcasts, twenty by O'Daniel. But their campaign was handicapped by its inability to collaborate with the Republicans. Most Regulars wanted to vote Democratic below the presidential level, and they would not pledge to vote for Dewey. Most Republicans wanted their party to keep its identity in order to enjoy future patronage in Republican administrations and in case a two-party system blossomed out of the political wars of 1944. Some GOP leaders thought O'Daniel blocked an effective coalition, evidently because the senator wanted to keep his base of support in the Texas Democratic party.[28]

Roosevelt and the Democrats won the election with about 822,000 votes, Dewey and the Republicans followed with over 191,000, and the Texas Regulars, who fielded no candidate, polled over 135,000. The Regulars' 12 percent of the vote forced them to disband officially in spring 1945, a necessary subterfuge for their intended infiltration, as a bloc, back into the Democratic party. Both Republicans and Regulars evidently found their strength in the silk-stocking precincts in the major cities, while black and working-class boxes were especially strong for Roosevelt (see appendixes 2, 3, 4, and 6). One Regular succinctly summarized the election: "Gentlemen," he announced, ". . . the yokels discovered that they can outvote us."[29]

The campaign was probably a decisive juncture in W. Lee O'Daniel's career. Shunned by many Senate colleagues who resented his holier than thou attitude and his criticisms of the Senate from within the Senate chamber, O'Daniel had also clearly lost his influence over Texans. His extremism was more noticeable than ever in his fanatical conviction that he possessed the "one and only truth" and in the frenzied air of many of his speeches. The nation "swarmed with parasitic government snoopers"; New Deal "smear brigades" were slandering him and his family; the rising tide of high prices after the war was planned by the government so that it could "hold onto power until it could lead the country into another war"; rationing was "a Communistic, totalitarian measure designed to beat the people of the U.S. into submitting to the edicts of an autocratic, bureaucratic dictatorship."[30]

The senator believed that an insidious web extended into every facet of American life. There was not just a plot here or there in American history; one vast communist conspiracy was the motive force in all history. The American civilization was on the verge of toppling. When O'Daniel announced that he would not be a candidate for reelection in 1948, he gave as his reason that there was only a slight hope of saving America from the communists. Perhaps there were other reasons for the senator's retirement. Some of the "blue chip boys," such as Carr P. Collins, had deserted his candidacy, doubtless recognizing a sure loser. The public-opinion polls credited him with only 7 percent of the electorate, surely an all-time low for

an incumbent United States senator. He had less than one-fifth the support
of former governor Coke Stevenson, who had been out of public office for
over a year.[31]

The political philosophy of the Texas Regulars and the front groups was
identical to O'Daniel's. Besides their obsession with the alleged Negro-New
Deal-labor union-communist conspiracy, the Regulars were a particular
threat to democracy in their attempt to corrupt the free press and subvert
the democratic election process. It is rather surprising that so many big
businessmen would spearhead such a movement. Corporations, after all,
are in the public eye, and openly playing ultraconservative politics might
hurt sales and business. Because of this, some of the business magnates themselves stayed out of the fray and allowed their commentators and lobbyists
to perform the heavy campaign work. For instance, Dallas banker Nathan
Adams made only one public appearance—at the draft-Byrd meeting—
while Humble executive Harry Weiss stayed completely out of the limelight but quietly donated thirty-five hundred dollars to the ADNC. Most
Establishment officials—such as Tom Connally and O'Daniel's successor as
governor, Coke Stevenson—cautiously chose to be quiet until the volatile
controversy was settled. (The governor's party allegiance was sorely suspect since it was his SDEC chairman who launched the Regular revolt, and
since he had suggested that both sets of electors be listed under the Democratic column.)[32]

Besides leading to the defeat of the extremist Regulars, the passions touched
off by the 1944 political wars did nothing to enhance the cause of any element in the Establishment. The SDEC fell into New Deal hands. Two vehement anti-New Deal congressmen were sent into retirement. Richard Kleberg
was defeated with the assistance of labor, Dr. Francis Townsend's pension
followers, and the Parr machine. And Martin Dies was hounded into with-
drawing from his race. The public image of Establishment champion Coke
Stevenson was probably tarnished in the short run. In a postcampaign
analysis Sam Rayburn wrote to a friend, referring to Stevenson and O'Daniel,
"that this election will prove the deathknell of certain mountebank politicians in Texas."[33] Neither Stevenson, O'Daniel, nor Kleberg won public
office again.

The turmoil of 1944 also may have hastened the retirement of the more
venerable conservative veteran, Hatton Sumners, whose stance illustrated
a certain political schizophrenia among Establishment leaders in 1944. As a
conservative Democratic congressman, Sumners agreed with much of the
O'Daniel-Regular approach, especially on labor issues. But he could not
bestir himsaelf to initiate legislation against strikers or to work against the
Democratic party. Although he still believed in 1944 that the "wild labor
crowd" wielded dangerous power, he had to fend off his own conservative
supporters because he had not tried to pass punitive labor measures over

President Roosevelt's certain veto. Sumners appeared reluctant to defy the commander-in-chief in wartime. And though he discovered that his closest advisers were of Texas Regular sympathies, he confided to one friend that O'Daniel's slashing attacks on Congress destroyed public confidence and played into the hands of the communists. Sumners found himself under strong challenge in the Democratic primary in 1944 from a former supporter who ran with the unofficial blessings of Dallas's burgeoning union constituency. After winning by less than a three-to-two margin, Sumners faced a Republican opponent who evidently garnered some backing from big business. Victorious in the general election but undoubtedly dismayed at the twistings of politics in Dallas and Washington, Sumners announced his retirement in 1946.[34]

Yet the Establishment suffered no permanent damage. Indeed a San Antonio pollster concluded that the local press effectively covered up for Coke Stevenson and that few citizens of the Alamo city ever learned that the governor fought Roosevelt.[35] The Establishment had learned that political control of the state did not ensure control of presidential politics and that party loyalty (and, to a much lesser extent, the New Deal philosophy) was not going to yield easily to the ultraconservatives' money or to their attacks. The impact of the Regulars and other Establishment ultraconservatives cannot be measured quantitatively, but their attitudes lingered. Their propaganda undoubtedly raised the consciousness of voters—in some fashion—for the trampling of academic freedom that took a dramatic turn that same year of 1944, the attempted antilabor legislation of 1945, the party bolting of 1948 and 1952, and the Texas McCarthyite activities of the 1950s.

5

Thunder on
the Right, 1940s

*Too many businessmen . . . hate and fear the New
Deal so much that they contribute money to support
blackguards whose chief stock in trade is professional
libel.*

> Hastings Harrison to Beauford
> Jester, June 22, 1946

The "slimy elements are boring from within."

> Oilmen Paul Roemer and C. F.
> Modglin to Hatton Sumners,
> March 27, 1941, lamenting New Deal
> permissiveness toward organized
> labor

The Christian Americans and Fight for Free Enterprise also played key roles in generating a reactionary mood in Texas during the war. They were primarily huckster groups operating on the right-wing fringe of the Establishment.

The Christian Americans traced their origin to the career of Vance Muse, a muscular, six-foot-four inch Texan who spent a lifetime lobbying for reactionary millionaires. His leading patron over the years was John Henry Kirby, a strong-willed oil and lumber baron from east Texas and Houston. Together they fought the threatened railroad strike and the Adamson Act of 1916, crusaded against all of Woodrow Wilson's allegedly antibusiness legislation, and worked in the 1920s for national sales tax legislation and the elimination of gift taxes. From 1926 to 1930 Muse and his sister, Ida Darden, and her husband, W. F. Myrick, raised almost nine hundred thousand dollars from Kirby and numerous other bankers and businessmen to fight for a higher tariff and lower taxes for the rich. The lobbying was of such a dubious nature that it was slowed in 1928 by the curiosity of a congressional investigating committee.[1] In July 1935, Muse and Kirby organized the Southern Committee to Uphold the Constitution with the hope of preventing Franklin

Roosevelt's reelection. Muse collected over forty-one thousand dollars for the SCUC in 1936, mostly from the DuPonts and other northern industrial interests. Even John Nance Garner, who was rarely concerned with defending the New Deal, was aroused by Muse's efforts. And the distribution of massive quantities of anonymous racist leaflets at the Macon, Georgia, convention of the SCUC attracted the attention of the Senate Lobby Investigating Committee headed by Hugo Black. Under Black's hammering, Muse admitted complete responsibility for the "picture of Mrs. Roosevelt going to some nigger meeting, with two escorts, niggers, on each arm." The SCUC was much discredited by the revelations of hate literature and northern financial backing by a so-called southern committee (a little more than six thousand dollars trickled in from Texas).[2]

Vance Muse was a professional extremist, a man who saw the world as filled with suckers and who learned to

> raise money with one hand while he was organizing committees, delegations, and conferences, espousing whatever measures he was espousing at the moment, with the other. He learned the tactful way of putting folding money where it would do the most good and how to say a nice thank you to state and local officials in return for favors received—and, not least important, how to convince big money men in the North that his projects were worth supporting.[3]

In 1936 Muse teamed up with Lewis Valentine Ulrey, a geologist whom he had met at the Macon convention. Ulrey was a former history professor at Valparaiso University in Indiana and a former Indiana state senator. In 1936 he was employed as a representative of Maco Stewart, oil, real estate, and banking multimillionaire, from Galveston. Unlike Muse, Ulrey was a true believer. During one interview he rapidly rattled off fifteen or more "communistic" laws and groups, including the child labor law, the NAACP, the Mexican Constitution of 1917, and "international-minded Jews." At the Macon convention Ulrey was remembered for his speech concerning "the coming Armageddon—the great struggle between Christianity and Jewish Marxism" and the capture of the New Deal by the Sanhedrin.[4]

Maco Stewart was Ulrey's "angel" in much the same way that Kirby was Muse's. Early during the depression, Stewart, a devout Baptist, came to believe that the churches were being penetrated by radicals and that something must be done to save the country for Christian Americanism. He felt that individual liberty was a product of Christianity, that the United States was a Christian land, and that the United States was the only nation with a real constitution. He organized and financed America, Incorporated to combat communism—which is the term he gave the social gospel—in the churches. Then Stewart realized that the communists were everywhere: churches, peace societies, schools and colleges, labor organizations, and both major parties. He financed literature, written by Ulrey, demonstrating that the New Deal, like communism, led to dictatorship and the extinction of liberty. Those who disagreed with him were either "shallow thinkers" or contained a "bit of radical taint in their blood."[5]

In November 1936 Muse and Ulrey chartered the Christian Americans as an educational, nonprofit, nonpartisan, and nonsectarian organization to distribute literature in favor of Americanism and righteousness. Although Muse was adequate at coining slogans, delivering harangues of gloom and doom, and writing withering letters, he was primarily a businessman. The talents of the more erudite Ulrey allowed Muse to concentrate on fund raising. He specialized in bringing in the contributions after the donors had been softened up by Ulrey's pamphleteering.[6]

The Christian Americans had no measurable impact in the 1930s. Muse's traditional patron, John Henry Kirby, was becoming discouraged. He apparently suspected that there was nothing he could do about Franklin Roosevelt and that Muse could not do anything either. In any event, Kirby was less able to offer assistance because of financial reverses suffered during the depression. Kirby died in 1940. Ulrey's patron, Maco Stewart, died in 1938, though Ulrey continued to serve Maco Stewart, Jr.[7]

The organization's newspaper, the *Christian American*, edited by the fundamentalist Reverend Harry Hodge of Beaumont's Sabine Tabernacle, discharged blasts against communism, atheism, Negroes, Jews, and unions. The paper warned, for instance, that since 1922 Russia had been establishing a Soviet republic in the southern states to be ruled by Negroes. Muse and Ulrey published a vivid map showing twelve million blacks ready to respond to a red call to arms. Civil war was imminent. Rural mail boxes were stuffed with sheets asking southerners and Texans if they wanted their loved ones working side-by-side with Negroes. The two crusaders also got credit for papering Caucasian political rallies and conventions with unsigned dodgers containing such captions as, "In grateful appreciation of our great commander-in-chief, Franklin D. Roosevelt, from the Negroes of Texas" and "A vote for Franklin D. Roosevelt is a vote for EQUAL RIGHTS for ALL—economic, social, and political."[8]

The Christian Americans were also concerned with the supposed international Jewish conspiracy. From 1937 to 1939 Ulrey wrote articles for the *Defender*, edited by Kansas minister Gerald Winrod. The reverend traced the founding of the red menace to the Jewish Illuminati back on May 1, 1776. The Illuminati, he said, went on to produce the French and Russian revolutions. Winrod, whom Ulrey considered a "real patriot," was indicted for pro-Nazi sedition during World War II. Ulrey charged that Colonel E. M. House had conspired with foreign Jews for the establishment of the League of Nations and complained that Roosevelt had sent two insulting messages to Hitler. He maintained, however, that he was not anti-Semitic and that it was only human nature that Hitler and the Germans should turn against the 1 percent of the population that owned the nation. A few years later, Mrs. Muse, a paid secretary for the Christian Americans, told a reporter that the organization could not afford to be anti-Semitic, "but we know where we stand on the Jews all right." It did not pay, she said to work with Winrod, Smith, Coughlin, and others up north because they were too outspoken and would get the organization in trouble. For public consumption, Muse declared that it was an old communist dodge to accuse his group of anti-Semitism. He said he respected the "decent Jew" and cited the Christian American circulation of the columns of George Sokolsky and David Lawrence. He added that "nearly 2000 years ago another man's neighbors accused him of being anti-Semitic."[9]

In 1941 the Christian Americans discovered the antilabor movement and did more than any other organization to awaken the South to the dangers of a unionized work force. (A growing number of southern Democrats in 1941 and 1942 not only feared the economic disadvantages of unionism for Dixie's corporations, but also opposed northern labor's encroachment in the high councils of the Democratic party.) The Christian Americans apparently assisted Governor O'Daniel in putting through the antiviolence-in-strikes law in the spring, but it was not until Labor Day, when Muse picked up a copy of the *Dallas Morning News*, that he found his new raison d'être. Major William Ruggles, editor of the *News's* editorial page, pleaded for an open-shop amendment to the Constitution. Ruggles wanted to prevent compulsory unionism and dues payments even though unions had to represent everyone in the plant or job site. Muse was so excited that he called Ruggles from Houston and wanted to know if the Christian Americans could take up the proposal as their cause. The *News* did not object. Muse visited Ruggles in Dallas several times, and the editor suggested to him the use of the "right to work" label, which he had employed three times in his editorial. Muse was evidently the first to use the term "right to work" as a full-blown slogan.[10] Senator O'Daniel, whom Muse and Ulrey rated equal in patriotism to Washington and to Jefferson Davis, took up the cudgels in Congress. The Christian Americans launched the project by deluging various states with literature and newspaper advertisements. One mailing item was a typical O'Daniel speech lambasting "labor union leader racketeers." The Christian Americans acquired a nationwide reputation as a menace to organized labor. William Green, president of the American Federation of Labor, referred to Muse as the "Fascist-minded" spearhead of antiunion lobbying before state legislatures. Philip Murray, president of the Congress of Industrial Organizations, John L. Lewis of the United Mine Workers, and the railroad brotherhoods all warned against him.[11]

Muse's efforts were bolstered in Texas and the Southwest by a wave of well-financed radio and newspaper accounts charging that war production was being hampered by strikes. Workers were accused of betraying Americans in uniform, and the administration was castigated as a pawn of organized labor. Much of the censure was directed at the forty-hour week, falsely claimed to be the maximum work week, though it was in fact the standard time for straight pay as distinct from commonly worked additional hours for overtime pay. The *Dallas Morning News* reached a nadir in its integrity when it editorialized against Rayburn and Roosevelt:

> Let the Speaker of the House each day place on the wall beside his chair, where Old Glory's furls are draped, a fresh list of dead heroes of America killed in battle and never fully supported by our country's efforts. And let the President of the United States face at his desk that roll call of the dead.[12]

Much of the Christian American propaganda attempted to stir racial hatreds without mentioning labor, but race baiting was the chief weapon of the antilabor forces in the South. Both white anxieties and black hopes were fanned by President Roosevelt's creation of the Fair Employment Practices Committee in June 1941, which called for racial equality in employment practices. Already torn by prejudice, black and white union men sometimes turned on each other because of Muse's efforts. Muse, of course, declared that "I like the nigger—in his place" and that the open-shop amendment "helps the nigger. Good niggers, not these communist niggers."[13]

Muse, rarely content just to write, plunged into feverish lobbying, but his foray into Louisiana in 1942 was a disaster. One solon on the floor of the Louisiana House of Representatives labeled Muse the "Christian American Heathen" who was fostering the hate laws of "Singing Lee O'Daniel Pass the Biscuits Pappy . . . the phony senator from Texas." The Louisiana legislature, not ordinarily noted for its liberalism, identified Muse's group as an organization that would "set capital against labor, Negro against white, Catholic against Protestant, and Christian against Jew." It asked the Federal Bureau of Investigation to investigate the possible subversive activities of the Christian Americans.[14]

Undaunted Muse redoubled his efforts the next year. Texas's labor regulatory law of 1943, the Manford Act, was the nation's first to use the phrase "right to work," and labor spokesmen claimed the Christian Americans were responsible. Muse, however, was so busy lobbying elsewhere that there is some doubt that he devoted much time to Texas. The Christian Americans, with considerable assistance from O'Daniel, claimed credit for 1943 regulatory laws adopted in Arkansas, Florida, Mississippi, Alabama, and several western states and constitutional amendments the next year in Arkansas and Florida. The two amendments banned the closed shop; the statutes varied from laws licensing union business agents and forcing them to open their records upon the complaint of any interested party to those that were patterned after the O'Daniel antiviolence measure. Muse liked to display a letter from a Mississippi state senator thanking him for his lobbying efforts, and he took delight in being in Montgomery, Alabama, in June 1943 when the legislature adopted a bill embracing many Christian American goals. The Texan promptly wired his wife in Houston, implying credit for the action. He said that some of the wording was identical to the Texas law and that the Alabamians referred to their bill as the "Pappy O'Daniel Christian American law." In Arkansas labor leaders thought they had beaten the Christian Americans, but O'Daniel's radio talks and Muse's lobbying turned the battle against them.[15]

Despite these events, there is considerable doubt that the Christian Americans were as influential as they claimed to be, except in Arkansas. Muse's telegram boasting of the Christian American triumph at Montgomery was simply a lure for rich contributors. A reporter was in Montgomery a few days later and was assured by a number of people that the bill would have passed with or without Muse, who had arrived for only the last three days of the debate. The real lobbying work was done by the powerful Associated Industries of Alabama. Throughout the south union regulatory measures were advocated by the American Farm Bureau Federation, chambers of commerce, the Southern States Industrial Council, and many southern politicians who recognized a winning issue.[16]

In 1944 Muse, like O'Daniel, refused to testify before the Senate committee investigating campaign expenditures, doubtless recalling the outcome of the 1928 and 1936 inquiries, but it is probable that the Christian Americans played a prominent role in the Texas Regulars movement. The committee found that the Christian American bank balance in Houston was $477.01 on April 4, 1944. The state convention was scheduled for Austin on May 23. From April 4 to May 25 a total of $13,415 was deposited in the Christian American account. The donations ranged from $1,000 to $4,550. During the twenty days before the Austin convention, $5,250 was taken out of the account in sums of $500 and up.[17]

Muse and Ulrey never divulged the financial backing of the Christian Americans, but in 1942 Muse boasted to a reporter of his connections with monied sources, stating that there were twenty-five wealthy men in twelve southern states whose names could not be revealed for obvious reasons. In 1943, Mrs. Muse told a reporter that he would be surprised how many important corporations supported their work. The Christian Americans managed to pay Muse $4,000 a year by his own admission and more according to others; his wife also drew a salary. Muse's assistant, Val Sherman, drew $300 a month. Ulrey drew his salary from Maco Stewart, Jr. Buck Taylor, the editor of a small Austin paper, the *Middle-Buster*, was hired to sound out the legislatures of Georgia and the Carolinas and received $1,500 for his three weeks' work. Finally the Christian Americans raised over $65,000 in the successful lobbying effort in Arkansas.[18]

But aside from the triumph in Arkansas and the hotly contested presidential race in 1944, when the coffers of the Christian Americans swelled, it is doubtful that Muse's group was well financed. Early in 1945 one Texan stated that anyone who could not raise more money than Muse did in Texas, with his causes, was only "small peanuts here." John Crossland, south Texas CIO regional director, described Muse as "pretty much of a shoestring operator since his financial angel, John Henry Kirby, died four years ago. We consider him a one-man goon squad for some ideas the real union-busting forces are trying to put across." Muse's claims of financial connections could easily have been braggadocio. Instead, the Christian Americans had to solicit primarily from rural, nonindustrial sections, from farmers and small businessmen who were still frightened by the word *union*. The quoted salaries might have pertained primarily to 1944. His son remembered that the famiy suffered a number of lean years because of Muse's refusal to settle down to a regular-paying job.[19]

Financing was not necessary for one type of influence that Ulrey exerted. In one of his more incredible appointments, Governor O'Daniel selected Maco Stewart, Jr., as chairman of the State Board of Education, and he in turn asked Ulrey to serve as his chief adviser on textbooks. In 1945 Stewart was apparently so busy with other matters that he requested Ulrey to take over his board work, which he did with a vengeance. Writing on the board's stationery, Ulrey informed J. K. Noble that his text on Russia was being rejected because of current diplomatic tensions between the United States and Russia. Noble took his case to the newspapers and to liberal organizations such as the Young Democrats and the Women's Committee on Educational Freedom. The resulting outburst was apparently sufficient to end the old man's influence.[20]

Another wartime lobbying project, carried on by both the Christian Americans and the Committee for Constitutional Government, was for the adoption of a resolution calling for a constitutional amendment limiting income, gift, and inheritance taxes to 25 percent. By January 1945, this resolution had slipped quietly through seventeen legislatures, sometimes in the final hours of the sessions. This was over half the number required for Congress to call a constitutional convention, but in the spring of 1943 the Texas senate tabled it, 29 to 3, and the house killed it, 58 to 52. During the next session the bill slipped quietly through the State Affairs Committee in the house, without a public hearing, but got only thirteen votes on the floor.[21]

Perhaps at first glance this proposition might not seem extremist. It might be considered, in the words of Anatole France, "a law of majestic equality, forbidding the rich as well as the poor to sleep under bridges, to beg in the streets, and to steal bread." Under the proposed amendment, however, Henry Ford, who paid about $800,000 tax on an income of about $1,000,000 in the 1940s, could be charged no more than $250,000; the average person, who paid about $175 on $2,000, could have his tax boosted to $500. But these observations would merely serve to label the amendment reactionary rather than extremist.[22]

The amendment was extremist, however, because of the fanatic and false propaganda behind it and because of the consequences it would have had on the political and social structure of the nation. As Wright Patman noted, if the income tax were limted to 25 percent, big business would easily have the economic resources to absorb and destroy small business, and the government would lack the wherewithal to pay off the national debt, aid veterans, pay social security, make soil conservation payments to farmers, provide help in constructing roads and harbors, and distribute numerous other benefits.[23]

The 1945 legislators paid closer attention to another measure favored by extremist groups, a right-to-work bill. Representative Marshall Bell proposed this open-shop legislation in January 1945, which would also eliminate the checkoff, the automatic deduction of union dues by employers (on behalf of the union). Bell believed that the nation was imperiled by unions and wondered what would have happened if American soldiers had gone out on strike during the recent German drive. Other legislators avoided the cloak of patriotism and frankly declared that they wanted to curb unions in order to attract industry to Texas. Bell insisted that the bill was his own product, but many other legislators had come to Austin already stocked with identical reasons for supporting the bill. A *Houston Press* staff correspondent pointed out that similar reasons indicate similar sources, and similar sources indicate a strong and well-organized presession lobbying campaign.[24]

As the right-to-work bill was introduced, prolabor legislators and union lobbyists in Austin accused Bell of working for Vance Muse's Christian Americans. Rumors were rife that Muse's group, along with the newly organized Fight for Free Enterprise and the National Association of Manufacturers, were spending thousands of dollars to pass the bill. The CIO was supposedly spending a great deal to defeat it. Taking account of this widespread gossip, Representative Ennis Favors of Pampa pushed through a resolution creating a committee to investigate all lobbying in connection with the right-to-work bill. Ironically Favors allegedly had to be bribed into introducing the bill.[25]

Bell told the committee that he knew nothing of the Christian Americans or Muse. He admitted that he toured the state before the session to talk to fellow legislators about strikes and labor conditions. Another witness, editor Buck Taylor of the *Middle-Buster*, denied talking to anyone about the right-to-work bill or having any business connection with the Christian Americans or Muse, but he did affirm his friendship for that "honorable Christian Gentleman."[26]

Harry Acreman, executive secretary of the Texas State Federation of Labor, declared that on the evening the right-to-work bill was discussed as a possible constitutional amendment, he saw Taylor talk to Bell, then walk out to the lobby and confer with Muse. Acreman also read into the record a letter from E. H. Williams, president of the AFL in Louisiana. Williams wrote that Taylor journeyed into Shreveport and Baton Rouge in 1943 expounding the Christian American antilabor program and trying to raise money. The labor forces, he wrote, stifled Taylor's efforts mainly by publicizing and scorning them.[27]

Muse testified that he had planned to mail fifty thousand circulars to influential people all over the state, urging citizens to tell their legislators to vote for the right-to-work bill and help slow down the forces of Sidney Hillman and Earl Browder. But, Muse said, contradicting Bell, a representative from Bell asked him not to mail the circulars, and only 450 were sent out. He added that he was not going to "mess up" anyone's bill. Muse also refuted his friend Taylor when he conceded that Taylor had been an agent for the Christian Americans in Louisiana and other states, but only to sound out southern sentiment for reduction in federal taxes. Taylor, he said, had not done anything in Texas for the Christian Americans.[28]

Another extremist organization, Fight for Free Enterprise, was spotlighted by the committee. FFE was chartered in Texas as "educational" in January 1944 and was led by William Walker and Phil Hopkins of San Antonio. Walker boasted that he had been connected with Joe Kamp's Constitutional Educational League in the East, which had recently been named in two federal indictments as a channel for Nazi propaganda. FEE claimed nine thousand members. Names of supporters were not made public, except for those on the advisory board. All of the board members came from south Texas and virtually all from San Antonio. According to one list, there were six contractors, three doctors, two judges, two cattlemen, and two produce merchants on the board, as well as assorted other businessmen.[29]

The goals of FFE included retention of the poll tax, disfranchisement of Negro voters in Democratic primaries, disfranchisement of federal employees in Texas elections, and enactment of a law requiring teachers to take an oath that they were not communists. In order to combat the alleged CIO-communist exploitation of the workingman, the group advocated laws forbidding the closed shop, requiring six years of Texas citizenship for holding office in a union, and requiring union officers and representatives to wear identifying head gear while on union business. The CIO men should wear "bright red or orange hats," the AFL "fawn, other light brown, or white hats," and the railroad brotherhoods "gray or black hats." Phil Hopkins described these latter proposals as "serious."[30]

Before the lobby investigating committee turned in its report, it received a letter from FFE advising that it was not lobbying for or against any bill in the legislature, but after the continuation of the committee had been voted down, FFE sent telegrams to all Texas senators urging passage of the right-to-work bill. It admitted spending seven hundred dollars in telephone calls that spring to drum up support for the bill. FFE also distributed a "Confidential Memorandum," unsigned but bearing its return address, declaring that "The Organization" was trying to save America from enslavement by the "Communistic Revolutionists, Extortionists, Racketeers, Thugs, Goons, and Common Thieves of the C.I.O." FFE identified itself only as "The Organization" in order to disguise itself from the machinations of the CIO-communist conspiracy. The reputed champions of free enterprise also bought radio time, erected billboards, and began a campaign to nominate antiunion Democrats in the 1946 primaries. Its most unusual ploy was wheedling a Texas charter for a splinter group organized by Hopkins in November 1945, called the "Congress of Industrial Organizations." A few days later the newly chartered corporation sued for an injunction against the CIO Oil Workers, demanding that they be denied use of the designation "CIO." Other CIO unions in Texas were warned to stop using the name, and radio stations were asked not to use "CIO" with reference to what the new corporation called "self-styled" CIO unions. Not until the next spring did Walker admit before a court that his bogus CIO had no members. FFE was then enjoined from using the CIO initials.[31]

The report of the lobby investigating committee cleared the unions, the Christian Americans, and FFE of the rumored bribery. But it added that although the Christian Americans apparently violated no penal statute, Muse's "high pressure propaganda methods" were unconscionable. The committee noted that the Christian Americans fostered racial dissension and dissatisfaction between labor and capital and that they cast reflection upon state and national public officials and distributed propaganda that was not constructive, educational, or in the best interests of the public. The five committee members called for further investigation, but the motion lost, 95 to 22.[32]

By spring 1945, some Texas employers had concluded that Vance Muse's name on a labor bill meant "the kiss of death." The bribery hearings slowed consideration of the right-to-work measure, and labor supporters engaged in innumerable delaying tactics. In the house, Marshall Bell was unable to stave off crippling amendments. The lower chamber voted 69 to 67 to exempt workers engaged in interstate commerce. This concession to the railroad brotherhoods amounted to class legislation, which undoubtedly would have been nullified in the courts. The amended bill passed 68 to 63. Senate procrastinators were equally successful, except that the bill came up for final vote on the last day of the session. But the chairman, Lieutenant Governor John Lee Smith, instead of immediately calling for a vote on the bill, made the tactical error of allowing time for debate. A prolabor senator, L. J. Sulak, proposed adjournment, and the motion passed before the chair realized what had happened.[33]

For all the financial backing, pervasive propaganda, and vigorous promotion and campaigning, the Texas far right seemed politically inept during the war. The antics of Muse, the CCG, and the FFE appeared to be merely sideshows, having no effect on the New Deal reforms and little effect on the Texas union movement. A number of the provisions of the Texas labor laws had been tossed out by the federal and state courts. By the end of the war the right wing had not only failed to accomplish much that was tangible but also seemed in danger of fading away. The Texas Regulars, even with O'Daniel's help, were crushed, and Muse had attracted so much unfavorable publicity that the Establishment champions of the open shop, his most cherished goal, avoided him. It looked as though Texas was becoming weary of such people, that the wartime boom, with its urbanization and industrialization, might fulfill progressive columnist Sam Hall's observation that "the liberal forces are slowly gaining strength."[34] This appearance was deceptive, since the ultraconservative elements—after a short pause—stormed back into the thick of Texas politics and helped curb any possible liberal resurgence.

6

The Martin Dies Story

*The Dies committee opened its doors to anybody
who cared to come in and call anybody else a red.*
Life 5 (September 5, 1938), p. 11

*Martin Dies named more names in one single year
than Joe McCarthy did in a lifetime. The membership
of the Dies Committee perfected all the gambits that
McCarthy would later use. . . .*
Robert Griffith, *The Politics of Fear*, 1970

It is possible that the feudalism contemplated by the extremist groups would be just one step removed from the time that some rabble-rousing orator and his followers would take over the nation. Some New Dealers, such as Secretary of the Interior Harold Ickes, feared that the man on horseback who might arise to "protect" the country was Martin Dies, congressman from an eleven-county district in southeast Texas. Dies's father had served the same rural, Piney Woods district during the progressive era and had amassed a record as a racist, isolationist, anticonservationist, and staunch opponent of women's suffrage.[1] The younger Dies inherited his father's ideology. Any alteration in the status quo of white supremacy, for instance, would only help the communists. Dies even kept a list of world figures who inspired hatred and incited racial antagonisms. The list included Stalin, Hitler, John L. Lewis, Ickes, Secretary of Labor Frances Perkins, and Harry Hopkins. (The same day that Dies released his list to the papers, Ickes went on the air to criticize the persecution of Jews in Germany.)[2]

Congressman Dies was supported by John Henry Kirby and the oil and utility interests. Considering his early record, they may not have been entirely pleased at first, for curiously enough, before 1937 Martin Dies cooperated with the New Deal's economic revolution. He was in full agreement with the Public Works Administration and with government regulation of banks and businesses. He proposed a comprehensive unemployment program of public works and wanted to use idle gold in Fort Knox to finance the relief program. He also asked Congress to increase gift and inheritance taxes, grant homestead exemptions on small farms and on homes worth five thousand dollars or less, and legislate tax differentials favoring small merchants.[3]

From the beginning, however, there was a contradiction between Dies's support for governmental controls over giant corporations in order to preserve democracy and opportunity and his opinion that any government that tried to abolish poverty and unemployment was a "dictatorship." And by the time Dies's first glow of national publicity came in the spring of 1937, Kirby's interest was redeemed. Dies helped knife the wages-and-hours bill and introduced a resolution to investigate the CIO.[4]

Dies is best known for his chairmanship of the House Un-American Activities Committee from its inception in 1938 until his temporary political retirement in 1944. The committee was authorized because many congressmen recalled that the previous similarly constructed McCormack-Dickstein committee kept its proceedings on a high plane, because of the potential threat of internal fascist subversion, and probably because of Vice-President Garner's hatred of the New Deal and its condoning of sitdown strikes. Garner knew that the Dies committee would soon be on the track of the New Deal and all its works. Majority leader Sam Rayburn, possibly concerned for President Roosevelt's program if Dies were vanquished on this emotional issue, also encouraged Dies's efforts. Dies delivered an anti-Nazi speech to help pave the way for passage. He made it clear that the authorized seven months would be enough time for his inquiry.[5]

The tone of the Dies committee hearings was soon revealed when one congressman accused child actress Shirley Temple of endorsing a French communist newspaper. Congressman Joe Starnes of Alabama also questioned the loyalty of Christopher Marlowe, whose plays were being produced by the Works Progress Administration Theater. Marlowe had died in 1593, but one of Dies's big successes was helping to kill the theater project. A hair tonic company, Kreml, was probed because of the similarity between its name and *Kremlin*.[6]

The congressman's favorite theme was the alleged widespread communist penetration of the New Deal government. At various times the Dies committee estimated that there were a thousand to fifteen hundred communists in the federal government and declared that some high officials in the Interior Department were members of communist front groups. Once Dies stated that the House Un-American Activities Committee was about to expose Soviet secret police operations in the United States and hinted that government officials were involved. He handed the State Department a long list of organizations that should be banned because they were agents of foreign governments. The American Civil Liberties Union headed the list. No evidence accompanied any of these revelations.[7]

The day after one of Dies's hearings, newspaper headlines announced that communists dominated the CIO. "Documentation" rested on the testimony of John Frey of the AFL, who hated the CIO. John Brophy, a lieutenant of John L. Lewis, was accused of communist leanings, but his parish priest announced that Brophy was a devout Catholic. Neither Brophy nor any member of the CIO nor any communist was called to testify in defense. Frey's charges stood in the record as fact. Dies demonstrated similar concern for individual rights and labor unions on several occasions. Most newspapers did not mention the superficial, inequitable manner of the hearings.[8]

Dies and his committee were a valuable campaign weapon for Republicans and Garner Democrats. Dies's efforts helped defeat liberal Democrats Frank Murphy for governor of Michigan and Elmer Benson for reelection as governor of Minnesota in 1938. The congressman's influence, however, was unsuccessful in unseating California Democrats—Senator Sheridan Downey and Governor Culbert Olson in 1938 and Congressman Frank Havenner in 1944. Dies, without evidence, accused these Democrats of accepting communist support.[9]

The Texas congressman even interfered with the defense effort. In 1940 his staff raided the German Library of Information in Washington, D.C., seizing the library's files. With considerable fanfare, they took from the files evidence that the library was a Nazi propaganda agency. Although this was common knowledge in Washington, Dies compared the keenness of his committee to the supposed laxity of the Justice Department.[10] The government, however, had long since planted agents in the library who gave them more confidential and important information than was ever put into the files. This source was completely cut off by Dies's raid. In fact all the government's traps were in constant danger of being prematurely sprung by a loudly publicized Dies raid. His goldfish-bowl methods tipped off some Nazi and Japanese agents, enabling them to flee the country. The president personally warned Dies to check with the Department of Justice first and also pointed out that innocent people were sometimes members of unworthy organizations, but the congressman rampaged on.[11]

In the summer of 1940, Dies proclaimed the discovery of Nazi influence in Texas, said that no testimony would be made public, but immediately began divulging testimony. He revealed that a chapter of the German-American Bund existed in Taylor, a central Texas town. The little town also supported the *Texas Herold*, a German-language weekly edited by Hans Ackerman, a German who had come to the United States sixteen years before. Ackerman apparently printed some articles supplied by the German consul at New Orleans. The consul had also urged a German-language newspaper in San Antonio to interpret the Third Reich more favorably, but the editor had rejected this pressure, and the consulate had already given up trying to influence him.[12]

Dies assured the bundsmen during one of his one-man committee sessions that he would not pass judgment until all the evidence was in, but then added that he was astounded at the extent of subversion in Texas. He compared the Texas fifth column with Belgium's before its fall and warned of a strong possibility that Texas would be destroyed from within.[13] The congressman's investigation did not increase his popularity among the German-Texans of the south-central part of the state, whose loyalties were unquestionable. The two hundred thousand German-Texans had had the highest percentage of war volunteers in the state in 1917-1918. Taylor housed a rather quiet branch of the *bund*, the only chapter in the state (and in the South). All the bundsmen were either aliens or naturalized citizens.[14]

In the midst of the testimony involving fascism, Dies released "evidence" of communism in Texas schools. The sheriff of El Paso provided Dies a long list of names of teachers and students who were communists. At one public school almost the entire football and basketball teams were on the list. The sheriff said that he had the minutes from a meeting of theirs in which they had laid plans for the governor's race of 1940. He added that Texas communists were promising the state's Mexicans that they could have Texas back when the revolution came. Other informants accused R. A. Stuart, member of the board that directed seven state teachers' colleges, of active communist work in Texas. Stuart demanded proof, which Dies did not have. Dies announced that if Stuart were guilty, he would be named and exposed; if innocent, it would be officially announced. There could be no doubt that Stuart was on trial by a one-man legislative committee.[15]

Seeds of sedition had also been planted at the University of Texas, Dies charged. In 1936 the Progressive Young Democrats at the campus had protested the selection of Roy Miller, a sulfur lobbyist, as financial director of the Democratic campaign in Texas. In revenge for this student attack, Miller's friends in the legislature had demanded an investigation of communism at the university. The House created an investigating committee headed by Texas state representative Joe Caldwell, which spent several days grilling economics professor Robert Montgomery and two members of the Progressive Young Democrats. The investigation was clearly aimed at these young liberals rather than at communism. Caldwell's probe fizzled in part because he based most of his questioning on stolen letters in his possession and in part because he was simply unable to find any evidence of communism in the letters or in the statements of the students.

Martin Dies picked up the discredited charges in 1940. He declared that there was a communist cell at the university and subpoenaed a dozen students and one professor. After taking their testimony, Dies told the press that there were two revolutionary groups on campus, Stalinists and Trotskyites, but, as usual, he had no proof.[16] Just a few days before Dies announced that he would be a candidate in the special senatorial election of 1941, the president of the University of Texas, Homer Rainey, challenged the red baiters to "put up or shut up," and the Texas house hinted that Dies ought to divulge his alleged evidence of subversive activities at the university. Dies said he would turn over the testimony only if the findings were kept secret. His investigators had found that one professor met regularly with several students to discuss Karl Marx, but Dies claimed he had rectified the situation. He admitted that no subversion existed at the University of Texas.[17]

Dies's sensational activities had inspired the creation of a "Little Dies" committee in the Texas senate. It was established in January 1941 and chaired by Clem Fain of Livingston. Fain's committee soon came up with a bill providing for the immediate dismissal of any schoolteacher or professor whose teachings were "inimical" to the Constitution. Economics professor C. A. Wiley testified at one of the few committee meetings open to the public that there was no certainty of what "inimical" meant. It might be construed to include the criticism of some part of the Constitution as obsolete or the proposal of an amendment. An addition to the Fain committee, Senator Jesse Martin of Fort Worth, charged that there was communism at the University of Texas no matter what President Homer Rainey said about red baiters putting up or shutting up. His charge came only five days before Dies's admission that there was no subversion at the university. After the congressman's statement, the "Little Dies" committee quietly folded.[18]

Dies's activities had also prompted other legislators to speak out against radicalism in Texas. State Representative Joe Ed Winfree of Houston was so upset with a "crazy" and "un-American" *Daily Texan* editorial criticizing Martin Dies's latest book that he threatened to close down the paper. The East Bernard legislator proposed a bill to levy heavy fines and up to ten years in prison for sabotage, criminal syndicalism, or waving the red flag. The honorable member from Corsicana introduced a bill legalizing the murder of instigators of any un-American activity in Texas (except by poison, he liberally conceded), but it failed to pass.[19]

Ironically there actually was an active communist group at the university in the 1940s—according to one former member of the Communist party—and it included a few professors as well as students. By 1948 the association had split into three cells of three members each, one of whom was in touch with one other cell. None of the bumbling legislative investigators ever found them out, though one of them voluntarily announced his affiliations in the late 1940s. The former member does not believe the cells were a menace to society.[20]

The furor over communism assisted Dies's publicity build-up for the 1941 special senatorial election. His negativism extended to accusing Lyndon Johnson of being duped by a Nazi agent (editor Ackerman), labeling Attorney General Mann stupid for putting communists on the ballot, and claiming that O'Daniel had his hillbilly band play while he tried to think of something else to say. According to the polls, which Dies thought were faked, his percentage of support decreased the longer he campaigned. It fell steadily from 27.9 percent on May 12 to 16.2 percent on June 28. Reporters, however, found that the Dies partisans had much stronger convictions about their candidate than any of the other voters. Many were superpatriots and firm supporters of the House Un-American Activities Committee. The committee's activities constituted the basis for most of the support he received outside his own district. In east Texas, where he did virtually all his campaigning, some of his audiences would frequently interrupt his fiery speeches with "pour it on" and "Amen." He was received more like a crusader than a political campaigner, and many people in his audiences always stayed to shake his hand.[21]

The election gave Dies 80,653 votes. He carried sixteen counties, including all eleven in his own district, three others in east Texas, one on the coast near east Texas, and one far away in southwest Texas. He fared considerably better with the average and above-average income groups, polling 23 percent of each, than with the poor and the "poor plus" (average annual income of $500 to $1,500) income groups, polling 11 percent and 13 percent, respectively. He captured about 18 percent of the rural vote and 14 percent of the town vote.[22] He could not have been heartened by such a performance, and it was eleven years before he ran statewide again.

Dies's greatest disability was that his potential constituency was the same one that "Pappy" O'Daniel had already sewed up on a statewide level: the fundamentalist, nonunion, Anglo rural areas and small towns. Moreover Dies simply could not match O'Daniel or Johnson on the hustings. Nor did it help any that he had ruined himself with the administration because of his red-baiting attacks against New Dealers. It was probably true, as Dies charged, that "word was spread in the right quarters that the election of Dies would mean that Texas would expect much less in federal handouts."[23]

During the war Dies stepped up his vendetta against the New Deal. He mobilized the congressional hostility against the administration that broke into the open in February 1943. He named forty government officials who allegedly supported left-wing or other causes, including one who advocated full-time, universal nudity. The House launched a loyalty probe and, by adding a rider to an appropriations bill, actually fired three men for harboring subversive views. Three years later the Supreme Court ruled that Congress, by punishing individuals without a trial, had violated the constitutional ban on bills of attainder.[24]

In 1943 and 1944 Dies also increased the tempo of his crusade against organized labor. The Political Action Committee of the CIO was, he said, communist inspired and had allocated $250,000 to defeat him. Sidney Hillman, head of the PAC, was replacing Earl Browder as the "Red Chief" of the nation. These charges came under congressional immunity. In 1943 the oil workers in Dies's district launched a drive to ensure that union members paid their poll taxes. On May 9, 1944, in his home county of Orange, a Democratic county convention dominated by the Refinery Employees Union of the CIO arraigned Dies as a demagogue. On May 13 Dies announced his retirement, citing ill health and a dread of becoming a professional politician.[25] Apathy and the poll tax usually had limited the voting in the district to some 5 percent or 10 percent of the population. The CIO poll tax drive in the oil regions registered 25 percent to 30 percent more voters than had ever voted before. The unions were shrewd enough to ask a distinguished county judge, J. M. Combs, to make the congressional race. The judge was neither a newcomer nor a laborite. He did not stand merely for unions. He represented everybody who was tired of Martin Dies, which meant the reputable citizenry as a whole.[26]

It is possible that some Establishment figures from the district were also fed up with Dies. A group of high officials from Gulf, Texaco, and Mobil, along with the Port Arthur postmaster and other Establishment bosses, allegedly talked among themselves one day about their congressman's shortcomings: Dies was making working people mad, and he was not getting any federal contracts for the district. A week later Dies bowed out.[27]

Dies's self-proclaimed retirement whipped him into a new fury against the New Deal and organized labor. The climax of his participation in the 1944 campaign against his own party was his appearance as a Texas Regular delegate at the state convention in September 1944. The pro-Roosevelt forces won the roll-call vote by twenty-nine votes out of sixteen hundred, but the tabulation took almost two hours. Procrastinating, the Regulars sent Martin Dies to speak, hoping to kill time until proxies could be rounded up. The congressman was booed off the stage.[28]

Dies and a three-man congressional subcommittee, two of whom had been defeated in their Democratic primaries with key help from the PAC, sought to prove that the PAC, besides being communistic, was an arm of the administration and thus a violation of the Hatch Act. The Dies committee leaked the information that a Dallas PAC leader, active in the campaign against incumbent congressman Hatton Sumners, had been on the payroll of the War Production Board for a couple of months after joining the political fray. Timed to benefit Sumners, who appeared to be locked in a tight race, the leak made headlines just before the election. Sumners won but probably would have anyway. Dies's report on the PAC was as futile as his speeches on behalf of the Texas Regulars. There were, of course, some communists in the CIO, but this union was an action organization, not an ideological junta, and had limited objectives of higher pay and shorter hours. The CIO no more refused help from someone politically different from most of the members than the Republican and Democratic parties refused communist votes in elections. Lewis and others used the communists because they were among the few experienced organizers available when the CIO cut loose from the AFL.[29]

Right-wing extremism was evident in Martin Dies's policies: racism, opposition to all immigration, slander against New Dealers and all opponents, violations of civil rights, extravagant and untrue findings of subversion, opposition to the existence of labor unions, attacks on academic freedom, and passionate religious fundamentalism. Just one or two or three of these policies might not constitute rightist extremism, but the combination of policies and the style in which he presented them revealed Dies to be an authoritarian similar to W. Lee O'Daniel.[30]

The Dies committee confronted the American public with the question of whether the end justifies the means. Communism was a real menace that had to be dealt with, but the procedure of the committee was itself a violation of American morality. It was a pillory in which reputations were ruined, often without proof and always without the legal safeguards that protected criminals. People were arraigned and charged, by legislators rather than jurors, for acts that were nearly always lawful. The Dies committee, in fact, pioneered the whole spectrum of slogans, techniques, and political mythologies that would later be called McCarthyism. The congressman and his committee popularized "guilt by association" and demonstrated the value of cultivating ex-communist witnesses. Dies, like McCarthy after him, frequently possessed allegedly reliable and startling evidence that he could not release at the moment. And fifteen years before McCarthy's heyday, Dies was already hypercritical of eastern politicians and New Deal "traitors." Dies also showed that the communist issue appealed strongly to the people of Texas and the United States. The Gallup poll consistently gave his committee high ratings.[31]

The depression and the war brought insecurity to millions, making it difficult to maintain tolerance. In such an unsettled era, differences of opinion could easily be interpreted as attempts to destroy what security remained. Dies tried to divert the people's attention from the flounderings of American capitalism by giving them a scapegoat for their troubles.[32]

Dies's molding of public opinion certainly affected the state and nation more than Vance Muse or even the Texas Regulars, although this is an estimate (bolstered by the Gallup ratings) of an intangible quantity. The red scare doctrine—more than Dies himself—was serviceable to the Texas Establishment, which feared not communism but rather the New Deal and the possibility of its extension. Dies was not regarded as an Establishment spokesman, since he never served as a state official, rarely attended the state conventions, and had already gravitated toward extremism by the late 1930s. Since the famous right-wing congressman bowed out of elective politics in utter impotence, however, it appeared that his demise, like that of the Texas Regulars, might foretell some liberalization in the state. But the Establishment was too well entrenched to allow that to happen. Dies's retirement did symbolize a weakening in the power of the red scare mentality, but only a temporary one.

7

The Coke
Stevenson Period

*In trying to prevent the funding of a professor's
project to trace the concept of human dignity from
Bacon to Locke, U.T. regent Orville Bullington declared,
"I don't think anybody'll spend $3 to read about
Bacon and Locke."*
Texas Spectator, *November 9, 1945*

*The conservative impulse and the reactionary
impulse do not, with some isolated and some ecclesi-
astical exceptions, express themselves in ideas but
only in action or in irritable mental gestures which
seek to resemble ideas.*
Lionel Trilling, The Liberal Imagination, *1950*

After "Pappy" O'Daniel was elected to the Senate, Lieutenant Governor
Coke Stevenson became governor. Hailing from a family with deep roots in
a frontier section of the state, Stevenson was reared on a ranch in Kimble
County. He worked his way up as a rancher, banker, lawyer, and legislator.
He was the first two-term speaker of the Texas house, 1933-1937, and was
elected lieutenant governor with W. Lee O'Daniel's endorsement in 1938.
He projected a relaxed, pipe-smoking, coffee-cooling image, and it was real,
though he also had a silent brooding side. Journalists labeled him "Calculatin'
Coke." There was nothing deceptive or pretentious about Coke Stevenson.
A staunch conservative, his administration ranks as classical Establishment.

Known as early as 1935 as a sulfur and oil man, the governor joined
Texas oilmen in 1944 in successfully opposing the Anglo-American Petroleum
Treaty because it provided for partial governmental control over the oil
industry. (Oilmen also feared that it would allow excessive imports from
the Middle East and therefore depress domestic oil prices, but neither they
nor Stevenson could be expected to publicize that fear.) Stevenson claimed
that this control would endanger the Texas economy and provide an opening wedge for international control over other businesses. The governor

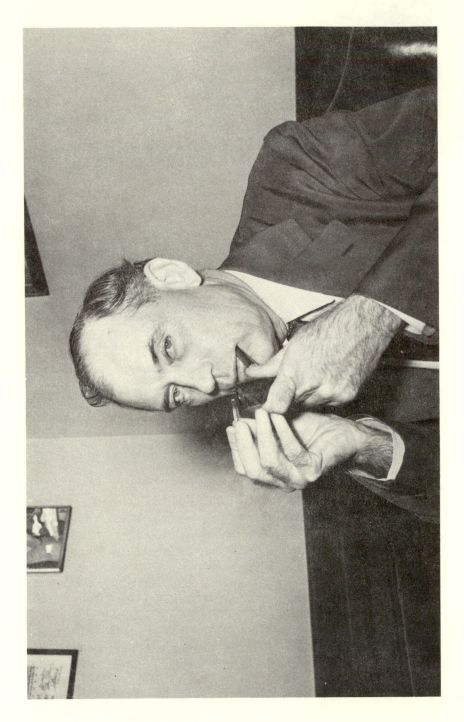

5. Coke Stevenson. *Texas State Archives.*

also had to cope with some scattered consumer and business pressure within the state to tax the oil industry. If ever there was a time when the wellhead oil tax could have been raised to the level of oil taxes in neighboring states, it was during the war. Enormous quantities of oil were being shipped out of state for a pittance, and even some businessmen urged the popular governor to raise the tax. The president of Superior Roller Company of Dallas urged the tax so that the state could "recover some of the money squeezed out of us by discriminatory freight rates." At the same time the manager of an independent oil company in Mexia and the head of a machine company in Dallas called upon Stevenson to increase the tax. The governor, who enjoyed a lucrative oil lease income, replied to all three men and completely ignored the oil tax portions of their letters, though he answered other items. He received a number of other telegrams and letters (from people whose professions were not identified) asking for a tax on oil or on gasoline shipped out of the state but made no move in that direction.[1]

Stevenson's conception of wartime government also followed the Establishment line, supported by Sam Rayburn and various corporate leaders, in his denunciation of gasoline rationing; it might be all right for other states, he said, but not Texas, where gas was the counterpart of "the saddle, the rifle, the ax, and the Bible that won Texas for the society we now have." The governor wrote to a traveling salesman that rationing hurt the economy and would not solve the rubber problem, then added that he did not think there really was a rubber shortage. (It was, in fact, so serious that Interior Secretary Ickes was stealing rubber doormats from the White House and turning them into the rubber pool.) Stevenson's thoughts were echoed by another west Texas frontiersman, the new lieutenant governor, John Lee Smith, who wrote Ickes that rationing represented the "fatuous fumblings of confused and capricious crackpots." Ickes replied, "As you go vociferously forth, draped in the outer garments of patriotism and the underwear of self-interest, please remember that our tanks and trucks and jeeps cannot burn as fuel the crocodile tears that you shed."[2]

The Stevenson administration's insensitivity—in an accurate reflection of Anglo-Texan opinion—was also evident after Texas's first lynching in the war years. Willie Vinson, a black Texan who was tentatively identified by a white woman as the man who had assaulted her, was seized in his Texarkana hospital bed, dragged by auto to a cotton gin, and hanged there on July 13, 1942. United States Attorney General Francis Biddle registered his distress, noted that Axis propagandists were exploiting the incident, and urged Stevenson to ensure prompt action against the lynchers. The governor replied that he had made a public statement on the matter; that was the only "action" he ever took on the issue. He added, in his letter to Biddle, that "certain members of the Negro race from time to time furnish the setting for mob violence by the outrageous crimes which they commit." Even a white man, he said, would have been lynched for this crime. That did not justify mob violence, he conceded, but it did show that "the Negro race was not the target." Three weeks later, he received a letter from Congressman Hatton Sumners, who observed that he had opposed federal antilynching bills a long time but that the states had an obligation to prosecute the culprits. Sumners added, "One of the reasons why, so it seems to me, that states are losing their governmental powers is because of nonexercise of those powers. Power will not remain where it is not used." Stevenson's inaction continued, but he was not always opposed to intervening in local affairs. Upon receiving a complaint from a Houston woman about blacks riding in Pullman cars, he sympathized with her and noted that he had brought the matter of local enforcement of jim crow laws to the attention of local authorities.[3]

A turbulent racial situation also arose in Beaumont, where an enormous influx of black and white workers crowded into the shipyards and refineries, creating housing shortages and transportation frictions. On the hot, muggy night of June 15, 1943, the city exploded. Stirred by the (false) charge of the rape of a white woman by a black man, over two thousand white shipyard workers threw down their tools, flung themselves into the streets, and soon ran amok in the black quarters. Three were killed and hundreds of whites and blacks injured before the long night ended. Lieutenant Governor Smith was out of the state, and the governor was also on his way out of Texas when he was informed of the riot. The governor indirectly informed the president pro tem of the Texas senate, A. M. Aikin, Jr., that he and the adjutant general's department could handle it. The leading student of the riot concluded that "the unperturbed Stevenson then continued his journey to the nation's capital while his own state blazed with racial violence," but Senator Aikin thinks that is an "inflammable" judgment. Smith returned to the state first, after the riot, and suggested that it was the work of fifth columnists. Two weeks later the FBI concluded that no fifth columnists were involved. The riot underscored the necessity for changes in Texas's race relations and indicated that the changes would occur without any assistance from the Establishment. Along with the May riot in Mobile, Alabama, the Beaumont affray revealed to white southerners that their boasts of racial control and feelings of contentment within the black community were based more on wishes than reality.[4]

Stevenson proved a bit more responsive in handling the numerous complaints from Mexicans and Mexican-Texans about discrimination in public facilities. Quite a few incidents were triggered by those small-town businesses in the southern half of the state that displayed signs proclaiming "No Mexicans." The governor's characteristic reaction, when such grievances were carried to him, was to point out that local "businesses are free to establish their own standards." He even tried to persuade the Mexican government that discrimination was rare. In 1943, however, Mexico announced that Texas would no longer receive braceros (Mexican citizens temporarily allowed to lend vital assistance in the low-paid task of picking crops). Texas's intolerable racism was cited as the reason. Stevenson reacted by approving the Caucasian Race Resolution, which forbade discrimination against "Caucasians" in public places (implying that it was all right with the state if discrimination against black Texans continued unabated). That same year, young Tom Sutherland, field representative for the State Department's Office of Inter-American Affairs, strolled into Stevenson's office and asked him to create a Good Neighbor Commission. Puffing on his pipe, Stevenson agreed and declared, "Meskins is pretty good folks. If it was niggers, it'd be different." The OIAA funded the commission, which performed credibly over the years in investigating discriminatory events and promoting local solutions. During the war years especially, with the cooperation of the Texas press, the commission enjoyed some success in educating Anglo-Texans about the necessity for fair play for Mexican-Texans and for those south of the border.[5]

After the war the spirit of common struggle faded away. And with the illegal entry of tens of thousands of "wetbacks" in the mid-1940s, the increasingly ineffective Mexican ban on braceros no longer mattered, and the farm employers of the Rio Grande Valley were less interested in being good neighbors. In 1945 a bill was proposed in the Texas senate to make it a misdemeanor to refuse service to Latin Americans in public places. The bill not only failed but also drew considerable criticism from the press. Even the pro-Latino *San Antonio Light* voiced doubts that antidiscriminatory legislation could replace education in fostering goodwill between Anglos and Latins. In the absence of civil-rights legislation, punitive powers for the commission, and a sympathetic press, the GNC's efforts tended to be scattershot.[6]

Stevenson was more sympathetic to labor, or at least the AFL, than his predecessor was. A good friend of Texas State Federation of Labor Secretary Harry Acreman, the governor strengthened the unemployment compensation system and, during the height of antiunion sentiment, negotiated a no-strike agreement with organized labor. Even so, in 1943, when the Manford bill sailed through the house and was rammed through the senate in unseemingly fashion by Lieutenant Governor Smith, Stevenson allowed it to become law without his signature. This important act required unions to file comprehensive annual reports with the state, forbade contributions to politicians and political parties, and prohibited any person convicted of a felony from serving as an officer or organizer of a union. All union organizers had to register with the state and obtain identification cards. The annual reports were to include all financial and organizational records, and all receipts and expenditures were to be itemized. The reports were open to grand juries and to judicial and quasi-judicial inquiries. They were virtually open to the public.[7]

Stevenson was particularly noted for his practice of governmental penury. He managed to govern Texas throughout the war without raising taxes. Revenues, of course, decreased, as the governor said they would. State services also decreased, but the governor did not say anything about that. Upon being accused of having no program, the governor responded that the free spenders of public money had never agreed with him and that he had a program of economy every day. He demanded tight budgeting by every state agency. He endorsed the pay-as-we-go amendment to the constitution, adopted in 1942, preventing state indebtedness. Costly special sessions of the legislature were virtually banned. Despite petitions from the Texas house and senate, the governor refused to call a special session to grant Texas soldiers overseas the right to vote without paying their poll tax. Even after the Supreme Court ordered Texas to integrate its Democratic primaries, the governor resisted the clamor for a special session that would ditch the primary system and return to the old convention process.[8]

On one occasion twenty-five or thirty river authorities faced severe financial difficulties that could be answered only by a special session. Their spokesman, banker Walter Hall, remembered:

> I asked him if he had any advice or counsel that he could give me to take back to my board of directors about how to plan for the coming year in the absence of money, how to plan to proceed with things we desperately needed to do, such as the acquisition of rights-of-way, the enlargement of canals, small pumping plants, and things of that nature. I remember so vividly Governor Stevenson, who was personable in many ways, but he sucked on a pipe pretty much and he had a very cold, calculating—some would say, a mean steely eye. He did not like to be asked the questions for which there were apparently no good answers. And when I asked him that question, he cocked his eye at me and he sucked on that pipe a time or two, and, believe it or not, he said to me, "Oh, Hall, those questions usually take care of themselves."[9]

Stevenson's economic strictures went beyond those of some Establishment leaders. R. L. Thornton, founder of the Dallas Citizens' Council (the city's Establishment), urged the governor to sign a bill that would elevate the pay of district judges from five thousand to six thousand dollars a year in order to keep capable people in the courts. Stevenson did not just refuse to endorse the pay raise; he actually increased the workload of the underpaid judges. When the judgeships were vacated due to death or resignation, the governor refused to fill the appointments. He asked neighboring judges to take up the slack.[10]

When faced with a choice between his usual government of indigence and his cherished individualism (in the form of demands for legislative reapportionment), Stevenson never wavered. The governor spurned postwar reapportionment pleas, despite an outrageous underrepresentation of west

Texas, south Texas, and the cities because of wartime growth. The legislature, to be sure, was primarily to blame. It had disregarded its constitutional mandate to reapportion after the 1930 and 1940 censuses, prompting one member to accuse his fellows of holding the constitution in contempt. Toward the end of the 1945 session, he apologized, remarking that the legislators acted "so utterly unconscious of a constitution that they could not possibly have had any intentional contempt for it." It was obvious that only a special session called for the purpose of reapportionment would do its duty. But the governor ignored the special session requests, even from entrenched Establishment figures, such as the appeals from Lubbock Representative Preston Smith "to a fellow West Texan," from the South Texas Chamber of Commerce, and from the American Legion commander of Houston. Stevenson justified his stand by leaking a letter to the press that cited legislative inaction. He also observed that Harris County's two additional members would probably be "elected by the CIO and other radical elements," so the state would be better off with continued rural representation.[11]

The most celebrated incident during the Stevenson years was the dismissal of University of Texas President Homer Rainey by the board of regents. James Allred had been governor when Rainey was named president, and the regents had been fairly liberal, but with the governorships of O'Daniel and Stevenson, the complexion of the board had changed. Just after O'Daniel's election, Orville Bullington, who made his millions in railways, banks, and flour mills, wrote to Dallas insurance magnate Carr Collins that he had a plan to cut the costs of higher education in Texas by more than half. Bullington asked his millionaire friend to arrange a conference for him with O'Daniel, and Collins was happy to do so. Bullington was a prominent Wichita Falls Republican who had been his party's candidate for governor in 1932 and who was on record that the New Deal was run by "gutter reds and parlor pinks." Judging by later events, O'Daniel must have been impressed by Bullington's views at their November 22 meeting. Bullington was endorsed for a seat on the university board of regents by oilman Jim West, a financial backer of O'Daniel. West also put in a plug for a friend of his and Bullington's, Dan Harrison, who made his millions in oil and cattle. Early in 1940 Harrison also received strong recommendations for a regent's post in letters to the governor from Houston state senator Weaver Moore and from D. K. Martin of the Alamo National Bank in San Antonio. Martin's letter also described a "far reaching evil," claiming that "unscrupulous, designing, subversive professors have been 'diggin in' in our schools more than we dare admit." He also thought he spoke for the medical doctors, especially E. W. Bertner, former president of the Texas State Medical Association, and that Harrison would meet with their "universal approval." Dr. Bertner of Houston was bitterly opposed to President Rainey and exerted a powerful influence on the selection of regents for the next several years. At the same time an incumbent regent, millionaire banker and oilman H. H. Weinert of Seguin, asked O'Daniel for a meeting to discuss university affairs, and added, "I do not believe that the freedom of the press gives some of the professors the right to attack the executive and legislative branches in the manner they do." Some professors, the regent thought, were "too radical." Another O'Daniel regent was Fred Branson, an employee of Galveston financier Maco Stewart, Jr., whom the governor selected for the state board of education.[12]

O'Daniel evidently decided that an assembly was necessary, so he secretly met with a group of his rich friends at the "Houston Gag Conference" in 1940 for the express purpose of placing reactionaries in control of higher education in Texas. They discussed how to limit academic freedom in the colleges, how to restrict the teaching of certain subjects, and how to get rid of certain professors. Having decided that they could not succeed by taking their plans to the legislature, they resolved to gain control of the college governing boards. The O'Daniel and Stevenson appointments carried out this resolve.[13]

At the first meeting of the regents after the Establishment had laid its plans in Houston, D. F. Strickland, a wealthy corporate lawyer and a lobbyist for the largest chain of movie theaters in the state, passed a small card across the table to Rainey. Written on the card were the names of four full professors of economics, each of whom had taught at the university for at least fifteen years. "We want you to fire these men," Strickland said. Rainey was amazed and asked why. "We don't like what they are teaching," the regent replied. Rainey told him that if he would prefer charges, a hearing could be held, but Strickland, of course, did not have any rational charges so he declined. Rainey refused to fire them.[14]

The chairman of the board in 1940, a holdover Allred appointee, was oilman J. R. Parten. He later recalled that dozens of businessmen that year had complained about the communist professors and most often demanded the termination of Dr. Robert Montgomery of the economics department. The chairman had read all of Montgomery's books and concluded that he was merely a New Dealer. Parten also had to cope with Martin Dies's accusations in May 1940 of communistic infiltration on the campus. Dies promised to send Parten a copy of his findings, but despite repeated requests, the transcript never arrived. In 1941 Dies finally agreed there were no communists at the university.[15]

In January 1941 Governor O'Daniel named two new regents for the university: Orville Bullington and Dan Harrison. Harrison took many of his ideas from his old friend, Bullington. From that moment on, the university was plunged into controversy. On one occasion, for instance, Bullington became disenchanted with the director of public relations at the university and, without notifying anyone, offered the job to another man, who turned

Shall we record in the minutes that Dr. Rainey had no comment?

—Reprinted from The State Observer, October 16, 1944. Paid for by volunteer contributions of University of Texas student body.

6. Homer Rainey and the Regents, 1944. *Courtesy of Bob Eckhardt.*

it down. The next day the regents abolished the position, without warning the man who held the job, without bringing a single charge against him, and without allowing him to come before the board and be heard. Bullington described the move as an economy measure.[16]

Several incidents contributed to Homer Rainey's academic demise in Texas. He had proposed consolidating (and enlarging) the Galveston medical school into the university proper, which was vehemently opposed by Houston and Galveston businessmen. The proposal also ran counter to the views of Dr. Bertner, who informed out-of-state educators in July 1944 that the university regents would soon fire Rainey.[17]

Another problem arose over an antilabor meeting allegedly called by mothers of servicemen, who offered "every citizen an opportunity to express his statements" on the issue. It was actually controlled by Dallas millionaire movie magnate, Karl Hoblitzelle. The meeting was called in a *Dallas Morning News* advertisement featuring big Japanese soldiers with rifles aimed at small United States soldiers with popguns. Dovetailing with the *News*'s ongoing antilabor crusade, the advertisement asserted that numerous Americans were dying needlessly because the union-dominated government would not allow anyone to work more than forty hours a week. Four University of Texas economics instructors were denied the privilege of taking the stand for two minutes to read the law, which provided for overtime pay beyond forty hours. But they were able to inform a reporter after the meeting that it had been stacked, that labor and the government had been denounced by preselected speakers. Since Hoblitzelle adhered to the customary Establishment views regarding free speech and since his interests in Austin were represented by his own lobbyist and a university regent, D. F. Strickland, it is not surprising that the board soon interrogated the instructors. During the course of the meeting W. Lee O'Daniel telephoned twice from Washington to speak to some of the regents. Only six regents were present, and by a four-to-two vote the instructors were "not rehired," as the *Morning News* phrased it. Rainey protested in vain against the termination of the untenured men.[18]

The regents responded to Rainey's protests by searching out ways to abolish the tenure rules so that they could easily rid themselves of all undesirable professors. They succeeded in weakening tenure but not in abolishing it. Strickland was so incensed at Rainey on the tenure issue that he wrote him that the president of the University of Texas had no business "urging or suggesting" anything at all to the regents. He added that if the abolition of tenure made it more difficult to recruit out-of-state professors, Texas would be better off. Thereafter the regents also refused to grant money for social science research, limiting their grants to the physical sciences.[19]

Rainey was also disturbed because the board questioned the English department's textbook committee in an attempt to identify the person whom they assumed had placed John Dos Passos's *U.S.A.* on the supplementary reading list for sophomore English classes. The board made it clear that they wanted to fire the individual, but since no one person was responsible, the regents settled on banning the "obscene" and "perverted" book. This purge of freedom of thought was aimed against a novel that soon won the Pulitzer Prize. The regents' action made it the most popular book in the state. It quickly sold out at all bookstores.[20]

Rainey denounced the censorship and presented a dramatic statement of all his grievances to a general faculty meeting on October 12, 1944. Having evidently waited for an overt act, the regents seized the opportunity to take action against the university president. Lutcher Stark, a lumber, oil, and banking multimillionaire who had not attended a meeting of the board in eleven months, made the motion to dismiss Rainey. By a vote of 6 to 2, November 1, 1944, Rainey was fired. No reasons were given. University students went on strike, and eight thousand marched in mute mourning from the campus to the capital and the governor's mansion. They marched in step to the slow roll of drums and the low moan of trombones by the Longhorn band playing Chopin's "Funeral March." The students carried a long, black coffin labeled "ACADEMIC FREEDOM IS DEAD." One sign asked, "WILL STEVENSON FIDDLE WHILE THE UNIVERSITY BURNS?" Austin city officials listed the procession as a legitimate funeral and cleared traffic from the streets.[21]

Governor Stevenson rose to this occasion with the skillful use of his favorite political tactic: doing nothing. One wit claimed that "no hole was too small for him to crawl through." He refused to take sides, stating that he was too experienced a rancher to burn his lips on a hot coffeepot. J. Frank Dobie, just back from England during the blitz, replied that plenty of people were getting burned by something much worse, people who were fighting for the same thing as the university—liberty to think as they please. The governor's beliefs were hardly secret, though, since he had appointed or reappointed some of the most reactionary regents. Although at least five of the trustees were Texas Regulars and seven were wealthy businessmen, Stevenson referred to them as "the most representative board" in many years. He wrote regent K. H. Aynesworth, in a private letter, that he agreed with him that the universities had surrendered to such bureaucracies as the American Association of University Professors and the American Medical Association, all of which were "foreign . . . undemocratic . . . and totalitarian."[22]

As the controversy raged, the regents were smoked out of hiding and forced to give reasons for the firing. One regent distributed a pamphlet across the state that quoted selected portions of *U.S.A.* It was designed to show Texans the foul language to which their children were exposed at the university. As one observer wrote: "This may be the only case on record of a university official's distributing wholesale what he thought, or at least said, was obscenity." The Texas senate committee on education, over the protests of Lieutenant Governor Smith, called hearings on the matter. Regent Bullington fanned the flames higher and smeared the university's name across the country by adding a new, sensational charge: under Rainey, the university had coddled a "nest of homosexuals" on the faculty. His charge was refuted by Rainey and by Homer Garrison, director of the Department of Public Safety, who had led the investigation. Bullington's senseless smear of the university, especially over a minor problem that had already been attended to, provoked one senator's cold rejoinder question: "Any other dirty thing about the university you want to volunteer?" Judge Strickland chimed in with the accusations that Rainey wanted to admit Negroes to the university and that communism was being taught in the economics department, but he was unable to cite any evidence. Regent Stark revealed the essence of Establishment thinking on the issue when he told the committee: "The president of the University of Texas occupies the position to the Board of Regents as a general manager of a corporation does to its Board of Directors."[23]

By the beginning of 1945, with the wrangle drawing nationwide adverse comment, the terms of three of the regents had expired, and three others had resigned. The governor's six new appointees were mostly ultraconservatives, but they were more politic than their predecessors. The new board opened up social science research funds and offered reemployment to the fired economics instructors, two of whom returned. The regents refused to reinstate Rainey, but they did adopt a statement in favor of academic freedom, proclaimed "an era of tranquility," and asked the faculty to advise the board in selecting a new president. In February 1945, a faculty committee was appointed, but months passed, and the acting president continued to be geneticist Theophilis S. Painter, who promised the faculty that he would not accept the presidency. His name was not among the twelve suggested by the faculty representatives.[24]

The crisis persisted. In January 1945, the newly organized Women's Committee on Educational Freedom had begun hammering away at the connections between most of the regents and the Texas Regulars. Concerned with the infringement of freedoms at the university, the seventy-five women demanded Rainey's reinstatement. They were mostly New Dealers, including Mrs. I. D. Fairchild of Lufkin, the former regent who had refused to vote to fire Rainey, Jane McCallum, a former secretary of state who headed the famous "Petticoat Lobby" in the 1920s, Clara Driscoll, national committeewoman from 1928 to 1944, and Minnie Fisher Cunningham, the incisive, vigorous former suffragette. In February the general secretary of the American Association of University Professors declared that the University of Texas regents regarded the school as a "proprietary institution." In July the

Southern Association of Colleges and Secondary Schools placed the university on probation. The actions of the two academic bodies had no legal standing but undoubtedly discouraged educators from accepting positions at the university.[25]

Early in 1946, with over a year's perspective in evaluating Rainey's presidency and the performance of the regents, journalist Weldon Hart wrote that the fray had been depicted in the Texas press as pitting the hard-headed, practical businessmen on the board against visionary professors. Yet, Hart wrote, the regents were just now aware of the atomic bomb and were now building the cyclotron that Rainey urged in 1940. The regents were now erecting emergency buildings to meet the housing shortage, after having rejected Rainey's housing proposal in 1943. The board had also launched a program for Negro education that Rainey had proposed earlier. The regents, in short, seemed to be sufficiently hard-headed but hardly practical. Rainey himself observed that state law forbade educators from sitting on the state board of education but did not prevent doctors from taking posts on the board of health or engineers from serving on the highway commission.[26]

Rainey began broadcasting on all the issues of the day in 1945, defending government price controls, expenditures for public health, and reapportionment of the legislature. There were persistent rumors that he would run for governor the next year. Establishment newspapers began to speculate that the broadcasts were sponsored by the "leftist" CIO, though they were in fact paid for by the Jaques Power Saw Company in Denison, Rainey's home town. In June 1945 J. Frank Dobie confided to Margaret Carter, leader of the Fort Worth chapter of the Women's Committee on Educational Freedom, that he thought Rainey should announce for governor early to keep Lyndon Johnson out of the race. But other progressives—including Jimmie Allred—thought that Rainey could not win. Allred preferred Johnson or (secondarily) himself. Cunningham apprised President Truman of the Texas political situation and then informed Rainey that the president "seemed to want us to succeed."[27]

Then in the spring of 1946, three events occurred in such rapid succession that some observers suspected a relationship between them: Rainey declared for governor, Painter was appointed permanent president of the university, and the AAUP blacklisted the university administration. The administration was kept under censure until 1953 because of "attempts by a politically dominant group to impose its social and educational views on the University." Regents Bullington and Strickland responded that little more could be expected from the AAUP, which they labeled a "CIO-like union."[28] With Rainey running for governor, the university dilemma was assured of scrutiny in the campaign.

After enjoying tremendous membership gains during the war, organized labor became another issue in the 1946 Democratic primaries. Prior to that year, Texas had had almost no strikes, but in 1946 workers, trying to keep up with the rising cost of living, were walking off their jobs all over the state and nation. Hundreds of workers successfully struck the Waco plant of General Tire and Rubber and the Fort Worth factory of the Consolidated Vultee Aircraft Corporation. By June of that year, Robert Oliver, director of the CIO organizing committee in Texas, seemed on his way to unionizing the rest of the state. In Texas and the South, the CIO aroused grave misgivings in part because it organized black workers, supported the Fair Employment Practices Committee, and sought to abolish the poll tax.[29]

Texans were also upset about civil-rights demands. They were disturbed over northern attempts to expand the FEPC and over the prospect of blacks voting for the first time in the Democratic primary (a result of the *Smith* v. *Allwright* case, 1944). Moreover, Heman Sweatt, a black Texan, publicly began efforts to enter the University of Texas law school in February 1946. The legislature desperately tried to stave off integration by creating a Negro law school on paper, while Governor Stevenson sounded out Houston oilman Hugh Roy Cullen on the possibility of transferring the University of Houston Negro College to the University of Texas.[30]

These three causes—academic freedom, labor union rights, and civil rights—were all more or less championed by Rainey but were all opposed to some extent by his four leading opponents. The other major candidates were the zealous lieutenant governor, John Lee Smith, snuff-dipping former railroad commissioner Jerry Sadler, state Attorney General Grover Sellers, and corporate lawyer Beauford Jester, a member of the state Railroad Commission. All four of the more conservative hopefuls concentrated their campaigns against Rainey. Governor Stevenson might have run again, but it would have been an uphill struggle, in large part because—as one politician phrased it—"Coke" was "in bad with the old people and he knows it."[31]

The odyssey of John Lee Smith—from popular lieutenant governor to electoral oblivion—is the strangest of the campaign stories. Smith had been gearing up for the governor's race for about three years, hoping to emulate W. Lee O'Daniel by riding the antilabor tide to victory. He repeatedly referred to wartime strikes (or sometimes just strikes) as "treason," leaving the clear implication that the strikers should pay the constitutional penalty— death—for that action. After the coal miners walked out in 1943, the lieutenant governor boldly proclaimed, "A firing squad would be a quick and effective remedy." He denounced Governor Stevenson's antistrike pact with labor as a farce. He appeared in full-page advertisements in the urban dailies with stories about a little white cross on Iwo Jima, a boyish face, and the sweetheart at home. The stories concluded," Surely they did not die to make other men pay tribute to labor racketeers before they can enjoy the God-given right to work." He delighted in spewing general statistics on the number of wartime strikes and the total man-hours lost, ignoring the facts that the unions did not sanction most of the strikes and that the national percentage of man-hours lost was less than one-tenth of 1 percent. (In Texas it was closer to one-hundredth of 1 percent.) The record in the United States was better than that of the vaunted British labor movement, and Britain was under a direct siege, with its national existence at stake.[32]

Probably as late as 1945 Smith was the leading contender for the governorship in 1946, especially if big-name possibilities who never entered the race are discounted (Johnson, Allred, Stevenson, and O'Daniel). Certainly the Texas Regular element in the Establishment, at least early in the race, preferred Smith. There was, in fact, a movement to put Smith in office before the election. Karl Hoblitzelle's regent-lobbyist D. F. Strickland wrote to Senator Tom Connally that Governor Stevenson ought to be named United States district judge. Smith would then become governor and thus be elected more easily the next year, though Strickland added that he thought Smith would be elected anyway. Strickland pointed out that Smith was the only man who had "guts enough" to prevent the takeover of Rainey, the CIO, "the communists and negros." Smith's wife wrote to Senator O'Daniel also urging the appointment of Stevenson to the San Antonio judgeship. She correctly observed that her husband, "has been fighting here in Texas along the same lines that you have fought for also."[33]

Those who wanted Smith elected, especially an unknown outfit called Advocates of a Greater Post-War Texas, spent thousands of dollars placing Smith's pictures and writings in half-page and full-page advertisements in newspapers all over the state. One or more of nineteen different articles appeared in nineteen newspapers between April 1 and mid-December 1945. The *Texas Spectator* estimated that they cost at least $12,034. None of the advertisements contained the words "advertising" and "paid for." Rather they were labeled "presented to the public." The lieutenant governor's papers do not pinpoint campaign donors, and Smith merely identified the Advocates as "about 50 or 60 friends, mostly small businessmen." But Smith was in close touch with Karl Hoblitzelle and D. F. Strickland, who were not "small." Strickland wrote Smith in the summer of 1945 about "the plan to let you make a series of speeches over Texas" but warned him in another letter that he could not win on criticism alone. Strickland also visited H. B. Guerra, the boss of one of the five "Mexican Counties," Starr, Zapata, Webb, Jim Hogg, and Duval. Strickland named the boss in each one and added, "These five counties always go together, and George Parr is the boss over the whole outfit. If you haven't already seen George Parr and these other leaders, I think you should do so immediately because if they once commit themselves to someone else, they will not change." He noted that Parr also controlled five thousand or six thousand votes in Jim Wells and Nueces counties. Some of Smith's other friends and supporters, whom he doubtless counted as small businessmen, were E. E. Townes and Strick-

land's fellow regents, D. K. Woodward, W. S. Schreiner, and Orville Bullington. All were very wealthy reactionaries. Still another friend, who wrote,
"I want to help organize and finance your campaign for Governor," was
George W. Armstrong. A multimillionaire oilman from Fort Worth, Armstrong achieved national notoriety a few years later when he offered oil lands
to a Mississippi college on condition that it champion white supremacy
and anti-Semitism.[34]

The Texas State Manufacturers Association was interested enough in
Smith's candidacy that it sounded him out in August 1945. One official was
so committed that he offered to raise money for Smith for 50 percent of all
money he collected. Smith confirmed the deal in January 1946: "You'll get
half the gross amount of all money you raise."[35] The official, E. J. Price,
doubtless neglected to inform would-be donors that he, Price, was skimming
off half of their contributions. There is no record of how much he collected.

Early in the campaign, however, Smith projected an image of extremism,
which the Establishment knew was not a winning stance in 1946. The lieutenant governor condemned organized labor, the closed shop, the Fair
Employment Practices Committee, Negro participation in the Democratic
primary, liberal schoolteachers, and new taxes. With the exception of new
taxes, which he merely censured, he labeled all these items and groups communistic. Smith charged that Homer Rainey had profusely praised the novel
U.S.A., which he said was part of the communist conspiracy. At a Smith
rally in Dallas, Hal Collins, a former aide to W. Lee O'Daniel, shouted,
"If Stalin was voting in Texas, who would he vote for?" Collins's western
band and a small group up front shouted back, "Rainey!" The lieutenant
governor announced in one speech, "I shall have nothing personal to say
against my opponents. So far as I know each of them are gentlemen and as
such are worthy of your respect." But in another speech he asserted that the
race was between communism and Americanism; and just in case anyone
doubted who the lone American candidate was, Smith pointed out that
weak-sister fence straddlers were as bad as communists.[36]

Being aware that east Texans were "more touchy" about the dangers of
integration than other Texans, Smith deliberately went into that section to
stir racial animosities. In Gregg County he announced, "I do not think the
intelligence of the Democratic party will be increased by bringing into it
150,000 negro voters." Rainey, he asserted, favored a state FEPC wherein
"white girls would be taking dictation from Negro men in your State capitol
and in the courthouse at Longview." Rainey would tear down the pictures
of Jefferson and Wilson and "hang in their places the pictures of some kinky-
headed ward heeler of the CIO-PAC."[37] In many of his speeches around the
state, Smith appealed for the alleged bloc vote of veterans, charging that
U.S.A. smeared the American Legion and "refers to soldiers of the First World
War as saviors of Morgan's Loans." No one pointed out that twelve years

FEATURE ATTRACTION

7. John Lee Smith Candidacy, 1946. *Courtesy of Bob Eckhardt.*

earlier, when pacifism was more popular, Smith had asserted that "we went to war as collectors for international bankers."[38]

Smith emerged, in short, as the personification of all the bitter fantasies and hostilities of the still-alienated Texas Regulars. He was always being asked if he was a labor baiter or Texas Regular. He was unable to control his contentiousness, his violent rhetoric, or his penchant for the most extreme position on a wide range of issues. As Jerry Sadler put it, Smith "poisoned himself right out of the race." A columnist noted, "He might have been easily elected if he had conducted himself more skillfully the last two years. He has talked too much." The *Texas Spectator* observed that Smith scared the "Blue Chip Boys" out of backing him seriously and that "John Lee . . . acted sort of like those unwise virgins of whom we are told in Matthew XXV. He just lit his lamp too soon and ran out of oil." A May 5 poll showed Smith with a higher percentage (11 percent) than anyone else who actually made the race except Rainey. He finished fifth with 9 percent.[39]

The spokesman for the Establishment, Coke Stevenson, probably never preferred Smith anyway. No later than mid-March, in fact, the governor forged a secret pact with Beauford Jester, in effect pledging Jester the Establishment's blessing. Stevenson told Jester that he would publicly keep alive the option of running again, which he evidently assured Jester he had no intention of doing, in order to prevent Rainey and others from announcing. This deception would also serve to "give things a chance to build up" for Jester. At the proper time the Stevenson forces, including many Texas Regulars, would swing toward Jester. Jester's advisers fretted that the delay just pinned down Jester's own supporters. Jester indiscreetly wrote to an adviser that the governor was trying to keep other candidates out of the race, highly inflammatory information to put in writing. Jester wrote again, cautioning his friend that "our enemies could ruin us if they saw my mention of the results of Coke's not announcing."[40] Rainey was, in fact, the last major candidate to announce; his May 23 opening was a month later than any other contender's, but it is extremely doubtful that his timing affected the outcome. Stevenson bowed out of the race a week later.

Technically Governor Stevenson made no endorsement in the campaign, but since he loathed Rainey, he could not resist meddling. He wrote open letters similar to this one to a minister in Mart:

> . . . Your letter also is evidence that you are not being fooled one bit by the agitation for "academic freedom." It is one thing to have full freedom to teach the truth as each of us understands the truth to be, and . . . another thing to take advantage of one's position in a public school to teach atheism, communism, and other isms that tear down and destroy all that you and I have been taught to believe in.[41]

Shortly before the balloting, he denounced atheism as subversive and not a part of academic freedom. Asked if he referred to Rainey, as all knew he did, he denied it. The low road was also represented by A. B. Stufflebeme, who delivered what one newsman labeled "a foul, dismal" radio address denouncing Rainey as an atheist. The charges of atheism, putatively rampant at the university, were just a typical Establishment tactic, designed to anger the public. In 1943 some twenty Austin ministers had signed an affirmation that the University of Texas was hardly "godless." Only 451 of the 10,150 students registered no church preference. In 1946 Austin ministers also testified that Rainey was a staunch Christian and an enemy of communism.[42]

One crucial matter that Jester and his advisers had to resolve was the timing of his leap onto the antiuniversity bandwagon. Presumably if he climbed on board too soon, he would be just another "anti" candidate, but if he hesitated too long, the popular issue might pass him by. He carelessly wrote to one of his columnist friends on March 7 that he was going to "allow" the University of Texas to "keep its dignity" for a while; then he planned to excoriate *U.S.A.* and academic freedom at the proper time. He was delighted that John Lee Smith was pioneering the attacks on *U.S.A.* and acquainting the clergy with the "wild passages." He added, "It may save us a lot of unsavory trouble later." Jester took the high road of moderation, delaying his slashing onslaught until May 26. Just after this speech, Lloyd Gregory, the managing editor of the *Houston Post*, wrote Jester that "John Lee realizes now that you took the play away from him."[43]

Grover Sellers, like John Lee Smith, wasted too much of his time attacking the university. Charging that the novel *U.S.A.* would break down the American home, Sellers ended his campaign speeches by dramatically requesting the ladies to leave. Then he donned white gloves to protect his hands from the "filthy" volume and read "obscene" passages from it. While this gambit attracted some attention, Jester was more shrewd in dwelling on the university troubles only long enough to establish his credentials. Jester chose to emphasize his stand against new taxes, always a basic issue with the voters. It also helped that oilmen were particularly interested in his candidacy. After all, even if he lost the race, Jester would continue to sit on the Texas Railroad Commission, which supposedly regulated the oil industry.[44]

Homer Rainey, as a deeply religious native Texan and self-made man, had much in his favor. He also still stands as the last truly liberal candidate in the state's history to have any significant press support. Many middle-sized urban dailies favored him, including those in El Paso, Austin, Waco, Corpus Christi, Wichita Falls, Port Arthur, Tyler, San Angelo, Paris, Sherman, and Denison. But Rainey was hurt by the labor and racial bugaboos, since many voters feared that he approved black entry into the university (which he was on record against) and wanted the CIO to take over the state.

It was the assaults on the Dos Passos book that really roused the countryside against him. Many of the "obscene" and atheistic quotes from the *U.S.A.* trilogy that were advertised by Jester's followers did not come from *The Big Money*, which was the only one of the three books placed on a University of Texas reading list (in one course). One particularly scurrilous pamphlet was evidently distributed with the encouragement of regents Strickland and Schreiner. Although the voters soundly rejected the extremist Smith and the demagogue Sellers, they were inevitably moved by the attacks. While Rainey led in the polls right up to election day, the electorate shifted to the man in the middle: Beauford Jester polled 443,000, Rainey trailed with 291,000, followed by Sellers with 162,000, Sadler 103,100 and Smith, 102,900.[45]

The same alleged issues prevailed in the runoff, as Jester flailed against communism, and Houston oilman Palmer Bradley, among others, lashed out against Rainey for stirring racism after Texas had enjoyed seventy-five years of peaceful race relations. Anonymous circulars and rumors accused Rainey of atheism, sexual degeneracy, and being a "nigger lover." The Establishment actually cared considerably less about race relations than about Rainey's promise to raise corporate taxes, including $30 million on oil at the wellhead, and to strengthen the antitrust laws, but these issues were not discussed by corporate spokesmen. The professor's candidacy probably hastened the reorganization of the Texas Manufacturers Association, carried out in the spring of 1946 under the aegis of Ed Burris. TMA committees were organized in every house and senate district and supposedly in every county for the purpose of defeating Rainey (as well as some legislative candidates). The moneyed interests were frightened enough of the mild progressive to donate an estimated $500,000 or more for his political demise. Rainey depicted Jester as a tool of the greedy corporations and tried vainly to exploit an embarrassing discovery about a Jester campaign manager. A prominent member of the Dallas firm of Watson Associates, handling Jester's publicity, was Phil Fox. Fox, it was revealed, had been a notorious Ku Kluxer and had served a stretch in the penitentiary in Georgia. This fact was as spurious an issue as communism, but nothing could have saved Rainey. Jester overwhelmed him about 701,000 to 355,700. Independent newsman Stuart Long saluted the "rulers of Texas" and their propaganda machine for convincing a majority of the electorate that an ordained minister was an atheist. It was, he wrote, their greatest triumph up to that time.[46]

This is the first election for a state office in the Establishment era in which a study of urban precinct returns ought to indicate some division along class lines. An embryonic liberal coalition (or at least liaison), composed of labor, minorities, and independent Anglo progressives, had formed in some cities. It was coalescing in support of racial moderation, a union movement unhampered by restrictive legislation, more state services, party loyalty,

Oh, I'll Take the High Road
And You'll Take the Low Road

8. The People's Path, 1946. *Courtesy of Bob Eckhardt.*

full employment, abolition of the poll tax, a shift in the tax burden from consumers to corporations, and casting off the domination of special interests. There are hints of the emerging (or reemerging) politics of economics in precinct returns from Dallas, Fort Worth, and Houston. The only Dallas boxes that Rainey carried, or even ran well in, were heavily infused with lower-income blacks, some Mexican-Americans and in two instances, organized (CIO) labor. The bloc of upper-class, white precincts that awarded New Dealer Allred a thumping majority over O'Daniel were now in the other camp. They trounced New Dealer Rainey in the runoff by better than a four-to-one margin, 7,979 to 1,812. This percentage was exceeded by only a few precincts in the county, nearly all of them in outlying small towns. In Fort Worth and Houston, where only first primary results are available, Rainey ran especially well in the black boxes. In Houston he also carried other precincts that were an admixture of union and nonunion labor and minority groups. Rainey's worst precincts in Harris County, along with the rural ones, were the urban upper-crust and professional neighborhoods, such as River Oaks and West University Place. Ten of these west side boxes obliterated Rainey, 6,099 to 1,681, with the other candidates trailing way behind. County returns also indicated voting along class lines. Mexican-American precincts in Nueces County, on the other hand, voted for Jester. Rainey was favored by Dr. Hector Garcia and his liberal friends, who had just founded the American G.I. Forum, but they were unable to overcome Jester's expensive campaign in the Mexican-American barrios. Even so, these Mexican-American boxes gave Rainey a much better percentage (43.5 percent) than he got statewide (33.7 percent). (See appendixes 2-5.)[47]

Both unions and blacks became scapegoats in Dallas. At precinct meetings on election night in the first primary, especially in the wealthy boxes, resolutions were adopted condemning the FEPC and the CIO. Dallas was the site of the most important and bitter congressional contest in the state, featuring the New Deal judge, Sarah T. Hughes, and businessman J. Frank Wilson. Judge Hughes, who led in the first primary by over a thousand votes, had tried to make peace and jobs the main issues. She had defended collective bargaining and price controls until reconversion was complete. But in the runoff, the judge was forced on the defensive and declared that she too opposed the FEPC, socialized medicine, and labor racketeers and favored the poll tax. The conservative Wilson, however, naturally benefited more from the clamor of the day, as he railed against the "left wing political terrorists of the CIO-PAC." Aided also by the endorsement of outgoing congressman Hatton Sumners, Wilson smothered Hughes by some 14,000 votes. Of the 62,468 votes cast in Dallas County, only some 3,260 of an expected 7,000 black voters showed up, and that was probably a greater number than the local CIO mustered. The Hughes vote correlated significantly with Rainey's.[48]

Probably few more than 75,000 Texas blacks, only 14 percent of their potential electorate, turned out at the polls, and Rainey received about 85 percent of their votes. The organized labor turnout was undoubtedly better than 14 percent, although one labor leader believed that less than 30 percent of the CIO's membership, which numbered 60,000 in Texas, had even paid their poll taxes. And while most labor leaders, especially in the CIO, favored Rainey, the membership did not deliver their votes to him as well as expected or as well as the blacks did. Labor-backed candidates across the state, nearly all of whom were also supported by minorities, lost four out of five congressional runoffs, three out of seven state senate seats (others were given up as hopeless and no endorsements were attempted), forty-seven out of seventy-one state house positions, and, of course, the governor's race. The 1946 elections, in fact, were generally disastrous for progressive candidates nationwide.[49]

The Establishment was completely triumphant. O'Daniel's corporate conservatism was already in the saddle when Stevenson took office in 1941, and the new governor's frontier individualism led the state down the same trail. Stevenson considered himself a Jeffersonian, opposed to government in principle, and did not even believe that the governor needed a legislative program or needed to be a party leader. In Jefferson's time he might have been a real democrat, but by ignoring government in the 1940s, he played into the hands of the special interest groups that dominated the state. He listed as his greatest accomplishment the transformation of a $34 million state debt in 1941 to a $35 million surplus when he left office in 1947, neglecting to bestow any credit on the booming wartime economy. He also neglected to mention the decline in state services or the poverty of a considerable number of citizens, especially east Texas blacks and Anglos and south Texas Mexican-Americans. In 1949, for instance, 85 percent of Texas blacks, 81 percent of the Mexican-Americans, and 51 percent of the Anglos made less than two thousand dollars a year.[50]

While Stevenson's socioeconomic policies did not differ markedly from O'Daniel's, Stevenson at least was more informal and always accessible to press and public. He even appeared to be a bit more independent of the lobby than the flour salesman, and except for the vital Rainey matter, he was less acerbic and frenzied in his approach to state affairs. He also deserves credit for sanctioning the Good Neighbor Commission, refusing to demagogue the labor issue, declining to reappoint Maco Stewart, Jr., to the State Board of Education, refusing to be stampeded into a special session for the purpose of abandoning the primary system, and pledging not to practice law in cases involving the various state boards and agencies that he had appointed.[51]

Though Stevenson avoided taking a public stand in the 1944 election controversy—years later he confessed privately to voting against FDR—the contest marked the return of meaningful ideological issues to the state's politics and proved that cooperation between the liberal and conservative wings of the party was going to be impossible.[52] The New Dealers won that round, but the firing of Rainey and Jester's victory over him showed the underlying reality of conservative dominance. Jester gave every indication of trodding in Stevenson's footsteps.

Texas's embryonic liberal-labor-minority coalition fit into the south's postwar pattern; as one historian noted: "This was as much a long shot in its own way as the independent electors' scheme. It required an increase in the voting of low-income groups, and it anticipated that low-income voters would see their self-interest in such a coalition."[53] Liberal hopes were dashed by antilabor obstacles and the vulnerability of low-income and laboring whites to racial and superpatriotic appeals. The *Texas Spectator* summarized the import of the decisive 1946 election as well as anyone:

> There has long been an alliance between the Eastern corporations and the gallus-snapping Texas politicians. The politicians furnish the corny appeals to provincial prejudice, the corporations furnish the money.
>
> As long as the candidates keep bawling about some mythical menace from a book, or from the Negro population, or from the PAC, a goodly number of the voters will be too alarmed or too confused to think of taxing the oil industry, or of doing something against discriminatory freight rates.
>
> The techniques get a good deal of help from the strict, deadpan coverage accorded by the daily press. However silly the outcries and ululations, they are recorded with a solemn respect.[54]

Perhaps the greatest tragedy in the conservative reality was the takeover of the University of Texas, a coup which was placed in context by historian Bernard DeVoto:

> In more hopeful times we used to believe that such an effort could never succeed—that truth must eventually win, that education could not finally be controlled, that freedom of thought and inquiry were in the end irresistible. We were wrong as hell itself. We have seen the forces of suppression win time after time, destroy a dozen nations, and come within an inch of destroying the world. They can still destroy it—and now we have seen them win here at home, in Texas. Education is no longer education in Texas. The University of Texas can no longer seek the truth, discover the truth, or teach the truth. It has been taken over by a dictatorship.[55]

8

"THE PEOPLE'S PATH":
The Jester Years

*It is not Raineyism or Jesterism—it is Texanism, and
we might as well admit it. We Texans would rather fight
than be fair. We ought to do more thinking about that.*
Dallas Morning News, September 12,
1946, on Democrats' intense partisanship

*Strikes are un-American because they are contrary
to the spirit of the constitution.*
J. A. Hill, president of West Texas State
College, during veterans' student strike
over the administration's ineptitude in
coping with housing and other needs—
Texas Spectator, December 27, 1946

*You shall not press down upon the Texas voter's
brow this crown of cactus thorns. You shall not crucify
decent government on a fiery cross.*
Parody of William Jennings Bryan's
cross of gold speech, *Houston Chronicle*,
October 1, 1948, on Lyndon Johnson's
alleged theft of South Texas votes with
the help of Justice Black, a former
Klansman

Beauford Jester was reared in Corsicana in a family that practiced the social
gospel, and his father was a Jim Hogg stalwart in the state senate as well as
lieutenant governor under Culberson. Young Jester was a smooth-talking,
wavy-haired glee club organizer at the University of Texas. He served in
World War I, did some farming, and later accumulated considerable wealth
as an oil industry lawyer and railroad commissioner.[1] Somewhat in keeping
with his family heritage, while trodding his self-styled "People's Path,"
Jester tried to follow a moderate course within Establishment confines. But
his efforts were wrecked by the antilabor tide that crested after World War II.

Moreover, though Jester sometimes seemed to wish otherwise, the climate of opinion in the state, created in less than a decade by rightists and Establishment conservatives, continued to be oppressive for academic freedom.

Even before taking office, Jester let it be known that he wanted to name his own regents, but the University of Texas board, keenly aware of state and national criticism, was seeking vindication. They craved the approval of two governors. When Jester persisted in talking independently, he drew the wrath of some ultraconservatives and prompted lame-duck Governor Stevenson, in January 1947, to announce the reappointment of Orville Bullington and W. S. Schreiner. In a surprise move, perhaps inspired by Jester, the Texas senate rejected Bullington. Schreiner's nomination stalled until Jester, who took office January 21, compromised in February by asking him to serve again. But the west Texas rancher, as the last of those who had fired Rainey, was a lonely regent. Schreiner was secretly bitter that the governor did not support the old board and was dismayed when the regents included J. Frank Dobie in the cross-the-board $200 salary increase. He resigned in July 1947.[2]

The university newspaper, the *Summer Texan*, begged the governor to appoint someone other than a rich businessman to the board, pointing out that preachers, farmers, housewives, and workers lived along the "People's Path" too. Jester responded by selecting another wealthy west Texas rancher, A. M. G. "Swede" Swenson. Schreiner congratulated Jester on his choice. "Swede," after all, knew the value of ranch lands and could help the board in managing its west Texas grazing leases, which Schreiner evidently believed was a major factor in the governance of the university.[3]

The new board was undoubtedly more moderate than its immediate predecessors, but it was nevertheless unable to avoid controversy. Professor J. Frank Dobie had been on a leave of absence for two years, when he requested a one-semester extension on the grounds that he had hay fever and wanted to finish writing a book. His colleagues and the dean recommended that the nationally famous scholar be accommodated. The board chose to exercise the two-year-leave rule, which was their official reason for dismissing him. Probably the real reason was that Dobie, a steadfast defender of academic freedom, had supported Homer Rainey in the 1944 controversy. He had also defended wartime strikes and the admission of blacks to the university.[4]

That same year the university also lost the services of a brilliant young English professor, Henry Nash Smith. In an open letter of resignation, Smith admitted that he was running out on his colleagues. He offered the extenuation that he was getting no scholarly work done, that "every week brought some new crisis, some insult to the faculty to be confronted," and he looked to his future: "I am not prepared to sacrifice these years to the University of Texas." He admired those who had the stamina to see it through.[5]

J. Frank Dobie believed that Smith was one of the brightest young scholars he had met at the university and, taking note of the Establishment's easy dominance over academia, he wrote:

> Under the conditions of this tranquility the faculty is free to count fruit flies, to publish statistics on the oil content of peanuts, to unwrap the swathings around Egyptian mummies—but not to unswathe the bindings that corporate enterprise tightens tighter and tighter around intellectual enterprise or to assay the oil content of certain American senators.[6]

On the labor front, the CIO had begun both a campaign against the poll tax and a large-scale union organizing drive. Between mid-May 1946 and the first week of February 1947, the Texas CIO chalked up sixty-four victories in various factories, the foremost effort in the South—14,500 laborers joined CIO affiliates. Operating out of their bases in Dallas and Houston, CIO organizers unionized several Waco plants and penetrated into the east Texas centers of Marshall, Longview, Tyler, and Lufkin. East Texans were not familiar with unions and were suspicious at first, but after CIO organizers visited them, the northern companies operating in the state had difficulty explaining to them why the pay scale was 25 percent to 50 percent less in Texas. The primary industries organized were oil (nine local unions), textiles (eight), steel (seven), automobile (six), and packinghouse (six). An outbreak of strikes also occurred as workers tried to keep up with the rising cost of living. Houston alone, which was hit by massive walkouts of telephone workers and public employees among others, lost an estimated $67 million in goods and services in 1946.[7]

The Establishment was horrified at these developments. Although Texas employers were enjoying their greatest profits in history, they seemed to resent any indication that labor might be gaining some competence and independence. As one friend wrote to Beauford Jester, many corporate leaders "are completely burnt up with these labor unions." Establishment chieftains even told each other that the mere presence of unions meant that Texas "has swung far to the left." Paul Holcomb, editor of the liberal *State Observer*, was splenetic, but not untruthful, when he wrote that union strength "alarmed these hypocritical, selfish, sanctimonious exploiters to a point where they demand action from their political stooges."[8]

The Establishment railed against the upstart laborites through the press, the courts, state agencies, the Democratic platform, and the legislature, among others. Perhaps a good deal of the credit for the soaring antilabor sentiment should devolve onto the state's monolithic press. Late in 1945 a scholarly four-month study was made of ten of the dominant metropolitan dailies (3,362 editorials were read). Of the 381 labor editorials, 295 were hostile toward labor's position, 82 took no position, and 4 were prolabor. The most emotional and bitter of the papers were the *Dallas Morning News* and the two San Antonio dailies. The Hearst-owned *San Antonio Light* went so far as to demand the abolition of all strikes, calling them part of the communist conspiracy. The Truman administration had proposed bills calling for full employment, the extension of unemployment benefits, a raise in the minimum wage to sixty-five cents an hour, and continued federalization of employment services during the period of reconversion. Of the 60 editorial references to phases of this program, 59 were in opposition.[9]

Also late in 1945, a short-lived independent weekly in Austin, the *Texas Spectator*, made a thirty-day study of the state's weekly newspapers. Small weeklies were revealed to be the biggest outlet for the "canned propaganda" of the National Association of Manufacturers. The NAM mailed out a weekly newsletter, permeated with antilabor columns and cartoons, and sent it in mat form; it was cheaper to make a metal casting from a mat than to put it in type. Fifty-two Texas papers, with a total circulation of ninety-seven thousand, used the mat in varying degrees. None of them gave a credit line to the NAM.[10]

Occasionally a press tactic backfired. At the General Tire and Rubber plant in Waco, for instance, the employers hired an expert to break the 1946 strike. The expert's first full-page newspaper advertisement asked why highly paid CIO workers were striking for more money; photostats of $100-a-week payroll checks were printed. Workers in local unorganized plants recalled their own wages of fifty cents an hour or less and joined the union. Employees of three textile plants, a clothing plant, a chemical plant, and a cotton oil mill came into the CIO within three months.[11]

The employers could not always count upon the courts either. In east Texas three CIO organizers and seven local union members were arrested for alleged "use of threats" on a picket line. Three other organizers and another local union member had thirteen felony indictments under the O'Daniel antiviolence law returned against them. Acquittals were won in all cases.[12]

Seemingly neutral state agencies were also manipulated for antiunion purposes. The Texas Employment Commission, for instance referred workers to jobs even when the regular force was on strike, in direct violation of an order from the Department of Labor. The possibility always loomed, however, that Labor would clamp down. The state Democratic platform, adopted in September 1946, proclaimed unalterable opposition to strikes, but platform planks are virtually meaningless rhetoric.[13]

The Establishment's most lasting recourse was legislative statute. By April 1947 the Fiftieth Legislature had passed the right-to-work law by a wide margin in both houses, and the bill had been signed by Governor Jester. Other antiunion laws passed that session included an anticheckoff law, forbidding union retention of part of the wages as union dues without the written consent of the employee; an anti-mass-picketing law, defining mass picketing as two pickets either within fifty feet of the entrance of the premises being picketed or within fifty feet of any other picket; a secondary boycott law, prohibiting that technique; and a law regarding unions as subject to the antitrust statutes. The antilabor legislation was climaxed when a prolabor member of the house, Isom Hydrick, offered an amendment to one of the above bills to abolish unions, confiscate union members' property, line all union members up against a wall and have them shot, and send their families to concentration camps. The house voted it down, 63 to 8.[14]

As Jester began signing antilabor bills into law, he became increasingly dismayed that his own labor proposals were shuffled aside in the legislature. Before he took office, Jester had received a summary of the so-called Minnesota labor law, providing for state governmental arbitration of many labor disputes. It had evidently reduced the number of strikes considerably in Minnesota. Jester was also impressed that the Texas Industrial Commission had quickly and successfully arbitrated the Odessa telephone strike in March. The commission, which was not called into being again for over seven and a half years, endorsed compulsory arbitration in utility disputes. Specifically the governor proposed that the state provide voluntary mediation and arbitration in disputes regarding current contracts, and compulsory and binding arbitration for public and quasi-public utility disputes. While the legislature procrastinated, Jester's assistant, William McGill, wrote Marshall Bell on May 19 that the governor's mail supported arbitration, that some of the bills the governor had signed did not relate to the causes of labor problems, and that until a well-rounded program was developed, Jester might be reluctant to approve "other repressive measures in this field which await his action." This warning probably prompted the deluge of corporate letters and telegrams on behalf of the two secondary boycott bills, which still lacked the governor's signature. Jester signed them on May 30, but two weeks later he contemplated a veto of still another secondary boycott measure that the legislature had passed. He signed it only because it reduced the penalty (required in one of the May 30 bills) for agreeing to engage in a secondary boycott from a felony to a misdemeanor.[15]

Meanwhile Jester's labor program floundered in legislative turmoil. Opposed by the TMA and Marshall Bell, the governor's bill passed to a third reading in the house but wound up on the suspension calendar and evidently died there. It hardly mattered, since it was never even seriously considered in the senate. The bill was introduced by Senator James Taylor of Kerens, the governor's spokesman in the upper house. But as gubernatorial assistant McGill observed incredulously in a memo to Jester, "Taylor didn't know what was in it and later found that he was against it!"[16]

The Christian Americans leaped to take credit for this spate of antiunion legislation. Vance Muse was so elated that he distributed a leaflet with pictures of house members who had voted against the right-to-work statute. The Christian American circular was labeled "Communists in the Texas Legislature," and/or it bore the photograph of one of Texas's few communists, Ruth Koenig, with the caption, "Where She Leads Us, We Will Follow." The other side told of the communist plan to raise taxes. When Muse walked into the house gallery shortly afterward, there was a brief and unrealized movement on the part of several legislators to remove him forcibly from the premises.[17] Christian American lobbying was abetted by that of the veteran racist Gerald L. K. Smith, who had joined the fundamentalist Reverend J. Frank Norris at his Fort Worth base in January 1947. Capitol newsman Hart Stilwell noted that there was "more sucker money in Houston" from frightened industrialists and angry businessmen, but that "Muse & Ulrey have bottled up the revolution there." Smith was actually welcomed to Texas by Governor Jester and other state officials, but one conservative lamented that "yokels like Smith make the public think that all honest conservatives are Nazis." Indeed Establishment forces, in and out of the legislature, did not need or solicit the extremists.[18] It is difficult to tell whether the far rightists' propaganda conjured up enough rural support to make them useful to the Establishment or whether the glare of adverse publicity about the rightists made them embarrassing—probably both are true.

Culpability for the regulatory laws properly belongs to the Establishment (including the press). The old, relatively responsible associations for employers and businessmen had lobbied diligently for the legislation. The Texas Manufacturers Association and the state's regional chambers of commerce were most prominent. They did not usually identify organized labor with the imaginary communist-Negro conspiracy. Instead they propagandized about the alleged exorbitant power of the growing unions and about the humane necessity of shielding the liberty of the laborers from abuses of this power. The implication was that management could no longer withstand union pressure for the closed shop, that legislation was necessary to protect the right of workers who wished to avoid union membership to obtain and hold jobs. This lobbying, with its appeal to liberty, not only attracted the legislators from business-dominated districts but also successfully exploited the agrarian individualism of the bulk of the legislature, which had not been redistricted since 1921.[19]

A single leader of the Establishment enjoyed much of the credit for the nine antilabor bills. Herman Brown, an intimate of Governor Jester, had been content for some years merely to maintain enough influence in the state senate to block whatever legislation displeased him. But with the opportunity in 1947 to ride public opinion toward positive action, his lobbyists worked feverishly for the antiunion laws. Probably a majority of Texans thought that labor (even the weak Texas union movement) had gotten rich and uppity during the war; it deserved disciplining. Herman

Brown, on the other hand, just engaged in "multi-million dollar war prof-iteering. He deserved sympathy and good will."[20]

While the Establishment wanted to curb union growth and preserve cheap labor, the extremists hoped the unions would be destroyed, and liberals and laborites warned that right-to-work impeded the essential exercise of collec-tive bargaining. Without the union shop, they said, some workers would take a "free ride" on the efforts of the unionized workers, thus impairing the effective freedom of all to bargain with employers. Working conditions would deteriorate, and wages would be depressed. Employers, they added, would hesitate to locate in a state where they would be confronted with industrial unrest and litigation, and workers without unions might go elsewhere.[21]

The irony of the right-to-work law was that it confounded all these groups; few of their hopes or fears were realized. In the traditional closed-shop areas, the right-to-work law has been generally disregarded, and the prac-tices that have continued appear illegal under federal as well as state legisla-tion. Workers and industries have continued to come into the state, and unions have continued to grow. There is no evidence that the law itself has helped lure industry to Texas. Cheap labor is still present, but primarily because of other factors, such as the absence of an effective minimum wage law and the immigration of thousands of illegal aliens. The passage of the right-to-work law, more than any other event, symbolized corporate, con-servative hegemony over Texas.[22] The Stevenson-Establishment wartime legacy, along with the effects of Martin Dies, "Pappy" O'Daniel, the Chris-tian Americans, and their ilk, clouded Governor Jester's attempts to mod-erate the harsher features of postwar Establishment government.

The governor was more successful in steering the Democratic party through the storms of the late 1940s. Despite conservative dominance of the statehouse, liberal-loyalist Democrats (loyal to the national party) con-tinued in control of the party machinery after the defeat of the Texas Regu-lars. In 1945 a subcommittee of the State Democratic Executive Committee condemned Governor Stevenson's choice for University of Texas regents, and the party leadership actually lobbied against them, although they were confirmed anyway. In 1946 resolutions were introduced calling for the abolition of the unpopular Fair Employment Practices Committee and the excoriation of the CIO's Political Action Committee for daring to intervene in Texas. They were hastily shunted aside and buried in subcommittee. The majority of the committee apparently favored Rainey for governor. And though Jester won a crushing victory in the July primary, it took two long roll-call votes to prove that Jester backers had a majority of the delegates at the state convention that fall. With the backing of most former Texas Regu-lars, whom the governor allowed back in the ranks in the name of harmony, several duly elected state senatorial district delegates were denied their seats. Some had been Rainey supporters. Yet Jester opposed the white primary resolution sponsored by the Fort Worth representatives. The September state convention was more attuned than the SDEC to the sentiments of Texas voters, since the convention resoluted against strikes and "bloc voting" by "colored citizens."[23]

Texas's Democratic partisanship was described by the *Dallas Morning News* as "hobnailed harmony." That is, the *News* took notice of the winner-take-all spirit of dictatorship that prevailed at party conventions. No one stopped to ask what was fair, only whether his side was in control. Intolerance was the byword at every level of the party; it was the same at precinct, county, and state conventions, and, the *News*, rightly added, it would have been the same under Rainey.[24]

Texas Regulars and other racists, meanwhile, began fanning the flames of rebellion once more. President Harry Truman began to recognize the nation's civil-rights problems after a series of racial murders in the South in the summer of 1946. Also, by January 1948, the White House feared the inroads into the crucial northern black vote by former Vice-President Henry Wallace and his new Progressive party. On February 2, 1948, the president sent to Congress a new recommendation for a ten-point program on civil rights. That same week, Jester seemed to justify the faith that the Regulars had placed in him. He joined other southern governors in castigating Truman's proposed antipoll tax and antilynching laws as violations of states' rights. The president's proposal for a permanent FEPC was considered a violation of "racial purity laws," and if enforced by special federal police, they would be "another Gestapo." State party chairman Robert Calvert concurred with the governor on the issues but took one position that the governor had not yet decided upon. Calvert disclosed that he would not bolt the party. As of March 11, the governor's civil-rights stand was favored by 1,271 letters from Texans and opposed by 190. Three days later Jester took another step toward the Regular position by announcing that he did not favor Truman's nomination.[25]

Some oilmen took up the states' rights battlecry because of their desire to exploit the oil-rich land off the Texas and Louisiana coast. Since they preferred state ownership to federal, they were irate over the 1947 ruling of the Supreme Court, comprised largely of Roosevelt-Truman appointees, which held that California did not own its so-called tidelands. (On that occasion, land commissioner Bascom Giles proclaimed that Texas should secede from the Union before surrendering its territory.) Some oil interests, however, feared repeal of the 27.5 percent oil depletion allowance if the tidelands issue were pressed too diligently. The zealous oil crowd that dominated the old Texas Regular faction talked of a third-party, Dixiecratic crusade, supposedly because of Truman's sudden opposition to state ownership of the tidelands. But they viewed the tidelands primarily as a tactical bludgeon against the administration and were prepared to "switch to civil rights" as an optional tactic if the oil issue was resolved by election time.[26]

Jester was obviously sympathetic to the philosophy of the Texas Regulars, but he undoubtedly perceived that race was not the flaming burden in Texas that it was in the deep South, and he still hoped to reverse Truman's course on the tidelands. Also the governor had a strong desire to be liked by as many people as possible and evidently did not have the personality to lead a revolt from party ranks. But the governor was quite capable of reaching a decision when the Regulars, who included many of his social and business friends, mounted pressure on him to bolt the party. Judge Merritt Gibson thought that Jester would be "pushed in front or pushed aside." Standard Oil counsel Palmer Bradley wrote to the Texas secretary of state that he was working in Houston for Jester's complete control of the May convention, "but we need to know what his program is." On April 6 Jester sent an emissary to Hugh Roy Cullen and sounded out the Houston oilman on the merits of a middle-of-the-road approach: fighting Truman from within the party. Cullen promptly threatened to bring W. Lee O'Daniel back to Texas and run him for governor. Undaunted, Jester suggested that Texas ought to take the lead in abolishing lynching and the poll tax and proclaim that bolting the party would be fruitless. In a series of private letters to other southern governors, he urged that they stay in the party and forge an alliance with western states at the national convention for the purpose of nominating military hero Dwight Eisenhower. The only secret part of the letter was Jester's account of his meeting with Governor Thomas Mabry and Secretary of Agriculture Clinton Anderson, both of New Mexico, who embraced the idea of an East-West bloc and a quiet promotional campaign for Eisenhower. Oilman George Armstrong publicly denounced Jester for submitting to the "Gangster Communists of the North and East," but the governor persevered.[27]

Since the Regulars could not take over the party by themselves, and since there was a strong labor-loyalist delegation at the state convention, the Regulars stayed hitched to Jester's team. At the Brownwood convention in May 1948, loyalist Democrats, who supported Truman's nomination, were defeated at every turn. (The convention was held in a converted mule barn, prompting some wags to take note of the antecedents.) One of the Texas Regulars, wealthy Houstonian Wright Morrow, was elected national committeeman. Resolutions were adopted expressing implacable opposition to civil rights, especially the FEPC, and to federal usurpation of states' rights. The delegates called for restoration of the two-thirds rule in the nomination of presidential candidates at national conventions. These were practically identical to Texas Regular resolutions of 1944. But Jester, though still bending his efforts for an Eisenhower nomination, was undoubtedly aware that the president had backtracked and gone silent on the race issue. Moreover the governor was under considerable pressure from the heavy minority of loyalists at the convention. Jester suddenly softened his original anti-Truman stance, and he bitterly disappointed the Regulars by persuading the delegates to send an uninstructed delegation to the Democratic national convention, a delegation that would presumably even be willing to vote for Truman. Nor would the convention allow Texans to cast a vote on whether they preferred a Regular or loyalist slate of electors.[28]

The ultraconservative Democrats kept up a drumbeat of criticism of Jester's position during the summer. Fort Worth oilman Neville Penrose wrote to the governor that he hoped SDEC chairman Bob Calvert (a Jester supporter) got on the National Democratic platform committee so that he could have two or three days' experience with the "city bosses, the niggers, and the Jews." The rich elite of the Regulars—Cullen, Bradley, E. E. Townes, and Arch Rowan, along with Houston millionaire banker James Elkins—decried Jester's stand. In league with South Carolina governor Strom Thurmond, they urged Jester to allow the SDEC to hold a referendum on electoral slates. But at the governor's insistence, the SDEC voted it down, 42 to 18. One friend of the governor, and an ex-president of the Daughters of the Republic of Texas, charged Jester with supporting a Moscow-controlled, communistic, police state. Jester doggedly informed some of his critics that he was working from within to rebuild the Democratic party.[29]

The governor joined a strange coalition of Democratic liberals such as Mayor Hubert Humphrey of Minneapolis, northern machine bosses such as Jake Arvey of Chicago, and southern conservatives such as Thurmond. They called upon Eisenhower to accept the Democratic nomination for the presidency, even though none of them even knew what the general stood for. Eisenhower renounced this effort on July 5, which discouraged Jester, but did not shake him from his determination to stay in the party. The bulk of the Establishment forces rode out the storm with Jester, even after the efforts for Eisenhower failed. R. L. Thornton, chairman of the board of the Mercantile National Bank in Dallas, informed the governor that he was "taking the right stand." Marshall Formby, general manager of KPAN in Hereford, confessed to Jester that he did not like all Democratic actions, but "I liked to have starved to death the last time they [the Republicans] took over."[30]

Pro-Truman, liberal-loyalist forces opposed Jester by voting for two candidates against him in the primary. Both Roger Q. Evans, a former legislator, and Caso March, a Baylor law professor, arraigned the People's Path as oil soaked and called for taxation of the oil and gas industry. Jester, who wanted no new taxes, pointed to the highways, hospitals, and eleemosynary institutions built during his tenure. The governor correctly boasted that it had been done without imposing any new taxes, though he neglected to point out that it was the expanded postwar economy that paid for the improvements. Partially because he did not choose to wage an active campaign, Jester's main problem was complacency among his followers. For instance, his Galveston fund raiser, Maco Stewart, Jr., insisted that no campaign was necessary and evidently did little on the governor's behalf. Benefiting from this complacency and from Jester's controversial middle-road position on Truman's candidacy, Evans and March polled some 467,000 votes to the governor's 642,000.[31]

At their national convention the Democrats were sufficiently frightened of oil money so that no mention was made of the submerged lands issue, but Texan and southern demands for the restoration of the two-thirds rule were tossed aside. Even more galling, Mayor Humphrey persuaded the convention, in a close vote, to adopt the strongest civil-rights plank ever offered by a major party. In the Texas delegation's disorderly caucus, Governor Jester and his followers lost an embarrassing 29 to 26 vote when state senator Joe Hill's strident anti-Truman resolution was substituted for a weaker one. The majority preferred to dwell on Truman's "false doctrines and political heresies," even though it was already known that he was going to win the nomination on the first ballot. And while the Texans bickered over whether to support Senator Alben Barkley for the vice-presidency, a runner announced that the Kentuckian had just been nominated by acclamation of the convention.[32] From the moment the southern delegates lost the civil-rights battle, the Dixiecratic third party was inevitable. At its Alabama convention it nominated Governor Thurmond for the presidency.

Texas's loyalist Democrats had to attempt a comeback, just as they had in 1944, to capture the Democratic state convention in September. Since Truman was the Democratic nominee and since Jester would not abandon the party, most Texas Democrats saw no choice except to join the loyalists in staffing the SDEC with loyal Democrats, firing Wright Morrow (though he refused to step down), and ousting those electors selected in May who had Texas Regular proclivities. The state convention drew up a platform that actually called for a gas tax but more predictably denounced the FEPC and federal interference in suffrage. Convention chairman Calvert ruled that the big Regular-dominated delegations from Houston and Fort Worth could not vote for themselves, since they were contested. They were soon evicted. The Dixiecrats marched out under the inspiration of Senator Joe Hill, who shouted, "You can't put me in bed with Truman and his Commiecrats." Among them was Neville Penrose, who had underwritten the rent for the convention's furniture and equipment. He called a truck and had everything hauled off. When Rayburn's table was carried away, he got up to protest and the movers took his chair. Adding machines and typewriters were also seized, along with the tablecloths and flowers, and the pipe organ was cut off.[33]

The most that Dixiecrats could hope for was to drain off enough Democratic votes to throw the election to Republican nominee Tom Dewey. The

GOP may well have promised the oilmen that they would turn over the multibillion dollar tidelands windfall to the states, whose royalties were only about a third the size of the federal levy. But the Texas Dixiecratic campaign was consumed with difficulties. "The backbone of our movement," Palmer Bradley admitted privately, "consists of the old Texas Regular crowd, but we don't want to be identified too closely with them." The old image dogged them, however, and the party continued to be called the Regulars. Moreover there was crippling infighting between the financiers and the political activists, which induced executive committee member Arch Rowan to resign after a clash with the Houston firebrand, Mrs. Sam Davis. More surprising was a problem in raising money. Houston multimillionaire oilman Glenn McCarthy accepted the chairmanship of the finance committee and promptly left town. Republican oilman Jack Porter's senatorial campaign diverted a considerable amount of oil money that would have gone into Dixiecratic coffers. Rowan initially suggested a budget of $220,000, but probably little more than $60,000 was actually raised, and virtually all of it came from Hugh Roy Cullen. Cullen thought he was merely loaning the money, but he received only about $4,500 back.[34]

Harry Truman was reelected in an upset over Dewey. The president scored the nation's most lopsided victory in Texas with 1,322,000 votes, while Dewey got 304,000 and Thurmond about 114,000 (6.5 percent). Although many Dixiecratic leaders had also been prominent in the Regulars in 1944, most of the voters who responded were quite different. The appeal of the Regulars was rather uniform across the state and involved the siphoning of votes that were ordinarily cast for Republican presidential nominees. Dixiecratic votes came from counties with large numbers of blacks; it was an east Texas racial backlash on the part of whites against the civil-rights turmoil of the day. The Dixiecrats, who never developed any positive proposals, probably placed far too much emphasis on race to do well in Texas, where blacks were too few in numbers to govern white political action. Thurmond's demise in Texas foreshadowed the fate of the diehard segregationists and the philosophy of massive resistance in the state in the 1950s. The Dixiecrats also failed in Texas for the same reasons they did elsewhere in the South: the strength of party regularity, fear of retaliation for desertion if the Democrats won, distrust of the Dixiecrats, and fear of putting the Republicans in office.[35] Oilmen did not bother with third parties again. After 1948 they did not need to. (See appendixes 3 and 6 for hints of urban voting patterns.)

The stormy year of 1948 also saw the most disputed senatorial election in the state's history. Senator O'Daniel, having correctly read the signs that showed that he could not beat anyone, bade a bitter farewell to elective politics. The *Lubbock Avalanche* labeled O'Daniel's decision to retire voluntarily as "the one most constructive act" in his ten years in politics. Coke

Stevenson had already announced for the office with one of his usual "homely, simple speeches," denouncing political promises, excessive taxation, and American communists. Congressman Lyndon Johnson hemmed and hawed, but finally decided to make the race against the favored Stevenson. Another entry was Colonel George Peddy, a well-heeled corporate lawyer who stressed cold war viewpoints.[36]

Johnson had a fair New Deal voting record, particularly for measures that might be described as "countryside" liberalism: farm-to-market roads, rural electrification, river development, and aid to the aged. But he had voted for the poll tax four times and lambasted Truman's whole civil-rights program as worthy of a police state. The congressman had not been regarded as particularly reliable by the oilmen, but he perceived that Texas was drifting to the right and that oil was the name of the game. He had a built-in connection to the oilmen after his close personal and financial friends, George and Herman Brown, became powers in the oil industry in 1947. (The Texas Eastern Corporation that they spearheaded purchased the Big and Little Inch pipelines.) By 1948 Johnson was privately telling friends that he really favored federal control of tidelands oil but was publicly campaigning for a bill to place the tidelands in Texas hands. Upon voting for the antilabor Taft-Hartley Act, and voting for it again to override Truman's veto, and using the phrase "labor leader racketeer," Johnson nailed down heavy corporate financial support along with endorsements from the Hearst newspapers in Texas.[37]

The race, then, was basically between Establishment conservatives, though most of the liberal-labor-minorities faction clearly preferred the enigmatic Johnson to "Calculatin' Coke." Johnson attracted much attention by campaigning in a helicopter, sometimes speaking to sixty thousand people a week. He may have been the first Texas candidate to use advance men to line up crowds and microphones. Stevenson erred by taking to the road in an old Plymouth, not outfitted with a loudspeaker, and shaking hands at gas stations and courthouses. After easing into a town, the governor would spend an inordinate amount of time chatting with old friends from legislative or wagon-hauling days. Moreover he wasted more than one weekend at his ranch, spraying cattle and such. Johnson also reaped many votes because of Stevenson's stubborn refusal, until late in the campaign, to endorse wholeheartedly the Taft-Hartley Act. The former governor had some reservations about the constitutionality of the law. More importantly he had promised a railway union leader that he would not embrace Taft-Hartley, which was doubtless a factor in his endorsement by the Texas State Federation of Labor. Johnson alleged a "secret deal" while simultaneously benefiting himself from the more effective silent help of the CIO. At least one Johnson brochure even berated Stevenson as the CIO candidate. Conservatives deserted Stevenson in droves.[38]

Two weeks before election day, some of the major oil companies, still doubtful of Johnson's reliability, made a move for Stevenson in east Texas. Johnson's District Three campaign manager in Longview wrote to Austin headquarters that "the big oil companies 'dumped' their money for Coke in the oil field here" and had obliterated all further attempts to raise money for Johnson. Some of this deficit, at least by the time of the inevitable runoff, was neutralized by Miriam Ferguson's endorsement of Johnson. "Ma" had never forgotten that Stevenson had not attended "Pa" Ferguson's funeral, in stark contrast to Johnson's attentiveness during Ferguson's last illness. The old Ferguson counties as a whole did not vote peculiarly, but elements of the rusting Ferguson machinery did crank up for their last hurrah, especially in several east Texas counties. Of the twenty counties that switched from Stevenson to Johnson in the grandest way, half of them were Ferguson's best counties.[39]

The runoff was one of the closest elections in American history. (See appendix 4 for a breakdown of the voting in one city.) Campaign manager John Connally was determined not to repeat the mistakes of 1941. Pro-Johnson election judges, perhaps in as many as fifty counties at one time, held back their complete returns from the Texas Election Bureau. Thus the Stevenson forces could not know how many votes they needed. The lead seesawed back and forth until four days after the election, when the TEB announced that complete returns gave Stevenson 494,330 to Johnson's 493,968. From Duval County the following message reportedly arrived at Johnson headquarters: "The moon is high. The river is low. How many votes do you need?" It was a reference to the well-lighted route across the Rio Grande for alien voters. Both Connally and Johnson may have even paid sudden visits to neighboring Jim Wells County, but it is also possible that neither was involved in the shenanigans that followed. In the next several days more late returns trickled in from such places as Zapata and Jim Wells counties, giving Johnson a lead of 162 votes. Right after the election Zapata County judge M. B. Bravo turned in a vote of 619 to 121 for Johnson and sent the congressman premature congratulations, but in the September 9 returns sent to the State Democratic Executive Committee— twelve days after the polls closed—Stevenson had mysteriously lost exactly 50 votes and Johnson had mysteriously picked up exactly 50 votes. The final Zapata return was 669 to 71. The amended return from Jim Wells County was even more breathtaking. Box 13 in Alice turned up 203 votes that had not previously been counted; 202 were for Johnson, 1 for Stevenson. The voters apparently voted in alphabetical order, signed their names to the poll list in blue-green ink (the rest of the precinct's list was in black ink), and all wrote alike. At least one of them was evidently deceased. In 1977 the Precinct thirteen election judge, Luis Salas, confessed that he saw the fraudulent votes added in alphabetical order and that on George Parr's orders, he certified them as authentic. Salas also charged that President Truman, while campaigning in Texas in September 1948, had promised Parr that he need not worry about any federal investigation of vote fraud charges. Truman, at the time, publicly embraced Johnson as the legitimate Democratic nominee.[40]

Stevenson angrily told reporters that the votes emanating from the Duval County area were for sale. Johnson retorted that if his opponent had such knowledge, he should give it to the grand jury. Stevenson himself had carried Duval by a grand total of 12,416 to 433 against sixteen opponents in his four previous statewide races, but the governor had never had any concerted opposition, and all of those votes had at least been turned in on time.[41]

Accompanied by ex-FBI man T. Kellis Dibrell and hardnosed former Texas Ranger Captain Frank Hamer (of Bonnie and Clyde fame), Stevenson stormed into the Alice bank past George Parr's armed gunmen. After seeing the preposterous voting list, Stevenson felt he had enough evidence for the anti-Parr County Democratic Executive Committee to throw out box 13. But the first of numerous temporary injunctions prevented the county committee from investigating the returns. Stevenson and Johnson then played all their cards before the State Democratic Executive Committee, which met in acrimonious debate all day long and well into the night of September 14. James Allred, John Connally, and several lawyers worked the committee for Johnson, while former Governor Dan Moody masterminded Stevenson's strategy. When the roll call vote was finally taken on whether to throw out box 13, Johnson won. Then one woman changed her vote and made it a tie. Chairman Robert Calvert called the names of absentees once more, not thinking anyone would answer. But Charley Gibson, who had been in the men's room, appeared in the back of the hall and cast a dramatic vote for Johnson. Other small dramas were crucial to the outcome. Johnson delegate Alvin Wirth, for instance, had a heart attack in a hotel lobby and surrendered his proxy as he lay on the floor. By a vote of 29 to 28, the SDEC certified to the state convention that Johnson was the nominee by a final margin of 87 votes. The state Democratic convention—enlivened by several fistfights—overwhelmingly endorsed the SDEC's decision after spending the whole day unseating hundreds of delegates who were pro-Stevenson (most of whom were Texas Regulars) and replacing them with pro-Johnson delegates (Jester-Truman loyalists).[42]

Stevenson's most obvious course would have been to contest the outcome in the state courts, and that was the only sure way of preventing the destruction of ballots within sixty days. No state judge, however, would have issued an injunction to keep Johnson's name off the ticket until all illegal ballots from around the state were thrown out. The general election might be over before this process was complete, and there was always the possibility—given widespread charges of fraudulent counts on both sides—that this form of recount would have confirmed Johnson's victory. The former governor preferred to zero in on the flagrant fast counts in the border counties. Thus Stevenson turned to the federal judiciary. He persuaded United States District Judge T. Whitfield Davidson, a rural east Texas Roosevelt appointee who had soured on the New Deal, to issue a temporary restraining order keeping Johnson's name off the ballot. After noting that no evidence had been submitted disproving Stevenson's contention that he had been robbed, Davidson appointed special commissioners to investigate the south Texas returns. The commissioners found that key witnesses were vacationing in Mexico and that many Jim Wells County ballot boxes were unlocked or had unsealed returns or keys attached; one was even stuffed with blank ballots. County poll lists were missing. The beginnings of the probe in Zapata revealed several irregularities, one of which was that one precinct's ballots had disappeared. But the investigation came to an abrupt end when Johnson's lawyers in Washington convinced Supreme Court Justice Hugo Black, an ardent New Dealer, to set aside Davidson's injunction and restore Johnson's name to the ballot. Black was sharply critical of the federal court for taking a hand in a state election contest. The Supreme Court cautiously confirmed Black's decision. Stevenson then turned desperately to the U.S. Senate Elections Committee, whose two investigators started impounding ballots. This action had no effect, since Duval's ballots were accidently burned by the janitor and some of the Jim Wells and Zapata ballots were lost (those entrusted with their safekeeping were baffled as to their whereabouts). The FBI also conducted an investigation, but it was desultory at best, perhaps because FBI director J. Edgar Hoover did not want to offend President Truman. Finally Stevenson endorsed Johnson's Republican opponent in November, but that, of course, was a futile gesture in one-party Texas.[43]

Just before the November balloting Johnson wrote a public letter to *Dallas Morning News* columnist Lynn Landrum, who had made a page-one headline demand that Johnson yield his nomination to Stevenson. Johnson observed that he had lost Kenedy County by a suspicious margin (52 to 8). that thirteen indictments regarding vote fraud had already been returned in Galveston County, which Stevenson carried overwhelmingly, and that "Coke" had a 466-vote lead from illegal ballots alone in Brown County (where six election judges had failed to sign their names on the ballots). Moreover in Dallas, where Stevenson got a heavy vote, twenty machines showed more votes counted than registered in a local contest, and the Dallas machines were cleared before the required sixty days had expired. The Brown County technicalities were the Johnson's camp ace in the hole, but in fact there was no hint of fraud in those six precincts, whose voters clearly preferred Stevenson to Johnson. There was no evidence of fraud in Dallas. Had the Galveston County irregularities been settled to Johnson's satisfaction, he would have netted some 700 votes, but these (and Brown County's too) were more than offset by the LBJ returns from some of the Ferguson counties and other controlled border counties (Starr, Jim Hogg, and Webb, for instance, weighed in with a margin of 9,388 to 1,560).[44]

Confessions from within the Johnson camp lent credence to Stevenson's charges. One former Johnson aide blurted, "Of course they stole the election. That's the way they did it down there." Johnson apparently confided to one reporter in whom he had enormous confidence, Dave Cheavens, that he was buying south Texas votes just as Coke was purchasing Gregg County votes (in and around Longview). Johnson reputedly vowed that "they" were not going to steal an election from him again. Jimmie Allred was quoted as summing up the dispute, "Well, Lyndon's backers thought Coke Stevenson had stolen the 1941 election in East Texas and they didn't see anything wrong with doing the same for their candidate in 1948." It is possible that if the vote count had been honest and accurate across the state, Johnson might have won the primary anyway, but the preponderance of evidence indicates that the victor should have been Coke Stevenson.[45]

With senatorial and presidential politics out of the way, Beauford Jester was able to turn his attention to the state's political needs. The governor shifted to the left a bit, perhaps persuaded by the relatively heavy 1948 primary vote against him and by the belief that the Dixiecrats were isolated and in disarray. At the behest of Jester an antilynching bill was passed, and a constitutional amendment abolishing the poll tax was submitted for a popular vote that fall. But Jester did not give the amendment high priority, and the Dixiecrats were more intact than most people realized. As a group the Dixiecrats, along with Phil Fox and various business organizations, worked diligently and successfully to defeat the amendment, taking advantage of the usual light voter turnout in off-year elections.[46]

The 1949 legislative session is best remembered as the one that overhauled the administration and financing of the public school system. The school reformers had to persuade the governor to become more interested in improving the schools than in stifling all new taxes. A deal had to be cut with Speaker of the House Durwood Manford, whose first priority was farm-to-market roads. It was said that Manford was willing to let the rural population grow up as ignoramuses just as long as they could drive to town on paved roads. And, of course, the governor and the lobby had to be assured that the oil, gas, and sulfur industries were not taxed for these improvements. Proponents also packed the galleries in order to keep vacillating members in line.[47] Finally the school reformers in the house had to cope with droves of house members who were suddenly absent on the day the Gilmer-Aikin bill came up for a vote. The absences would prevent passage, since there was no quorum on the floor. The truants hid out in bars, motels, and their other usual haunts. Remaining legislators voted a call of the house, which gave the sergeant-at-arms the authority to track down the missing members and bring them back—by force, if necessary. One historian observed:

> Most of them came quietly, but at one tavern three of them tried to hide behind the bar. When [Sergeant-at-Arms] Murphey and his helpers rousted them out, one ran through the tavern owner's living quarters where the lady of the house was trying to get her baby to sleep. In his haste he awakened the child and plunged into a clothes closet. Fearful of being trapped there, he emerged almost at once and rushed, with Murphey close on his heels, out the back door, through a slough of ankle-deep mud, and into a creek bed, where he was captured. Another ran into a clothesline full of diapers and had to get a fresh start. . . . The third fugitive fell under a big live oak tree where chickens habitually roosted.[48]

The Gilmer-Aikin law more than doubled the state's spending for public schools overnight, providing for minimum salaries based on professional considerations. It also streamlined the administration machinery, consolidated hundreds of school districts, and lessened the chances of political selections of textbooks. Many liberals were convinced that the law was Establishment folly, but an objective observer commented a few years later, "They were mistaken. Since private schools are scarce in Texas, businessmen had as much to gain as anybody else from a truly efficient public school system. They therefore supported the movement with complete sincerity."[49]

In retrospect, though, Gilmer-Aikin was just another law, like the Texas constitution itself, that was regressive and out of date the day it was adopted. Since it was steered through the senate by Senator James Taylor, who was literally in the pay of the Texas Manufacturers Association until January 1949, it is not surprising that it was financed by selective consumer taxes, a fact that no doubt heightened the sincerity with which businessmen supported it. The minimum salaries in the richest natural resource state in the Union have never even reached the national average. And it was just as true in 1949 as it was a quarter of a century later that the school districts that made the smallest effort in levying taxes were rewarded the most lavishly by the state. The heralded features of changing the state board from appointive to elective and the state commissioner of education from elective to appointive were meaningless tinkering. Some legislators, as well as Governor Jester, may have favored the switch partially in order to get rid of state school superintendent L. A. Woods, who made numerous enemies while protecting the rights of black teachers and speaking out for Homer Rainey. One member of the Gilmer-Aikin Commission, Texarkana school superintendent H. L. Stillwell, openly told everyone within earshot that he was searching for a way to oust Woods.[50]

Also by the spring of 1949 Jester and the University of Texas hierarchy were prepared to abandon their Dixiecratic rhetoric and bow peacefully to pressures for integration. President Painter advised Regent Woodward that two black students who were applying to the Galveston medical school were ranked competitively with white students. Woodward informed Jester that the state was "clearly under obligation" to provide them with medical education equivalent to that of the University of Texas medical branch at Galveston. The governor replied that unless the legislature created a medical facility at the existing black college, Texas State University for Negroes, and unless its board agreed to it by September 1, "Negro students with proper scholastic averages will have to be admitted" in Galveston. Integration of the medical school began that August, when one black was admitted.[51]

One of the last problems Jester wrestled with was a bill transforming Lamar Junior College into a four-year technical college. One might think that if the governor of a state saw no educational need for a college and evidently viewed it as a budget-wrecker, that would be the end of the matter. But this particular college bill had been rammed through the legislature by Lieutenant Governor Allan Shivers, which prompted aide Weldon Hart to remind Governor Jester:

> Speaking of popularity, we will lose our Hooper rating with Mr. Shivers if you veto Lamar College. This is something to consider in light of the fact that we have (1) some unfinished business this session, (2) we are almost sure to have a special session, sooner or later, (3) we may have a second regular session next January. It is not timidity, but discretion that leads me to point out that Brother Shivers can operate in reverse as well as forward gear.
>
> Whatever you do about Lamar College, I deem it highly advisable that you confer deeply with Shivers before you act.
>
> If you are going to veto it, you ought to look him in the eye and tell him why. If your reasons are good, he will have to respect your honesty and good intentions, if he does not share your views. At least you will have met the issue, i.e., Shivers, face to face.
>
> If you are going to sign it, you ought to do a little bargaining first—enlisting Shivers' aid for the higher education survey, the tax study, the water study, and the eleemosynary building program. He can be helpful, and he ought to be pledged.[52]

Jester went against his own judgment in signing the bill.[53] A month later, on July 11, 1949, he died of a heart attack. He was, at least, one of those southern leaders who realized that the political agitation provoked by the New Deal could not be answered with only a rebel yell. Compared to O'Daniel and Stevenson, Beauford Jester was clearly willing to expend state revenues for what he perceived to be necessary services. When a leading Establishment figure, Executive Vice-President Maston Nixon of the Southern Minerals Corporation, reproved the governor for excessive spending, Jester replied that Nixon's concept of spending "would have meant dispensing with any idea of repairing or expanding our disgraceful eleemosynary system, giving pay raises to badly pinched state employees, [or] increasing support to higher educational institutions." Moreover even after Jester signed the series of antiunion bills, he was still able to communicate with labor leaders. After a December 1948 meeting with some nine union spokesmen, Jester evidently concluded that he and the legislature at least ought to think about reconsidering some of the antilabor laws. And unlike the other Texas governors of the primitive years, Jester would sit down and talk with black political activists, and he adhered to a modern concept of states' rights. Although he spoke of the need to preserve "racial purity," he thought that repealing the poll tax, passing an antilynching bill, and establishing a better voter registration system would not only "modernize" the state but would also "take the wind out of the sails of Northern Democrats and Republicans who are always insisting on them." Jester also maintained his fidelity to the Democratic party, which O'Daniel and Stevenson had been unable to do. As the *Wichita Daily Times* phrased it, Jester's "state of mind toward Texas and its problems is higher-minded than that of either of his two immediate predecessors."[54] Unfortunately Jester's connivance in the maintenance of corporate hegemony over the University of Texas, his signature on more antiunion bills than that of any other governor in the nation, and his disparagement of civil rights besmirch his record. Even so, had he lived, his moderation (by Texas standards) might have dampened some of the ultraconservative outbursts that followed.

9

Red Scare
Politics, 1950s

*Joe McCarthy—a real American—is now officially
a Texan.*

New York Times, October 22, 1953,
upon Governor Shivers's presentation
of citizenship certificate along with a
$6,000 Cadillac to McCarthy

*It's a subversive organization made up of old bags,
the wives of ignoramuses and the newly rich.*

Maury Maverick, Sr., describing the
Minute Women, 1954

Americans were shocked in the late 1940s by a series of disastrous events overseas—the Berlin blockade, the communist coup in Czechoslovakia, the fall of China to the red forces, and the explosion of an atomic bomb by the Soviet Union. Just as most citizens became convinced that the communists comprised a grave external threat to the United States, spectacular spy disclosures escalated public fears on the home front. In 1945 the FBI found secret government documents in the offices of the editor of a pro-communist magazine. In 1946 the Canadian government unmasked a Soviet spy ring that had operated in the higher levels of the administration. In 1947 President Truman launched a zealous loyalty probe for all federal employees and talked of American purity and inevitable United States victory over the godless communists. (One cannot overlook the role of Texans in this phase of the Truman administration. Will Clayton, assistant secretary of state, advised the president that the foreign aid bill was doomed unless Truman set forth "to scare the hell out of the country." Attorney General Tom Clark emphasized the seriousness of internal subversion.) And in 1948 Alger Hiss, a distinguished civil servant in the Roosevelt and Truman administrations, was accused of subversion and eventually convicted of perjury.[1]

These sensational affairs created a volatile political situation in the country, which was most ably exploited by Senator Joseph McCarthy of Wisconsin.

Early in 1950 McCarthy began a five-year rampage, using the issue of communist subversion in government (and education and other institutions) as an easy answer for America's apparently vulnerable position in the world. Hurling one unsubstantiated charge after another, McCarthy soon became a hero to a large segment of the excited and confused public. The critics of McCarthyism defined the senator's techniques (pioneered by Texas congressman Martin Dies) as the use of indiscriminate, often unfounded accusations, and blatant sensationalism—ostensibly justified in the suppression of communism.

As the red scare mania was absorbed into the national mood, people avoided politically controversial subjects, and the political spectrum shifted to the right. The moderate politics of Truman gave way to the reactionary politics of McCarthy. The same process occurred in many states. In Texas the relatively moderate political stance of Jester was replaced by the shriller rhetoric of Allan Shivers.

McCarthyism around the country was also a product, in part, of a continuing hostility to the New Deal. Texas politics, of course, had its own heritage of ultraconservatism, much of which—Martin Dies's career, Texas Regular and Dixiecratic crusades, and W. Lee O'Daniel's escapades—had eventually been stopped by Democratic loyalist opposition. The pent-up furies represented in these lost causes began flourishing on the local level and were often abetted by local elites.

Education, especially its political components, was particularly subjected to irrational attacks. Self-styled patriots established committees to examine textbooks for evidence of socialistic ideas, forced libraries to censure books written by alleged communists, persuaded legislatures to devise loyalty oaths for teachers, and demanded that school boards dismiss controversial educators.

In Texas Houston was the hotbed of this fervent activity. In the fall of 1948, when the Houston school board entertained a proposal to accept federal aid for lunches, a venomous conservatism suddenly festered and scarred the city for years to come. The chairman of the board damned federal aid to schools as a destroyer of initiative and individuality and a creator of infernal inspections and regulations. One board member claimed, "It is not the school's responsibility to provide for indigent pupils." Using lunchroom profits, the board launched an advertising drive to collect private funds for lunches, but the city did not have the initiative to come up with the money. Houston's fear of federal controls was so complete that the board refused to require federal inspection of the meat that they bought. On at least one occasion the district purchased meat—beef, it supposed—from the Superior Meat Company that turned out to be horse meat. An entire generation of impoverished Houston children ate little or nothing during the noon hours while millions of other American children received their lunches free. Finally in 1967 a conservative board evidently concluded that hunger did not pro-mote individuality. Federal aid for lunches was voted in.[2]

Elsewhere in the state, in 1949 the Texas Daughters of the American Revolution had investigated Frank Magruder's popular *American Government* text and discovered that its patriotism was suspect. Lucille Crain re-vealed this information in her new quarterly newsletter, the *Editorial Reviewer*. Though her report was filled with glaring inaccuracies, her crusade attracted nationwide attention. Many critics never bothered to read the book, but by 1950 it was banned in Houston, three out-of-state towns, and the whole state of Georgia.[3]

Magruder's text was in fact a conservative book that had been used since 1937 in Houston and had the approval of 90 percent of the teachers. The author could not have realized that he was playing with social dynamite when he paid a casual compliment to the United Nations, which at that time was dominated by the United States and its allies. The Houston school board had its own opinion about the United Nations; there were communists in it. The board was also offended by a paragraph noting that government con-trols increase as society becomes more complex and added that "the country is capitalistic with strong Socialistic and even Communistic trends." Magruder's phraseology was a bit misleading, since the trends he cited—such as power projects and old-age assistance—could have been accurately described as welfare-capitalistic, but it should have been too trivial to attract attention. Yet it was largely on the basis of this one paragraph that the Houston school board, with only a single dissenting vote, rejected the Magruder text. Hous-ton civics teachers taught mostly without a text for the next two years. Professor Magruder promptly purged the book of its offending remarks, and it was allowed back in most schools.[4]

The most important of the national extremist groups that sprang up in the early 1950s, destined to exert notable influence in Houston and San Antonio, was the Minute Women. The group was chartered in September 1949 in Connecticut by Suzanne Silvercruys Stevenson, a sculptress and upper-class refugee from Belgium. The evangelistic woman modestly dubbed herself the "Paul Revere of the Fair Sex." Her connection with McCarthyism was clear enough, since her most treasured possession was a letter that the senator wrote her. In it McCarthy advised that organizations that fought the com-munists would be smeared but that they would have the satisfaction of hurt-ing the reds. When prospective recruits balked at joining the Minute Women, members gave them a glimpse of "the" letter.[5]

Minute Women pledged to vote in every election and intended to re-move every vestige of communism from federal and state governments and the local schools. A list of succinctly phrased principles, which the group dubbed nonpartisan, included states' rights, fairer taxes, and "right to work." The group literature elaborated on some of these principles and revealed the true meaning of the terms. States' rights actually meant continued racial segregation and support for the states in the tidelands battles with the federal government. Fairer taxes referred to the Minute Women's desire to repeal the graduated income tax. "Right to work" cloaked the Minute Women's hope of stamping out unions.[6]

Although the women were supposed to support the traditional American way of life, Stevenson selected a Council of Eleven who chose all local, state, and regional chairmen. Elections and bylaws were banned. There was no constitution and no parliamentary procedure to guide meetings. The agenda was predetermined by the chapter chairman and her executive committee; motions from the floor were prohibited. Stevenson commented, "It is odd, but it's the only protection we have against ever being taken over by the Communists. . . . Even garden clubs in the United States have allowed themselves to become infiltrated by Communists."[7]

The totalitarianism, in fact, was not odd, since the policies of left-wing and right-wing extremists are sometimes identical. A series of Minute Women newspaper advertisements, for instance, called for support of legislation to curb President Truman's authority to send more troops to Korea without the consent of Congress. Communists adopted the advertisements as propaganda against United States intervention in the Korean War. One of the original leaders of the Minute Women promptly resigned, charging that the others were following the "Communist party line." Minute Women policy also coincided with that of the communists when they denounced President Truman's proposal for universal military training.[8]

Minute Women meetings, usually held without public announcement, took place in the local American Legion or Veterans of Foreign Wars hall or in a member's home. The members opened the evening's battle against communism by singing the Minute Women song to the tune of "America, the Beautiful":

> As Minute Women now we pledge
> Unitedly to stand
> And strive with loyal hearts to guard
> Our most beloved land.
> America, we hear thy call—
> America, for thee—
> We pray for might to keep alight
> The torch of liberty.[9]

Ralph O'Leary, a *Houston Post* reporter who wrote a series of articles pinpointing the Minute Women's activities in his city, believed that Stevenson's most remarkable innovation was never to use her organization as a pressure group. Minute Women always acted as individuals. If five hundred women were to make individual phone calls of protest to a governmental agency, it would have considerably more effect than a similar number of calls from an organization; the same was true of letters to newspapers. Stevenson preferred that Minute Women use postcards to express their views on current events since a card was likely to be read by half a dozen persons on its way through the mails.[10]

The estimated nationwide strength of the group varied, but it was clearly strongest in California, Connecticut, West Virginia, Maryland, and Texas. Houston's chapter of the Minute Women was the first and most vigorous in the Lone Star state. O'Leary's investigation revealed that by the fall of 1952, the organization had about five hundred members, many of whom lived in River Oaks and other exclusive residential districts. About one-fourth were wives of physicians or oil industry executives and personnel. Many members of older patriotic groups and the wives of men belonging to such groups were attracted. There was a substantial faction from parent-teacher organizations and other groups in the educational field, including one school board member and two wives of board members. Several wealthy male lawyers and businessmen attended a number of Minute Women meetings. A fraction of the women hailed from less affluent circles; among them were elderly widows, boardinghouse operators, seamstresses, and operators of small speciality shops, many of whom depended on the River Oaks trade for their livelihood. The Minute Women were also aided by unorganized remnants of the defunct Dixiecrats.[11]

At least one meeting of the Houston Minute Women was infiltrated by an observer from the Anti-Defamation League of the B'nai B'rith. The speaker, according to the spy, urged that the Federal Security Administration be abolished, since it reeked of socialism and had supported Howard University, a black school. The observer was appalled that the women believed that the FSA was an arm of the United Nations. In conversation after the speech, the women revealed that they genuinely believed that communists and socialists were already in complete charge of the entire federal governmental structure and of many colleges and public schools. The eighty or so women and twenty men seemed determined to fight this takeover.[12]

Houston's Minute Women were deeply opposed to left-wing speakers visiting the city, though they always denied having any connection with the protests that arose. Years later, however, one of their charter members admitted that they had initiated chain letters and telephone campaigns against individuals or issues when alerted by their leaders and that Jesse Jones's *Houston Chronicle* "gave us wonderful publicity to get the public aroused against outside speakers." One of the militant women—Helen D. Thomas, Vance Muse's niece—distributed leaflets attacking the Quakers as leftists just before they held their second annual Institute on International Relations in Houston in June 1952. Among other allegations, she charged that the Quakers were cited by the House Un-American Activities Committee in 1938 as "working for the suppression of capitalism and imperialism by the establishment of a new social and international order." Another typical charge was that Alger Hiss, "between trials," attended a summer Quaker meeting in Vermont and delivered a speech advocating world government. The Quakers denied that their American Friends Service Committee had ever been cited as subversive by any government agency. They noted that Thomas was relying upon the testimony of one witness, Walter S. Steele, editor of an ultraconservative magazine. They added that there was no basis for the assertion and that the House committee never took action on it. Concerning Hiss, the Quaker statement explained that he was invited before his indictment and spoke before his conviction. At the time he spoke, he was still employed by the Carnegie Endowment for International Peace, whose board of directors included Dwight Eisenhower and whose chairman was John Foster Dulles. The Friends added, "Presumably both groups were following the American principle that a man is considered innocent until he is proven guilty."[13]

Inspired by Thomas's writing, about twenty Minute Women and male allies, led by attorney John P. Rogge, heckled a noncommunist, pacifist speaker and accused him of preaching communism and treason. The second night, this same speaker was seized by the arm and wrestled to the floor momentarily by a legionnaire. Anna Lord Strauss, United States delegate to the United Nations General Assembly, was accused of communism during her speech. The only actual communist present, the counselor for the Yugoslav permanent mission to the United Nations, was completely undisturbed during his part of the speaking program.[14]

As a result of the unruly Houston meeting, those of the Quaker speakers who were scheduled to appear the following week at Southwest Texas State Teachers College in San Marcos were informed that the meeting was canceled. Some months later the Quakers prematurely distributed announcements that the third annual Institute on International Relations would be held in June 1953 at the previous site, St. James Episcopal Church in Houston. There was an immediate attack in the form of an anonymous four-page brochure, which repeated all the old discredited charges and added that the Quakers did not hire halls but rather sought the facilities of tax-exempt churches and universities. Many citizens, it continued, were attaching "safeguard pledge slips" to their contributions to tax-exempt organizations. The recipient had to pledge that its facilities were not open to any individual or organization that had been cited as a "communist front" in the files of the House Un-American Activities Committee. St. James Episcopal Church, which had not given full permission for the meeting, was in the midst of a fund drive for its hospital. The Quakers were denied the site.[15]

The Minute Women, several legionnaires, attorney Rogge, and others also attempted to prevent Dr. Rufus Clement from making a Sunday address on race relations at the First Methodist Church in February 1952. Dr. Clement, a black, had been president of Atlanta University for sixteen years and was an ordained minister. He was attacked as having a communist-front record. The charges disintegrated in the face of unusually powerful support for his loyalty from the governor of Tennessee, a United States district judge, highly placed legionnaires, and the presidents and trustees of several universities.[16]

The Minute Women and their allies were primarily concerned about alleged subversion in the public schools. A reference book, *Our Changing Social Order*, disappeared from high school libraries when one man objected to the contention of the author that it was impracticable for anyone with an income as low as twenty-five hundred dollars a year to own a home unless he was a farmer. The protester was a real estate dealer whose name school officials could not remember. A teacher's guide was almost unshelved when a school board member objected to a conservationist statement that "minerals do not rightly belong to any one group or people or to any one nation." Local radio announcer Joe Worthy was caught up in the spirit of the day and tried to found a "Watchdog Association" of "informers in all classes," including kindergartens, to ferret out the "poison being taught in our schools."[17]

Any connection between the public schools and the United Nations continued to be resented, since the Minute Women held that the "Russian-instigated U.N. is running the Korean War with the purpose of destroying us." In March 1952 Assistant Superintendent J. O. Webb, acting without the approval of the superintendent of schools, eliminated the United Nations examination contest, by means of which students could win college scholarships and trips abroad. It and its predecessor had been held in the schools since the early days of the League of Nations. Some months later all information about the United Nations contained in the regular curriculum was dropped.[18]

In November 1952 four candidates ran for the school board chiefly on an anti-United Nations platform. The hyperconservative slate had the financial backing of many of Houston's veteran anti-New Deal millionaires, including oilmen Hugh Roy Cullen and Glenn McCarthy, banker and attorney James Elkins, and Lamar Fleming, Jr., a business partner of *Houston Chronicle* owner Jesse Jones. The candidates, all of whom were Minute Women or husbands of them, charged that the nationwide conspiracy of creeping socialism could be halted only by rejecting federal aid to education, cleansing school libraries of subversive literature, and attacking the United Nations Educational, Scientific and Cultural Organization. The fiery leader among the candidates was Dallas Dyer, who noted that she had read ten UNESCO booklets and warned that "their purpose is to train children to think, not as

citizens of America first, but as the citizens of all countires—of the world."
She feared that these booklets might creep into the Houston schools.[19]

The moderate opposition tried to emphasize that the conservatives had
poorly administered the finances of the district, but they could not avoid
the McCarthyite issues. They took the position that the school board should
always be on alert for subversion in the schools but that the accusations of a
drift toward socialism were contemptible efforts to undermine public faith
in the schools. One moderate reminded Houstonians that if socialism had
crept in, it was the fault of the conservatives who had been on the board for
years. Dyer's opponent pointed out that the UNESCO charter forbade intervention in the local affairs of member nations and that the booklets she had
read were printed reports of seminars that had nothing to do with Houston's
teachers or their methods.'[20]

Since the election was held simultaneously with the presidential balloting,
which always attracts more voters than a local contest, eight times as many
people voted in the 1952 school board election as in any other previous one.
Dyer and another McCarthyite were elected, but moderates won the other
two slots. The personal popularity of individual candidates was evidently
more important than other factors. The results were indecisive, since the
board's voting alignment could not be safely predicted. There was, however,
no doubt of the board's generally conservative bent. Moreover with the
election out of the way, the Minute Women turned with a vengeance to
school district problems that had been postponed.[21]

The Minute Women's most spectacular accomplishment was pressuring
the school board into investigating and firing deputy superintendent of
schools George Ebey, a liberal who had arrived from Oregon in 1952. Instrumental in the probe was a brochure charging Ebey with being a weak
combatant of communistic influences in an organization to which he once
belonged, the American Veterans Committee. The brochure also devoted
considerable space to racial matters. Attorney John Rogge, acting as spokesman for groups he refused to identify, told the board that Ebey was soft on
communism and on white supremacy. The attorney revealed one allegedly
"dangerous" quotation from an Ebey speech given over six years earlier in
which the educator stated that "the Communist Party is to be abhorred,"
but that free thought and free speech should not be suppressed to fight communism. The school board finally authorized an exhaustive inquiry into
Ebey's past by ex-FBI investigators, who submitted a slipshod 348-page
report that cost the city almost six thousand dollars. The investigators made
no attempt to evaluate the accuracy of the testimony that they took; their
report was, in fact, a collection of personal opinions sprinkled liberally with
innuendo and hearsay, usually slanted against Ebey. At least seven school
administrators and board members in Oregon protested that the questioners
took no notes, made up quotations, and generally warped the interviews

beyond recognition. Even so, the report cleared Ebey of all charges of disloyalty, showing, for instance, that he opposed one candidate for the AVC board solely because the man was a communist. Apparently his most serious offense was that he had been in charge of instruction and curriculum in a Portland, Oregon, school that placed American children of Asian descent in the same classes with Anglo-Americans. He had also permitted a black to teach at the school.[22]

Despite the hysteria of his opponents, Ebey did have considerable support in Houston. A number of businessmen, including the president of the Dannenbaum Manufacturing Company and the personnel director of Houston Natural Gas Corporation, deplored the malicious attacks against the deputy superintendent. Ministers protested the smear, and the CIO predictably joined the fray against the "Petticoat front of the Minute Women."[23]

With all the facts and wild accusations before them, the school board— bombarded by Minute Women phone calls, letters, and telegrams and bolstered by the important support of Jesse Jones's ever-reactionary *Houston Chronicle*—voted 4 to 3 to fire Ebey on the spurious grounds that he was not suited to handle personnel matters. The story flashed across the country, and one national news magazine after another recoiled. Even some Texas papers—the *San Antonio News* and the *Houston Post*, among them—were ashamed of their state.[24]

The National Education Association, damned by the Minute Women as an "American Gestapo," and by the *Houston Chronicle* as a communist front, investigated the case upon the request of the state and local teacher associations. Its report pinpointed the deleterious influence of the Minute Women and concluded that the school board had acted "precipitately" in the dismissal of Ebey. An NEA poll of 1,918 Houstonians in the school system tallied 258 teachers who had been pressured to support a political candidate or to slant courses to a certain political belief, 259 who had been asked not to support the Houston Teachers' Association, and 844 who feared that they might be fired because of their social or political beliefs. All told, 1,112 teachers had personally experienced "unwarranted pressure." The leading pressure sources were principals, board members, and school administrators along with such outside forces as the Minute Women, the American Legion, and *Houston Chronicle*. The *Chronicle* lashed out against the NEA for holding secret meetings in Houston and for not allowing the Minute Women to testify or to "know who their accusers were. Certainly that is not the American way." The *Chronicle* never did criticize John Rogge for refusing to identify the people whom he said supported him in his attacks on Dr. Ebey.[25]

Ralph O'Leary's exposé of the Minute Women in October 1953 and the publicity of the NEA investigation in January 1954 did not end the group's ability to foment public mischief. In March 1954 two Reagan High School

English teachers were fired—largely at the instigation of the Minute Women—because they had read excerpts from D. H. Lawrence's writings in their classes. The principal, who had secretly investigated the teachers but found nothing against them, informed one of them that carrying Lawrence into a classroom was tantamount to practicing communism. The charge did not go very far in explaining the fact that Lawrence's writings were suppressed in communist countries. Moreover the only passages read in class merely poked fun of Benjamin Franklin's thirteen moral points. One Lawrence expert wrote a letter to the *Houston Post* challenging the communist charges and was promptly deluged with Minute Women propaganda. He was informed that subversives were everywhere, that parents could not be too careful about what their children were exposed to, and that he was just another "duped liberal."[26]

The turmoil inflicted more damage on the McCarthyites than they realized. As the president of the Houston Teachers' Association put it, Ebey's martyrdom forced "into the light of day many pale grub worms previously only suspected," and most of them were unable to stand the light. In the next school board election, November 1954, Houston voters stunned the reactionaries by electing two members of the moderate slate to the board. The new board demoted J. O. Webb, who had arbitrarily banned the United Nations contests, and allowed the superintendent to appoint a committee to review the contest material. One committee member, the principal of Milby High School, announced that "the UN started out by having a lot of lousy people on it and they did a lot of lousy thinking." Nevertheless tests for the contests were available in March 1955, but only four of Houston's sixteen thousand students competed. The moderates lost control of the board in the 1956 elections not because of the declining, factionalized Minute Women but because of a last-ditch segregationist crusade.[27]

The only other Texas city that suffered serious abuse from the Minute Women was San Antonio. By late February 1952, three months after the chapter was organized, the Minute Women had enlisted some 415 members in the Alamo city. While they were organizing, they ran into eloquent opposition from Thomas Pape, associate editor of the *Alamo Register*, the official paper of the Catholic archdiocese of San Antonio. Pape evaluated the Minute Women's program, as outlined by Stevenson who was visiting the city, and pointed out that her sales tax—the poor man, having less to spend, pays less—overlooked the fact that many Americans must spend their entire salaries to support their families, but the rich do not have to. Stevenson, a Catholic, also called for total free enterprise, which, the editor noted, "reached its peak with 96-hour workweeks in the last century" and which was also contrary to an encyclical issued by Pope Pius XI. Another Minute Women plank was states' rights, which was set forth in such a way that it meant opposition to federal civil-rights legislation. Pape declared that the states' rights champions had no valid opposition to federal civil rights if they did not try to persuade their own state legislatures to pass civil-rights laws. The editor added that the teachings of the church regarding the brotherhood of all men were too well known to repeat. The Minute Women were opposed to socialism and communism, which Pape thought was commendable except that they suffered from the delusion that Truman's Fair Deal program was socialism, even though some of the legislation proposed had been called for by the American bishops as far back as 1919.[28]

The group shrugged off such opposition and soon delved into book censorship. In 1953 Myrtle Hance, an elderly widow who was the leader of the local Minute Women, presented the city council with a list of about six hundred books in the city library that, she alleged, were written by communist sympathizers. The list included Einstein's *Theory of Relativity*, Thomas Mann's *Joseph in Egypt*, Norbert Wiener's *Cybernetics*, Louis Untermeyer's *The Treasury of Great Poems*, and books on sculpture, the mentally ill, alcoholics, child care, architecture, and mystery novels.

Hance recommended that these books "be stamped on the inside cover with a red stamp, large enough to be seen immediately, showing that the author has Communist front affiliations, and the number of [HUAC] citations." (The stamp was reportedly developed by J. C. Phillips, editor of the *Borger News-Herald* and chairman of the "Americanism Commission" of the Texas American Legion.) Hance also stormed into two local high schools and demanded that she be allowed to examine all their books for evidences of red bias.

The cry for book stamping was taken up in May 1953 by Mayor Jack White, whose wife was a Minute Woman. Several council members agreed, but acting city manager Wylie Johnson thought the books ought to be burned. Mayor White reconsidered and thought maybe burning would be better. These tactics triggered a reaction, and hundreds of townsfolk held mass meetings and denounced the council. The city's newspapers, even Hearst's, called for a free library. Former congressman and mayor Maury Maverick soon thought the bookburners were on the run because they had gone so far as to attack a number of the rich Establishment leaders. By June Mayor White and the council quietly passed the word that they were not going to press the matter.[29]

By the fall of 1953, the mayor and city council had replaced most of the liberal library board, slashed the library budget, and launched a quiet, indirect attack. Gift books had to be approved by a committee dominated by Minute Women and their supporters. Audiovisual services were abolished, since educational television was considered liberal. House Un-American Activities Committee reports were required to be taken out of the obscure

government documents library and placed in the main library, and they had
to be bound, prominently displayed, and advertised with ten by twelve inch
signs.[30]

In February 1954, however, the veteran library board chairman, M. M.
Harris, persuaded the panel to adopt the American Library Association's
standards for book selection. It was a 6 to 5 vote against censorship. And
since all eleven members conceded that they were "against using books for
fuel," the Minute Women, according to the press, had lost the battle. Two
months later it looked as though this vote had been another false turning
point, though, since most of the Harris majority was not reappointed, and
Harris himself resigned when he learned that the mayor was not going to
reappoint him. The library controversy, however, had helped trigger a
campaign by the newspapers and various civic groups for the formation of
the Good Government League, a new and more moderate Establishment
group, which won the first of its continuing series of electoral victories in
the summer of 1955. In June they appointed a new library board, which
was opposed to stamping, burning, and other mutilation.[31]

Lobbying at the state level in November 1953, the Minute Women pressured the state textbook committee to recommend the elimination of both
the United Nations Declaration of Human Rights and interpretations of it
from world history books. The militant women considered the declaration
a leftist, integrationist document. The State Board of Education considered
the textbook committee's recommendation, but in the crucial maneuvering,
the members infuriated the Minute Women. The board voted 9 to 6 not to
table Houston lawyer Jack Binion's motion to leave the declaration in but
to delete editorial comments. Simultaneously the Minute Women attempted
to elect Mrs. C. R. Larimer of Houston as president of the Texas Parent-
Teachers' Association. Although motorcades were organized on her behalf,
she lost the presidency 3,213 to 608. These defeats appeared to terminate
Minute Women influence on agencies that operated statewide.[32]

The very loosely knit Establishment in the Rio Grande Valley was also
infiltrated by the rightists in the early 1950s. In November 1951, newspaper
magnate R. C. Hoiles of Santa Ana, California, spent about $2 million of
his estimated $20 million fortune in purchasing the three leading papers in
the valley: the *Brownsville Herald*, the *McAllen Monitor*, and the *Valley
Morning Star* in Harlingen. It was assumed that Hoiles would be just another
absentee owner, especially since he assured employees that no changes in
personnel were planned. Hoiles, however, fired the three editors and immediately launched a vigorous attack on public schools and public taxes. In
his crusade to abolish the public schools, he maintained that public school
teachers could not teach the "American way of life" because they did not
understand the Declaration of Independence; if they could read and understand the declaration, he reasoned, they would not be public school teachers.

He added that the public schools were socialistic institutions and a violation of the Bible. (It was not meek, he said, to force the majority to pay school taxes, whereas Scripture clearly states, "Blessed are the meek, for they shall inherit the earth.") The California publisher also made it clear that he opposed defense bonds, paper money, Community Chests, libraries, public hospitals, social welfare laws, organized labor, majority rule, police departments, the armed forces, the United Nations, Judaism, Catholicism, the Federal Council of Churches (Protestant), and the mixing of Anglo-Americans with Negroes or Mexican-Americans.[33]

Opponents of Hoiles rallied around Roy Hofheinz, former member of the legislature, Harris County judge (1937-1945), owner of valley radio station KSOX, and later mayor of Houston and manager of the Astrodome. Beginning a series of radio broadcasts in December 1951, Judge Hofheinz reminded the public that the author of the Declaration of Independence, Thomas Jefferson, had founded the tax-supported University of Virginia. He pointed out that schools were no more socialistic than such widely accepted federal institutions as the military forces, highways, post office, and weather bureau. The valley Establishment, led by the merchants, boycotted the Hoiles papers. Some nine thousand dollars was raised in a public sale of paid-up subscriptions to a nonexistent newspaper, in the hope of establishing one. In February 1952 Hoiles and Hofheinz debated the public-school issue with a thousand people looking on and some thirty-five hundred listening on the radio. Hoiles was interrupted only once with a few claps while Hofheinz was interrupted several times. Hofheinz believed that he could drive Hoiles out of the valley.[34]

Hoiles, however, was more flexible than Hofheinz imagined. By the summer of 1952, the Californian had dropped the writings of David Baxter, his most vicious columnist, and had begun soft-pedaling the various controversial issues. By the fall of 1952, at least temporarily, he was printing a better newspaper than his predecessors and had even appointed a Jewish editor for the three papers. Hoiles remained an extremist in his columns, but less obtrusively than before. The boycott expired.[35]

In Dallas the conservative Establishment came under fire from the right and failed to meet the challenge. One controversy was sparked by John O. Beaty, a right-wing professor of English at Southern Methodist University. In 1951 he had published *The Iron Curtain over America*, an extensive anti-Semitic diatribe. In its autumn 1953 issue, the Southern Methodist University literary quarterly, *Southwest Review*, printed an article critical of Beaty's book. The professor retorted in a pamphlet, *How to Capture a University*, that the Jews dominated SMU, as well as Dallas's chapter of the Institute on American Freedom. His chief target was Stanley Marcus, president of the Nieman-Marcus stores and the only liberal member of the local Establishment. Since Marcus was an Establishment man, and since the chapter included Mayor R. L. Thornton, the acrimony should have soon died. But the Establishment organ, the *Dallas Morning News*, editorialized the incident as a liberal-conservative conflict and suggested that SMU make up its mind between the two. Such misrepresentation and indifference on the part of the Establishment newssheet served to nurture right-wing attacks.[36]

In the spring of 1954 the three-year-old Dallas Council of World Affairs, which sponsored such speakers as Henry Cabot Lodge, was vilified as a communist front. The executive director of the council, H. Neil Mallon, had attended a convention sponsored by the Foreign Policy Association; Brooks Emeny, president emeritus of the FPA, was also present. At one time Emeny had been on the board of directors of the Institute of Pacific Relations—and so had Alger Hiss. From Alger Hiss to Brooks Emeny to the FPA to a single convention of the FPA to the executive secretary of the Dallas Council on World Affairs to the council itself, a clear red trail was drawn. Besides it was common gossip in Dallas that Mallon was selling industrial equipment to the Russians (he was not). The Dallas Council on World Affairs was able to get a fair hearing and be cleared only because its board included honorary members from the Establishment. And even at that, the board had to announce its formal disassociation from the FPA, which included among its many distinguished members Secretary of State John Foster Dulles.[37]

Perhaps the exigency for Texas's apparent hypervigilance was best realized by a member of the State Board of Education, who surveyed the public schools in February 1954 and found one communist out of sixty thousand people. That one was fired.[38] Yet the near-hysterical McCarthyite outbursts of the early 1950s were met by local Establishments with either indifference or connivance. In Houston and San Antonio, where the controversies were hottest, the common people showed more courage and faith in democratic processes and proved to be less reactionary than their elite leaders. In fact McCarthyism in Texas and the nation was not sustained by mass grass-roots support but rather by elite groups.[39] The fears of the public seemed abated by the mid-1950s, but little thanks for this is owed to the local Establishments or to the Shivers administration.

10

"OIL FOLKS AT HOME":
The Shivers Administration

> *The writer feared that Governor Jester was flying around too much, that it was dangerous, because "Allan Shivers would become Governor of Texas. Of Texas, sir. Allan Shivers!"*
> Unsigned letter to Beauford Jester, October 6, 1947

> *". . . the [presidential] fight in Texas is hotter than in the nation generally because Texas magnifies everything."*
> Time, September 29, 1952

> *"It is like a bunch of kids wanting to play cowboy and Indian. All want to be cowboys. I think we need more Texas Republicans, but I don't want to be one."*
> Columnist Allen Duckworth, quoting an advocate of two-party government, 1947

After Governor Jester's sudden death in July 1949, he was succeeded by Lieutenant Governor Allan Shivers, a tall, dark man of considerable ability. Shivers was born poor and paid for his University of Texas education by working in the Texas Company refinery in his home town of Port Arthur and by selling shoes in Austin. He developed his political pragmatism at the university. On one occasion his campus political group was considering an alliance with a sorority. A great discussion was going on about the advisability of this, when young Shivers stood up and reputedly said, "Bring them in; a whore's vote is as good as a debutante's in an election." He won the student body presidency in 1932, and just four years later he unseated a favored incumbent as state senator from highly industrialized Jefferson County. Shivers was still fairly hard pressed for money until he married into the multimillionaire Rio Grande Valley family, the Sharys, in 1937.

9. Allan Shivers Rolls His Own. *Texas State Archives.*

Some labor leaders were suspicious of Shivers from the beginning, distrusting him for wearing pearl grey spats and sporting an expensive walking cane on the streets of Port Arthur. He cast his votes for union interests during his early years in office but abandoned labor as soon as he felt secure in his position. He voted for the sales tax in 1939, and O'Daniel and Manford antilabor bills in 1941 and 1943. Yet in 1945 he was one of ten senators who prevented that chamber from voting on the right-to-work bill, and the liberal *Texas Spectator* did not rank him as one of the "busy friends of the corporations." As dean of the senate, he was the choice of nearly all his colleagues in 1946 to run for the lieutenant governor's slot vacated by John Lee Smith. He won handily and ruled with iron control during the notorious 1947 session of the senate, which passed nine antilabor bills and knifed the gas gathering tax passed by the house. He did favor jury service for women and was on record against the poll tax. Shivers's biographers claim he was ahead of his time in advocating constitutional amendments establishing annual sessions and annual salaries for legislators, but as they also note, he did not try to prevent the business lobby from slaying them in the 1949 balloting.[1]

But Shivers was no mere pawn of businessmen and powerful interest groups. Indeed, as governor, Shivers soon considered it one of his biggest jobs "to call in businessmen and convince them that spending was necessary." Late in 1949 Shivers was confronted with the opinion of Ed Burris, president of the Texas Manufacturers Association, that the TMA was upset over the governor's "constant mention of taxes." Burris believed that no new taxes were needed; rather the governor should just recommend an across-the-board 10 to 15 percent cut in appropriations in the second year of the biennium. Some $3 million to $5 million could be saved by not buying any textbooks, for example. Burris also conveyed a veiled threat to the executive office: unless appropriations were slashed, railroad commissioner Olin Culberson would "wean away conservative support" and defeat Shivers in the next election. Burris added in January 1950, as another example of savings, if appropriations were decreased 15 percent, the needs for eleemosynary operations would be reduced by $2.5 million. Also in January the Fort Worth Chamber of Commerce came up with a similar retrogressive plan. Shivers's aide, Weldon Hart, wrote a memo to the governor noting that the chamber's plan could work only by closing all state departments for one year and state colleges for six months and repealing the soil conservation and rural road building programs. Hart doubted that even the Fort Worth businessmen would really want to go quite that far.[2]

Meanwhile, late in 1949 the governor thought it prudent to send a trusted friend, public relations man Jake Pickle, into towns and cities throughout the state for political reconnaissance. Pickle sought out the leading attorneys, doctors, editors, and bankers—the Establishment in each town—and submitted detailed reports from and about dozens of top men in Texas's local Establishments. Commissioner Culberson, according to Pickle, enjoyed some oil support in Wichita Falls and Tyler, and had dispatched a "hatchet man" to spread "dirty stuff" against Shivers in Canton, but neither he nor any other potential candidate was a serious threat. In Dallas assistant district attorney Henry Wade promised valuable help: he would mail the governor a list of the city's 180-man ruling elite with the proviso that the roster be kept confidential. As a result of his survey, Pickle offered the kind of practical advice that all governors must have. For instance, since Shivers had married a Catholic, which brought about considerable underground grumbling, Pickle advised silence while the bigotry built up; then—just before the vote—he should give a "Little Red Arrow Character and religious speech." Pickle proposed to put "every Baptist in the state on the broadcast," though Catholicism should never be mentioned. Another bit of advice for the governor was to "take the lead for one or two liberal things," such as eleemosynary appropriations or old-age pensions, to undercut the opposition and make the people feel that Shivers was "their liberal leader."[3]

In January 1950, on the eve of a special session of the legislature, Shivers became the first governor to call the major industry lobbyists to the mansion and outline his demands. Ed Burris's hesitancy dissolved, and the whole group readily acceded to the Shivers program, which largely bypassed new taxes on natural resources, especially in proportion to the rocketing postwar profits in oil and gas. The burden of financing the governor's reforms was placed on consumer taxes, particularly an increased cigarette levy. The reforms included long-overdue increased appropriations for eleemosynary institutions, school salaries, retirement benefits, highways, and old-age pensions. The 1951 legislature passed an omnibus bill that actually increased oil, gas, and sulfur taxes 10 percent, though it also levied selective sales taxes on a couple of dozen other items. The governor was irate when the legislature defeated a gasoline sales tax and passed a gathering tax on natural gas piplines, similar to the one proposed by Governor Allred in the 1930s. The legislature carried this fight into special session, which lowered expense allowances from ten dollars to five dollars a day. Many of the pipeline taxers, who came to be known as the Gashouse Gang, rented an old boarding house at 1700 Rio Grande and thereby cut expenses. Twenty-two of them lived there at one time and lounged on borrowed furniture and apple crates. Some elements in the liquor lobby kept them supplied with drink and the Farm Bureau sent baskets of groceries. The liquor lobby, of course, wanted to avoid further taxation of their product. They were keenly aware that the Gashousers had proposed a liquor tax bill, but they knew the solons were not serious about it if the gas tax was adopted. Also, the liquor folks simply enjoyed the fracas. The Farm Bureau was interested in the farm-to-market roads that the bill was designed to pay for. The legislators generated considerable public support and rammed the bill down Shivers's throat, but it was quickly challenged in the courts. Finally Attorney General John Ben Shepperd, who had lobbied against the gas tax on the floor of the house while serving as secretary of state, was called upon to defend the law before the Supreme Court. The Court found the law unconstitutional.[4]

In one of the more prescient letters of the time, J. Webb Howell, the conservative president and manager of the Bryan Cotton Oil and Fertilizer Company, sent encouragement to the Gashouse bellwether, blind representative Jim Sewell of Blooming Grove. Howell believed that Texas should "conserve and tax natural gas" before it was exhausted. He thought it "criminal" for the "big companies to get this gas for a mere song and deliver it to the coal regions." With gas leaving the state at the rate of seven billion cubic feet a day, Howell thought it was anybody's guess as to how long it lasted.[5]

The top leadership of the Gashouse Gang soon disappeared from the legislature. Sewell accepted appointment as county judge of Navarro County; the incumbent judge was offered a better job in Tyler. D. B. Hardeman of Denison, regarded by colleagues and reporters as one of the most talented house leaders in years, was given a new district. The gerrymandering suddenly presented him with new constituents. The oil and gas lobby moved into the new district like an avalanche and crushed Hardeman in the 1952 primary. One house member commented, "This ought to show who owns the seats in the Texas legislature." Senator George Nokes of Corsicana was also thrown into a district where he could not win. Because he needed a paying job, he retired from the legislature. Shivers may have had a hand in these developments. He undoubtedly intervened to put the house under better control. Taking advantage of the many new members, the conservatives at the next session organized and put through a rules revision requiring six days' written notice of a motion to refer a bill from one committee to another. This terminated the committee-shuffling technique used by Shivers's enemies.[6]

Governor Shivers also deftly emasculated the Good Neighbor Commission. As lieutenant governor and a landed aristocrat from the valley, Shivers had been embarrassed by GNC studies that spotlighted the exploitation of Mexican labor by south Texas farmers at the illegal wages of ten cents to twenty-five cents per hour. Shivers retorted that the Mexicans and Mexican-Americans on his estate made forty to fifty cents an hour and that the wage report, which he labeled as outside the "proper realm" of the GNC, just "stirs people up." Shivers connived in the forced resignation of GNC executive secretary Pauline Kibbe in September 1947, in exchange for which the GNC was made a permanent state agency. Commission chairman Bob Smith, a self-styled "oil operator" from Houston, confirmed the deal in a letter to Shivers—"For your confidential information, this has all turned out as planned"—though Shivers naturally denied that any arrangement existed. Under the new director, Tom Sutherland, the GNC avoided the Mexican labor issue but continued to search into discriminatory practices and lobby against school segregation.[7]

Suddenly in January 1949, the Longoria case burst onto the nation's headlines. Felix Longoria, killed in action on Luzon, was denied burial services by the Three Rivers, Texas, funeral home. The case could probably have been adjusted without publicity, but Dr. Hector Garcia of Corpus Christi decided to make a national issue of it. A wealthy agitator and friend of Sutherland's, Dr. Garcia still directed the Mexican-American veterans' organization, the American G.I. Forum. Both the Good Neighbor Commission and the American G.I. Forum held that the Longoria family was the victim of ethnic discrimination, but a legislative committee took 372 pages of testimony and "whitewashed" the case, in the word of a dissenting committee member. The results were that Senator Lyndon Johnson arranged for Longoria's burial in Arlington National Cemetery and Lieutenant Governor Shivers resolved to rid the state of an investigative Good Neighbor Commission. Also, by the time Shivers was governor, the Truman administration was hinting at a possible federal probe of migratory labor scandals, and Shivers may not have wanted Sutherland, or anyone who worked with Garcia, in a position to cooperate with the inquiry. Sutherland could simply have been fired, but in the wake of the Longoria and Kibbe cases, that would have been a political debacle for the new governor.[8]

The governor solved his problem by splitting the Good Neighbor Commission in two. Beginning in January 1951, the GNC would handle the international aspects of Latin Americans' difficulties in Texas, for example, the crossings of Mexicans. The commission was placed under the chairmanship of ex-Dixiecrat Neville Penrose, and the new executive director was the governor's aide, John Van Cronkhite. Penrose was rather active in promoting the chamber of commerce approach toward ethnic tensions by urging towns and cities to form local human relations councils, but the GNC's *Weekly Report* revealed less and less news about discrimination and the activities of the American G.I. Forum. The network of local councils and the mandate to handle Texas's domestic Mexican-American affairs was granted to the new Human Relations Council under Sutherland. But the Council was created with the built-in vulnerability of being privately financed, mostly by its board chairman, Bob Smith. Smith was a rich, brawling Shivers supporter who was willing to spend a good deal of his own money in order to do something for Mexican-Texans, but he refused to commit his financing beyond a month-to-month basis. By October 1951 Shivers's aide Weldon Hart lamented that the HRC was floundering, plagued by internal frictions as well as a lack of stable financing.[9] In a memo to Hart, Van Cronkhite pointed out that the HRC had at least proved to be politically profitable, since:

1. We DID use the H.R.C. as a means of dumping Sutherland out of the state government;
2. The H.R.C. was originally used to a small extent for political expediency in a campaign year;
3. We had the problem of what to do with Bob Smith and again solved that problem by using the H.R.C.[10]

Soon after Sutherland was diverted to the shaky organization, Van Cronkhite persuaded Smith to halt his monetary backing altogether, and the HRC quietly vanished.[11]

The governor had a bit more trouble in taking over the Democratic party machinery, but he finally did it at the state convention in Mineral Wells in September 1950. Though the governor was quite popular with the voters, he did not hold a sizable majority against liberal and former Dixiecrat forces at the convention. Determined not to be cut off from party machinery as Coke Stevenson and W. Lee O'Daniel had been, Shivers became—after a hard fight—the first governor to purge State Democratic Executive Committee nominees who had been elected by their own senatorial districts. In the process, one delegate launched a scathing attack against Mrs. Sam Davis, a former Dixiecrat and the Democratic committeewoman from the posh River Oaks section of Houston, and was interrupted when another woman seized him by his lapels and grabbed an ashtray with the apparent intent of beating him. Other delegates pulled her away. Continuous screams, catcalls, and yells created the usual Texas Democratic hubbub. Shortly after becoming governor, Shivers pledged himself to strict party loyalty as long as he was a public figure, and the Mineral Wells convention saluted him for "his unquestioned loyalty to the Democratic party."[12]

Shivers won easy reelection contests in 1950 and 1952. In the first year he was opposed by Caso March, a young Baylor law professor, who drove around the state with steer heads and fox tails tied to his car. The governor, who attempted to manipulate labor into neutrality, was insulted that the AFL and CIO endorsed March, and both he and veteran labor leader Hank Brown related years later that it probably made him feel more conservative in his politics. A more serious challenger, Ralph Yarborough, appeared in 1952. Yarborough hailed from a pioneering east Texas family, had graduated with highest honors from the University of Texas law school, served as district judge of Travis County, and saw considerable combat service in World War II. Having also been an assistant attorney general under Allred, Yarborough had his eye on the attorney general's post. The Shivers administration was concerned about this threat to Establishment candidate John Ben Shepperd. One of the governor's aides thought that a Texas supreme court opening "may be the solution to the Ralph Yarborough competition to Shepperd if Yarborough had just as soon be a Supreme Court Associate Justice." But with the indirect encouragement of Sam Rayburn, who had reasons for wanting Shivers tied down in a race, Yarborough announced for governor. Yarborough waged a lonely campaign and was buried by the conservative turnout but did manage to win a half-million votes.[13]

Shivers faced larger problems in the early 1950s as it became evident that he and the Establishment were on a collision course with President Harry Truman's Democratic administration. Truman, concerned about national security and conservation, wanted direct federal access to the supposedly oil-rich tidelands. (The word *tidelands* was Texas's misnomer for a seabed that was never exposed by the tide but rather was continuously under water.) Since state ownership soon appeared dead in the courts, Governor Shivers had once endorsed one of Sam Rayburn's compromise proposals, which would have given the federal government 27.5 percent of the revenue within the ten-mile limit and Texas 27.5 percent from the outer continental shelf, but with no legal recognition of Texas's ancient claim that its boundary was ten and a half miles out in the ocean. Throughout this maneuvering, however, Attorney General Price Daniel continued to make headlines by stubbornly clinging to the state's contention that the Republic of Texas had been guaranteed a ten and a half mile limit when it entered the Union in 1845, which was accurate. But federal jurisdiction over the offshore lands was upheld by several Supreme Court decisions. The 1950 ruling prompted two hundred citizens of Nocona to demand Texas's secession while railroad commissioner Ernest Thompson and Congressman Lloyd Bentsen, Jr., called upon Texas to exercise its unique right of dividing into five states (with ten senators committed to state ownership of the tidelands).

Even more deeply involved in the clamor for the "return" of the tidelands were Texas's newly rich oilmen, ever growing in numbers and influence. Oil cast a large shadow over a caucus between Shivers and Daniel shortly after Shivers became governor. Daniel quietly threatened to run against him unless he changed his position on the tidelands. By the fall of 1951 the governor was excoriating Truman's efforts at "nationalization" of the oil industry and his proposed "dictatorship over fuel production." He even confided to one of his millionaire banker friends that Dwight Eisenhower (who had his own close ties to Texas oilmen) as Republican nominee would provide "a very good chance of bringing Southern Democrats and Northern Republicans together in some permanent manner." The governor had already thrown in with the oil-and-ranch Texas Regular-Dixiecratic faction of the party, which had little hope for Shivers at the time he became governor.

Ultraconservative chieftains in the early 1950s included Palmer Bradley and Lamar Fleming, Jr., of Houston, Clint Small of Austin, Clint Murchison of Dallas, Curtis Douglass of Amarillo, and Arch Rowan of Fort Worth (a power in three different congressional districts).[14]

The oil lobby had lost some of its leverage over Texas's two premier Establishment spokesmen in Washington, Speaker Rayburn and Senate minority leader Lyndon Johnson, but as it turned out, the oil faction triumphed without them. Rayburn was angered by the attacks against him on the part of the *Dallas Morning News* and by the oil industry's general lack of appreciation for his role in preserving the lucrative oil depletion allowance and the community property law and in trying to work out a mutually advantageous tidelands trade. As late as the spring of 1951, the Speaker was inclined to let someone else worry about offshore oil lands. Former New Dealer Johnson had "solidified his support with the oil boys" after the close 1948 election, but he had to work within the framework of the national Democratic party if he hoped to retain his influence and realize his ultimate ambition of becoming president. Johnson went so far as to refuse a 1949 appeal from Daniel to seek a Supreme Court postponement of the tidelands case. Suddenly in the summer of 1951, Rayburn and Johnson awakened to the thunder of the oilmen and, by May 1952, had pushed a bill through Congress that ensured Texas a ten and a half mile limit. Truman vetoed the measure and, in a stinging message, accused Texas and other coastal states of "robbery in broad daylight." The president's action ended any last hopes that Texas Democrats would present a united front in the 1952 election.[15]

Governor Shivers's party regularity was already doubtful by the summer of 1951 when he signed a bill allowing candidates of one party to cross-file as candidates of other parties, and much of the politicking the next two years revolved around allegiance to the Democratic party. The liberal-loyalist faction, suffering no illusions about Shivers, organized as the Loyal Democrats of Texas in order to challenge the governor. Led by the curmudgeon Maury Maverick and Austin attorney Fagan Dickson, among others, the LDT wanted all Texas Democratic delegates to the national convention to take a party loyalty pledge to support the nominess of the convention. They also opposed Shivers in that they condemned McCarthyism, wanted to amend the Taft-Hartley law, and favored a civil-rights plank in the national platform. Rayburn informed prominent Democrats that the cross-filing bill was destroying the Democratic party and that he was very much in favor of the LDT. Yet Rayburn took no action for months on end and ultimately stood by while events slipped through his hands. When the governor attacked the Supreme Court for its tidelands ruling, denounced the administration's foreign policy, and cursed the "pauperizing burden of confiscatory federal taxes," Rayburn, Johnson, and Truman evidently

10. Loyalist Bolt, 1952. *Texas AFL-CIO.*

thought he was just gearing up to defeat incumbent Senator Tom Connally. Shivers also lulled the Washington crowd with hints of voting a straight Democratic ticket.[16]

As early as January 1952, the governor was plotting vaguely with the Dixiecrats to bolt the national Democratic ticket. By early February Shivers was aware that some of his conservative loyalist followers were upset with him for avoiding the party loyalty oath, but the governor refused to budge. In late April Johnson tattled on Rayburn by informing Shivers's aide Weldon Hart that Rayburn was not supporting the LDT, which was certainly true. Shivers knew the loyalists were impotent without the prestige and guidance of Rayburn. Doubtless comforted by the knowledge that they had snookered the opposition, Shivers and his Dixiecratic allies overwhelmingly controlled the state Democratic convention in May. They selected delegates to the national convention who were not pledged to sustain the Democratic ticket. Maverick and the liberals bolted, exchanging a few fisticuffs with conservatives as they marched out into a rain and elected their own delegates to the national convention.[17]

At the national Democratic convention, according to Rayburn, Shivers told him privately that he intended to support the Democratic ticket. The governor gave the same assurance in answer to the bumbling questions of Senator Earle Clements of Tennessee, a member of the credentials subcommittee. It seems unlikely that the Shivers delegation would have been seated over the Maverick one (which had the encouragement of President Truman) had not Rayburn and Clements exacted such a pledge, but the governor denied making it in both instances. Keeping an eye on the Yarborough race, Shivers needed to be seated in order to maintain his credentials as a good Democrat. Shivers definitely pledged that the Democratic nominee would be listed under the Democratic title on the Texas ballot, and he told the national convention that he had always voted Democratic, but he cleverly avoided a direct statement of support. By this time Shivers was widely suspected of "moving every pebble and cowchip in Texas" to deliver the state's electoral vote to the Republicans.[18]

Knowing that the Democrats were unlikely to select a candidate who pleased the oil interests, Shivers (by 1952) never planned on supporting the party nominee. The Democratic nomination went to Illinois governor Adlai Stevenson, who made it clear that he would not accept outright state ownership of the tidelands. Shivers understood and expected this stance and eventually became one of three southern governors to endorse Republican nominee Dwight Eisenhower, who favored state ownership of the tidelands. Texas Dixiecrats had wanted the Democrats to nominate Hubert Humphrey "on a negro equality platform," in order to trigger a third-party, southern rebellion, but since that did not happen, they strung along with Eisenhower.

In Amarillo, where the state Democratic conclave was held that fall, the airport was described by an elected official as "choked with oil company planes." They had flown in delegates from all over Texas. Shivers did resist the friendly attempts of the reactionaries (Rowan, Bradley, Douglass, Small, Fleming, Jr., Townes, and Gibson, among them) to list Eisenhower as a Democratic nominee as well as Adlai Stevenson. Instead, for the first time in the state's history, the Democratic convention endorsed a Republican for the presidency. Every Democrat running for state office, except agricultural commissioner John White, allowed his name to be cross-filed as a Republican. The entrapment of Democratic party machinery was facilitated by the location of the Republican and Democratic party chairmen in the same Dallas law office. They were partners. Stevenson's margin over Eisenhower, revealed in a poll in early August to be 50 percent to 33 percent, faded fast.[19]

Sam Rayburn rushed into the breech with too little, too late. The Speaker's idea of a presidential campaign was to persuade all congressmen to take to the stump for Stevenson, but he was not even successful at that. Three Democratic congressmen went on record as refusing to vote for the Democratic nominee. One of them, Lloyd Bensen, Jr., informed Rayburn at the last moment that he would not campaign for Stevenson but that he had voted absentee for him. Rayburn also wanted Lyndon Johnson in the forefront of the fray, but the senator made only slight exertions for the party ticket. Rayburn unwisely assumed—in the fact of mounting evidence to the contrary—that most of the state's Democratic officials were as loyal to the party as he was. The national committeewoman, Mrs. Claude Hudspeth, not only blocked Lillian Collier and her liberal friends from achieving any campaign status, but also telegrammed Rayburn to remove her name from the delegate list in District Twenty because Maury Maverick's name was on it. Some liberals chafed under "Mr. Sam's" leadership. Maury Maverick, Jr., a member of the Gashouse Gang, thought that Rayburn was "kissing Shivercrats" and compromising the Stevenson campaign.[20]

Democratic machinery was also hampered by mechanical failures. Not until mid-September did the Democratic National Committee inform all department heads not to communicate with Dallas attorney Wallace Savage, the state party chairman who was heading the Texas Democrats for Eisenhower. Three weeks before election day Cottle County had no Democratic campaign stickers or brochures. One of Rayburn's campaign managers, in charge of five counties, lamented that a deluge of Stevenson material arrived five days before the election even though they should have had it at least six weeks in advance; he concluded that "this is one of the worst organizational setups I have ever been in."[21] Perhaps the situation was best summed up by Margaret Carter, an ally of Collier's, in a letter to Jim Wright (who was elected Fort Worth's congressman the next year):

> While he [Sam Rayburn] was stranded at his Adolphus Hotel headquartrs
> without the support of the people he had made influential and prosperous by
> channeling New Deal patronage to them, he was savage about the "fat cats"
> who had let him down and cordial to the assorted Democrats who wanted to
> work for Stevenson. But our whirlwind makeshift collaboration did not pro-
> duce a victory.[22]

Texas oilmen saw to it that the tidelands issue dominated the 1952 election. They preferred state jurisdiction to federal because the required state
royalty for producers was 12.5 percent, whereas the required federal royalty
was 37.5 percent. Since this point was not an exciting one to debate before
the electorate, it was thought better to conjure up an emotional or patriotic
aspect of the issue. As it happened, royalties from Texas state lands were
used to support the public schools—thus the children of Texas could be
described as the true victims of federal control. With the financial support
of millionaire oilmen, such as Palmer Bradley and Clint Murchison, the
potent public relations firm of Watson Associates printed a campaign newspaper showing an evil-looking Adlai Stevenson sneering at a classroom of
Texas children and saying, "Tideland funds for those kids? Aw, let them
pick cotton." Billboards dotted the state informing the public that Ike
would "return" the tidelands to the schoolchildren of Texas. Television
specials taking the oilmen's side were shown repeatedly in the last few
weeks of campaigning until, as one baffled parent put it, "My kids came
running in from the TV set like Paul Revere, tears streaming from their eyes,
saying, 'Pa, they're trying to take our tidelands away!'" Loyalist Democrats retorted that in two years, state rentals and royalties had actually
provided the schoolchildren with six-tenths of one cent apiece. Rayburn
also tried to counter the high-pressure advertising campaign by hinting once
more at repeal of the oil depletion allowance, but given the tidelands issue
and the prospects of Eisenhower victory, Texas oilmen were no longer afraid
of switching from Democrats to Republicans. Oil demagoguery was supplemented by speeches on the part of Governor Shivers and other Texas
Democrats for Eisenhower. They denounced and linked together corruption
in Washington, the Fair Employment Practices Committee, the CIO, the
Americans for Democratic Action (a liberal group), communism, and the
tidelands "theft." With these tactics the Eisenhower forces defeated the
Democrats 1,102,000 to 970,000. The Republicans soon delivered the tidelands to Texas.[23]

Stevenson ran well among traditional Democrats and minority groups,
both of which were most numerous in east and central Texas and in the
boss-controlled counties of deep South Texas. The Democratic nominee

was predictably strong in the urban labor precincts, but he lost most of the larger cities and even the highly industrialized counties of the Gulf Plain.[24] (See appendixes 5-8 for suggestions of voting trends among select urban groups.)

By 1952 a few oilmen such as Hugh Roy Cullen hoped Shivers would lead the Establishment forces into the Republican party. The Republicans had not only carried Texas in 1952 but also had ousted their own encrusted patronage machine and had become a party that actually wanted to win elections. But as Shivers noted, the Eisenhower majority was a victory for the man, not the party. The reality was that the GOP had merely recruited "presidential Republicans," especially in the big cities and in the Panhandle. The vote showed a high correlation with the Texas Regular returns of 1944 but supposedly not with the racist-burdened Dixiecratic results of 1948. The conservative majority of Texas voters, like Shivers, remained steadfastly Democratic in their balloting for all other offices. The one-party Democracy was deeply rooted in Texas's political folkways and habits, and changing the system is still proving to be a long and tortuous process. Thirteen years after the election, Shivers recalled that he had "always" thought the two-party system would be best for the state, but in fact the one-party system was consistently defended by the Shivercrats. Their pamphlet for Shivercratic precinct workers urged conservatives to stay in the party, which was going to win sooner or later, and prevent it from going socialist. After all, as Shivers's state Democratic chairman lamented to the governor, two-party counties have a "highly political atmosphere."[25]

Politics had a hand in the 1952 retirement of one of the old-line loyalist Democratic spokesmen, Tom Connally, who had served four terms in the Senate. Certainly one reason Connally refused to run again was the opinion of his friends that he could not beat Attorney General Price Daniel, since Daniel had successfully linked him with Truman's unpopular policies, especially foreign policy. Also, Connally mailed a campaign advisory to his long list of supporters with disastrous results (a large percentage of letters reputedly came back marked "addressee deceased" or "addressee moved— no forwarding address.") Daniel really wanted to be governor, but, with tears in his eyes, he could not talk Shivers into running against Connally, as Shivers recollected years later. Daniel thought that only Shivers could beat Connally, but the governor assured Daniel in November 1951 that anybody could beat Connally because the veteran senator had not kept his fences mended.[26]

Connally was such an ancient blatherskite that his retirement was probably merciful for the state and the Senate. Late in his last term he attempted to reply to a criticism from Senator Ken Wherry, the mortician from Pawnee City, Nebraska:

Connally: I feel very much like an old lawyer in my section of the country.
             He had as his legal antagonist a very loud and enthusiastic lawyer
             who shouted and foamed at the mouth in addressing the jury, and
             when it came the turn of the lawyer to answer him he stood up
             and said, "If you please, bow-wow-wow. Now that I have an-
             swered my opponent I shall discuss this case."
Wherry: Bow-wow-wow-wow-wow
Connally: Mr. President, I do not like to discuss this question in any but the
             most serious fashion.
Wherry: Will the senator yield for another question?
Connally: Oh, yes.
Wherry: The Senator's answers are just as clear as "bow-wow-wow-wow"—
             just as clear.
Connally: Well, I use that kind of language and that kind of explanation—
             "bow-wow-wow-wow."[27]

Connally's departure was hastened because the most important fence
that had fallen was the senator's link with the oilmen. Actually he had
served the industry well, notably in passing (without benefit of hearings)
the Connally Hot Oil Act of 1935, which in effect guaranteed federal protection for the companies' price fixing. The senator also pleased Texas's
conservatives by turning against labor in the 1940s. During the war years he
and O'Daniel supported the Republican-southern Democratic conservative
coalition more often (seventy-four votes) than any other southern duo. As
chairman of the Senate Foreign Relations Committee, he doubtless lost
touch with oilmen by engaging in such dubious projects as helping write
the United Nations charter. He continued to cater to the oil industry, but
with decreasing effectiveness. In April 1951 Connally's interstate oil com-
pact renewal bill had passed but was caught on a potentially dangerous snag
in the Justice Department; the senator's office did not even know the bill
had been referred to Justice. It was also in 1951 that Connally made the
absurd claim that the powerful tidelands oil lobby did not exist. That very
lobby (through Clint Small) was even then informing Governor Shivers that
it would support him for reelection or for Tom Connally's seat because it
wanted a strong, safe leader. When Shivers chose reelection, the lobby
swung to Price Daniel for senator because he too would support whichever
presidential nominee delivered himself to so-called states' rights on the tidelands question. Connally, complete with old-fashioned string bowtie and
flowing white mane, also entertained old-fashioned notions of Democratic
party loyalty. To the oilmen, the last of the flowery orators in Congress
was just an aging, unreliable windbag. One account has it that the oilmen
gave him the word in a Texas back room early in 1952. Displaying the cash
they had collected to beat him in the primary, oil's political agents bludgeoned
him out of running.[28]

Daniel's oil and gas support in 1952 was impressive. Hugh Roy Cullen turned over $5,000, Humble Oil lobbyist Walter Woodul and family contributed $3,600, El Paso Natural Gas president Paul Kayser, $3,500, oil lawyer Palmer Bradley, $2,500, and oilman George Strake, $2,500, among others. The support more accurately might be labeled spectacular, when one considers that Daniel faced only token primary opposition from east Texas congressman Lindley Beckworth, who was little known outside his district and ran on a shoestring. Daniel dismissed Beckworth as a tool of the CIO or "the wasteful, corrupt Truman crowd" and charged the congressman with being soft on the tidelands, spending, taxing, and socialized medicine. Beckworth carried all eight counties in his district but was defeated by over a three-to-one margin.[29]

The Establishment still faced troubled times. Had Governor Shivers chosen to retire by the time of the next election year, 1954, he could have rested on a record similar to Coke Stevenson's. Shivers had presided over a scandal-free administration for over five years, just as Stevenson had, and had steered the Establishment through a crucial political crisis by successfully backing the Republican presidential nominee in 1952, just as Coke had preserved conservative hegemony during the firing of Rainey and the revolt of the Texas Regulars. Shivers exuded a greater ultraconservative ideological appeal than Stevenson, yet at the same time he was more willing to expend state funds for various services. Upon deciding to run for governor again, however, Allan Shivers plunged the state into murkier depths than the Junction frontiersman would ever have tolerated. Unlike Stevenson, Shivers ended his elective career demagogically defending a suddenly corrupt administration.

11

The Shivers-
Yarborough Shootout, 1954

Sometimes a man just gets to wondering if the Lord is taking sleeping pills or something. He sure isn't keeping check on politics down here in Texas.
> Maury Maverick, Jr., to Janet Sewell,
> August 27, 1953

The successful businessmen of Texas are the only Texans who have and give the kind of money needed to finance an expensive statewide campaign.
> Probusiness *Brownwood Banner*,
> July 29, 1954

. . . you go to the people who have the money.
> Allan Shivers reminiscing on the
> 1954 campaign

There has been a heck of a lot of fraud perpetrated on Texans.
> Secretary of State Tom Reavley to
> Insurance Commission chairman John
> Osorio, January 8, 1956

Rightist extremism made deep inroads into community affairs in the early 1950s, creating an environment that would leave its mark on the Shivers administration. In Houston, Dallas, San Antonio, the Rio Grande Valley, and other locales such bitter controversies raged, particularly around educational institutions, that extremism seemed almost to govern the state. It was in this atmosphere in 1954 that the ambitious governor declared his candidacy for an unprecedented third term. Not only was this a violation of Texas tradition, but also the governor's administration was racked with scandal. This setting did not augur well for a clean-cut primary based on meaningful issues.

Shivers was sufficiently worried about his reelection chances that he adroitly reversed his spending policies. On March 8 he met with some forty-four of Texas's leading oil, gas, sulfur, and brewery barons, and their attorneys and warned them that the administration had to be able to claim that it had accomplished something or Shivers might well be defeated by the challenger, Ralph Yarborough. The governor told the corporate executives that teachers had to be granted a pay raise and that the state had to hike appropriations for schools and eleemosynary buildings, all of which had been denied the previous year with Shivers' blessings. The governor also told them that these proposals had to be financed by a new gas gathering tax to replace the old one tossed out by the courts, a higher corporation franchise tax, and a heavier beer tax. Since the governor and the big corporations—the Establishment—controlled the legislature, the program was soon adopted and Shivers's political credentials were refurbished for the upcoming campaign.[1]

As the primary campaign got underway, Yarborough talked about such progressive proposals as a gas pipelines tax and greater expenditures for education, but since Shivers had preempted these issues somewhat, Yarborough lost no time in finding other matters to question the governor about. To begin with, the collapse of various insurance companies operating in Texas, which harbored more companies than the rest of the United States combined, was reaching alarming proportions (seventeen in seventeen months). Texas was winning the reputation of having the worst insurance laws in the nation. The Texas Mutual Insurance Company, for instance, was organized with $500 cash and a loan of $19,500 but was so imaginatively managed that it went bankrupt owing $1.2 million. Moreover until the summer of 1954, several insolvent insurance companies operated in Texas without governmental interference. One company, Lloyd's of North America, paid $1,000 a month to John Van Cronkhite, Shivers's former campaign manager and a long-time Shivers employee. Van Cronkhite was hired by Lloyd's to ensure "cordial relations" with the state Board of Insurance Commissioners. The governor had been warned years earlier by two of his top men in Nacogdoches that Van Cronkhite was a "damn crook," but Shivers evidently thought little about it, since he continued using the man in his campaigns. In April 1953 Shivers was informed of the company's insolvency but did nothing about it as long as Van Cronkhite was receiving the "public-relations fee." Early in 1954 Lloyd's either fired Van Cronkhite, or he severed relations with the company. In any event, the payments stopped, and the state government examiners poured over the Lloyd books. The company was liquidated in June 1954. Yarborough, meanwhile, called for a "complete investigation of the insurance mess" and eventually charged the governor with allowing "fixers and influence peddlers to operate in Austin."[2]

The governor was also embarrassed by some of his business deals, especially by one of his real estate transactions. In 1946, when he was running for lieutenant governor, Shivers had bought an option on 13,500 acres in the Rio Grande Valley from millionaire citrus grower Lloyd Bentsen, Sr., for $25,000. (Bentsen had earlier made a fortune in the "immigrant land business," selling valley land without the vital water rights.) Six and a half months later Shivers sold his option—one day after it had expired—back to a Bentsen-owned company for $450,000. Three months after Shivers became governor, the State Board of Water Engineers granted precious, but restricted, water rights on the Bentsen land. Because of the lack of water in the Rio Grande River, this was the first time in more than twenty years that the board had granted a new permit. Shivers had not appointed any of the board members, but they knew very well that he would be governor when they came up for reappointment. According to Shivers, who was never able to think of any reason for the 1,700 percent increase in the value of the option, Yarborough's criticism of the deal only showed that Yarborough did not believe in "our American system of free enterprise." Years later Shivers defended the land transaction by noting that it had occurred before he was lieutenant governor. Shivers was drawing a very fine line; he sold the option in December 1946 when he was lieutenant governor-elect and his inaugural was four weeks away.[3]

Despite the potency of these issues, the mounting red scare in Texas doomed Yarborough's chances. The near-hysteria was triggered by a recognition strike by some 430 CIO retail workers in November 1953 against twenty Port Arthur stores. Several of the early strike leaders who came to the city to supervise the picketing and boycotting were apparently communists, or at least had been at one time. These men were quickly replaced, but the tainted connection enabled Attorney General John Ben Shepperd, a Shivers supporter, to speak of the "proven Communist leadership" of the strike. Shepperd added the unsupported claim that the union was "bent on organizing in every petroleum and coastal area of this state." Shivers reiterated these accusations as a guest on H. L. Hunt's Facts Forum program on December 1.[4]

The governor appointed a five-man industrial commission to investigate the infiltration of the communists into coastal unions. The appointees included two conservatives from the South Plains—a rancher, C. E. Fulgham, and an oil field supply company president, E. G. Rodman—an American Legion commander from deep east Texas, L. E. Page, a conservative newspaper editor, Walter Buckner, and the president of the Texas State Federation of Labor, William J. Harris. Ten days later the commission issued a preliminary report decrying the "clear and present danger" that communist-dominated unions would move into Texas. It recommended outlawing the communist party. Instead, keeping a sharp eye on his reelection chances, the governor convened a special session of the legislature and listed as one of his high-priority items a bill making membership in the Communist party a crime punishable by death.[5]

One episode during the hearings on these bills reveals the aura of extremism in which they were passed. Representative Bill Daniel, brother of Senator Price Daniel, was apparently disquieted by an unexpectedly large crowd at one hearing. Suddenly he launched into a speech; he recalled an incident in Washington when Puerto Rican nationalists shot some congressmen and reminded the audience of the perils of being a member of the Texas legislature. Warming to his subject, he glared at the assembly and demanded, "Is there a Communist in the room?" Amid stunned silence, he repeated the question several times, staring fixedly at one end of the room. Nobody pleaded guilty, but his repeated questioning and staring eyes made one man so nervous that he arose and said, "I'm no Communist." This response created a nervous titter, which annoyed Daniel, and he snapped, "You've all got your coats on; how do I know you're not carrying guns?" Representative Daniel, who had his coat on himself, was finally pacified when the committee chairman ordered a paper passed around the room, urging everyone to write his name and address for security purposes.[6]

The legislature balked at the governor's recommended death penalty and made the maximum punishment for Communist party membership a fine of $20,000 and twenty years in prison. These Loyalty and Subversion acts of 1954 also established penalties for "subversives," a term that was never defined. In addition, upon the affadavit of one "credible" witness and the application of a district attorney, a local judge could order the search of any establishment and the seizure of any kind of writing, recording, or picture. The raiding of private homes required an affidavit from two "credible" witnesses. The final bill that made communism a felony sailed through the senate 29 to 0 and the house 127 to 7. A few journalists who usually supported the governor, such as KTBC news editor Paul Bolton in Austin and Tomme Call, the editor of the San Antonio News, confided to Shivers their fear that the communist-control legislation might erode civil liberties.[7]

Shivers's actions prevented many Texans from seeing that the governor was making no attempt to enforce the eight antisubversion laws that were already on the books. Outlawing the Communist party, for instance, would not have been necessary if the law requiring all communists to register had been enforced. These two laws, in fact, conflicted, since the new one made it a felony to be a communist, while the old one required communists to register, which meant that they would be incriminating themselves. It also was overlooked that the state industrial commission admitted that it could find no current communist influence in Texas unions and that Shivers confessed in January that no un-American activities committee was needed in Texas because of the dearth of communist activities. Several ex-Communist "witnesses," who had appeared in other states, regaled the commission and the legislature with tales of communism in unions, and one charter member of the party asserted that Texas was a focal point of communist concentration. But none could pinpoint any subversive activity in Texas. Further, despite a request from the CIO, the governor refused to allow the industrial commission to investigate the causes of the Port Arthur strike. Coastal cities were in the forefront of the state's business and industrial development and were at the cutting edge of the union movement, but Shivers knew very well that coastal unions were anything but intrinsically communistic. It was just that waitresses, sales clerks, and maids making twenty-five dollars or less for forty-four hours or more per week were not apt to be overly concerned about the ideology of union organizers. Veteran labor spokesmen in the area recollect that the early strike leaders did not attempt to inculcate communism among the workers.[8]

Governor Shivers rode the red scare by proclaiming that he had exposed Port Arthur's "communist-dominated" union, which had crippled that city, and had "scuttled" the union's "well-laid plans to spread its tentacles all along the Gulf Coast and eventually into *your* community." In regard to communistic unions, the governor pledged that "we're going to crush them under the heel any way we can." Shivers also asserted that "while I know my opponent is not a Communist, I feel that he is a captive of certain people who do not approve of being tough on Communists." Since the majority of union members, along with most blacks, liberals, and party loyalists, supported Yarborough, Shivers occasionally extended his misleading linkage of unions and communists to embrace "the ADA, the NAACP, and all the rest of that kind." The governor's persiflage was supplemented by propaganda from such sources as the American Legion and the Texas Manufacturers Association and by an obliging series of articles by Robert Baskin in the *Dallas Morning News*. Also, Port Arthur jeweler Ann Lanz wrote to other Texas jewelers that the picketers had cost her thousands of dollars but that tax-deductible "Port Arthur Lanz Fund" checks could be sent to the chamber of commerce.[9]

Although the red scare mania was honed into a powerful anti-Yarborough tool, perhaps an even more important factor in the first primary were the ethnic controversies. In the midst of the campaign the Supreme Court issued its famous ruling that the nation's schools must be integrated. At first Shivers commented more temperately on the case than most southern governors. He noted that there were no quick and easy answers, that desegregation was a long-term affair, and that Texas should certainly not abolish its public schools. The next week the press discovered that the governor's son, John, attended St. Edwards High School, the only integrated one in Austin.[10]

Almost a month later, as his campaign faltered, Shivers seized upon the race issue as a windfall. In his Lufkin speech of June 21, the governor proclaimed:

> All of my instincts, my political philosophy, my experiences and my common sense revolt against this Supreme Court decision. It is an unwarranted invasion of the constitutional rights of the states, and one that could be disastrous to the children and to the teachers of both races.
>
> My administration has already told the local school districts that, as far as the state of Texas is concerned, there are no changes to be made in the way we are conducting our schools.[11]

In several succeeding speeches the governor lambasted the NAACP for not only favoring desegregation in schools but also in residential areas and in social activities. He repeatedly pledged himself to local control of schools, though he had already dictated to the school districts that they could not integrate even if they wanted to (some did want to). Shivers successfully threw Yarborough on the defensive by demanding that he tell the people how he felt about segregation.[12]

Unwilling to write off the black vote completely, Shivers campaigners circulated an anonymous pamphlet, *The Big Lie*, in black neighborhoods. It charged that Negroes had been lied to by Yarborough, who had finally admitted that he favored segregation. Shivers, it said, had always befriended Negroes and had promised that the Ku Klux Klan would not be tolerated. And, the pamphlet continued, the governor wanted the segregation issue handled locally, where Negroes would have a real voice in it. It was more in keeping with the thrust of the campaign, however, when some Shivercrats sent a well-dressed black man through east Texas in a new Cadillac bearing Yarborough bumper stickers. He would stop often at service stations manned by whites, order a dollar's worth of gas, then rudely demand faster service while claiming that he was in a hurry to get back to his work for "Mr. Yarborough."[13]

Aware that Texas voters overwhelming opposed integration, Yarborough evaded the race issue as long as he dared. He was finally quoted as opposing "forced commingling" and favoring separate but genuinely equal schooling, but he refused to attack the Supreme Court or to pledge to fight to preserve segregation. Yarborough thus lost the support of many white conservatives who felt that he should have taken a stronger segregationist position. Yet his moderate stand also cost him the backing of numerous white and black liberals who were chagrined that he had not openly hailed the Supreme Court's judgment.[14]

Governor Shivers's cause was also bolstered by deliberate, secret intervention from the White House. Yarborough had discerned that the departments of Justice and Interior were reluctant to recognize that Texas's boundary extended three leagues into the ocean, so the candidate accordingly accused Eisenhower of "welching" on the tidelands and implied that Shivers placed far too much trust in the Republicans. Eisenhower's press secretary, James Hagerty, then recorded in his diary that "in an attempt to help Shivers . . . the President had Price Daniel in" and permitted him to announce later that the president favored Texas's three-league boundary. Hagerty added, "This had a good effect in Texas and helped Shivers tremendously." (Daniel, incidentally, also assured reporters that his White House appearance had nothing to do with any political race.) But a few days later, on July 19, an Interior Department spokesman, citing Justice Department advice, once more shot down Texas's tidelands claim, in an interview with a reporter. As Hagerty privately noted, "We got frantic calls from Shivers' people in Texas." One of the governor's Republican strategists wrote to the White House, "This has become a big moral issue in Texas and could well cause the defeat of Governor Shivers Saturday unless corrected." Interior officials hastened to issue corrective statements, followed by one on the part of Eisenhower himself, on July 22, two days before the Texas balloting.[15]

The vote in the first primary, July 24, showed that Yarborough had forced Shivers into a runoff. Shivers polled 668,913 votes, Yarborough 645,994, J. J. Holmes (an Austin contractor who was particularly agitated by "gruesome, rapacious, hideous, immoral, degrading, foul" comic books) 19,951, and Arlon "Cyclone" Davis, Jr. (son of a former Texas congressman and an auto mechanic who lived and worked under the Cadiz Street viaduct in Dallas) 16, 254. Yarborough was strongest in central, east, and north Texas, in a bloc from Texarkana west to Wichita Falls, south to San Saba, then east to Jefferson County. Shivers carried most of the Gulf Coast, west Texas, and the boss-ridden border counties. The South Plains and the Panhandle were divided. Yarborough was hurt by low turnouts in labor and black precincts in the four big cities, while Shivers racked up high percentage turnouts in the silk-stocking precincts. Weldon Hart, one of the governor's top aides, studied the returns and found an issue that had not been discussed as extensively as the others. He informed Shivers that there was a "striking parallel" between Yarborough's counties and those that voted for Adlai Stevenson in 1952. Moreover the Shivers counties that had favored Stevenson were very close, as were the Yarborough counties that Eisenhower had carried. Shivers was wounded by party loyalty sentiments more than he could have realized at the time of the tumultuous Republican victory of 1952. Indeed, incumbent Texas governors forced into runoffs had always failed at the polls. State senator Doyle Willis advised Sam Rayburn that if he could persuade the Kilday machine in San Antonio to switch sides and if the Speaker himself would openly endorse Yarborough, the challenger would win.[16] Willis may well have been right, but neither of his conditions was met.

Upon giving the primary results to Eisenhower, Hagerty wrote "He was considerably interested and told me to talk to [Sherman] Adams further tomorrow to see if there was anything more we could do to help Shivers in the runoff." Since Eisenhower and Shivers were members of opposing political parties, and since there were suspicions that the two were cooperating anyway, the president felt obliged to tell the press that no one in his party had said anything to him about the Texas election. The only written request that the Shivers forces addressed to the White House during the runoff was that the attorney general say nothing about the tidelands "until August 28th" (voting day).[17]

During the first primary, one of the governor's friends, Joe T. Cook, secretary-treasurer of Shivers's Times Publishing Company and editor of the *Mission Times*, wrote to his fellow editors that "Allan Shivers speaks our language because he is in the publishing business." Suddenly it was learned during the runoff that state contracts had been awarded to the Shivers company. The governor denied being a stockholder in his company. But affadavits of ownership filed with the Post Office indicated otherwise, as Yarborough informed the public on several occasions during the runoff. Years afterward Shivers changed his story when he remembered that his "manager," Joe Cook, bid on the state printing contract without him (the governor) knowing anything about it.[18]

Agitation of the race issue continued into the runoff. Some Yarborough supporters, for instance, published a circular that was evidently distributed in several white neighborhoods in the eastern half of the state. It pictured the black leaders who had endorsed Shivers, invaded the privacy of the governor's family by pointing to his son's attendance at a racially mixed school, criticized the governor for obeying a 1950 Supreme Court order that blacks be admitted to the University of Texas, and splashed a picture of him eating with Negro Texas soldiers in Korea. Years later the governor recollected that the brochure was distributed in Fort Bend and surrounding counties and caused him to lose them all by overwhelming majorities. The evidence does not bear him out, since Shivers did, in fact, carry Fort Bend and all five adjoining counties by comfortable margins.[19]

Some of the governor's campaigners also continued to play with the race issue. A Jasper lawyer proposed to Shivers that some "negroes" be influenced to create a Yarborough-for-governor organization, which would publicize Yarborough's opposition to segregation in rural east Texas and trigger a white turnout for the governor. Conversely, Shivers operatives published a reprinted article from Carter Wesley's *Informer*, the largest black newspaper in the state. The leaflet declared that the black Golden Rule Civic Club endorsed Shivers because the governor was paying to have one son educated at Austin's only integrated high school. The circular was obviously intended for distribution in black neighborhoods. The nadir of the campaign occurred when Shivers's headquarters mailed a retouched photograph of Yarborough to many newspapers. In the picture Yarborough's skin was darkened, his nose flattened, and his cheekbones altered, all in an attempt to make him appear to be a black man. Few editors, however, used it.[20]

With fewer than two weeks remaining in the runoff, Weldon Hart was not satisfied with the campaign. He wrote to the governor:

> You badly need a burning issue for the last 10 days, such as segregation furnished in your closing First Primary drive. I don't believe that old dog will hunt again. A sort of standoff has been achieved, as far as public statements are concerned. . . .
>
> The "outside labor bosses" haven't scared the voters much, as too many of them either don't believe the threat is real or don't see how they are involved either way.
>
> I submit for your consideration a doublepronged program to bring the labor issue closer to home by:
>
> 1. Using the Port Arthur Story as a threat to businessmen everywhere;
> 2. Using the farm labor unionization threat, especially in West Texas.
>
> Both approaches have their hazards. It will be hard to develop the Port Arthur Story fully without flatly being *against* the unionization of the class of workers organized by the DPOWA. So far you have just been against the union because it was Red-controlled. This plan would involve being against the union, period.
>
> Even more hazardous is the farm labor question, because of your personal involvements. Certainly you would be open to counterattack. However, I'm afraid it's the only thing we have that can be made to appeal to the West Texas (especially South Plains) farmers, who are pretty solidly against you now and getting more so, according to reports. If properly predicated upon what you have already said about labor bosses, etc., and tied in with the Port Arthur Story in some way, perhaps we can avoid being too vulnerable to charges of self-interest. Anyway, it would be nice to have the other side doing some explaining and counter-charging instead of us.[21]

Hart's plan, embellished by public relations experts, was more or less followed. As the campaign intensified, teams of Port Arthur businessmen were put on television and radio all over the state. They described their city as a ghost town because of the communist picketing and charged that the unions promoted "hate, fear, and violence." They told mass meetings of small merchants, corralled by the governor's local organizations, that their towns were next if Shivers were not reelected. They told of blacks on the picket lines and showed pictures of white women and Negro men on the lines together (union officials said the pictures were faked). They revealed that the high school football team could not attend the annual banquet in its honor because the banquet was held in a picketed hotel, but they neglected to reveal that the players had voted not to cross the picket line. A television film called "The Port Arthur Story" accused the CIO of "personally supervising the death of a city" and showed deserted streets in the coastal town.

Yarborough charged, and it was later admitted by a Shivers staff man, that the film was taken at 5:00 A.M. He also confessed after he had left the Syers, Pickle, and Winn advertising firm, "I had to take 30 minutes of film to get a few seconds when there was no smoke coming out of the smokestack at one plant." In separate broadcasts the governor added that the people in the "Communist-launched" war in Port Arthur favored Yarborough, along with all the "Reds, radicals, Communists, and goon squads" in the state. Yarborough, Shivers said, thought it was silly to look for communists under the bed; he did not have to, the governor explained, because these people were in bed with him. Shivers concluded that a network of red unions was being erected along the whole coast—"the pushing of a single button in Moscow" would paralyze Texas. A booklet, *The Port Arthur Story*, was so distorted that the president of the Port Arthur Chamber of Commerce cautioned civic leaders about its harmful effects on business.[22]

Elaborate pamphlets, accompanied by a letter from a Port Arthur merchant in the same line of business, were mailed to virtually every small businessman in Texas, warning that Yarborough's election would portend the unionization of the state. The CIO did hope to organize retail workers, but it could do that no matter who was governor. Leaflets depicting the CIO as a black tornado descending on a lonely Texas farmhouse were sent to all rural free delivery boxholders—some 700,000—warning that unless the farmers voted for "Shivers and Texas," CIO pickets would invade the farms. In fact, the CIO did not even have an active farm workers' affiliate in Texas. It was a clever attempt to take farmers' minds off the drought, since Shivers had consistently refused to sponsor any kind of state drought or water conservation plan and had delayed the flow of emergency federal aid.[23]

The Shivers forces informed doctors that Yarborough would favor chiropractors; chiropractors were told that he would favor M.D.s. Truckers were told that he was friendly with the railroads; railroad men were told that he wanted to increase the load limit on trucks. The governor had the support of the Women's Christian Temperance Union, as well as the beer and liquor lobby; his operatives told the wets that Yarborough was dry and told the drys that he was wet. Although these tactics might be chalked off as campaign lying typical of politics everywhere, the anonymous threats and abusive midnight phone calls to Yarborough supporters could not be so easily dismissed. Nor could the firing of employees with Yarborough stickers on their cars, or the unsubtle warnings to state employees that Texas did not have a secret ballot be excused as legitimate.[24]

Shivers needed a hefty turnout in Dallas to overcome Yarborough sentiment in the surrounding countryside, so it should have come as no surprise that Yarborough's local campaign manager, a small businessman, was compelled to resign because Lone Star Gas threatened to sever his contract. The largest loanshark in Dallas forced his employees to drive cars festooned with Shivers stickers. Besides endorsing Shivers, the *Dallas Morning News*

The word has come down to Texas from the C.I.O.-P.A.C., Labors' League for Political Education and other leftist groups that there isn't room for Allan Shivers in their national Democratic Party and that he must be defeated for Governor. In the Saturday Evening *Post* of June 5, 1954, on page 135, former Vice-President Alben Barkley, the grand old warhorse of the Democratic Party, tells how this same group told him that he could not run for the party's nomination for president at the national convention in 1952. Alben Barkley, one of the country's great Democrats, said that he could not believe this could happen in America—but it did. Texas voters, on July 24, will show the C.I.O.-P.A.C. it can't happen in Texas by re-electing Allan Shivers.

11. Anti-Ralph Yarborough Cartoons, 1954. *Texas AFL-CIO.*

serialized the Martin Dies story, ran articles about the improving economy, and accused Yarborough of favoring a sales tax (which he was specifically pledged against). The *News* did concede that there were Texans for Yarborough who were not "reds . . . radicals or goon squad supporters." The governor carried Dallas by a majority of nineteen thousand votes.[25]

Most of the crucial, menial chores in the campaign were handled by women. The Texas Democratic Women's State Committee, run by Lillian Collier, Minnie Fisher Cunningham, and others, were vehemently bent on electing Yarborough. Hundreds of them took care of much of the stamp licking, envelope stuffing, telephoning of voters, neighborhood meetings, and transporting of voters to the polls. The Shivercratic forces countered with such local outfits as San Antonio's Womanpower for Eisenhower organization, which operated out of its old 1952 headquarters.[26]

In South Texas the patróns opted for Shivers. Some Yarborough literature was a bit extreme in accusing the border bosses of engaging in "slavery with illegal aliens" and of not caring whether communists and dope runners crossed into the United States. But an honest count was assured only in Duval and two other counties—and there only because court cases were pending and Texas Rangers guarded the polls. Yarborough was running a risk by even daring to appear in some border communities. After being warned not to show up in Laredo, Yarborough was greeted by small explosives that were touched off near the speaker's platform. A huge cross, doused with gasoline, was set afire behind where he was speaking.[27]

During the last week of the runoff the governor's staff recalled Jake Pickle's old advice about trotting out Baptist speakers to head off a possible anti-Catholic backlash against Shivers. At least two such speakers delivered statewide, partially canned, mudslinging attacks against Yarborough. A. B. Stufflebeme, who had played the same role against Rainey, claimed to be an everyday, early-rising, God-fearing dirt farmer, who, as it happened, was also president of a bank. Jack Dillard, secretary of the Baylor alumni, charged that Yarborough, whom he did not know, was rich and aloof, when in fact those were two characteristics of his own candidate.[28]

In the waning weeks of the runoff, Yarborough was deluged by the Shivers juggernaut. Of the one hundred daily newspapers in the state, ninety-five editorialized for Shivers. Display advertisements for the governor, in some cases as many as ten, were placed in every paper. Radio and television completed the media blitz. On the Friday before voting day, hundreds of stations ran one-minute Shivers entries at every program break at a cost of ten to fifty dollars an hour per station. Thirteen years after the event, Shivers calculated that $600,000 might have been spent on his behalf, but that was an underestimate. A tantalizing glimpse into campaign financing is afforded in a report to the governor by H. E. Chiles, Jr., on August 13, 1954. It reveals that seven west Texas cities plus Dallas, Fort Worth, and Tyler had suggested local budgets—just for the last two weeks of the campaign—totaling

$225,000. Since two weeks amounted to only one-sixth of the active campaigning and since the metropolitan areas of the ten cities comprised less than a fourth of the state's population, a cautious conclusion would be that the Shivers forces made a multimillion dollar effort in the two primaries. Yarborough may have spent half a million in losing to the governor, 775,088 to 683,132.[29]

In 1951 the Texas election code was changed to eliminate the ceiling on campaign expenses and to require candidates to report all contributions and expenditures. Penalties for false statements could run up to five thousand dollars and five years in prison. While itemized financial statements from campaigns immediately became more realistic, candidates were still reluctant to allow money to flow too freely in public view. The voters might think that the rich candidate and his friends were trying to purchase the office. Governor Shivers reported receipts of $1,000 each from such oil and gas magnates as H. H. "Pete" Coffield, Frank Wood, Arch Rowan, Guy Warren, H. E. Chiles, Jr., C. T. McLaughlin, Joe Zeppa, and W. W. Wise. The governor also wrote thank-you letters to the following Establishment donors, among others, whose names are not listed as contributors in the files of the secretary of state: Edgar Brown, oil and timber entrepreneur and president of the Orange National Bank ($1,000), Ben Carpenter, vice-president of Southland Life ($1,000), Jack Binion, corporate lawyer ($1,500), J. Lee Johnson, Amon Carter's son-in-law ($1,000), Houston Harte, publisher ($500), Charles Beard, president of Braniff ($500), oil men Bud Adams and John Mecom ($1,000 each), and H. L. Hunt, Palmer Bradley, Lloyd Bentsen, and Hugh Roy Cullen (each of whom was thanked for helping in a "very material way" or in Cullen's case, for "splendid support"). An attachment to Beard's receipt stated "don't list." Campaign contributors were also responsible for reporting their contributions, and if they failed to do so, they were civilly liable to each opponent for double the amount of each unreported contribution. Corporate donations, of course, continued to be against the law. The Kuehne, Brooks and Barr architectural firm sent the governor $100, and the Ard Drilling Company of Abilene chipped in with $200, but neither is listed as a contributor. The Ard money was accompanied by another $200 from A. R. Elam, and a memo attached by the Shivers staff said "list Elam for $400," but his name is also missing from the official list of contributors. Shivers was neither the first nor the last candidate in Texas to accrue far more campaign money than he reported, but he seems to be the only one who left evidence of it. Ralph Yarborough, whose papers are unorganized and unavailable to researchers, also received some hefty donations in 1954, such as $3,000 each from some of the Houston area's wealthy, among them, Mrs. Frankie Randolph, Will Clayton, J. R. Parten, Paul Dougherty, and Percy Strauss. Most of organized labor's political action money was spent by the unions, often at the local level, so it did not have to be reported to the secretary of state's office.[30]

The geographical breakdown of the balloting was much the same as in the first primary. Existing precinct returns studies suggest that Yarborough, as expected, was backed by the classical urban liberal coalition that had been forming since the mid-1940s, but the turnout, as usual, was not high. In the four largest cities, black precincts supported the challenger 27,495 to 3,485 in the runoff, while Bexar County's twenty-two Mexican-American boxes went for him 8,413 to 2,841. Relatively low-income districts in the cities, especially labor precincts, gave Yarborough whopping majorities. Wealthy urban boxes favored Shivers overwhelmingly. University Park in Dallas, for instance, gave the governor a margin of 5,672 to 802. (See appendixes 6-9 and 12.) Much of Yarborough's large "home folks," rural east Texas constituency was liberal on economics but conservative on race. The judge's sizable vote among drought-stricken farmers reflected the economic woes of West Texas, but this was a passing phenomenon. These farmers and cattlemen did not become a permanent part of the liberal voting coalition. Texas's politics of economics was a bit blurred in that Yarborough also had the support of assorted groups and individuals who were not motivated primarily by economic issues—for example, some party loyalists and citizens who were appalled by the scandals.[31]

Not until after the runoff was it learned that in the eighty-three counties where Republican primaries were held, only token turnouts were sought by the GOP. In fifty-two counties the Republican primaries were called off at the request of the Shivers leaders. Only 9,300 votes were cast in the Republican primary. Texas's other 150,000 to 200,000 very conservative Republican voters either abstained or joined the Democratic primary.

A few weeks after the second primary, an Associated Press reporter, Max Skelton, interviewed dozens of people in Port Arthur. He proved once and for all that communism was not the cause of the continuing union-management stalemate but rather that it was simply a "determined, bitter struggle" between the retail merchants and the CIO. Far from being a ghost town or a city of fear, Port Arthur had few vacant buildings, and people walked the streets, day and night, just as they did anywhere else. By January 1955 fourteen stores had agreed to unionize, and the strike was about over.[32]

In a state the size of Texas, it is impossible for any candidate or manager to keep a continuing check on the ethical level of the campaign in every area. As the days roll by, the campaign becomes obscured by crises and opportunities, provocations and temptations. With the election nearing, tension increases, and an unethical tactic begins to look like an underhanded but useful chance; it finally becomes an unpleasant necessity. The candidate, of course, does not know of everything that is done on his behalf, perhaps not even half of everything. There is no reason to believe that Shivers approved or even knew of The Big Lie pamphlet or that Yarborough knew anything about the circular depicting the governor's "race-mixing" record.

Shivers did, however, preview "The Port Arthur Story" and approve its showing. One of his staff members claimed that the governor did not know that some of the pictures were faked, which indicates that the public relations experts were careful not to tell him. Quite possibly the governor was careful not to ask. Even Shivers partisans admitted privately that the antiunion attack was overdone. Perhaps the most pertinent postelection analysis was offered by one of Shivers's lieutenants: "Allan really doesn't like to demagogue, but he was about to lose the race."[33]

The Yarborough campaign jolted the Establishment in other arenas besides the governor's race. Conservative congressman Ken Regan of Midland was probably a casualty of the Yarborough turnout in his west Texas district. Regan was replaced by the much more moderate J. T. Rutherford, who built his winning margin in counties with large numbers of oil workers and pipeliners. Wingate Lucas, the leader of antiunion Democrats on the House Labor and Education Committee, was ousted by moderate-liberal Jim Wright in the Tarrant-Parker counties district. It was a humiliating defeat for Amon Carter's Seventh Street crowd at the hands of the labor-liberals, who were also turning out because of the Yarborough race. In Dallas labor-liberal-minority forces experimented for the first time with what became known as the rebuilding strategy in the 1960s: defecting from Democratic ranks when faced with reactionary candidates from both parties, resulting in the election of the Republican. Theoretically the defeated Democratic party would then be rebuilt by liberals. Conservative Democrat Wallace Savage, who thought that ballot splitting was fine in 1952, would not even confer with labor after surviving a bitter primary against a labor-backed candidate. Savage might have beaten Republican challenger Bruce Alger except that Phil Fox allegedly assured Savage that the Democratic nomination was tantamount to election and thus he should not dignify the various charges with a reply. It was also crucial that the CIO worked hard for Alger and that other liberals "went fishing" by the thousands on election day. Equally instrumental, and another harbinger of Establishment problems in the 1960s and 1970s, was the overwhelming vote for the GOP candidate in the silk-stocking boxes. In a shocking upset, Alger defeated Savage about 28,000 to 25,000 votes. Most CIO leaders were pleased with the result at the time, but the tactic did not liberalize the Democratic party in Dallas, and the hyperconservative Republican, Alger, stayed in office for ten years. On the other hand, Alger was totally ineffective, never passing or even influencing any legislation. He was once on the short end of a 378 to 1 vote, futilely attempting to block free milk for schoolchildren. Savage, in contrast, probably would have been an effective operator for the Dixiecratic faction.[34]

A final result of the tumult was that several Yarborough Democrats, feeling manipulated by the conservative press in 1954, decided to underwrite a liberal-loyalist newspaper. Frankie Randolph of Houston became the chief financier of the *Texas Observer*, which, with Ronnie Dugger as editor, bought out the *State Observer* in December 1954. The paper often played a key role in developing stories that the corporate dailies were slow to touch, especially stories that embarrassed the Establishment.[35]

The close election illustrated the eclipse of the Shivers administration. Besides the obvious effect of the scandals, the governor's standing (both before and after the election) with one large segment of the population, farmers and ranchers, suffered from his handling of the great drought that began spreading over the Southwest in 1951. As late as October 1952, the governor wrote to Congressman John Young and others that he was "personally against asking the federal government for favors," even though he admitted that farmers and ranchers were in dire need. Yet the state programs, such as they were, came very close to being farcical. In November 1953, the legislature appropriated ten thousand dollars to study water resources projects while the California legislature was granting five hundred thousand dollars. During the Shivers years, in fact, no comprehensive water program was ever developed nor was a state disaster fund established. Shivers was certainly not entirely to blame for state inaction, since the legislature is also charged with the responsibility of serving the people. This miserly approach by the state's executive and legislative branches was traceable to the fears of the corporate lobbies that tax increases would be necessary for the building of dams, for water studies, and similar programs and that the companies might have to help pay for them.[36]

It was also disadvantageous for the administration that the programs that did operate in the state seemed to run afoul of greed or red tape. The federal hay program bogged down because of the government's own rigid eligibility requirements, because hay dealers pushed up prices, and because the railroads, which agreed to pick up half the freight costs in November 1953, rescinded their action nine months later. In 1956 the Texas State Drought Committee of the Department of Agriculture recommended forty-seven counties as eligible for the Drought Emergency Feed Program. The USDA in Washington, D.C., approved fourteen counties, some of which were much less needy than many of those denied. Even the Texas representatives of the agricultural agencies were mystified, though they could not be quoted. As William McGill wrote to the governor, it was difficult to explain this process "to farmers and stockmen in counties that drew the black beans." While it was true, as Price Daniel charged in 1956, that federal relief "is often too little and too late," it is nevertheless worth noting that in the course of his years in office, Governor Shivers managed to rise above principle and, after a late start, secured $7.5 million in federal drought relief grants.[37]

Shivers's power continued to unravel in his last term because of still more corruption. The story was broken by the new editor of the *Cuero Record*, Kenneth Towery. The *Record* was an insignificant paper in a small town in the south Texas brush country; thus it took several days before the inert

Texas dailies caught the whiff of scandal. Towery became suspicious of wrongdoing when he learned that a half-dozen of Cuero's most respectable businessmen were entertaining a score of blacks and Mexican-Americans in private bottle clubs (public saloons being illegal). Since it had never previously occurred to the Anglos to treat the "niggers" and "meskins" as human beings, Towery investigated and discovered that the minorities were war veterans who were being induced to sign papers for reasons that were rather vague. Some of them thought they were going to get free land or bonuses from the state. Some of them did, in fact, receive money, but not from the state. They were paid by the racketeers who were interested in their signatures on applications for state loans with which to buy land.[38]

Just after the war, state land commissioner Bascom Giles proposed a constitutional amendment whereby Texas would appropriate $100 million to help veterans buy land cheaply. The efforts of Giles, who was not a veteran, were resented by some spokesmen for veterans, including iconoclastic Mark Adams in Austin. Adams did not believe that veterans needed the subsidized real estate gimmickery. But the amendment passed, and the state began to purchase land for resale to veterans, at 5 percent down, 3 percent interest, and up to forty years to pay the note. The Land Board, composed of the land commissioner, the attorney general, and the governor, had to approve both the land purchases and the applications for loans by veterans. The investigations triggered by Towery revealed that promoters bought land or land options at market prices, subdivided the tracts, duped groups of veterans into signing the papers for as little as twenty-five dollars or forged their signatures, had the land appraised at sky-high values by Giles, and sold the land to the state at the artificially swollen prices. Giles declined to take his oath of office on January 1, 1955, and later admitted that he had accepted bribes to approve the schemes of the land speculators. Three other land office employees soon resigned.[39]

Towery received a Pulitzer Prize for his exposé, but it was more in keeping with the traditions of the Texas press that *Cuero Record* publisher Jack Howarton urged the reelection of Congressman John Bell, who had been instrumental in creating the land program and who had then become involved in the land frauds. Bell confessed to taking about $28,000 in "attorney's fees" from the guilty landsharks. He was indicted for conspiracy to defraud the state of $154,100 (just in one deal), but it was quashed on a technicality over the qualifications of one of the grand jurors. The publisher conceded that Bell was at least "morally wrong," but after all, graft was "common practice" for at least three-fourths of the Austin and Washington representatives. It was just "unfortunate" for the congressman that his deal "came to light." Whatever their shortcomings, however, Texas voters are not tolerant of opening plundering, and John J. Bell was retired by public demand.[40]

Since Shivers and Attorney General John Ben Shepperd were also on the

Land Board, many Texans naturally began to assume that they too were guilty. Even the Establishment legislature was forced to question them about their activities. They explained copiously that they had seldom attended the board meetings; other obligations frequently required them to send stand-ins. They declared that they had not been suspicious of Giles. The House Special Investigating Committee disclosed that in the "normal course of their duties" the board members would not have discovered fraud. The files and records did not contain irregularities, and knowledge of them could only have come from outside sources. It seemed astonishing to many observers, however, that Shivers, Shepperd, and their stand-ins never glanced at the minutes of previous meetings, which showed that Giles had incorporated approvals of suspicious deals into the minutes after the board meetings. The legislature reprimanded Shivers and Shepperd for not keeping closer watch over the board's affairs. Shivers's popularity plummeted from 64 percent approval in early January 1955, to 52 percent in May, 45 percent in August, and 22 percent in September.[41]

By the summer of 1955 Shivers was sufficiently weakened by the scandal that he compromised with Rayburn and Johnson. Dixiecratic national committeeman Wright Morrow was sacrificed and replaced by a lifelong Democrat acceptable to party leadership, Lieutenant Governor Ben Ramsey. By also paying lip-service to party loyalty, Shivers was readmitted to the bosom of the Democratic party, but he was still widely distrusted by loyalists. He brought no strength to the party, especially since the insurance scandals broke out again.[42]

U.S. Trust and Guaranty and a subsidiary failed almost simultaneously in December. The failure of the parent firm affected 128,000 depositers who had invested over $5 million with it. Other insurance companies quickly followed it into bankruptcy. The failures could have been accepted by the public, but it soon became apparent that Shivers's insurance board had performed peculiarly. The legislature was predictably slow in probing the frauds, since a number of legislators were involved in insurance operations and since the investigating committees were staffed by the governor's friends. One investment expert, employed to evaluate the insurance problem, hastened to assure the new insurance commission chairman, Shivers's close friend John Osorio, that "all of the members of our legislative committee feel that we are personal friends of yours and Allan Shivers." After seven weeks of research, the appalled investigator added, in a "personal and unofficial" letter to the commissioner, that in one insurance company prospectus:

> There is no certified balance sheet, earnings report, statement as to how much commission is being paid, proceeds to the company, and in fact if a securities dealer belonging to our association put out such an item he would receive

severe penalties. . . . in my opinion . . . it borders on fraud. . . . goes back to
my remarks . . . that apparently whoever is approving prospectuses and
securities under the Board of Insurance Commissioners must be quite inex-
perienced and does not realize what losses he is allowing the people of Texas
to take.[43]

The previous insurance commissioners, however, had known very well
what they were doing: accepting gifts and tips from insurance companies
while conniving to cover up the machinations of dishonest promoters. U.S.
Trust and Guaranty and its subsidiary, for instance, had been under surveil-
lance for well over a year, and a report six months earlier showed them to
be insolvent. The board had done nothing. Many companies had also given
legislator-lawyers "retainers" to represent them before the Insurance Board
and other state agencies.[44]

The next year, 1957, still another legislative investigating committee discovered a "gross breach of public trust" in the "substantial payments made
under questionable circumstances by the I.C.T. Insurance Company and/or
other Ben Jack Cage companies" to one former insurance board commissioner, the son-in-law of another, and two board examiners. Cage, starting
with a bank loan of $200,000, had erected a seventy-four-company insurance
empire in six years. In 1957 he was indicted in Austin for bribery and indicted and convicted in Dallas of embezzlement before departing permanently
for Brazil. Still more legislators were listed as receiving attorneys fees and
loans that were never repaid.[45] Much of the rising public indignation was
aimed against Shivers, who had not only appointed the board commissioners
but also defended them even after it was revealed they had been incom-
petent and corrupt.

Shivers stayed in office too long, and it was, perhaps, his repeated victories that made him overweening. This arrogance of power was reflected
in his coddling of the red scare mentality even after it was on the wane in
1956. The *Texas Observer* noted, for instance, that Shivers's secretary of
state, Tom Reavley, had revised the labor organizers' permit application
to remove most of the questions about communist associations and membership. Alerted by the newspaper item, the governor quickly revoked the new
application form. A more serious abuse of governmental prerogatives
occurred after Shivers received a rambling letter from a Chicago attorney
who asserted that the communist influence on Adlai Stevenson was traceable in part to the Wirtz family. Willard Wirtz, the letter continued, taught
law under a "red dean" now at the University of Texas. The professor was
identified in the letter, and a margin note, probably written by Hart, labeled
him as an anti-Shivers, Yarborough man. Shivers ordered that the letter be
turned over to the director of the Department of Public Safety, Homer

Garrison, who was instructed to investigate the entire law faculty at the University of Texas, using the FBI and other sources, and report back to the governor. For that matter, the usual Establishment cronyism sometimes resembled misfeasance, as in the case of a bank charter "for our friends in Hooks," as former Secretary of State Howard Carney put it in a memo to the governor. Carney reminded Shivers that the governor had already lined up state treasurer Jesse James's vote and that John Ben Shepperd had "voted with us last time," but he wanted the governor to ask Shepperd to help again in order to cinch the charter. The merits of the bank's application appeared irrelevant.[46]

The conservative governor ironically felt that his greatest accomplishments were the vastly increased appropriations for eleemosynary institutions, prison reforms, highways, and old-age pensions. They were financed regressively, to be sure, and to some extent the programs were simply the result of public and political pressure. By educating Texans on the alleged desirability of voting for Eisenhower, and by pointing out that there are loyalties in life greater than party affiliation, Shivers probably provided some impetus for the growth of the two-party system, although that was manifestly not his intent. Shivers also had a point when he recommended that executive agencies be made part of the governor's official family. Constitutionally Texas had a limited governor, Shivers observed, but the people had come to hold the governor responsible for the administrative functions of other agencies. The governor recognized that state agencies often functioned as if others did not exist and tended to become semi-independent fiefdoms. Yet the complaint is a bit strange coming from a governor who was so domineering that, as one conservative columnist conceded, he "practically dictated all major actions of the legislature."[47]

What Allan Shivers did want to recognize is that the governor, simply by virtue of his position as chief executive of the state, is responsible for setting the ethical tone of Texas' government. After Shivers's quick $425,000 profit in the valley land option deal, the state's numerous insurance and landsharks, some of whom were the governor's friends and appointees, might almost be forgiven for thinking it was open season. Moreover Shivers's McCarthyite political practices place him in the mainstream of the red scare, one of the most monumental threats to democratic processes in the nation's history. While his rhetoric never reached the depths of O'Daniel's, Shivers's refusal to move hard and fast against corruption and his igniting of repressive impulses cause him to rank alongside "Pappy" as the men who did the most to brutalize modern Texas politics.

12

Turning Points, 1956-1957

The voice of the demagogue has been heard
throughout our state. The people listened—
then voted for the path of moderation. Let
demagogues everywhere listen and take notice.

> Lyndon Johnson, upon the defeat
> of the Shivercrats in the state
> Democratic convention, May 1956

Once again the Democratic party has saved
the nation from Texas.

> Tom Connally, after observing Lyndon
> Johnson's bewildering, losing effort at
> the national Democratic convention,
> August 1956

They have stolen votes from counties which
they never stole of yore
Van Zandt, Hidalgo, Harris, and a half a dozen more
There has been no steal so flag-a-rant since 1954
As Lyndon let us down

(Chorus)
Deal and Compromise forever
Deal and Compromise forever
Deal and Compromise forever
For Sam will see you through

> Sung to the tune of "The Battle Hymn of
> the Republic," Bexar County liberals
> commemorated Johnson-Rayburn theft
> of the state Democratic convention,
> September 1956

During the presidential election year of 1956, Sam Rayburn and Lyndon Johnson, with their national party orientation and keen memory of the 1952 debacle, could not afford to allow Allan Shivers to exercise the traditional

governor's prerogative of controlling Democratic machinery and chairing
the state delegation to the national convention. Nor did they want the re-
surgent labor-liberals, buoyed by the Shivers scandals, to gain the upper
hand. (Rayburn had been pressured by the liberals into sponsoring a shadow
party organization, the Democratic Advisory Council, run by Navarro
County judge Jim Sewell, among others.) Rayburn did not cope with either
threat until early March, when he hit upon a gambit that promised to cut
down the Shivercrats and assimilate the liberals; he announced that Johnson
would be Texas's favorite son for president and would also serve as chairman
of the delegation at the national convention. Shivers was irate, since he
again planned to head the Texas convention forces. Johnson, with his
national prestige and ultimate presidential ambitions at stake, could hardly
refuse to come to the aid of his party, but he did not accept the honors
immediately. Indeed Johnson tried to appease Shivers, while the governor
was excoriating Rayburn as unprincipled. It is likely that Johnson went the
extra mile because Rayburn had tossed him into a bloody fray that—no
matter who won—would cause him to lose many friends who were also
among Shivers's followers. Evidently Rayburn had not consulted Johnson
on the decision.[1]

Shivers seized upon Johnson's feverish desire for compromise and began
stringing the senator along. On March 29 Shivers surprisingly announced,
regarding Johnson, "I would not deny to him for an instant the honor of
representing Texas as the chairman of its delegation to Chicago."[2] Shivers
did not mean a word of it, but it served to keep Johnson's phone calls coming into Austin. The negotiations, of course, were carried on privately and
sometimes through other parties. During the first week of April 1956,
Johnson learned from Herman Brown, who was acting as an intermediary,
that Shivers would agree to Johnson and Ernest Thompson's being cochair-
men of the delegation. Rayburn was apparently willing to go along with
that. Evidently Shivers was just postponing confrontation for another week,
possibly hoping to delay the Johnson forces' merger with Rayburn and the
DAC. Shivers and his followers were striving to obtain control of the upcoming May 5 precinct conventions and May 22 state convention in order
to deliver Democratic machinery to the Eisenhower cause that autumn.
Such plans necessitated that the delegation chairmanship not be yielded to
others.[3]

Most Texas labor-liberals were dismayed when Rayburn tossed Johnson's
hat into the ring. As DAC political organizer Kathleen Voigt put it, they
favored a "weekend romance with Lyndon, but didn't want to marry him."
But the DAC and the labor leaders—Jerry Holleman of the AFL and Fred
Schmidt of the CIO—forged an uneasy alliance with the Johnson-Rayburn
Establishment in attempting to scourge the Shivercrats. But because of mutual
distrust and political differences, consummation of the arrangement was
awkward. Exact details are hazy. Evidently most of the liberal-labor faction,

which was chronically addicted to bitter in-fighting, agreed not to resist Johnson's candidacy for favorite son and delegation chairman if the senator allowed the DAC to take a fair share of party offices.[4]

Shivers and Johnson carried the burden of debate during the primary, and the governor and the senator did differ on a few issues. Shivers felt strongly—contrary to Johnson's wishes—that the Texas delegation should not be pledged to the Democratic presidential nominee. He was dismayed that Johnson had embraced federal aid to education and had not demanded restoration of the two-thirds rule or endorsed "interposition," a vague assertion of the paramountcy of states' rights in regard to segregated schools. But toward the end of the primary, the issues were lost in a sea of rhetoric. Shivers accused Johnson of being "vicious," a tool of the leftists, and of having won the 1948 senatorial election with "fraudulent votes." Shivers questioned Rayburn's patriotism, linking his name once with Santa Anna's, and also charged that Rayburn placed the welfare of the Democratic party over that of the nation. Johnson accused Shivers of having the most corrupt administration in Texas's history, and Rayburn reproached the governor's "insane attacks" and his "rat alley politics." The name calling presumably revealed a great depth of feeling on the part of all hands, but such was the case only between Rayburn and Shivers. Shivers and Johnson later agreed that they should never have broken, that there was no real reason for the split.[5]

The governor was "on the trail of evidence that Walter Reuther and the CIO were sending large sums of money into Texas." He produced photostats of bank deposit slips, without saying how he acquired them, showing that the Detroit office of the UAW had deposited a thousand dollars in the account of the Rio Grande Valley Democratic Club, which intended to round up as many valley liberals as possible for the precinct meetings on election night. Liberal-dominated precincts would select anti-Shivers delegates to attend the state Democratic convention. The governor professed to be offended that Reuther would "pour" this kind of money into "one county." Shivers's charge may well have been true, though he neglected to add that the deposit was legal. The governor also made no mention that $13,007.87 that he had paid for radio and television advertising had been paid back to him by Bill Blakley, the multimillionaire owner of Braniff Airlines whom Shivers appointed to the United States Senate seven months later.[6] Shivers had been reimbursed by one man in one county. Both the UAW and Blakley payments simply reflected politics as usual.

The combined liberal-Establishment forces routed the Shivercrats, but the "strange new political world," as ADA organizer George Lambert phrased it, proved illusory. Just before the county conventions were held, Johnson summoned Holleman, Schmidt, and Voigt to the LBJ Ranch, evidently selecting three of the liberal leaders with the widest contacts, and cajoled them about the paucity of Johnson favorite son support among most liberals.

The senator wanted the Texas national delegation to vote for him on every ballot, while most liberals were reluctantly ready to concede him only the first ballot vote. The labor leaders kept eating Johnson's steaks, drinking his liquor, and saying "no." As soon as they left, Johnson cursed them repeatedly as sons-of-bitches and then began to take action. Lambert soon found it "disturbing" that Johnson had "hired a man named John Connally" to produce some delegates to the state convention and/or maneuver them away from labor-liberals.[7]

At the state convention Connally's success became evident when the delegates overrode a band of hard-core liberals and voted to go "all the way with LBJ," voting for him as president as long as he was a candidate. The liberals, excluding some DAC leaders, were also beaten in attempts to oust the hyperconservative State Democratic Executive Committee members, as well as all candidates who refused to pledge themselves to support party nominees. The Establishment-liberal accord was further weakened when liberal-labor-loyalist delegates, mostly urbanites, rebelled against a Johnson ploy. The senator demanded (with Rayburn and his restraining hand absent from the convention) the appointment of former Congressman Lloyd Bentsen, Jr.'s wife as national committeewoman. Beryl Ann Bentsen may have been a loyal Democrat, but she was ultraconservative and inactive in party affairs. Certainly her claims to party reward were insignificant compared to those of the liberal leader, Frankie Randolph. The wealthy daughter of a Texas lumber baron, Randolph became a full-time volunteer organizer who led the Harris County Democrats in gaining control of Houston, precinct by precinct. For once the liberals were strong enough to prevail, with help from moderates who were dissatisfied with Johnson's high-handed manner of running the convention. Randolph was elected to the disputed post. Other than this one contest, Johnson got everything that he wanted. Shivers, on the other hand, lost out entirely, and reflected years later that since he favored Ike all along, he really had "no business" trying to control Democratic proceedings.[8]

Meanwhile the scandals that had hounded Shivers out of the gubernatorial primary gave encouragement to the liberals. Any conservative candidate, it was thought, would be handicapped by being in the same faction with Shivers. The foremost liberal politician in the state, the inevitable nominee of his faction, was Ralph Yarborough, who had never quit running since his defeat two years before. The Establishment candidate was Senator Price Daniel, who, after winning the tidelands battle, was no longer interested in staying in Washington. Several reactionary candidates entered the fray, including "Pappy" O'Daniel and the west Texas rancher and writer, J. Evetts Haley.

Both Haley and O'Daniel rode the race issue for all it was worth. Haley labeled integration a communist plot to destroy the white race and called all those who did not believe in interposition "communists." He demanded the impeachment of every school board that had ordered desegregation. If the federal government tried to enforce the Supreme Court's ruling on integration, Haley proposed to meet them at the Red River with Texas Rangers. O'Daniel ran his old-time hillbilly road show and ranted about "blood running in the streets" because of the communist-inspired Supreme Court decision. He added, "Pretty soon there'll be little parties . . . nature will take its course, they intermarry and the mongrel race takes over."[9]

The two leading contenders fought it out on higher ground, though Daniel often seemed confused over the identity of his opponent. Though challenged by Yarborough, he usually spoke as though he were running against the NAACP and "Walter Reuther of the CIO." Daniel knew that the CIO had merged with the more conservative AFL but managed to overlook it in his campaign rhetoric. The Daniel forces paraded a photograph of Reuther giving a seventy-five thousand dollar check to NAACP officials. They did not point out that the transaction took place in Detroit and had nothing to do with the Texas elections. The NAACP, in fact, had not endorsed Yarborough, since he had come out against "forced" integration. Once again Yarborough's racial stand caused disaffection and apathy among urban liberals. Yarborough tried to stress his proposals for soil and water conservation, old-age pensions, an antilobby law, and more money for schools, teachers, and public health, though he probably did not help his cause when he referred to Daniel as "junior" and to former backers who switched to Daniel as "turncoats." Daniel appealed for the farm vote by charging that the CIO was about to take over the state's farms and ranches. The senator's campaign did have a positive side, reflected in his pledges for a lobby control law, school improvements, narcotic control, old-age pensions, and water conservation. Daniel was driven to take advantage of the Davy Crockett craze by hiring Fess Parker to preside at a rally at the Alamo, while Yarborough retaliated with a band called the Cass County Coon Hunters. Backed by big oil and other corporate interests (including thousand dollar contributions from Texas Eastern Transmission vice-president Charles I. Francis, Rex Baker of Humble Oil Company, E. B. Germany, Lamar Fleming, and corporate attorney Leon Jaworski) along with the customary monolithic support of the Texas press, Daniel breezed in with a plurality. He carried the three most populous counties in polling nearly 629,000 votes, while Yarborough finished with about 463,400. O'Daniel captured much of the rural-old folks-segregationist bloc, carrying sixty-six counties with 347,750 votes. Haley got nearly 88,800. Thus Daniel and Yarborough were thrown into a runoff, with Daniel heavily favored.[10]

The runoff primary between Yarborough and Daniel was even more hotly contested than the first. Daniel secured Shivers's endorsement, while Yarborough picked up O'Daniel's. O'Daniel, who had earlier criticized Daniel for party jumping, intended to run as an independent in the November general election and announced that Yarborough would be an easier

opponent to defeat than Daniel. Yarborough and O'Daniel shared no ideological common ground, but in the heat of the fray, Yarborough told a
group of "Pappy's" first primary supporters in Georgetown that he wanted
the opportunity to carry out O'Daniel's plans. Daniel continued manufacturing
an issue out of the very existence of the CIO and, after analyzing his one-
sided defeat in black precincts in the first primary, he stepped up his segregationist approach. Ironically, conservative black editor Carter Wesley
started a write-in campaign for himself in his *Houston Informer* and hurt
Yarborough in the city's black boxes. Yarborough ran out of money and
had no significant press support, yet he almost beat the Establishment. He
polled 694,830 to Daniel's 698,001. Daniel undoubtedly suffered because of
the public reaction against Establishment scandals. Some conservatives
claimed it was that close because Yarborough benefited from such returns as
the Negro box in Tarrant County that went for him 1,036 to 26, with many
of the names allegedly in alphabetical order. But these incidents were more
than offset by the white bloc vote from such areas as Highland Park and by
the usual returns from the boss-controlled counties of south Texas.[11] (See
appendixes 7, 10, and 12.)

In such a close race the unanimity of the press was crucial. Several trivial
incidents that occurred before the primaries illustrated the natural bond
between conservative politicians and Texas newspaper editors. Senator
Daniel was shocked by a *Fort Worth Star-Telegram* editorial on December
1, 1955, which sounded to him as though it had been written by someone on
the staff of Jimmy Phillips, a conservative state senator who was thinking of
running for governor. Daniel asked a good friend, wealthy insurance man
Raymond Buck, to investigate quietly the motives behind the editorial. After
talking to the editor, Buck soon replied that the paper was not committed
to Phillips but that it did like Daniel in the Senate and feared that if Daniel
resigned, he might be replaced by someone worse. The *Star-Telegram*,
however, eventually endorsed Daniel. Meanwhile *Houston Post* editor
William P. Hobby promised Phillips his support but switched to Daniel.
The *Lubbock Avalanche-Journal* ran a column that praised Phillips highly,
but after Daniel declared for governor, the Lubbock paper declared that if
Phillips stayed in the race, he would just be a hatchet man who would split
the conservative vote and allow Yarborough to win. Finally after learning
that the oil industry had thrown in with Daniel, Phillips backed out of the
race, but he continued to feel that it was the press that had broken the back
of his campaign.[12] In fact, the high-powered conservative had press connections that the lesser-known conservative could not match, and Yarborough
(and other liberals) had no connections whatever.

The second primary had to compete for the people's attention with the
Democratic national convention. The liberal-moderate delegation followed
Johnson and Rayburn loyally, voting for Johnson for the presidency in the

face of Adlai Stevenson's overwhelming first-ballot strength. They also stood behind their two leaders through a bewildering chain of votes on the vice-presidency, backing losers all the way.[13]

After his ignominious setbacks at the national convention, Johnson faced a chaotic home front in Texas. The labor-liberals were poised to take over the party machinery at the fall state convention, and Johnson, Rayburn, and Daniel had pledged that all legally elected delegates would be seated. Johnson, however, undoubtedly shared Rayburn's notion that the left could be ignored because they had nowhere else to go. The sensitive senator had already fallen out with the liberals anyway, since they did not render him the kind of absolute, continuous loyalty that he demanded. Randolph, the labor leaders, and other liberal spokesmen were not sufficiently subservient because they continued to demand immediate replacement of the Shivers-controlled Democratic Executive Committee, whose presidential sympathies were largely Republican. There were rumors, spread by Shivers, among others, that a liberal SDEC might go so far as to unseat Daniel and designate party loyalist Yarborough as the official Democratic nominee for governor. This notion, which was not entertained by many liberals, may have spurred the Daniel forces into serving as conciliators between the Johnson-Rayburn and the Shivers camps. Shivers favored Eisenhower's reelection, but that was too trifling a matter to prevent the Establishment from healing itself in the face of its enemy.[14]

The real reason that Johnson discarded his pledges was heavy-handed advice from his corporate financiers and other friends around the state, who wanted party machinery to remain in conservative Democratic hands at all costs. Given his corporate power base in the state and the fact that Establishment financing was more important for his future ambitions than the (at best) uncertain support by labor-liberals, counting out the old DAC crowd was not a difficult decision. Moreover Johnson and Rayburn used their mastery to force Price Daniel into a weak endorsement of the national Democratic ticket.[15] The liberals had no leverage that could hold the Establishment leaders to their pledges. Johnson, Rayburn, Daniel, and Shivers apparently agreed to steal the convention from the labor-liberal faction if there was no other way to win it. There was no other way.

The Establishment was so fearful of turmoil that a chain link fence topped with barbed wire was erected around the old Fort Worth auditorium. Once, amid rumors that liberals were going to seize the rostrum, one man in the balcony watched closely with his pistol drawn. Convention fireworks revolved around the disputed Harris and El Paso delegations, though progressive forces had evidently won both of them narrowly. As the convention opened, Lyndon Johnson's minions were preparing to throw both of them out. El Paso County Judge Woodrow Wilson Bean secretly proposed to Lyndon Johnson that his liberal delegation be seated in return for its voting for the seating of the Harris conservative delegation. Johnson, seizing the opportunity to acquire a pipeline into the liberal camp, picked up the telephone and informed the credentials committee that the El Paso liberals were the official delegation. But Bean could no more control liberals than Johnson could. The El Paso contingent did not know of Bean's deal and obviously would have disapproved it, but Bean advised them that it was only after they were seated that a top official told him that El Paso had to vote against the Harris liberals. When the senator learned that the El Paso delegation would not assist him, he summoned Bean before him, gave him a lecture on the virutes of integrity and loyalty to Lyndon Johnson, reconvened the credentials committee after it has been permanently adjourned, and had them strip the El Paso liberals of their official status.[16]

In Harris County the *Houston Chronicle* conceded that the liberals had won the county convention, and four Houston newspapermen at the state convention confided the same opinion. Indeed the conservatives' charges of fraud were confined to eight precincts, whose votes were insufficient to alter the outcome. Fifteen other precincts, which were not represented by any protestors, were charged only with technical violations of election procedure. Yet the outcome was predestined, since the Harris conservatives could vote on the group to be seated and cast a decisive 270 votes for themselves. The Establishment stole party control from the liberals, 1,006 to 869.

From that point on in Texas's political history, it was an article of faith among Texas liberals, who had entertained some doubts about Lyndon since 1948, that Johnson could never be trusted. Most of them agreed with W. O. Cooper of Dallas, who said, "I have lost my last entrail on the battlements under the leadership of Johnson and Rayburn. I have never seen people kick their political friends in the teeth with the kind of vengeance that was done in Fort Worth this day."[18]

After this brazen caper, there was no hope of a united Democratic campaign on behalf of the presidential nominee, Adlai Stevenson. Johnson did not make much of an attempt to attract conservative support for the Democrats and ignored the embittered liberals. On the other hand, liberal distrust of Johnson probably helped the Republicans, since liberals hesitated to send their money or even their names to the State Democratic Executive Committee. Governor Shivers endorsed Ike while labeling Stevenson "unstable," but his support had nothing to do with Eisenhower's sweeping victory. Yet liberals could take heart from the 1956 campaigns, because every state senator seeking reelection who had been even marginally connected with the insurance or land scandals was defeated. Moreover the defeats in the state convention and the general election inspired liberals, as distinct from loyalists, to come up with their first effective statewide organization that worked separately from the Establishment's party machinery. Austin attorney Creekmore Fath suggested local clubs under a loose central council,

12. Establishment Politics, 1956. *Courtesy of Bob Eckhardt.*

following the organization of the California Democrats. This movement, christened the Democrats of Texas, continued the harassment of the Texas Establishment from the left.[19]

To the embarrassment of the Establishment, Judge Ralph Yarborough became the favorite in a special senatorial contest to fill Daniel's vacated seat. Called for April 12, 1957, it was a special election rather than a primary, which meant that there would be no runoff. The high man won, even if he received a low percentage of votes. The conservatives could not follow their usual pattern of rallying behind the front-running conservative from the first primary in order to crush the liberal survivor of that primary. Worse from the Establishment view, the other declared contenders were a young Republican, Thad Hutcheson, and the former chairman of the House Un-American Activities Committee, Martin Dies.

Dies had not changed much over the years. In 1952 he lobbied the legislature to prevent redistricting, a successful violation of the state constitution, which created a congressman-at-large seat. It was an easy race, since no one of stature opposed him. By that time Texas voters were well aware of the Soviet theft of American atomic secrets, of the Hiss trials, and of the presence of communist spies in the land. There was a feeling in the state that Martin Dies had been abused, that he was a prophet without honor in his own land, and that the electorate owed him an apology.[20] After the election Dies made his usual promise to disclose startling information of subversion involving important people; then he learned that the Un-American Activities Committee did not want him back. He had to accept a post on the committee on merchant marine and fisheries (Ida Darden, in the effervescent *Southern Conservative*, wailed that the only subversive fish was Truman's "red herring"). Dies never did unveil the "startling information." The hapless and innocuous Communist party, hopelessly infiltrated by FBI agents, was driven underground by a 1954 law that Dies helped pass. He was also instrumental in scuttling the proposed civil-rights law of 1956.[21] Given these achievements, he won easy reelections in 1954 and 1956, and by 1957 he felt ready for the Senate.

Being well aware that Dies was an impotent campaigner and snakebitten with right-wing rhetoric, as well as being personally abhorrent to Sam Rayburn, the Establishment put heavy pressure on Dies to withdraw from the race in favor of Lieutenant Governor Ben Ramsey. The pressure was exerted by Senate majority leader Johnson, Speaker Rayburn, Governor Daniel, Brown and Root lobbyist Frank Oltorf, and the speaker of the Texas house. But Dies held firm. Then a new strategy was hit upon: Establishment leaders decided to order the Texas legislature to change the election law and require a runoff. Emergency conditions had to exist before the legislature could consider a bill out of its proper order, so Governor Daniel obligingly declared that the election proposal was an emergency, citing no grounds whatsoever. The house voted to require a runoff, 90 to 57. But the measure needed 100 votes in order to take effect immediately. Under more intense pressure, the house voted for it, 103 to 44. Also, Establishment financiers and congressmen lured Agricultural Commissioner John White into the feverish last-day lobbying in the house and into the Senate race itself, in an attempt to draw off Yarborough's rural support.[22]

In the minds of most conservatives the "gut-Yarborough" bill was designed to prevent the election of a liberal, and Dies, for one, honestly admitted it. House sponsor Joe Pool of Dallas, who coveted Dies's congressional seat, said he favored it in order to uphold the principle of majority rule. (Pool was chairman of the Texas House Investigating Committee during the Shivers administration scandals, but the committee never seemed to find the time to look into them. It did investigate lewd and horror comic books). Lyndon Johnson said little publicly about the Pool bill and nothing about majority rule, doubtless recalling that he won his first race with 28 percent of the vote in a special election. Alone among Establishment leaders, Rayburn bore Yarborough no animus, but he did genuinely fear the election of the Republican. Much of the Establishment, by this time, would not have been particularly displeased by a Republican victory, since Hutcheson and all Texas Republicans entertained about the same political views as did conservative Democrats. (Conservative Democrats were the most likely source of Republican votes and Texas was generally conservative.) But Johnson and Rayburn really did not want Hutcheson because his election would mean that the Republicans would organize the precariously balanced U.S. Senate and Johnson would be reduced to minority leader. (Both the Johnson forces and top Republicans spent part of the ensuing campaign trying to persuade the oil and gas industry that only their party could enact a gas bill.)[23]

But in the corridors around the Texas senate, Weldon Hart, Shivers's top aide when he was governor, was seen lobbying against the Pool bill. Several observers recalled that Shivers had not only fallen out with Establishment leaders over his support for Eisenhower but also that he was incensed that Governor Daniel opposed several of his last appointees in January 1957. Thus for his own reasons Shivers apparently convinced a few state senators to vote against the alteration of the election law. According to Yarborough, some Shivercrats, among them Senator H. H. Weinert, simply did not believe in rigged elections. The vote to take up the house bill out of order (necessary for immediate approval) was favored 18 to 13, but it needed 21. Four of the nay votes were unexpected by the sponsors. Six freshmen senators, keenly aware of the charges of corruption hurled against the legislature in the recent land and insurance scandals, also voted against the bill. Moreover the John White strategy may have backfired. His candidacy, which appeared to indicate that the liberals were split too, may have cooled the enthusiasm of some for legislative tampering. The "gut-Yarborough" bill failed to pass.[24]

When the Establishment tried to crank up its political machinery in order

to change an election law in the middle of an election, at least one conservative spokesman thought it was a bit shabby. In resigning his membership on
the State Democratic Executive Committee, Ben Bock of New Braunfels wrote
to the chairman of that body:

> When your office called me to get everyone I could to wire my representative
> to vote for the Pool bill I was told it was what the Governor wanted, but I
> could not use the Governor's name. This sounded strange to me. If he was for it
> I could not understand why we could not say so. I could not get out here and
> talk out of both sides of my mouth, even though I personally wanted the bill
> passed, so I was not much help.[25]

After citing another secret attempted putsch on the part of the governor,
Bock noted that he could not sell a program with an anonymous sponsor
and that it was not his way of doing business. Several conservative papers,
such as the *Houston Press* and the *San Angelo Evening Standard*, thought
the legislature had sunk quite low when it tried to destroy a candidate and
that, as one put it, the effort would be a "grotesque specter hovering over
every election in the future."[26]

Yarborough, as the leading candidate, issued few statements that could
be challenged. He had the all-out backing of labor and the new DOT, but
still had no significant press support. The judge's increasingly efficient
organization, however, was placing press releases in local newspaper offices,
and the papers were using them. Perhaps the most colorful candidate was
Hutcheson, who was conspicuous in a field of twenty-two Democrats. He
talked mostly about reducing government expenditures and proposed a
constitutional amendment requiring a balanced budget. Dies ran a well-
financed campaign and enjoyed the somewhat reluctant endorsement of
most of the big city dailies. But his negativism, which had not been so obvious in his virtually unchallenged races for congressman-at-large, seeped
out in the course of the campaign. He claimed that only he could halt the
"communization" of the country, though the radicals were trying to "liqui-
date" him. Dies's chances were also hurt because he followed the customary
Establishment tactic of refusing to resign one office while running for another, thus preventing a simultaneous election for his successor. If Dies
went to the Senate, there would have to be another statewide election for
congressman-at-large. Texans had suffered through four statewide elections
in 1956 and were not eager to repeat in 1957.[27]

Yarborough polled about 364,600 (38 percent), Dies approximately
290,800 (29 percent), and Hutcheson 216,600 (23 percent). In the election,
Dies and Hutcheson had split the conservative vote and had given the post

13. Ralph Yarborough Triumphant, 1957. *Texas AFL-CIO.*

to a liberal. Yarborough ran well in the big cities, where the labor-liberal-minority coalition was concentrated. In sixteen predominately Mexican-American precincts in San Antonio, for instance, he trounced Hutcheson 3,200 to 461, though Hutcheson won a plurality in Bexar County. Yarborough also led in the rural areas, in part because he had long favored drought relief and boosting the income tax exemption from six hundred to eight hundred dollars. Hutcheson ran second in the ten largest cities and also picked up votes in south Texas and the Panhandle, seats of growing Republicanism. Dies ran strongest in the countryside, especially his native east Texas.[28] The election of Yarborough, of course, was a stupendous victory for progressives over the Establishment. (See appendix 11.)

The labor movement was also successful in 1957 when it consummated the first legislative compromise with management in the Establishment era. The Texas state AFL-CIO and the TMA agreed on a workers' compensation bill that increased benefits by 40 percent, granted medical coverage, and devised a system of adequate funding for the Industrial Accident Board. The bill was enacted into law and since that time, especially since the late 1960s, the AFL-CIO and TMA have successfully cooperated on several workers' compensation and unemployment compensation measures and helped persuade the legislature to adopt them.[29]

Meanwhile on another political front, Establishment meddling in higher education continued unabated during the Shivers years. Legislative investigations and inadequate financing reflected contempt for the universities. In fact the legislature's search for reds, which never uncovered a single communist, cloaked the state government's failure to increase appropriations. Chancellor James Hart, who in 1951 was the victim of a whispering vendetta accusing him of being a communist, resigned his post in 1954 when he was ordered by the regents not to fight for higher appropriations. The humanities suffered the most. The University of Texas English Department, which was at the center of the Rainey controversy, paid its members less than seven dollars for each classroom hour taught in 1952-1953, while the engineering faculty and staff were paid over nineteen dollars. Of the 215 English sections, 177 had more than 20 students; only 100 of the 232 engineering sections had more than 20 students. And English was, of course, vital to everyone whereas the engineers were catering to fewer than 2,000 students. Even eight years after the Rainey fight, the university had not pressed forward, despite its physical expansion. But all higher education was penalized, not just the humanities or the University of Texas. In 1956 dollars, Texas spent 6.5 percent less per student in 1955-1956 than in 1931-1932 (just before the legislative investigation of the mid-1930s, which was followed by others in the 1940s, as well as the attacks of Martin Dies and the firing of Rainey). Even a business spokesman admitted in 1959 that "every budget for ten years has been balanced in Texas at the expense of colleges mainly."[30]

In 1956 the Establishment taught the colleges about freedom of the press. University of Texas student editor Willie Morris wrote occasional columns in the *Daily Texan* advocating higher state taxes on oil, gas, and sulfur and opposing the Fulbright-Harris bill, which would have freed natural gas prices from federal controls. Suddenly the regents—all Shivers appointees—handed down a censorship edict. Their censor refused even to print several paragraphs on freedom of the press written by Thomas Jefferson, but he did allow Morris to run blank spaces and editorials entitled "Let's Water the Pansies" and "Don't Walk on the Grass." One oilman-regent observed, "We feel the *Daily Texan* is going out of bounds to discuss the Fulbright-Harris natural gas bill when 66 percent of Texas tax money comes from oil and gas." Even some of the Establishment press, such as the *Fort Worth Star Telegram*, thought that this move was too severe, but the *Dallas Morning News* thought the coercive conformity was fully justified. Possibly inspired by the regents' attitudes, Logan Wilson, the university president, forbade the faculty from publicly supporting or opposing candidates for governor, lieutenant governor, and the legislature. The regents, however, lacked the will to enforce the first dictate, and the faculty refused to be emasculated by the president.[31]

In Lubbock, Texas Tech regents were also caught up in hyperconservative actions. J. Evetts Haley had been recommended for the board by only one man, Tech president Clifford Jones, and Shivers appointed him in 1955. In July 1957, Haley may have been instrumental in persuading the rest of the Tech regents to fire three professors. The most prominent was Dr. Byron Abernethy, a government professor and floor leader of the liberal forces, who gave an eloquent address at the September 1956 Democratic convention defining the loyalist arguments. Also dismissed were Dr. Herbert Greenburg, a blind psychologist who had conducted studies in integration, and Per Stensland, whose adult education program had succeeded in direct opposition to a Haley-supported Americanism Institute on campus. The entire adult education program, which was sponsored by the Ford Foundation, was abolished. None of the professors was given prior notification of his dismissal and none was granted a hearing. Another peculiarity was that the regents had copies of Abernethy's income tax returns. At first no reasons were cited for these sudden dismissals, but there was sufficient outcry to force the board to conjure up an explanation: the professors played politics. Thus Haley, who had not resigned from the board when he was a candidate for governor the year before, reasoned that such freedom was in poor taste for liberals and integrationists. When Haley's term expired in 1958, Governor Daniel did not reappoint him. Though Tech remained on the American Association of University Professors censured list for ten years, and the forces that Haley reflected did not disappear, at least the regents did not indulge in any more ostentatious firings.[32]

The storms in Texas higher education died down after 1957, and the Establishment ruled with a lighter touch. State spending for higher education increased enormously, especially under Governor John Connally (1963-1969). Willie Morris wrote in 1967 in his autobiography that repression had passed and academic freedom was firmly guaranteed. Unfortunately the very next year University of Texas regent Frank Erwin helped terminate an untenured instructor, Larry Caroline, who talked of revolution while off campus, and attempted to curb activism by ruling that no more than three "non-student, non-employed guests" could attend a campus meeting or event.[33] His three-year tyrannizing, however, was pale alongside the continuous onslaughts of the 1940s and 1950s. Former governor Shivers became chairman of the board in 1973 and generally presided with a defter touch than Erwin, though he too harkened back to a darker era when he paid little attention to faculty opinion in selecting Lorene Rogers as the university president in 1975.

Another postwar Establishment problem and a leading issue of the day was the white public's tolerance of black activities. Texans accepted the *Smith* v. *Allwright* decision with better grace than the states of the deep South. A 1946 poll revealed that 44 percent of white Texans endorsed the decision. Blacks voted without much difficulty in the 1946 primary, especially in the cities. In some cities, such as Dallas and San Antonio, black voters had long been numerous enough to bargain successfully for improved schools, parks, public housing, and health care. In Dallas and Houston in 1947, black deputy poll tax collectors were appointed. In 1948 San Antonio elected a black to its junior college district board. In its first newsletter in 1949, the Texas Commission on Interracial Cooperation observed that race relations had definitely improved in the last ten years. Establishment leaders, especially Governor Jester, acquiesced in the trends.[34]

One of Governor Shivers's businessmen followers advised him in 1950 to cultivate two prominent Texas black leaders, Carter Wesley and Hobart Taylor, because they had the "right attitude" about segregation and because they exercised (he thought) "almost absolute control over their potential 650,000 voters in Texas." The governor's opinion of blacks, however, left little room for such overtures, at least in 1950. Some blacks were evidently threatening to file suit in order to establish their right to use state parks, and the Texas parks board had advised Shivers that there was no law or rule requiring segregated parkways and picnic grounds. Even if there had been, the Supreme Court had ordered equal facilities in public institutions for all races. There was no hope of providing duplicate facilities under the parks budget. Shivers's private response to the adjuring of the blacks was "let them sue and be damned." He had to yield, of course, and blacks were soon complimenting him for allowing them to share the parks.[35] Establishment adaptability disappeared altogether after the Supreme Court ordered school desegregation in May 1954, though for a year or so Shivers's rhetoric was more heated than his actions. Texas racism reached its dramatic turning points in the middle and late 1950s.

By the summer of 1955 the red scare was waning, the tidelands settlement had eroded concern for states' rights, and corruption was embarrassing the Shivers administration. Segregation offered a rallying point for the governor. In July 1955 Governor Shivers appointed the Texas Advisory Committee on Segregation, packed with segregationists who were charged with developing solutions to the school crisis. The committee promptly threatened school districts that had integrated by accusing them of violating the Gilmer-Aiken act. This threat was soon demolished by the Texas Supreme Court in the Big Spring case of *McKinney* v. *Blankenship*, which held that the "dominant purpose" of the law was "to guarantee to each child of school age in Texas the availability of a minimum Foundation School Program." This decision did not alter the governor's course. Late in 1955 Wallace Savage, Shivers's chairman of the SDEC, correctly informed the governor of what he doubtless already perceived: that the segregation issue was the "best single one to weld together conservative forces."[36]

In February 1956 Shivers called for the placement of segregationist referenda on the July primary ballot. Since the governor still controlled the SDEC, they placed three referenda on the ballot. The voters were to decide whether they favored state "interposition" to prevent "illegal federal encroachment," though both these phrases were vague. They were also asked whether they wanted stronger state laws forbidding racial intermarriage and whether they thought the legislature should exempt children from compulsory attendance at integrated schools. The racist referenda carried by about four-to-one margins, but interpreting the returns was not as simple as it seemed. The vote came mostly from east Texas. One-third of the people casting ballots in the governor's race did not bother to vote on the integration question. Three counties, most notably Bexar, refused to put the petitions on the ballot. And some moderates proposed to "smother [interposition] by embracing it." Scores of school districts had already peacefully integrated. An earlier poll indicated that 35 percent of Texans thought that gradual integration should begin in schools where there was only slight opposition to it, and 14 percent favored integration regardless of opposition. Indeed, throughout the 1950s there was a movement in Texas toward gradual acceptance of integration, except during 1956.[37]

Supposedly bolstered by the returns on the referenda and shrugging off his crushing defeat in the spring convention, Shivers pursued interposition to its dismal climax in Texas. By August 1956 the Committee on Segregation's legal and legislative subcommittee had quietly submitted its report to the governor and his staff for censoring.

Weldon Hart was appalled by the report's long-winded explanation of the

14. Mansfield School Supplies, 1956. *Courtesy of Bob Eckhardt.*

old nullification doctrine and by the incessant assertion of state authority over localities, contradicting Shivers's statements that segregation was a matter for local people to decide. The final report did abandon nullification but recommended that the state coerce local districts into establishing or reestablishing segregated systems, force them not to count whites in black schools, or vice-versa, in the average daily attendance figures, and compel them to deny student transfers for an undefined duration. The subcommittee also wanted psychologists to advise local districts, prompting Hart to suggest sarcastically that this service be extended to the legislature and the governor's staff. The report was released just as Texas faced its first real crisis over integration.[38]

Mansfield, Texas, in 1956 was a sleepy farm town of some 1,450 people, seventeen miles southeast of Fort Worth, with a school district that numbered 688 whites and 58 blacks. The blacks attended a separate school, which had no indoor toilets, and if they wanted to go to high school, they had to ride a public-service bus to Fort Worth. Whites saw nothing wrong with busing. In the fall of that year, Mansfield was the first district in the state ordered by a federal court to allow black attendance at the neighborhood public school. The school board acquiesced. But as cross burnings and other incidents indicated that a crisis was building, the mayor, chief of police, and others in the town's power structure literally left the community. Fanatics took over the town and its newspaper. While a hundred or so other Texas districts desegregated quietly that fall, mobs of three hundred to four hundred per day ringed the Mansfield school and prevented any possible black enrollment. The mobs hanged a black in effigy, roughed up several reporters, cameramen, and the assistant district attorney, and threatened the sheriff with violence if he tried to uphold the law by escorting black students to school. Signs were carried aloft, reading, "A dead nigger is the best nigger." Vigilantes met all cars entering Mansfield; suspected Negro sympathizers were hustled out of town. Governor Shivers, referring to the lynch-minded mob scene as "orderly protest," defied the law of the land by dispatching Texas Rangers to uphold segregation and authorized the Mansfield school board to transfer the black students to Fort Worth. Shivers undoubtedly felt fairly secure that President Eisenhower was not going to uphold the Constitution either, considering that the election was just two months away and that Texas and the southern states had many voters who were interested in segregation. (Eisenhower took no action until the next year at Little Rock, Arkansas, where Governor Orville Faubus's actions were possibly inspired by Governor Shivers's.)[39]

The replacement of the Shivers administration with that of Daniel signified a basic change in the state government's philosophy on segregation. Daniel promised to support local school boards in their decisions, which indicated that he would guard segregation in most districts, but also integration in a growing number (over a hundred by the time he took office). Moreover the new attorney general, Will Wilson, did not agree with John Ben Shepperd's contention that Supreme Court decisions did not apply to Texas.[40]

As Daniel took office he was badgered by the press to say something about segregation, but he merely noted that there were other fields in which the legislature should work. Defying the *Dallas Morning News* and other racist forces, the governor arranged with legislative leaders to have the controversial segregation bills postponed until late in the session. Hard-core segregationists were beaten 85 to 52 in the house when they tried to present an interposition measure. But late in the session east Texans introduced a dozen bills, which, among other things, would have barred members of the NAACP from public employment, withheld state funds from integrated schools, allocated state funds to educate pupils in private schools, and required integrationists to register with the secretary of state (known as the "thought permit" bill).

The defeat of these particular bills was the result in large part of the power of the Texas church lobby, whose conscience was awakened by the legislative racism. Organized labor and the Young Democrats also lobbied to good effect. Two filibusters, ramrodded by freshman state senator Henry Gonzalez of San Antonio, the first Mexican-American elected to the Texas senate this century, were also important in burying all but two of the bills. Three more passed in special session despite another filibuster by Gonzalez. One segregation bill that passed provided for local option elections on integration, which evidently meant that the citizens would vote to decide whether the Constitution was in effect in their school district.[41] Governor Daniel signed the bills into law in 1957, but since they were patently unconstitutional, they were never carried out. Thereafter no state Establishment leader waged a racist campaign, stood in a schoolhouse door, or attempted to do much of anything to prevent the inevitable crumbling of segregation. Indeed, in that same year, Senate majority leader Lyndon Johnson broke with southern sentiment and steered a civil-rights bill through Congress. No other Texas senator had cast a vote for civil rights since 1876, but Johnson and Yarborough provided 40 percent of the southern votes for the 1957 voting rights law. (Johnson referred to the measure as a "civil-rights bill" in letters to proponents and a "right to vote" bill in messages to those who feared it was a civil-rights bill.)

Johnson's refusal to sign the notorious southern manifesto, which denounced the Supreme Court's position on integration, caused night riders to burn a cross on the lawn of his ranch. Only five of Texas's twenty-two congressmen signed it. Race ceased being a statewide factor in elections after 1956, and by failing to embrace the South's tactics of massive resistance, Texas drifted further away from southern moorings. The state's governors

15. Price Daniel, Sam Rayburn, and Lyndon Johnson, 1960. *Texas AFL-CIO.*

in the 1960s and 1970s shunned inflammatory racial statements, appointed a number of black and brown Texans to various governmental posts, and generally attempted to cultivate minority support. And minority group members were elected to Congress and the legislature in increasing numbers.[42]

In the pivotal year of 1956 Lyndon Johnson, Sam Rayburn, and Price Daniel took over the state's politics from the Shivercrats. Though they were all backed by the same or virtually identical corporate intrests, the trio were not nearly as interested as Shivers in maintaining a red scare mentality. The public's actions at the polls, especially the election of Yarborough, indicated that the Shivers-Dies-O'Daniel kind of extreme conservatism had expired. Even labor and management had reconciled their differences, for the first time, over an important legislative matter in 1957. Similarly, the spectacular phases of the Establishment takeover of higher education ceased after 1957, just as the active intransigent resistance to the civil-rights movement degenerated into prolonged inimical contrariness. One columnist expressed the feelings of many contemporaries when he credited liberal pressure for having promoted many of the changes that were occurring and that finally "history had to take over."[43]

13

Whither the Establishment?

. . . ruling groups have so inveterate a habit of being wrong that the health of a democratic order demands that they be challenged and constantly compelled to prove their case.

V. O. Key, *Southern Politics,* 1949

"But no matter how appalled you are by what you see down there in that strange chunk of the United States, still, you're interested. Aren't you?"

"Fascinated. But rebelling most of the time."

"What could be more exciting! As long as you're fascinated and as long as you keep on fighting the things you think are wrong, you're living."

Leslie Benedict and her father in
Edna Ferber's *Giant,* 1952

The impact of Establishment rule on the Texas citizenry added another chapter to the long, dismal history of the failure of American states' rights conservatism. Some of the factors that made Texas so conservative became operative only in the primitive years: rapid and turbulent economic change (especially the rise of the oil industry), the use of unprincipled public relations men by politicians, the handiwork of right-wing hucksters, and the newspapers' swing toward reaction. The conjunction of these forces with other underlying ones—"Texanism" and the politically calamitous mingling of traditionalistic and individualistic subcultures with no leavening of the moralistic influence—seemed to ensure that Texas would fail to meet the state responsibilities that go along with state rights. If a government exercises more power than a situation calls for, it is tyrannical, but if a government does too little to promote dignity, the final result will also be tyranny. In its 1944 and 1954 integration decisions, for instance, the Supreme Court performed the functions of the state governments because the states had failed to provide civil rights to all citizens.

The Establishment inherited a situation wherein Texans had accepted a low level of taxation as customary, although Governor Allred had tried to change it. This system was perpetuated and made more regressive. The combined local and state tax burden was 6.4 percent in 1942, eighth lowest in the nation, and had inched up only to 6.7 percent in 1953, twelfth lowest. Long before the general sales tax was adopted in 1961, the corporations saw to it that taxes in Texas were not based on ability to pay but on the people's inability to control the lobby. Selective sales taxes brought in half the total revenue of the state by 1954, while mixed sales and natural resources taxes brought in another 18 percent. The regressive structure (whereby the impact of the tax decreases as income rises) was clothed in the rhetoric of civic duty. As Paul Carrington, at that time immediate past president of the Texas Association of Commerce, wrote to Governor Jester, his organization favored "no new taxes" and urged legislation "only for the general good of all people." In Texas the cry of "no new taxes" amounts to class legislation, since the state taxes its corporations so lightly compared to individuals. Lobbyists and conservatives today like to argue, just as they did twenty years ago, that people pay all taxes, that natural resource taxes are just passed on to consumers. If that were true, then why is it, when such a tax is proposed, that producers immediately protest that they cannot stand further taxes?[1]

The ultimate index of Establishment rule is the level of oil taxation, which, despite repeated attempts by liberals and moderates, has not changed since 1951. Indeed the regulation pipeline portion of the tax has not been altered since 1935. Oil, like most other commodities, can be taxed at different junctures as it moves toward the consumer. Crude oil may be taxed at the wellhead, refined gasoline may be taxed at the refinery or at the service station pump, and oil company income may be subjected to a profits tax. The point of taxation has a decided influence on the state's income and on the distribution of the tax burden. A sales tax on gasoline at the pump is simply incorporated in the price that the car owner pays for fuel. Except for travelers who buy gasoline in Texas, the money the state receives from this levy comes from Texas consumers. A wellhead or refinery tax, however, would become part of the price structure of gasoline wherever it was eventually purchased in the United States. Texas would be allowing other Americans to share the tax burden—all those who purchased gasoline refined from Texas crude (wellhead tax) or in Texas refineries (refinery tax). Conservative journalist Byron Utecht argued in 1949 that if Texas succumbed to temptation and taxed natural resources, other states would retaliate. But Michigan and New York, to take just two examples, had already long since derived income from their taxes on autos and cameras, respectively, thus taxing all the nation's car and camera purchasers, including Texans. By similarly taxing oil production or refining, Texas could generate income for education and other state services while at the same time placing a smaller burden on individual Texas motorists.[2]

Yet Texans in the 1940s and 1950s seemed unaware of a number of salient facts about the oil industry. Historically, for instance, three-fourths of Texas oil was owned by "Wall Street," in the broad usage of that term. Even the so-called independents, such as Humble Oil Company and Magnolia Refinery, were branches of Standard Oil of New Jersey. Also, a low percentage of oil stock was owned by Texans. Nor did the Texas public seem to know or care that the oil lobby, over the years, was in the forefront of the fight to stave off an income tax and, eventually as part of the same battle, to foist off on the state a general sales tax, which it successfully accomplished in 1961. In a sense, Texas has paid an enormous penalty for being so rich in oil.[3]

The taxation of oil, of course, is interrelated with conservation. Texas, according to one geologist in the 1940s, "has permitted a depletion of her natural resources at a rate unequaled in the world's history," but the state seemed peculiarly unaware that this irreplaceable resource (and tax base) would dry up in a few decades. The Establishment position, developed in the 1940s, was summarized by railroad commissioner Olin Culberson while testifying against an oil treaty with Britain. When asked whether there should be any importation of oil from abroad—which would conserve American supplies—Culberson replied, "Not so long as our domestic production, Senator, will take care of our domestic demands."[4] In the oil crunch of the 1970s Americans began paying the price of the Establishment's "drain Texas first" policy.

The proposed treaty, in fact, triggered the founding of the Texas Independent Producers and Royalty Owners Association, which has incessantly agitated for curbs on oil imports. Meanwhile the Railroad Commission, charged with regulating the oil industry, had long been the captive of the regulatees. Two groups of oil producers, in a fit of boosterism, even took out a full-page advertisement in the *Texas Almanac, 1972-1973*, to proclaim, "Since 1891 the Texas Railroad Commission has served the oil industry."[5] The original goal of serving the citizenry and regulating the oil industry seemed to have been lost in the shuffle.

In keeping with its nethermost tax efforts, Texas provided few services for its citizenry. Texas had a low per-capita income, which in turn (according to political science studies) was related to its right-to-work law, an above average number of people not covered by the federal minimum wage, and its lack of an income tax, minimum wage law, merit system, fair employment practices statutes, and interparty political competition. While the Establishment was willing to spend money for highways and farm-to-market roads, its services to people were distinctly secondary as the chart demonstrates:

Texas's Ranking among the States

	1941	1946	1950	1955	1957
Aid to dependent children	39	46	42	43	42
Old age assistance	27	37	37	37	37
Aid to the blind	20	37	36	36	36

	1940-1941	1944-1945	1948-1949	1952-1953	1958-1959
Expense per pupil in public schools	34	35	36	32	32

Moreover, it was the only state generally in the bottom quartile that was urban, industrialized, and rich in natural resources. In the 1940s and 1950s Texas not only ranked first in oil but also in gas, sulfur, cattle, cotton, and wool. (Epitomizing the spirit of the era, one new oil millionaire questioned some of the state's low rankings, but added that if they were true, it meant that Negroes and Mexicans were being counted and thus the figures were of no significance.)[6]

The Establishment not only dispensed economic injustice to Texas consumers and the lower class but also intervened in social activities in an arbitrary and repressive fashion and occasionally tolerated corruption. If it is a government's function to preserve and extend individual freedoms, state and local leaders have no business engaging in political scare tactics, witch hunts, book censorship, the suppression of academic freedom, or the passage of extreme antiunion legislation or loose subversion laws allowing searches and seizures in private homes. Moreover all too often an insensitive ruling elite evolves when, as Lincoln Steffens put it, business seeks "privileges," requiring the corruption (broadly speaking) of public officials—seamier examples being the veterans' land deals and the insurance scandals—and resulting in the merger of business and politics. Or as C. Wright Mills phrased it, today's corporate world is "organized irresponsibility," where "political institutions and economic opportunities are at once concentrated and linked."[7]

The consequences of such political immoderation are not as wicked as they look on paper, however. Lawrence Peter noted with some exaggeration, "neither sound nor unsound proposals can be carried out efficiently because the machinery of government is a vast series of interlocking hierarchies, riddled through and through with incompetence." Boards of regents and investigative commissions, for instance, are often manned by "utter irrelevantists," who do not make the slightest pretense of doing their jobs (though regents can be galvanized into action by a Strickland or a Haley).[8] Moreover, irrelevant or unenforceable laws and rules are simply ignored by both the bureaucracy and the citizens. Thus in Texas controversial books were back in circulation almost as soon as they were allegedly suppressed, University of Texas social science faculty continued voicing liberal sentiments if they pleased, and very few, if any, private homes were raided. Scores of local unions went right on negotiating closed-shop agreements, and, in fact, by 1955 organized labor was growing faster in Texas than anywhere else except possibly California.[9]

The form of present-day Texas politics took shape in the postwar decade. The election pattern for conservative dominion was first established in the 1946 gubernatorial primary and has been repeated in every such Democratic fracas—1954, 1956, 1962, 1968, and 1972—that has not involved incumbents (who are traditionally reelected). Several conservative candidates split the conservative vote in the first Democratic primary, allowing the lone liberal challenger to get into the runoff with the leading conservative. The conservative vote and money and newspapers then coalesce behind the conservative candidate in the second primary, defeating the liberal, who invariably runs out of money and who never had any press support. The conservative survivor is not necessarily the most conservative person in the race, but his views have seldom displeased the interest groups. Senatorial primaries have been more complex, but no nonincumbent liberal has ever won a runoff.

Texas's current three-tiered political structure—comprised of the two Democratic factions and the Republicans—was launched in 1952. Suddenly the Republicans became a party that attempted to win some elections, and they were on the winning side in Texas with the Eisenhower victories. In 1957, for the first time since Reconstruction, the Republican party—operating as a party—determined the outcome of a statewide election in Texas (splitting the conservative vote, allowing Yarborough's triumph). The future appeared bright, especially when the Democrats' internal feuding permitted the Republicans to elect John Tower to the Senate in 1961 and 1966, and he rode in again on Nixon's coattails against a moderate Democrat in 1972. The Texas GOP also elected a few legislators and congressmen, and it pulled over 45 percent of the vote in several gubernatorial and senatorial elections in the 1960s and 1970s. But the Republicans were not able to expand much beyond their country club base in the 1950s, in part because the Eisenhower administration tended to deal with Texas's dominant Establishment Democrats to the disadvantage of the nascent Republicans. During and since that time the Republicans discovered that they cannot promise or deliver anything that Establishment Democrats have not already promised or delivered. Also the Texas GOP does not always seem to be sure that it really wants to approach elections with the serious intent of winning them.[10]

Establishment Democrats disagree so fundamentally with most national party nominees that they often bolt to the Republicans or ignore presidential elections, though they remain in the Democratic party and vote for conservatives in the primaries (if they bolt, they do so after the primary). The bolters can be traced back to J. Evetts Haley in 1936 through the Regulars and Dixiecrats of the 1940s, but they became more significant in 1952 when Governor Shivers endorsed Eisenhower for president. Shivers has continued taking this stand except when Lyndon Johnson ran in 1964. More typical has been the politics of loyalist lassitude practiced by Johnson in 1952, 1956, 1968, and 1972, Daniel in 1956, John Connally in 1968, and Dolph Briscoe in 1972.

It was in the mid-1950s that the Establishment began to digest several hard political facts. While the conservative elite had successfully muted economic issues (as best they could) in such crucial elections as those in 1946, 1952, and 1954, the election of Yarborough demonstrated that workers, minorities, and small farmers could turn out in sufficient numbers to defeat the conservatives, especially if there was a Republican drawing off votes from conservative Democrats. Texans, in fact, might even be as liberal as northerners on economic questions, a notion that no Establishment leader ever had much reason to ponder. In a classical study in 1956, V. O. Key determined that adults from the southern and border states were at least as progressive on economic matters as nonsoutherners, but that the South seemed more conservative because blacks and whites in the working class usually did not vote. Three political scientists studying Texas politics reached the same decision, and scattered turnout percentages in appendixes 7, 9-11, and 15 seem to sustain that conclusion.[11]

Until the mid-1950s labor and minority groups had been shut off from meaningful participation in the governing of Texas, providing faint comfort for the pluralist school of political science, which holds that a determined group can exert meaningful influence on the political system. Indeed, though liberal Democrats put together their labor-minority-loyalist coalition in the 1940s and early 1950s and overcame their lack of money and media support to score some victories in 1956-1957, even those triumphs were both the alpha and omega of the liberal movement. The liberals never won another important statewide race for any post other than Yarborough's. But in the mid-1950s Texas did at least develop a pluralist politics, since the labor liberals supported a more or less full-time leadership cadre, a fairly effective propaganda machine, a network of internal communication, and a membership that thought it could win elections on occasion. The new moderate Establishment leadership was sophisticated enough to finesse the labor-liberals, to allow some of them to influence public policy on occasion, and thus to divert those who seemed amenable to compromise. The Democratic factions have been able to put it all together on behalf of presidential nominees whenever a Texas Establishment figure has been on the ticket, 1960 and 1964, or whenever the Democratic ticket is headed by a candidate who is not perceived as left of center, as in 1976.

A political scientist, Martha Dickenson, recently applied aggregate data analysis, showing the relationship between voting and socioeconomic factors, to every Texas election from 1944 through 1972. She discovered that V. O. Key's prediction of emerging ideological clashes, with liberals and conservatives battling along socioeconomic lines, was borne out in Texas politics from 1944 through 1956. Given the absence of precinct studies, and the difficulty in ferreting out precinct returns, Dickenson confined her analysis to county returns. The counties providing the greatest conservative support in that period were located in south Texas, the far west, and along the Gulf Coast. Liberal counties lay in central, north central, and east Texas (though the latter counties were certainly not liberal on racial issues). Compared to the conservative counties, the liberal counties had lower incomes, less urbanization, more minorities, and more manufacturing. But a dramatic realignment occurred after the 1956 elections. Liberal support shifted to the southern, southwestern, and scattered south-central portions of the state, as well as to the Gulf Coast. The Panhandle, west-central counties, and scattered ones in the southwest became conservative bastions. Moreover the liberal-conservative economic cleavage could no longer be identified. Liberal counties remained higher in manufacturing and percentages of minorities and impoverished people, but surprisingly they also had significantly higher percentages of white-collar workers and of people making fifteen thousand dollars or more per year. Ordered political competition and the stable, dependable vote for Democratic conservative governors that prevailed from the mid-1940s through the early 1950s had been replaced by a state of flux. After 1956 the electorate shifted radically to support candidates of varying ideological persuasion.[12]

Also nearly half of the conservative counties from 1944 through 1956 were 30 percent or more Mexican-American, but after that fully half the liberal counties were 30 percent or more Mexican-American. During and after the 1956 elections, these counties also turned far more Democratic in presidential races than they had been previously. Ultimately some of them broke free of Anglo-Establishment manipulation. The German-American counties also moved away from Republicanism toward the state mean Democratic vote.[13]

It would not necessarily be expected that Dickenson's findings would be reflected in the returns from the ideologically motivated, interest group precincts listed in the appendixes, but some shifting is detectable in these precincts. The most important post-1957 alteration is that Establishment Democrats have encroached on the traditionally liberal domains in the urban labor and ethnic boxes. All the premier Establishment leaders of the 1960s formed alliances with factions within the black, Mexican-American, and labor communities. The Establishment was first obliged to court these liberal groups because conservative participation in the Democratic primaries declined some 281,000 between 1956 and 1962. Indeed John Connally survived the 1962 gubernatorial primary against liberal Don Yarborough only because of inroads among the minorities and in the brass-collar counties, especially in central and north-central Texas.[14] Establishment trespassing on formerly liberal turf was also important in Preston Smith's triumph over Don Yarborough in 1968 and Dolph Briscoe's over Frances Farenthold in 1972. (Contrast the post-1957 elections in appendixes 11 through 13 with earlier returns.)

The other noticeable shift involved the destination of those affluent conservatives who dropped out of the Democratic party. Beginning particularly with the special elections to the United States Senate in 1957 and 1961, Republicanism gradually prevailed in the wealthy urban precincts, especially in Dallas, Houston, and the Panhandle-Plains cities. During the heyday of the Establishment, Republicanism among the rich was mostly confined to presidential races. In November 1956, for instance, Price Daniel lost only one small precinct by two votes to his Republican opponent out of 311 boxes in Harris and Tarrant counties combined. Lyndon Johnson evidently had the distinction of being the first Establishment politico to lose the urban silk-stocking precincts to a Republican. Seven of the richest boxes in Tarrant County, for example (precincts 76, 81, 95, 108, 115, 116, and 117), gave Jack Porter 4,012 votes to Johnson's 2,115 in 1948. Johnson in 1948, however, could have been perceived by many of the wealthy as a liberal. Wallace Savage, running for congressman in Dallas in 1954, was the first conservative Democrat who was a victim of wealthy Republicanism. Bruce Alger carried the nineteen richest precincts in the county against Savage and thirty-seven of the wealthiest fifty.[15] Republicanism became quite common in affluent precincts in the 1960s and 1970s (see appendixes 10-15). During those years Texas elected and reelected a number of GOP stalwarts, but Republicans seemed to reach a ceiling between ten and twenty house members and four or five state senators and congressmen. This limited movement in the direction of a two-party system is ideological to the extent that it is motivated by the belief that the national Republican party is more conservative than the national Democratic party.

The Texas electorate probably still casts some votes along economic lines, if and when the voters can perceive ideological differences between the candidates. Indeed one explanation for the lessening of ideological voting is that several of the leaders of the new moderate Establishment since 1956 have not provided much of an ideological target. By fluctuating between liberal and conservative positions, these leaders have been perceived by the bulk of the electorate as flexible, though they were often perceived as vacillating by hard-core liberals and conservatives. Lyndon Johnson, who became the dominant figure in the state in 1956, was mentioned earlier as having a voting record that embraced "countryside" liberalism. Liberals chastised him and Speaker Rayburn (who died in 1961) for not going far or fast on such issues as integration, federal aid to education, or repeal of the poll tax, but they were never as rigid on these issues as most southern conservatives. On the other hand, they proved their Establishment credentials by voting for bills that provided tax relief for corporations, especially the oil and gas industries. Also, with that one exception in the spring of 1956, they always came down hard on the side of conservatives at the state Democratic conventions.[16]

Price Daniel, who was elected governor in 1956 and served three terms, supported most corporate programs and always worked for conservative policies at state conventions. Yet he fought the general sales tax relentlessly, calling instead for a tax bill that would have been half on business and half on sales. When he saw that the corporate lobbies were determined to ram through a retail sales tax, he openly indicted the "interstate oil and gas lobby," but he did not veto the bill. For several years he tried to persuade the legislature to pass an abandoned property act, similar to those in thirty-six other states, which would have allowed the state treasury to requisition unclaimed bank and utility company deposits. Citing proof that dozens of banks had seized dormant funds with unconscionable service charges, he bitterly criticized the banking lobby for opposing and defeating the bill. Later he got it passed. Daniel and his legislative allies put through a lobby registration law; it was not as strong as the governor wanted, but it was the first such law in twenty-seven years. He also reorganized the Board of Insurance Commissioners and secured a water plan that was the first of its kind in Texas.[17]

An even more significant and exciting demonstration that Texas was breaking away from omniscient conservative domination was the election of Ralph Yarborough to the United States Senate in 1957. At one postelection party a veteran Yarborough supporter harkened back to Jimmie Allred's last election in 1936 and said, "It's been a long, long time." A Humble oil lobbyist who visited a riotous Yarborough headquarters on election night was puzzled and noted, "No big shots there, just people." It was an entirely new phenomenon to him and to the rest of postwar Texas.[18]

Yarborough, an out-and-out liberal, fought and voted for virtually all labor, education, and welfare measures. He sponsored Senate passage of the minimum wage expansion bill of 1966, the Occupational, Safety, and Health Act of 1970, and federal funding for bilingual educational programs. He authored the GI bill for cold-war veterans, a struggle that took years, since the executive branch and many other congressmen opposed it. He also fathered the Padre Island National Seashore and laid much of the groundwork for the Big Thicket National Forest. His long survival in a state that continued to be conservative seemed to defy reason. Aside from pointing out that politics often defy reason, one explanation offered for his success was that he presented a nonideological image. According to one authority, Yarborough's campaign manager in 1958 deliberately set up the candidate to "masquerade as a middle-of-the-roader." Also Yarborough often voted against liberal-backed foreign aid measures and was careful not to attack the oil and gas industry. Dickenson notes that Yarborough consistently surpassed the base liberal support available in Texas and obviously drew many of his votes because of other factors besides liberalism.[19] Her statistics, however, do not actually prove that he was able to do this because of a nonideological approach.

Perhaps Yarborough was the beneficiary of a new random factor in the state's post-1956 politics, unleashed as the grip of ideology loosened. Yarborough seemed to owe his victories in part to the fates or luck. He won in 1957 because the conservatives split their votes and the law for special elections did not provide for a runoff. The *Dallas Morning News* observed logically that conservatism was still dominant in Texas and that "Yarborough the liberal" could not win in 1958 unless Texans changed their thinking "materially." His opponent was "Dollar" Bill Blakley, one of the richest men in the nation, who hewed to the conservative line of the day by denouncing labor, integration, and federal aid to education. Yarborough trounced him. One decisive factor was the surprise endorsement of Rayburn, who may have resented the Blakley campaigners' spreading rumors that he silently favored their man. Another bit of good fortune was the war scare in Lebanon, which occurred in the waning days of the Texas primary. Yarborough borrowed navy films on Lebanon, which he showed on television just three days before the balloting, giving the people a true picture of the situation and calming their widespread fear of war. Republicans thought that they would nail the "socialist Yarborough" in the general election, but did not even come close.[20] It also just happened that 1958 was a liberal year around the country. Millions of Americans voted against the Republican recession, and Texans are hardly immune to such trends.

Yarborough's next election was in 1964, shortly after Johnson became president. Johnson wanted credentials as a liberal and needed labor support for his programs in Congress. He believed that he might not get either if his Establishment friends in Texas knocked off the prolabor senator. Governor John Connally was anxious for reactionary valley congressman Joe Kilgore to wipe out Yarborough in the primary, but Johnson squelched it.[21] Even then Yarborough might have lost to the vigorous Republican conservative, George Bush, except that, once again, it was a liberal year all over the nation. It was the year of the Goldwater debacle, when the Democrats blitzed almost every state. Yarborough rolled in with the Johnson tide. The next time Yarborough came up, 1970, he lost many former supporters, especially among union and east Texas voters, to Establishment conservative Lloyd Bentsen, Jr. Bentsen, who painted Yarborough as an opponent of school prayers and a devotee of extensive integration, defeated the senator handily. But 1970 was a conservative "law and order" year across the land. The Nixon administration was at its peak strength, and even if Yarborough had survived the primary against Establishment conservative Lloyd Bentsen, Jr., he undoubtedly would have lost the general election to George Bush. Bentsen was correct when he observed that Yarborough was too liberal for Texas.

If the Establishment cannot count on the stable electoral support of the 1944-1956 period, it is necessary to ask why no liberal candiate other than Yarborough has ever won a major statewide election. Defections to the Establishment form part of the answer, but also the progressives are coming closer to winning. Between 1942, when Allred almost beat O'Daniel, and 1954, when Yarborough got within range of Shivers, no one running on a liberal platform pulled over a third of the votes of his Establishment opponent in any statewide race. But since 1954 every gubernatorial race not involving an incumbent has been fairly close between liberal and conservative candidates (on two occasions incumbents were ultimately displaced by other conservatives). Among the closer ones, Yarborough almost edged Daniel (1956), Don Yarborough polled 49 percent of the votes against Connally (1962) and 45 percent against Preston Smith (1968), and Frances (Sissy) Farenthold threw a real scare into Briscoe (1972). Sooner or later the liberals will either win the governorship or, more likely, Establishment candidates will edge ever deeper into the moderate camp and compromise the liberals' electoral efforts.

The two governors who followed Daniel, to be sure, showed few signs of drift toward moderation, though both made some inroads with factions within labor and minority groups. One was John Connally, who served in conservative Democratic fashion from 1963 to 1969. On fiscal matters alone, for instance, he and the legislature lowered the taxes on state banks and sulfur companies, raised taxes on clothing items costing ten dollars or less, doubled the sales tax, and granted the highest legalized interest rates in the nation. There was no evidence that he was concerned that Texas was the last of the ten largest states without a minimum wage law or that Texas ranked last in weekly compensation for injured workers. Connally seemed to exemplify another theory explaining the possible absence of ideological voting: that the post-1956 Texas political system is a battleground of personalities. It has been hypothesized that factions can emerge based primarily on the personal magnetism of particular candidates. Most candidates have at least tried to "build personal followings by employing the image-making techniques of personal relations firms, survey research, and television."[22]

Connally's administration, in fact, may have been little more than an expensive mirage, which began with Billy Graham prayers, parades with floats, drill teams, and mounted posses. There followed years of charisma, beautiful speeches, and publicity. The two accomplishments of which he was most proud, the creation of the Coordinating Board of Higher Education (given the controversial power to limit courses and degree plans) and of Hemisfair, were rammed through because of his domineering personality. The coordinating board has been widely ignored by legislators, colleges, and governors, including Connally himself. Hemisfair was originally designed to be a people's-oriented fair, but degenerated into the $10 million "Connally's Carnival," planned "by big business, for big business and to profit big business." The building supposed to display historical and cultural items featured a wall-sized Texas flag in glaring neon and a huge color portrait of Connally.[23]

After being wounded by Oswald during the Kennedy assassination, Connally was probably unbeatable, even without the press agentry hoopla. The manufacturing, oil, banking, and insurance lobbies begged him to run again, but he decided to retire from a post that bored him.[24] The Establishment has not been quite the same since Connally's departure, especially since his conservative successor stigmatized the state government.

Governor Preston Smith, 1969-1973, and the 1969 legislature were so inept and so desirous of avoiding the anger of the corporate lobbies that they could not even come up with a tax plan to finance the state budget. Forced to call a special session, Smith joined with Speaker of the House Gus Mutscher and Lieutenant Governor Ben Barnes in support of a bill to place food under the general sales tax. This proposal was regressive, since it would have penalized the lower- and middle-income groups, who spend a larger proportion of their income on food than do the wealthy. The food tax squeaked through the senate, 15 to 14, but passage was delayed by a weekend filibuster led by Oscar Mauzy of Dallas. The crucial postponement allowed a public furor to arise, and when the house convened on Monday, the representatives were deluged with letters and telegrams sent by irate taxpayers. The "housewives' revolt" induced the house to kill the measure, which was a defeat for the lobby and the Establishment.[25]

Also in 1969 Frank Sharp, who controlled the National Bankers Life Insurance Company and the Sharpstown State Bank in Houston, successfully lobbied a bill through the legislature that was designed to exempt state banks from the regulations of the Federal Deposit Insurance Corporation. Meanwhile Smith, Mutscher, and a few other state officeholders bought NBL stock through the same broker with loans from the same bank (Sharpstown), which asked for no collateral. A few weeks later most of the officials sold the stock at identical (now inflated) prices at the same time to the same buyer, Jesuit fathers. The religious order was gulled by Sharp into buying the stock at about five dollars per share above the then-current market price. Though Governor Smith was one of the big winners, with a fast profit of over sixty-two thousand dollars, he vetoed Sharp's bill. After these revelations became public in 1971, Smith, Mutscher, and others were scourged from office in 1972.[26]

While the Establishment obviously missed the presence of someone with Connally's acumen, no permanent damage was done. Citizens unfamiliar with Texas politics probably assumed that the Sharpstown scandal at least crippled the lobby, but such was not the case. At the height of the scandal the business lobby defeated a corporate income tax by twenty-three votes in the house, then pushed through a tax bill—which took effect immediately— that put most of its $662 million burden directly on consumers. The legislature of 1973 did adopt a good deal of ethics legislation, however: a financial disclosure law, a campaign reporting measure that requires the names and addresses of all contributors, and a so-called lobby control law that provides for no ethics commission and no disclosure of lobbyists or beneficiaries. The corporate lobby is quite able to live with it.[27]

By the time Smith left office, Texas raised 70.1 percent of its taxes through the regressive general and selective sales taxes, compared to the average state's 55.5 percent. From Connally's last term through Smith's two terms, state sales taxes leaped over 41 percent per thousand dollars of income compared to a 22 percent average among all states. And 659 Texas cities had added a 1 percent local sales tax. The combined regressive effect of this structure was revealed in a 1972 survey of Dallas, where a family of four making $2,000 a year paid 12.6 percent of its income in state and local sales and property taxes (excluding selective sales taxes); a family that made $5,000 paid 6.9 percent, $10,000, 4.6 percent, $15,000, 4.6 percent, and $25,000, 3.8 percent. Texas was one of the four remaining states without a corporate income tax, though it did have a corporate franchise tax.[28]

The recent administration of Dolph Briscoe (1973-1979) did very little that the corporations found objectionable. In fact, it did little at all except try to hold the line on taxes. Briscoe took credit for avoiding new taxes but never mentioned that public education acts had required local property tax increases. Since Briscoe doubled expenditures by executive administered departments after four years in office, his claims of good fiscal management actually hinged on double-digit inflation and increased revenues traceable to the high price of oil and gas. His school finance proposal of 1977 would have given the 272 richest school districts more additional state aid, $230 per pupil, than it would the 273 poorest districts. The governor's request for $825 million in new highway aid—before any other state needs were even considered—was a capitulation to the highway lobbies,

prompting one senator to suggest changing the state flower from the blue-
bonnet to the concrete cloverleaf. The legislature altered the governor's
requests but did not change the thrust of them. Despite advances, then, in
political civility, education, and civil rights, the tax structure and governmental priorities of the mature Establishment of the 1960s and 1970s are
almost as retrograde as in the otherwise darker political period of the 1940s
and 1950s.[29]

There were, however, indications of creeping moderation in the Briscoe
government. Occasionally the governor appointed a superior person to a
state post, such as Joe Christie to the insurance board, though he selected a
man who had moved to California for one position and a dead man for
another. Briscoe's lieutenants ran the fairest state conventions in modern
times. As the first governor to bring organized labor wholly into the Establishment, Briscoe and his administration may serve as a bridgeway to a
more liberal future, at least in appointments. Presumably Establishment
Democrats are being pulled toward moderation by the lure of slowly growing liberal strength and pushed by the slow increment of conservative deser-
tions to the Republicans (John Connally's 1973 defection being the most
spectacular). The long-term effects of industrialization and urbanization
(including a fairly heavy influx of managerial, professional, and technical
people from Republican states) are supposedly fostering a two-party system.[30] By the late 1960s court-ordered reappointment had smashed the rural
conservative suzerainty over the legislature, which had slowed effective
political organization of industrial areas. About the same time, court-ordered
single-member districting began thwarting city oligarchs in their customary
selection of entire legislative delegations.

In this story of state politics, little has been written about local elites,
but theirs is a necessary supporting role for the Establishment, especially in
picking legislators. The powers of the local establishments also seem to be
disbursing. In Dallas, for instance, the city fathers, who formally organized
in 1937 as the Dallas Citizens Council, historically controlled the city's bond
issue elections, legislative delegations, the mayorship, and local congressional seats. But the federal courts ordered single-member districts for state
senators in 1966, state representatives in 1972, and city councilmen in 1975,
each of which was bitterly fought by such current Establishment leaders as
the multimillionaire businessmen John Stemmons and Bob Cullum. Local
leaders decry the corrupt ward government that will allegedly make Dallas
into another Chicago, but several of these leaders over the years have wielded
clout that Mayor Daley would have envied. The whole city of Dallas, in a
sense, was just one big ward run by rich, white, conservative Democrats.
In ordering individual districts, the courts noted that blacks, Mexican-
Americans, liberals, and Republicans had been excluded from representation. They are now represented. The Establishment was also shaken in 1971
by the defeat of its mayoralty candidate, who was backed by the two Dallas

Once in a large state not so far away, there was a governor shrouded in mystery.

When the people would cry out, their answer from the mysterious governor would sometimes be silence...

GOVERNOR! THE SOUTH TEXAS FARM WORKERS ARE REVOLTING!

YOU CAN SAY THAT AGAIN...

...and sometimes be a profound enigma.

GOVERNOR, THE SCHOOLS ARE OUT OF MONEY...

VERY WELL. IF IT'S HIGHWAYS THEY WANT, THEN HIGHWAYS THEY SHALL HAVE.

16. The Briscoe Administration, 1977. *Cartoon by Ben Sargent, copyright* Austin American Statesman, *reprinted by permission.*

dailies and had a campaign fund of $250,000, at the hands of a sportscaster who spent about $15,000. Another blow was the 1972 defeat of Congressman Earle Cabell by Republican Alan Steelman. One of the issues was Steelman's opposition to building the Trinty River barge canal, a long-time favored project of the Establishment, and the canal bonds were voted down the next year. The Establishment attempted a massive telephone campaign the night before the balloting, but its traditional tactic of intimidating election workers lacked the old magic. Republic National Bank, for instance, asked its employees to man the phones—240 showed up, but 148 did not.[31]

In 1976 the old-line Establishment wanted to defeat a gadfly businessman in the mayor's race and did so in an extremely close and disputed election, but the victory hardly seems likely to revive the elite's glory days of the 1940s and 1950s. And though Steelman declined to run for reelection in 1976, he was replaced by a progressive Democrat, the first liberal congressman in the city's history. And in 1978 a conservative Democratic congressman, over half of whose district lay in Dallas County, was ousted by a moderate.

There is evidently some prospect for progressive change in Texas, and it
lies with the state's new, young, second-echelon leadership. None of them is
a liberal, but each is making moves that would have been political suicide
for straight-out Establishment predecessors. Attorney General John Hill
was an outspoken advocate of strong utility commission regulation during
the 1975 legislative session and simultaneously asserted his own regulatory
powers in a successful fight to lower Southwestern Bell's intrastate telephone
rate increase. Hill also—quietly—did as much or more than any other person to put together the new state constitution (which was rejected at the
polls). In 1973, after market prices for gas skyrocketed, Hill and land commissioner Bob Armstrong filed fair market value lawsuits against twenty-seven
major gas producers. The gas and oil royalty on state lands was raised
from one-sixth to one-fifth of market value, and the state is even taking
royalty payments in gas, which it will market directly. These settlements
added an immediate $30 million to the Permanent School and University
Funds. Armstrong has also initiated an environmental review of all state
tracts up for lease and has generally changed the Land Office from a record-
keeping and collection agency to one that actually manages the land. Joe
Christie, appointed chairman of the state insurance board early in 1973,
reduced casualty insurance rates, cracked down on deceptive insurance
advertising, attempted to make insurance policies readable, forced Allstate
Insurance to pay $4 million in policy dividends that were owed to Texas
motorists, and successfully lobbied for the legalization of health maintenance
organizations (prepaid medical plans with the emphasis on preventive
services). State comptroller Bob Bullock launched a massive reorganization
of his agency, breaking up the empires that had proliferated under the
previous incumbent. Bullock's most spectacular actions have been the clos-
ings of some 575 businesses around the state (as of mid-January 1978) for
cheating the treasury out of sales tax revenues. Their liabilities totaled over
$3 million, most of which will be recovered either by payments from the
businesses or by public auction of their goods. The comptroller has even
suggested that the state stands to lose billions of dollars in possible income
by letting major oil companies rather than a public body build and own a
"superport" on the gulf. Bullock enjoys considerable support among both
liberals and business interests, but it is difficult to walk that tightrope for a
long period. Price Daniel, Jr., son of the former governor, presided as a
reform-minded speaker of the house after the Sharpstown infamy and
vainly attempted to curb the exorbitant powers of the speaker by serving
only one term. His political retirement was only temporary. Each of these
five men is ambitious, and it speaks well for the state that one or more of
them will probably be governor someday. Lieutenant Governor Bill Hobby,
who probably has the fewest progressive instincts among this group, is at
least fair-minded and is capable of listening and compromising.[32]

The defeat of Price Daniel, Jr., for attorney general in the Democratic primary in May 1978 staggers his political career, while Joe Christie's demise in the senatorial primary marks his political retirement. Armstrong and Bullock enjoyed uncontested victories for their current posts and will make their moves in the future. John Hill's stunning upset of Dolph Briscoe in the gubernatorial primary places Hill well on the road to the governor's mansion. Though Hill will avoid taxing the corporations, he will undoubtedly reorient the state's spending away from highways and toward education. Those who guide the state, however, will have to accomplish great deeds in order to overcome the heritage of the demagogues and the slow progress since then, for the dignity of Texans has rarely been advanced in the political arena.

Thus, the dangers of the historian treading into the swamp of contemporary politics are obvious. The relatively progressive second echelon leadership has been shattered, not only by the defeats of Daniel and Christie but also by the public revelation of Bullock's ill health, the realization that Bob Armstrong probably cannot raise the several million dollars that are evidently necessary to wage a successful campaign for the highest offices in Texas, and the razor-thin, spectacular triumph by Republican Bill Clements over John Hill in the general election of November 1978. Hill was victimized by the polls that showed him way ahead, low voter turnout—especially in minority precincts (see appendix 15)—Clements's slick seven-million-dollar campaign, and specifically Clements's success in portraying himself as the conservative in the race against a big-spending liberal. Richard Nixon proclaimed Clements's election as the nation's most significant Republican victory in a generation, but it does not necessarily herald meaningful political change within Texas's Establishment politics. It is more apparent than ever that big money distorts Texas campaigns and limits political access to the rich or to those whose beliefs cater to the rich. Also, while Clements's coattails helped John Tower slip back into the Senate by an eyelash margin, there is no evidence that Clements will make any more effort than Tower to foster a genuine two-party system in the state. The abrasive Dallas oilman's primary commitment seems to be to recruit conservative Democrats and Republicans in the project of slashing state expenditures. About the only hopeful sign on the political horizon in Texas in 1979 is the possibility that public opinion may force the governor and the legislature to enact a tax on oil and gas that leave the state, but perhaps even that would be a case of too little, too late. In a very real sense, Texas's natural resources have already been frittered away, and the politicians cannot bring them back.

As the first Republican governor of Texas in 105 years, Bill Clements may profit by recalling that his GOP predecessor, who was also elected by a very slim margin, served one four-year term and was then run out of town by popular demand. On the other hand, Clements can rest easy with the knowledge that his future potential opponents—Lieutenant Governor Hobby, Speaker of the House Billy Clayton, and Attorney General Mark White—are all about as conservative as the governor and arouse no enthusiasm among progressive elements of the population. They may well fall prey to one of those crippling problems that plagued Texas Republicans for so many years—failure to offer a meaningful alternative.

Appendixes

The locations of the precincts listed in twelve of the following appendixes were pinpointed in commissioners' court minutes, lists of voting sites in newspapers, precinct analyses in the papers of Margaret Carter of Fort Worth, the late George Lambert of Dallas, and the Texas AFL-CIO, and in Lance Tarrance, Jr., ed., *Texas Precinct Votes '66* and *Texas Precinct Votes '68*. The ethnic and economic designations are derived from those same precinct analyses, occasional newspaper stories, and interviews with veteran political activists. No statistical analysis was employed, but the designations in Dallas in the 1950s correlate very well with the census tract data revealed by Bernard Cosman in his master's thesis, "The Republican Congressman from Dallas" (University of Alabama, 1958).

Although precincts may retain the same numbers through the years, their boundary lines may well be altered, and, of course, neighborhoods may deteriorate or improve economically or change in ethnic makeup. The Park Cities precincts in Dallas have changed their numbers several times and their boundary lines on occasion, but they are always identifiable and have been among the county's handful of wealthiest precincts since their founding in the 1910s and 1920s. Precinct 115, Westover Hills in Tarrant County, has kept the same number and boundaries since its establishment in 1943 and is still one of the richest in the county. The same appears to be true of several Harris County boxes organized at least by 1940: 87 and 133 (West University Place), 89 (South Side Place), 40, 143, and 148 (Rice University area), and 135 (River Oaks area). On the other hand, Fort Worth's two Texas Christian University area boxes—81 and 108—are rather smaller than they were in the 1940s, but they are still the heart of the old precincts. They are much less conservative in the 1970s than in the 1940s because of an influx of both young people and the aged into apartment houses.

The black precincts in Fort Worth kept their numbers but probably changed their boundaries somewhat over the years, while those in Dallas were altered drastically both in borders and enumeration. All black boxes are nevertheless well identified in any given year, and all are evidently over

90 percent black. At least four black precincts in Harris County retained their same numbers and roughly the same boundaries between 1946 and 1966: precincts 24, 25, 47, and 48.

The labor boxes are the most tenuously labeled. Probably the majority of voters in the Jefferson County labor wards represented organized labor, mostly oil workers. The Harris County labor precincts of the 1940s and 1950s (including oil workers), the Dallas labor precincts (with auto workers), and the Fort Worth labor boxes of the same period (including machinists and packinghouse workers) may have averaged a third union labor, with the rest being working-class white. In Fort Worth in the late 1950s and early 1960s, according to labor leaders Frank Barron and Garland Ham, the labor precincts were changing into lower income and nonunion working-class boxes. The packinghouses were closing, and good union contracts at General Dynamics and Bell Helicopter triggered a dispersal of union workers to the more affluent suburbs. The Dallas labor precincts at the Ford plant (218 and 222) became minority boxes in the 1960s and early 1970s after the plant closed, according to Dallas AFL-CIO Secretary-Treasurer Gene Freeland. The labor precincts in appendix 13 are best described as working-class white, with some union labor, and by 1972 they were about 20 percent black. Of the Harris County labor boxes used in the appendixes, the ship channel precincts (64 and 66) were abandoned by refinery people in the 1960s and early 1970s and are becoming minority boxes. Galena Park (81) and Pelly (101) have remained working-class white, infused with many union families, according to Ceole Speight of the Harris County AFL-CIO.

Precincts are the smallest voting units, and a rigorous analysis of them during an election is far more valuable than a county study. Considering population turnover through the years, however, along with shifting precinct boundaries, a limited number of examples, the imprecise "silk stocking" and "labor" designations used herein, and a paucity of census data support, these appendixes should not be considered anything more than suggestions or hints of voting behavior among particular urban groups.

One valuable source reached me too late to influence the appendixes: Numan Bartley and Hugh Graham, *Southern Politics and the Second Reconstruction* (Baltimore, 1975). Page 43 contains supplementary race and class data from Fort Worth and Waco regarding the 1954 gubernatorial primary (appendix 8) and the 1957 senatorial election (appendix 11), and page 135 illuminates Houston precinct returns in the 1968 governor's race (appendix 14.) In appendix 15 the Tarrant County labor precincts are working-class white, with a heavy sprinkling of United Auto Workers, from the Arlington east side, while those in Dallas are from the white sector of Pleasant Grove as of 1978.

Dallas, Park Cities Area	Presidential Election, November 1940		Democratic Senatorial Primary, July 1942			Second Democratic Senatorial Primary, August 1942	
Precincts	**FDR**	**Willkie**	**Moody**	**Allred**	**O'Daniel**	**Allred**	**O'Daniel**
26	573	274	196	127	114	292	156
59	853	549	323	222	170	460	193
60 ⎫ Highland	405	927	443	138	178	399	274
61 ⎬ Park	396	526	293	109	119	305	171
62 ⎭	398	527	273	104	112	291	160
63	882	782	472	318	198	659	268
72	602	589	400	293	166	588	228
90			117	38	58	112	87
93	47	2	86	39	42	104	53
118	643	612	392	198	170	481	226
Totals	4,799	4,788	2,995	1,586	1,327	3,691	1,816
Percentages	50.1	49.9	50.7	26.8	22.5	67.0	33.0
Dallas County returns & percentages	49,431 / 74.9	16,574 / 25.1	12,242 / 31.3	12,290 / 31.5	14,536 / 37.2	21,450 / 58.5	15,201 / 41.5
Fort Worth, Colonial Club-Westover Hills sector							
81	444	294	253	167	95	322	141
95	329	412	262	140	117	257	193
108	501	233	186	176	91	308	129
115			33	6	28	22	27
116			35	27	7	48	25
Totals	1,274	939	769	516	338	957	515
Percentages	57.6	42.4	47.4	31.8	20.8	65.0	35.0
Tarrant County returns & percentages	35,615 / 82.7	7,474 / 17.3	8,902 / 29.4	12,101 / 39.9	9,330 / 30.8	17,640 / 63.4	10,184 / 36.6
State returns & percentages	905,156 / 81	211,707 / 19	178,471 / 18.4	317,501 / 32.7	475,541 / 49	433,203 / 49	451,359 / 51

The above silk-stocking precincts include all of those that Willkie won in the two counties. Election results are from the *Official Returns* in the county clerks' offices. The wealthy nature of the Dallas precincts was confirmed by Gene Freeland, Dan Wicker, and the George Lambert Papers, those in Fort Worth by Margaret Carter, the Margaret Carter Papers, and Ben Procter.

Houston Precincts, 1942, 1944, 1946

Precincts	Democratic Senatorial Primary, July 1942			Presidential Election, November 1944			Democratic Gubernatorial Primary, July 1946		
Minority and labor	Moody	Allred	O'Daniel	FDR	Dewey	Regulars	Jester	Rainey	Others
24							123	876	
25							4	369	
30							276	829	
47							36	226	
48							17	1,720	
75							213	546	
85							250	368	
66 ⎫	56	380	256	1,114	93	131	187	312	
81 ⎬ labor				886	79	70	362	643	
101 ⎪				568	37	97	228	273	
64 ⎭	40	359	168	792	81	92	250	233	
Totals	96	739	424	3,360	290	390	1,946	6,395	
Percentages	7.6	58.7	33.7	83.2	7.2	9.6	23.3	76.7	
White upper class and professional									
40	182	217	201	427	219	511	498	164	
129	28	49	56	80	51	89	112	28	
148	86	175	158	562	290	853	678	190	
143				769	317	1,028	1,023	276	
136				989	314	537	694	250	
89	57	93	64	170	81	155	189	64	
133				1,113	310	566	714	231	
87				762	325	707	879	328	
135 ⎫ River				446	330	1,617	778	92	
155 ⎭ Oaks							534	58	
Totals	353	534	479	5,318	2,237	6,063	6,099	1,681	
Percentages	25.8	39.1	35.1	39.1	16.4	44.5	78.4	21.6	
Harris County returns &	8,190	31,408	22,111	71,077	11,843	21,095	34,010	27,587	20,759
percentages	13.3	50.9	35.8	68.3	11.4	20.3	55.2	44.8	

Most 1942 precinct results are either unknown or, in the first group, do not measure the minority vote, since blacks could not vote then. The 1944 results are available, but it is not known what percentage of the vote was black at the time. Every Harris County precinct in which the Regulars had a plurality is included here. A few precincts in both the Jester and Rainey camps had more one-sided margins than those listed above, but their composition and location were not well identified. The also-ran candidates were omitted from the 1946 computations. They took almost 20 percent in the labor precincts, but considerably less in the black and silk-stocking boxes. Precinct information comes from interviews with Franklin Harbach, John Crossland, and Louis Kestenburg, from the *Houston Post*, July 27, 1942, July 29-30, 1946, *Houston Chronicle*, July 24, 1942, July 28-30, 1946, *Houston Press*, August 23, 1946, and Harris County *Official Returns*, 1944.

Dallas County Urban Precincts, 1944, 1946, 1948

Precincts	Presidential Election, November 1944			Second Democratic Gubernatorial Primary, August 1946		Presidential Election, November 1948			
White upper class and professional	FDR	Dewey	Regulars	Jester	Rainey	HST	Thurmond	Dewey	Wallace
26	696	287	111	528	185	372	110	479	6
59	1,034	647	215	642	176	223	90	412	4
60	565	864	439	1,209	171	135	93	763	2
61	448	416	215	659	145	227	159	608	11
62	421	457	216	698	137	209	168	734	6
63	1,071	919	362	1,225	331	339	200	845	10
72	908	928	381	959	182	412	178	1,243	8
90	526	275	98	445	143	458	97	476	5
93	247	373	233	558	83	152	97	540	6
118	801	793	259	1,056	259	252	181	943	5
122				381	68	234	172	857	9
Totals	6,717	5,959	2,529	8,360	1,880	3,013	1,545	7,900	72
Percentages	44.2	39.2	16.6	81.6	18.4	24.0	12.3	63.1	.6
Minority, some lower-income white and labor									
5	297	56	26	113	186	346	24	99	5
6	416	55	6	53	444	1,285	13	180	26
7	372	63	14	120	433	278	25	75	10
19 } labor	776	94	39	334	349	546	68	170	6
51 }	957	161	63	497	230	491	94	183	4
24	483	85	34	137	307	243	52	130	3
25	622	141	40	261	312	364	64	235	7
45	809	120	24	202	603	948	2	89	25
46	699	113	32	287	300	466	47	94	5
66	652	81	30	257	388	605	37	66	6
69	169	25	6	287	300	289	22	58	2
Totals	6,252	994	314	2,548	3,852	5,861	448	1,379	99
Percentages	82.7	13.1	4.2	39.8	60.2	75.3	5.8	17.7	1.3
Dallas County returns & percentages	60,909	21,099	11,781	42,670	18,917	47,464	10,162	35,664	536
	64.9	22.5	12.6	69.3	30.7	50.6	10.8	38	.6

The four Dewey precincts in 1944 were the only ones he carried in the county, but by 1948 he took the above eleven plus twenty-four others (out of 143 boxes). The ten Rainey precincts were his only ones in the county. Precinct information comes from interviews with Gene Freeland, Ruth Ellinger, Howard Broyles, and Dan Wicker, and from *Official Returns*, 1944, 1946, 1948, Dallas County Clerk's Office. Minor party candidates are omitted from general election computations.

Fort Worth Precincts, 1944, 1946, 1948

Precincts	Presidential Election, November 1944			Democratic Gubernatorial Primary, July 1946			Second Democratic, Senatorial Primary, August 1948	
	FDR	Dewey	Regulars	Rainey	Jester	Others	C. Stevenson	Johnson
White upper class and professional								
81	504	112	455	128	358	177	387	210
95	281	86	536	99	473	195	391	168
108	416	77	297	155	298	213	382	235
115	9	11	74	4	66	15	55	11
116	195	30	103	183	585	381	617	384
117				119	307	184	415	312
Totals	1,405	316	1,465	688	2,087	1,165	2,247	1,320
Percentages	44.1	9.9	46	17.5	53.0	29.5	63.0	37.0
Labor (Northside)								
48	420	39	57	88	120	189	199	137
49	446	26	52	141	103	206	176	183
50	454	33	46	133	13	109	83	116
51	343	19	23	133	89	164	224	200
121				95	85	126	154	151
122				78	62	136	125	101
123				65	64	148	132	87
Totals	1,663	117	178	733	536	1,078	1,093	975
Percentages	84.9	6.0	9.1	31.2	22.8	45.9	52.9	47.1
Black (Southside)								
5	229	10	33				65	85
56	227	22	12	205	21	29	50	95
58	291	35	17	201	42	65	67	114
59	266	50	8	463	15	49	84	262
73	589	61	51	243	90	150	146	139
120 Como				161	95	88	140	135
Totals	1,602	178	121	1,273	263	381	552	830
Percentages	84.3	9.4	6.4	66.4	13.7	19.9	39.9	60.1
Tarrant County returns & percentages	36,791	4,113	10,161	11,514	16,734	18,498	22,741	18,092
	72.1	8.1	19.9	24.6	35.8	39.6	55.7	44.3

Results taken from *Official Returns*, Tarrant County Clerk's Office, 1944, 1946, 1948. Precincts identified in the Margaret Carter Papers and by Margaret Carter. Results of the 1946 runoff are not available nor are the returns from the first forty-five precincts in the first primary. In 1944 two other wealthy boxes (76 and Arch Rowan's 69) plus two other boxes of unknown composition gave the Regulars 390 votes, Republicans 92, and Democrats 498. The Democrats did not come close to losing any other precincts in Tarrant County to the combined Regular-Republican forces.

Nueces County Urban, Mexican-American Precincts, 1946 and 1952

Precincts	Democratic Gubernatorial Runoff, August 1946		Presidential Election, November 1952	
	Rainey	Jester	Stevenson	Eisenhower
13 Robstown	27	8	298	27
33	75	123	277	51
44	139	192	749	127
46	89	162	409	52
47	86	202	512	40
49	152	190	414	45
56	148	111		
60	42	51	636	87
61	86	120	1,237	107
5	194	187	234	82
Totals	1,038	1,346	4,766	618
Percentages	43.5	56.5	88.5	11.5
County returns & percentages	5,468 43.0	7,244 57.0	20,156 51.3	19,124 48.7

All except one of the above precincts are in Corpus Christi. The 1946 boxes are identified as Mexican-American by Dr. Hector Garcia, and the results are from the *Corpus Christi Caller*, n.d., Shivers Papers, 4-15/242. The 1952 table is from David Strong, "The Presidential Election in the South, 1952," *Journal of Politics* 17 (August 1955): 376. Precinct 30 at Holy Cross School is labeled Latin-American by Strong, but Dr. Garcia believes it was mostly black. It voted for Rainey 239 to 45 and for Stevenson 347 to 12.

APPENDIX 6 Sampling of Nearly Fifty Houston Precincts, 1936-1954

Average Home Valuation	Democratic Percentage for President					Democratic Percentage for Allan Shivers, 1954	
	1936	1940	1944	1948	1952	First Primary	Runoff
Over $30,000	57	29	18	7	6	81	81
$19,000	71	47	35	29	13	79	80
$15,000	81	58	50	25	22	79	77
$13,000	79	60	52	23	22	73	73
$10,000	86	74	64	33	26	59	68
$9,000	90	80	68	40	33	55	56
$8,000	93	85	79	61	50	53	42
$7,000	93	88	78	57	49	45	45
$5,000	94	89	84	66	60	36	31
Under $5,000	91	89	87	72	60	37	35

From Samuel Lubell, *Revolt of Moderates* (New York: Harper and Brothers, 1956), pp. 186, 282.

APPENDIX 7 Dallas County Urban Precincts, 1952, 1954, 1956

Precincts	Presidential Election November 1952			New Precinct Numbers	Second Democratic Gubernatorial Primary, August 1954			Second Democratic Gubernatorial Primary, August 1956		
University Park (Upper-Class White and Professional)	Eisenhower	Stevenson	Turnout		Shivers	Yarborough	Turnout	Daniel	Yarborough	Turnout
122	2,377	341		122	416	48		425	40	
				123	936	102		932	109	
118	2,102	334		124	489	30		522	34	
				125	713	110		700	123	
72	2,631	470		130	909	134		1,011	139	
				131	636	70		638	54	
63	1,803	332		132	935	152		948	129	
123	1,462	347		133	638	156		730	155	
Totals	10,375	1,824			5,672	802		5,906	783	
Percentages	85.0	15.0	93.0		87.6	12.4	77.0	88.3	11.7	56.0
Minority, labor, some lower income white										
51	570	535		218	209	264		225	235	
19 labor	537	726		222	216	352		229	424	
82	648	668		432	386	526		360	473	
141	489	609	85.6	431	353	584	57.9	394	508	46.6
17	379	402		221	114	210		123	215	
69	214	658		403	98	343		138	554	
6	113	1,408		165	23	732		13	710	
7	243	378		164	88	168		97	150	
24	243	273		163	111	173		94	186	
45	94	1,405		308	30	659		14	733	
				309	5	498		3	623	
Totals	3,530	7,062			1,633	4,509		1,690	4,811	
Percentages	33.3	66.7	81.1		26.6	73.4	57.7	26.0	74.0	45.0
Dallas County returns & percentages	118,218	69,394			57,737	38,782		68,409	48,017	
	63	37	87.5		59.8	40.2		58.8	41.2	

This chart is derived from precinct analyses by George and Latine Lambert in the Texas AFL-CIO Collection, 110-8-9-5, 110-26-10-7, and the George Lambert Papers, 127-30-4, and from *Official Returns*, 1952 and 1956, Dallas County Clerk's Office. There were more one-sided precincts in both camps, but the above lists are illustrative. Precinct 45 had to be excluded from the turnout computation. For a more detailed analysis for 1952, see Donald Strong, "The Presidential Election in the South, 1952," *Journal of Politics* 17 (August 1955): 373-375. See also Bernard Cosman, "The Republican Congressman from Dallas" (Master's thesis, University of Alabama, 1958), pp. 20-108.

Precincts	Presidential Election, November 1952		Second Democratic Gubernatorial Primary, August 1954		Presidential Election, November 1956	
	Eisen-hower	Steven-son	Shivers	Yarbor-ough	Eisen-hower	Steven-son
Upper-class white						
81	1,057	223	639	119	1,032	223
95	1,098	140	671	71	934	163
108	1,104	360	554	198	867	325
115	127	8	87	1	132	2
117	2,211	532	769	192	1,127	399
129	970	675	343	59	1,193	167
130 } Tanglewood	392	47	297	31	560	100
134 }			428	55	734	127
Totals	6,959	1,985	3,788	726	6,579	1,506
Percentages	77.8	22.2	83.9	16.1	81.4	18.6
Black						
5	63	273	9	54	98	154
56	43	397	14	211	56	152
58	62	419	17	265	178	307
59	39	720	15	424	154	494
73	445	199	66	277	228	315
120	530	610	228	456	366	599
127	27	313	10	253	136	394
Totals	1,209	2,931	359	1,940	1,216	2,415
Percentages	29.2	70.8	15.6	84.4	33.5	66.5
Labor						
48	269	303	102	162	145	189
49	205	461	118	229	165	215
50	331	446	60	304	185	254
51	289	534	215	444	467	641
121	461	410	188	244	359	395
122	310	381	129	223	263	267
123	236	412	91	268	161	312
128	300	367	109	280	293	413
Totals	2,401	3,314	1,012	2,154	2,038	2,686
Percentages	42.0	58.0	32.0	68.0	43.1	56.9
Tarrant County returns &	63,680	45,968	34,653	29,310	66,329	43,922
percentages	58.1	41.9	54.2	45.8	60.2	39.8

Chart derived from precinct studies in the Texas AFL-CIO Collection, 110-26-11-7, and the Texas Social and Legislative Conference Files, 120-1-15.

Second Democratic Gubernatorial Primary, August 1954: Jefferson County Urban Boxes

Precincts	Yarborough	Shivers	Turnout	Percentage Women Poll Tax Holders Compared to Men
Labor				
33	520	178		
35	248	106		
38	120	36		
45	375	129		
55	587	287		
Totals	1,850	736		
Percentages	71.5	28.5	72.6	51.3
Black labor				
56	369	104		
58	687	80		
Totals	1,056	184		
Percentages	85.2	14.8	61.7	43.7
Black				
34	76	5		
59	1,005	72		
18	639	36		
12	639	35		
Totals	2,359	148		
Percentages	94.1	5.9	57.5	44.6
Yarborough composite				
Totals	5,265	1,068		
Percentages	83.1	16.9	63.8	46.9
Upper-class white				
44	159	635		
49	352	862		
50	284	864		
2	128	389		
4	155	697		
5	88	785		
6	101	400		
7	205	1,035		
Totals	1,472	5,667		
Percentages	20.6	79.4	67.7	86.6

Precincts	Yarborough	Shivers	Turnout	Percentage Women Poll Tax Holders Compared to Men
Jefferson County returns &	21,079	21,205		about
percentages	49.8	50.2	74.6	62

This chart is derived from union precinct analyses in the Texas AFL-CIO Collection, 110-26-11-4. The population characteristics came from Mrs. R. Z. Dutton and Mr. and Mrs. E. R. McAdams. The precincts are the candidates' best in percentage returns.

Houston Precincts, 1956 Gubernatorial Races

Precincts	First Democratic Primary, July		Second Democratic Primary, August		Turnout August	November	General Election, November	
White upper class	Daniel	Yar-borough	Daniel	Yar-borough			Daniel	Bryant
87	596	131	765	183			1,009	506
89	272	36	306	53			424	168
133	707	189	842	308			1,416	621
135	736	39	935	50			986	463
143	707	93	856	130			1,185	454
148	791	121	958	149			1,400	618
217	391	30	435	31			498	236
234	1,131	75	1,392	101			1,619	958
Totals	5,331	714	6,489	1,005			8,537	4,024
Percent-ages	88.2	11.8	86.6	13.4	47.4	79.4	68.0	32.0
Black								
24	18	204	14	254			319	163
25	30	489	10	655			740	368
47	42	261	16	358			381	282
48	5	340	4	372			527	39
Totals	95	1,294	44	1,639			1,967	852
Percent-ages	6.8	93.2	2.6	97.4	28.1	47.1	69.8	30.2
Labor								
64	122	241	136	362			601	150
66	149	358	127	354			790	165
81	197	201	250	382			753	164
101	286	383	458	652			1,136	241
Totals	754	1,183	971	1,750			3,280	720
Percent-ages	38.9	61.1	35.7	64.3	39.1	57.5	82.0	18.0

Precincts	First Democratic Primary, July		Second Democratic Primary, August		Turnout August	November	General Election, November	
Harris County returns & percent- ages	59,344	46,149	69,473	71,301			165,872	60,824
	56.3	43.8	49.4	50.6	41.5	66.7	73.2	26.8
State returns	628,914	463,416	698,001	694,830	52.8	65.3	1,350,736	261,283

Chart taken from brochure in Texas AFL-CIO Collection, 110-26-11-2. Minor candidates eliminated from percentage computations. The eight silk-stocking boxes are in
Harris County's top twenty precincts in percentage for Daniel, while the four black ones
are in Yarborough's best thirty. There were 259 precincts. The lesser candidates in the
state received 484,540 votes in the first Democratic primary and 112,072 in the general
election. The state turnout figures are only estimates, since the number of voters exempt
from the poll tax (those aged sixty and over) is unknown. The *Texas Almanac, 1958-
1959*, p. 453, added a 25 percent factor to the poll taxes in 1956.

Precincts	Special Senatorial Election 1957				First Democratic Gubernatorial Primary, 1962			
Upper class white	Hutche-son	Dies	R.Yar-borough	Turn-out	Con-nally	Daniel	D.Yar-borough	Turn-out
95	228	422	60		288	124	23	
81	247	338	74		310	113	71	
108	186	281	124		225	115	82	
115	37	59	0		95	16	4	
117	214	397	130		395	124	84	
129	371	279	66		503	167	33	
130	160	205	36		470	141	46	
134	163	200	57		328	129	90	
Totals	1,606	2,181	547		2,614	929	433	
Percent-ages	37.1	50.3	12.6	57.5	65.7	23.4	10.9	(unavail-able)
Black								
5	3	3	87		59	0	74	
56	5	5	70		46	1	24	
58	49	7	203		74	3	147	
59	34	5	313		168	1	146	
73	46	23	310		275	6	144	
120	64	6	380		296	14	245	
127	1	1	225		175	3	196	
Totals	202	50	1,588		1,093	28	976	
Percent-ages	11.0	2.7	86.3	42.3	52.1	1.3	46.5	about 45.0
Labor								
48	20	52	73		75	36	25	
49	32	39	87		77	9	32	
50	47	29	149		110	19	82	
51	43	109	219		230	93	122	
121	48	104	117		138	50	48	
122	26	51	94		103	22	46	
123	18	55	100		126	46	65	
Totals	234	439	839		859	275	420	
Percent-ages	15.5	29.0	55.5	40.3	55.3	17.7	27.0	(unavail-able)

Precincts	Special Senatorial Election 1957				First Democratic Gubernatorial Primary, 1962			
Tarrant County returns & percent-	11,645	19,486	17,940		28,957	9,239	14,910	
ages	23.7	39.7	36.6	46.2	54.5	17.4	28.1	54.7

Chart taken from precinct studies in the Margaret Carter Papers. Minor candidates are omitted from all calculations except the turnout figures. The returns from seven other known labor boxes in 1957 did not alter the percentages for the candidates but did raise the overall labor turnout figure to 46 percent.

**Urban, Conservative Democrats'
Decline in Select Precincts**

	1954 Runoff Governor	1956 Runoff Governor	1958 Senate	1962 Runoff Governor	1962 General Election, Governor
25 conservative precincts, Harris County	Shivers 17,070	Daniel 18,576	Blakley 13,843	Connally 8,804	Connally 6,543
	R.Yarborough 2,687	R.Yarborough 3,061	R.Yarborough 4,272	D.Yarborough 3,183	Cox 19,028
10 Tarrant County conservative precincts	Shivers 6,095	Daniel 6,152		Connally 3,572	
	R.Yarborough 1,943	R.Yarborough 2,060		D.Yarborough 1,519	
11 Bexar County conservative precincts	Shivers 4,957	Daniel 5,046		Connally 3,827	Connally 2,764
	R.Yarborough 931	R.Yarborough 794		D.Yarborough 1,152	Cox 8,013
26 Dallas County conservative precincts	Shivers 18,145		Blakley 14,481	Connally 9,683	
	R. Yarborough 3,339		R.Yarborough 3,731	D.Yarborough 2,486	
Black precincts, four largest cities	Shivers 4,147			Connally 11,024	Connally 40,177
	R.Yarborough 27,495			D.Yarborough 16,254	Cox 2,554
26 Bexar County precincts, mostly Mexican-American (22 precincts in 1954 and 1956)	Shivers 2,841	Daniel 4,032		Connally 8,603	Connally 16,908
	R.Yarborough 8,413	R.Yarborough 7,980		D.Yarborough 6,447	Cox 1,348

From Larry Goodwyn, *New Shapes in Texas Politics*, 1963 booklet in the George Lambert Papers, 127-30-7.

Selected Precincts, Dallas and Fort Worth, 1968 and 1972 Gubernatorial Races

Dallas labor precincts	*Second Democratic Primary, June 1968*		*Second Democratic Primary, June 1972*		*General Election, 1972*	
(Pleasant Grove)	**D. Yar-borough**	**Smith**	**Faren-thold**	**Briscoe**	**Briscoe**	**Grover**
327	251	368	224	380	555	838
328	187	199	171	303	440	711
329	228	225	221	324	517	681
330	195	280	212	378	544	811
331	270	283	251	401	711	1,003
Totals	1,131	1,355	1,079	1,786	2,767	4,044
Percentages	45.5	54.5	37.7	62.3	40.6	59.4
Dallas County returns &	47,540	80,141	80,153	90,489	160,980	245,178
percentages	37.2	62.8	47.0	53.0	39.6	60.4

Forth Worth black precincts	*First Democratic Primary, May 1972*		
	Barnes	**Farenthold**	**Smith, Briscoe, others**
5	109	43	21
56	65	29	29
58	175	62	97
59	218	140	71
73	183	88	65
120	641	253	183
127	680	340	157
1	67	45	63
119	271	59	29
89	347	270	143
61	61	22	35
Totals	2,817	1,351	893
Percentages	55.7	26.7	17.6 (7.5% for Briscoe)
Tarrant County returns &	25,313	34,852	54,508 (46,375 for Briscoe)
percentages	22.1	30.4	47.5 (40.4% for Briscoe)

Figures are from *Official Returns* from the county clerks' offices. Minor candidates in the 1972 general election were discounted in the percentages.

APPENDIX 14 Urban Upper-Class Precincts in Gubernatorial Elections, 1966, 1968, and 1972

	Pcts.	Tarrant		Pcts.	Dallas		Pcts.	Harris	
1966		Con-nally	Ken-nerly		Con-nally	Ken-nerly		Con-nally	Ken-nerly
	95	446	302	1123	854	475	217	764	519
	115	147	76	1130	670	402	135	881	526
	129	703	450	1131	530	319	87	626	495
	130	1,113	773	1132	679	360	89	247	230
	134	532	296	1133	647	356	133	537	377
Totals		2,941	1,897		3,380	1,912		3,055	2,147
Percentages		60.8	39.2		63.9	36.1		58.7	41.3
County		69.4	30.6		70.8	29.2		69.2	30.8
State		73.8	26.2		73.8	26.2		73.8	26.2
1968		Smith	Eggers		Smith	Eggers		Smith	Eggers
	95	316	737	161	581	1,141	217	429	802
	115	306	458	163	583	1,126	135	493	1,037
	129	598	1,254	171	464	776	87	493	954
	130	1,063	2,344	172	602	1,050	89	237	434
	134	681	1,005	174	647	1,224	133	564	779
Totals		2,964	5,798		2,877	5,317		2,216	4,006
Percentages		33.8	66.2		35.1	64.9		35.6	64.4
County		50.1	49.9		48.3	51.7		47.4	52.6
State		57	43		57	43		57	43
1972		Briscoe	Grover		Briscoe	Grover		Briscoe	Grover
	95	359	652	161	507	1,609	217	330	969
	115	883	1,936	163	538	1,526	135	321	802
	129	664	1,459	171	536	1,466	87	390	1,090
	130	670	1,724	172	520	1,247	89	177	545
	134	583	1,064	174	409	797	133	427	916
Totals		3,159	6,835		2,510	6,645		1,645	4,322
Percentages		31.6	68.4		27.4	72.6		27.6	72.4
County		44.3	55.7		39.6	60.4		43.9	56.1
State		51.6	48.4		51.6	48.4		51.6	48.4

Figures are from *Official Returns* from the county clerks' offices, and, in the instance of Harris County in 1972, from Ceole Speight in the Harris Council AFL-CIO office. See also Lance Tarrance, Jr., ed., *Texas Precinct Votes '66* (Austin: Politics, 1967) and *Texas Precinct Votes '68* (Dallas: Southern Methodist University Press, 1970). The Dallas County precincts are all from the city of University Park.

APPENDIX 15 Dallas and Tarrant County Urban Precincts, 1978 Gubernatorial Election

Precincts	Tarrant County			Precincts	Dallas County		
Upper Class White	Hill	Clements	Turn-out	Upper Class White (Univ. Park)	Hill	Clements	Turn-out
95	124	411		1,160	280	720	
115	279	692		1,162	183	861	
129	347	924		1,163	327	1,182	
130	315	1,058		1,164	272	1,062	
220 } Arlington	150	432		1,171	245	1,055	
228 } west side	287	781		1,172	321	842	
Totals	1,502	4,298			1,628	5,722	
Percentages	25.9	74.1	56.4		22.9	77.1	62.3
Black				**Black**			
5	52	0		3,310	271	61	
58	134	9		3,318	628	36	
59	205	6		3,321	312	19	
73	110	6		3,324	735	33	
120	764	23		3,325	740	32	
127	685	27		3,339	230	3	
Totals	1,950	71			2,916	184	
Percentages	96.5	3.5	30.2		94.1	5.9	28.4
Labor				**Labor**			
100	413	375		3,330	389	390	
145 } Arlington	512	423		3,331	555	436	
210 } east side	272	254		3,343	269	280	
225	249	249		3,345	271	235	
Totals	1,446	1,301			1,484	1,341	
Percentages	52.6	47.4	40.3		52.5	47.5	35.0
County returns & percentages	63,649	70,689			108,584	154,884	
	47.4	52.6	42.5		41.2	58.8	43.7

The returns, taken from the *Fort Worth Star-Telegram*, November 8, 1978, and the *Dallas Morning News*, November 9, 1978, are unofficial. Turnout computations are derived from voter registration figures supplied by Houston Wade and Sybil Boyd at the Dallas and Tarrant county courthouses. Minor party candidates are discounted in all computations. The Dallas black precincts roughly embrace those listed in appendix 7. The statewide turnout was about 41.3 percent, with Clements edging Hill 1,183,564 to 1,165,127.

Notes

PREFACE

1. Malcolm Moos, ed., *H. L. Mencken on Politics: A Carnival of Buncombe* (New York: Vintage Books, 1960), p. 193.

CHAPTER 1

1. Theodore H. White, "Texas: Land of Wealth and Fear," *Reporter* 10 (June 8, 1954): 35; Louis J. Halle, "What's Eating Us?" *New Republic* 151 (September 19, 1954): 19.

2. John Bainbridge, *The Super-Americans* (Garden City, New York: Doubleday, 1961), pp. 17-18; White, "Texas," p. 35.

3. White, "Texas," p. 35; John Gunther, *Inside U.S.A.* (New York: Harper and Brothers, 1947), pp. 815, 822; Mark Nackman, *A Nation Within a Nation* (Port Washington, New York: Kennikat Press, 1975), pp. 4-5.

4. Edgar Shelton, "Political Conditions Among Texas Mexicans Along the Rio Grande" (Master's thesis, University of Texas, 1946), p. 117. For educational statistics regarding Chicanos, see Stanley Arbingast, Lorrin Kennamer, and Michael Bonine, *Atlas of Texas* (Austin: Bureau of Business Research, University of Texas, 1967), pp. 29, 49, and Harley Browning and S. D. McLemore, *A Statistical Profile of the Spanish Surname Population of Texas* (Austin: Bureau of Business Research, 1964), pp. 29-30.

5. See *Dallas Morning News* series, August 18-24, 1974; *Texas Observer*, April 25, 1975); H. H. Martin, "Tyrant in Texas," *Saturday Evening Post* 226 (June 26, 1954): 20-21, 45-54; Shelton, "Political Conditions," pp. 44, 76, 80, 104-107; D. F. Strickland to John Lee Smith, January 17, 1946, John Lee Smith Papers, Southwest Collection, Texas Tech University, Lubbock; Neal Peirce, *The Great Plains States of America* (New York: Norton, 1973), p. 361; Gordon Hunter, column, *Houston Chronicle*, December 18, 1977; Sam Kinch, Jr., column, *Dallas Morning News*, February 15, 1976; Kaye Northcott, column, *Texas Observer*, February 22, 1976; for typical tales of Duval County fraud, see the Duval folders, Allan Shivers Papers, 4-10/26, 4-15/338, Texas State Archives, Austin, as well as innumerable accounts in Dudley Lynch, *The Duke of Duval: The Life and Times of George B. Parr* (Waco: Texian Press, 1976).

6. Ron Laytner, column, *Vancouver Sun*, July 7, 1973.

7. Ibid.; "Houston's Civil War," *Newsweek* 77 (May 3, 1971): 54, 59; Don Myers,

column, *Fort Worth Press*, May 8, 1974; Jim Barlow, column, *Fort Worth Star-Telegram*, October 11, 1970; David McComb, *Houston, the Bayou City* (Austin: University of Texas Press, 1969), p. 215; Sheldon Hackney, "Southern Violence," *American Historical Review* 74 (February 1969): 906-925; D. W. Meinig, *Imperial Texas* (Austin: University of Texas Press, 1969); Tom Curtis, "Support Your Local Police," *Texas Monthly* 5 (September 1977): 83-89, 156-164.

8. Lonnie Roberts, letter to the *Dallas Morning News*, March 19, 1966.

9. V. O. Key, *Southern Politics* (New York: Alfred A. Knopf, 1949), pp. 254, 259, 269-270; Gunther, *Inside U.S.A.*, pp. 845-846; *Houston Chronicle*, September 14, 1947.

10. Quoted in Robert Martin, *The City Moves West: Economic and Industrial Growth in Central West Texas* (Austin: University of Texas Press, 1969), pp. 162-163; Mody Boatright, "The Myth of Frontier Individualism," *Southwestern Social Science Quarterly* 22 (June 1941): 14-32; Jules Loh column, *St. Petersburg Times*, December 1, 1963.

11. Quoted in William D. Kelley leaflet, November 20, 1961, General Edwin A. Walker Collection, Anti-Defamation League Files, Southwestern Office, Houston, Texas; Jim Mathis, column, *Houston Post*, October 12, 1964; J. A. Burkhart, column, *Texas Spectator*, May 24, 1948.

12. Daniel J. Elazar, *American Federalism: A View from the States* (New York: Crowell, 1966), pp. 86-103; Dan Nimmo and William Oden, *The Texas Political System* (Englewood Cliffs, New Jersey: Prentice-Hall, 1971), pp. 50-52.

13. Nimmo and Oden, *Texas Political System*, pp. 53-54; David Nevin, *The Texans* (New York: Morrow, 1968), pp. 182-183; Jack Walker, "The Diffusion of Innovations Among the American States," *American Political Science Review* 63 (September 1969): 880-899.

14. Charles J. V. Murphy, "Texas Business and McCarthy," *Fortune* 49 (May 1954): 101; White, "Texas," pp. 13-14, 34; *Texas Almanac, 1976-1977* (Dallas: A. H. Belo Corporation, 1967), pp. 188-192; James Soukup, Clifton McCleskey, and Harry Holloway, *Party and Factional Division in Texas* (Austin: University of Texas Press, 1964), p. 50.

15. Robert Engler, *The Politics of Oil* (Chicago: University of Chicago Press, 1961), p. 351.

16. White, "Texas," p. 35. Both White and Peirce, *Great Plains States*, depended on veteran Austin newsman Stuart Long for some of their insights.

17. Bill Brammer, column, *Texas Observer*, May 2, 1955.

18. Stanley Kelley, Jr., *Public Relations and Public Power* (Baltimore: Johns Hopkins, 1956), p. 204.

19. *Texas Spectator*, January 27 (Landrum quote), May 12, 1947; other quotes from George Fuermann, *Reluctant Empire* (Garden City, New York: Doubleday, 1957), p. 130; White, "Texas," pp. 34-35; Saul Friedman, "Tussle in Texas," *Nation* 198 (February 3, 1964): 115. For a short, quantitative study showing that newspapers affect both the knowledge and the attitudes of the reading public, see James Brinton and L. N. McKown, "Effects of Newspaper Reading on Knowledge and Attitude," *Journalism Quarterly* 38 (Spring 1961): 187-195.

CHAPTER 2

1. Margaret Carter, column, *Texas Observer*, January 24, 1964.

2. V. O. Key, *Southern Politics* (New York: Alfred A. Knopf, 1949), p. 262; Rupert N. Richardson, Ernest Wallace, and Adrian Anderson, *Texas, the Lone Star State* (Englewood Cliffs, New Jersey: Prentice-Hall, 1970), pp. 292-299.

3. Key, *Southern Politics*, p. 262.

4. Quote is from Hart Stilwell pamphlet, *Texas* (Austin: Texas Social and Legislative Conference, 1949), p. 12.

5. Key, *Southern Politics*, pp. 262-265.

6. Seth Shepard McKay, *Texas Politics, 1906-1944* (Lubbock: Texas Tech Press, 1952), pp. 290-293; interview with Harry Acreman, Dallas, August 28, 1969; interview with Ralph Yarborough, Corpus Christi, July 18, 1969; Raymond Brooks, column, *Austin American*, November 24, 1966; *Texas Observer*, October 2, 1959; J. L. Calbert, "James Edward and Miriam Amanda Ferguson" (Ph.D. diss., Indiana University, 1968), pp. 277-278; Robert Martindale, "James V. Allred" (Master's thesis, University of Texas, 1958), pp. 58-59; interview with John Crossland, Houston, August 17, 1971, University of Texas at Arlington Oral History Project.

7. David Williams, "The Legend of Lyndon Johnson," *Progressive* 21 (April 1957); 20-21; Rowland Evans and Robert Novak, *Lyndon B. Johnson: The Exercise of Power* (New York: New American Library, 1966), pp. 7-8; Booth Mooney, *The Lyndon Johnson Story* (New York: Farrar, Straus, and Cudahy, 1956), p. 36; Robert Sherrill, *The Accidental President* (New York: Grossman Publishers, 1967), p. 107; David McComb interview with Claude Wild, Austin, October 3, 1968, Oral History Collection, Lyndon B. Johnson Library, Austin; James M. Smallwood, "Texas Public Opinion and the Supreme Court Fight of 1937" (Master's thesis, East Texas State University, 1969), pp. 16, 38-40, 78-82, 109-111; Alfred Steinberg, *Sam Johnson's Boy* (New York: Macmillan, 1968), pp. 105-113. The first five sources perpetuate the myth that Johnson's opponents were all anti-New Deal.

8. Williams, "Legend," pp. 20-21; *Vital Statistics of the United States* (Washington: Government Printing Office, 1939, pt. 1, p. 17.

9. Carter, *Texas Observer*, January 24, 1964; Jasper Shannon, *Toward a New Politics in the South* (Knoxville: University of Tennessee Press, 1949), pp. 38-53; Ralph McGill, *The South and the Southerner* (Boston: Little, Brown, 1949), pp. 161-163; Dewey Grantham, *The Democratic South* (Athens: University of Georgia Press, 1963), pp. 74-75.

10. "Texas," *Fortune* 20 (December 1939): 82; Donald Dodd and Wynelle Dodd, *Historical Statistics of the South, 1790-1970* (University, Alabama: University of Alabama Press, 1973), pp. 66-73; Ralph Steen, *The Texas Story* (Austin: Steck Company, 1948), pp. 382-383.

11. Quote is from J. B. Shannon, "Presidential Politics in the South," *Journal of Politics* 1 (May 1939): 147; Joseph Alsop and Turner Catledge, *The 168 Days* (Garden City, New York: Doubleday, 1938), p. 69; Tom Stokes, "Garner Turns on F.D.R.," *Nation* 144 (June 26, 1937): 722-723; Robert S. Allen, "Roosevelt's Defeat—the Inside Story," *Nation* 145 (July 31, 1937): 123-124.

12. Shannon, "Presidential Politics," p. 149; Tom Connally and Alfred Steinberg, *My Name Is Tom Connally* (New York: Crowell, 1954), pp. 138-146.

13. Shannon, "Presidential Politics," p. 149; Alsop and Catledge, *168 Days*, p. 285; Allen, "Roosevelt's Defeat," 123-124; Mary C. Monroe, "A Day in July: Hatton W. Sumners and the Court Reorganization Plan of 1937" (Master's thesis, University of Texas at Arlington, 1973), pp. 29, 88-89; Booth Mooney, *Roosevelt and Rayburn* (Philadelphia: Lippincott Company, 1971), pp. 89, 94-97. See also James T. Patterson, *Congressional Conservatism and the New Deal* (Lexington: University of Kentucky, 1967), pp. 77-127. Bascom Timmons, *Garner of Texas* (New York: Harper's, 1948), pp. 218-224, does not agree that Garner publicly opposed Court reform or that he failed to work for compromise on it.

14. Shannon, "Presidential Politics," pp. 149-150; *Nation* 145 (August 7, 1937): 144; *Austin American*, July 10, 1938.

15. Richard Henderson, *Maury Maverick: A Political Biography* (Austin: University of Texas Press, 1970), pp. 163, 177-183; Heywood Broun, "A Sock for Garner," *New Republic* 99 (May 24, 1939): 72; Heywood Broun, column, *Washington Daily News*, February 8, 1939; Ronnie Davis, "Maury Maverick Sr.: The Rise and Fall of a National Congressman" (Master's thesis, St. Mary's University, 1966), pp. 38-51. See also H. W. Kamp interview with Paul Kilday, August 28, 1965, North Texas State University Oral History Collection, Denton, and Robert Christopher, "Rebirth and Lost Opportunities: the Texas AFL and the New Deal, 1933-1939" (Master's thesis, University of Texas at Arlington, 1977), pp. 108-109.

16. See H. M. Baggarly, column, *Tulia Herald*, April 18, 1865; George Fuermann, *Reluctant Empire* (Garden City, New York: Doubleday, 1957), p. 62; Wilbourn Benton, *Texas, Its Government and Politics* (Englewood Cliffs, New Jersey: Prentice-Hall, 1966), pp. 127-128; Stilwell, *Texas*, pp. 14-15; *Texas Observer*, June 12, 1970; Neal Peirce, *The Megastates of America* (New York: Norton, 1972), p. 503.

17. The quotation and other items are from Selig Harrison, "Lyndon Johnson's World," *New Republic* 142 (June 13, 1960): 16; Theodore White, "Texas: Land of Wealth and Fear," *Reporter* 10 (June 8, 1954): 31-32; Douglass Cater, "The Trouble in Lyndon Johnson's Back Yard," *Reporter* 13 (December 1, 1955): 32; James Conaway, *The Texans* (New York: Knopf, 1976), p. 6, coined the phrase "subrosa accord."

18. Howard Zinn, *The Southern Mystique* (New York: Simon and Schuster, 1974), p. 21; Jimmy Banks, *Money, Marbles and Chalk* (Austin: Texas Publishing Co., 1971), pp. 131-132, on the 8-F crowd; and Conoway, *Texans*, pp. 102-104.

Much of this concept of a state Establishment coincides with the state and national sociological models of C. Wright Mills as refined by William Domhoff. See William Domhoff, *Who Rules America?* (Englewood Cliffs, New Jersey: Prentice-Hall, 1967), pp. 135-137, 140.

19. Carl Rister, *Oil: Titan of the Southwest* (Norman: University of Oklahoma Press, 1949), pp. 317-320; James Clark, *Three Stars for the Colonel* (New York: Random House, 1954), p. 11; Ronnie Dugger, "Oil and Politics," *Atlantic* 224 (September 1969): 76; *Texas Merry-Go-Round* (Houston: Sun Publishing, 1933), pp. 120-121.

20. Rister, *Oil*, pp. 321-324; Stilwell, *Texas*, p. 9; Fuermann, *Reluctant Empire*, p. 102; Owen P. White, "Piping Hot," *Collier's* 95 (January 12, 1935): 10-11, 30; Amon Carter to Sam Rayburn, February 1, 1943, to Coke Stevenson, February 8, 1943, to Harold Ickes, February 27, 1943, and to Earl Godwin, October 15, 1943,

Coke Stevenson Files, box 133, Texas State Archives, Austin; Gerald D. Nash, *United States Oil Policy* (Pittsburgh: University of Pittsburgh Press, 1968), pp. 144-146; Barbara S. T. Day, "The Oil and Gas Industry and Texas Politics, 1930-1935" (Ph.D. diss., Rice University, 1973), pp. 310-318; U.S. Congress, Temporary National Economic Committee, *Hearings, Investigation of the Concentration of Economic Power*, part 15, Petroleum Industry, 76th Cong., 2d sess., 1939, pp. 8232-8233.

21. Robert Engler, *The Politics of Oil* (Chicago: University of Chicago Press, 1961), p. 352; H. W. Kamp interview with Ed Gossett, June 27, 1969, Dallas, North Texas State University Oral History Collection, Denton; *Texas Almanac, 1936*, p. 324, and *Texas Almanac, 1939-1940*, p. 289. In 1951 Gossett decided to take another job—with Southwestern Bell—at $25,000 a year. As the curmudgeon John C. Granbery wrote, "His job will be to scare Texas city councils into another round of rate increases, so he will be continuing the role he has played in Congress." See *Emancipator*, July-August 1951.

22. U.S., *Congressional Record*, 75th Cong., 1st sess., 1937, 81, pt. 4, 4180-4184; Willie Morris, "Legislating in Texas," *Commentary* 38 (November 1964): 41-42; William Payne, columns in *Emancipator*, January and February 1939; quote is from A. H. Wheeler, column, *Texas Citizen*, January 4, 1941; William Rives, column, *Dallas Morning News*, February 26, 1947. Rives evidently broke the Calvert story, but Calvert remembers the account in the *Texas Spectator*, March 10, 1947, as the best summation; interview with Robert Calvert, Austin, December 23, 1976.

CHAPTER 3

1. Seth Shepard McKay, *W. Lee O'Daniel and Texas Politics, 1938-1942* (Lubbock: Texas Tech Press, 1944), pp. 13-14; Owen P. White, *Texas* (New York: G. P. Putnam's Sons, 1945), pp. 252-253.

2. McKay, *W. Lee O'Daniel*, pp. 45, 393.

3. Ibid., pp. 14-23, 31-32; Frank Goodwyn, *Lone Star Land* (New York: Alfred A. Knopf, 1955), pp. 251-252; *Austin American Statesman*, November 23, 1975.

4. McKay, *W. Lee O'Daniel*, pp. 14-23, 31-32.

5. Ibid., pp. 34-35; Goodwyn, *Lone Star Land*, pp. 256-258.

6. George Fuermann, *Reluctant Empire* (Garden City, New York: Doubleday, 1957), p. 19; *New York Times*, July 25, 1938.

7. Goodwyn, *Lone Star Land*, pp. 258-259.

8. Ibid., p. 261.

9. *Dallas Morning News*, February 15, 19, 1940, January 3, 1941; *Southern Patriot*, February 1944; Dorothy Neville, *Carr P. Collins* (Dallas: Park Press, 1963), pp. 55, 58-59, 69; John Ferling, "The First Administration of Governor W. Lee O'Daniel" (Master's thesis, Baylor University, 1962), pp. 19-20; Sam Kinch and Stuart Long, *Allan Shivers: the Pied Piper of Texas Politics* (Austin: Shoal Creek Publishers, 1973), p. 33; Dick West, column, *Dallas Morning News*, May 24, 1969; T. A. Price, column, *Dallas Morning News*, August 14, 1938.

10. McKay, *W. Lee O'Daniel*, pp. 48-49; *Texas Almanac, 1939-1940*, pp. 359-365.

11. Quote is from Paul Bolton's file, KTBC-TV, quoted by Ronnie Dugger, column in *Texas Observer*, March 28, 1956; interview with John Crossland; Fred Johnson to W. Lee O'Daniel, June 17, 1938, and Mrs. O'Daniel to Johnson, June 17, 1938, W.

Lee O'Daniel Files, box 240, Texas State Archives, Austin; McKay, *W. Lee O'Daniel,*
pp. 32, 40, 105; *A Warning to the Workers of Texas* (Dallas-Fort Worth union pamphlet, 1938), and John Oglesby to officers and members of Carpenters local 1266,
n.d., Brotherhood of Locomotive Firemen and Enginemen Files, 38-1-7, Texas Labor
Archives, University of Texas at Arlington. From the stump, O'Daniel reputedly
answered labor questions by relating tearfully that his father had been buried in
overalls; see Wayne Gard, "Texas Kingfish," *New Republic* 104 (June 23, 1941): 849.

12. H. T. Loveless, January 28, 1939, Herman Brown, January 26, 1939, Hughes
Tool company union, January 24, 1939, to W. Lee O'Daniel, W. Lee O'Daniel Files,
box 240; union telegrams to O'Daniel are in box 233; McKay, *W. Lee O'Daniel,*
pp. 149-152, 161-164; *Dallas Morning News,* April 4, 1939.

According to the Jeffersonian Democrats' records, West donated almost $28,000
to the movement that accused Franklin Roosevelt of brutal dictatorship (among its
milder epithets), though West was mostly a conduit for oilman Joseph Pew and the
notorious Liberty League. See Jeffersonian Democrats' Correspondence, "Expenditures and Donations," folder XXXI, and W. P. Hamblen to J. Evetts Haley, August
20, 1936, folder XI, Barker History Center, University of Texas Archives, Austin.

13. Interview with William J. Lawson (O'Daniel's private secretary), Austin,
September 14, 1976, on the origin of the transaction tax; Rep. S. J. Isaaks to L. N.
Jones, June 16, 1939, Rep. R. G. Piner to Joe Kennemer, June 14, 1939, and Rep.
Mat Davis to Mrs. Roger Camp, March 31, 1939, W. Lee O'Daniel Files, box 202;
Kinch and Long, *Allan Shivers,* p. 32; McKay, *W. Lee O'Daniel,* pp. 116, 135, 139,
166-167, 188, 195. The "Immortal 56" were named by themselves and by journalists
after the "Immortal 40," the 1912 Texas delegation to the Democratic national convention, whose cohesiveness and perseverance for Woodrow Wilson was instrumental in Wilson's nomination.

14. McKay, *W. Lee O'Daniel,* pp. 203, 206-207, 236.

15. Ibid., pp. 192-193; box 189 in the O'Daniel Files is filled with voluminous
pension mail, and in some of it the governor's office advises the potential pensioners
to take up the issue with their legislators; box 203 in the O'Daniel Files contains
scores of letters from the governor's office enclosing lists of those voting against
SJR 12; most of the hostile letters and petitions are in box 202 of the O'Daniel Files,
including those from Fannin and Hale counties, April 10 and 11, 1939, respectively;
Gustine to Sen. Metcalfe and Rep. Howington, February 1, 1939, O'Daniel Files,
box 235; *Mt. Vernon Optic-Herald,* July 7, 1939, O'Daniel Files, box 234.

16. McKay, *W. Lee O'Daniel,* pp. 225-231; U.S., Congress, Temporary National
Economic Committees, *Hearings, Investigation of the Concentration of Economic
Power,* part 15, Petroleum Industry, 76th Cong., 2d sess., 1939, pp. 8232-8233.

17. T. E. Huffman to W. Lee O'Daniel, April 4, 1939, O'Daniel Files, box 202.

18. John W. Connelly to John C. Granbery, April 25, 1940, John C. Granbery
Papers, Correspondence, Barker History Center, University of Texas Archives,
Austin; golden rule quote in *Dallas Morning News,* April 5, 1940; Milk quote in
Ferguson brochure, 1940, Brotherhood of Locomotive Firemen and Enginemen
Files, 38-2-1; Thistle Patch quote in *Austin American,* July 1, 1940, and Thompson
to Winchester, Brotherhood of Locomotive Firemen and Enginemen Files, 38-2-2;
three Ferguson brochures, 1940, campaign material, 2-22/701, Texas State Archives,

Austin; Lynn Landrum, column, *Dallas Morning News*, July 27, 1940; Kinch and Long, *Allan Shivers*, p. 32; Walter Davenport, "Where's Them Biscuits, Pappy?" *Collier's* 105 (January 6, 1940): 22; *Fort Worth Star-Telegram*, July 30, 1940; Tom Brewer interview with Allan Shivers, April 12, 1965, notes that O'Daniel helped defeat a number of house and senate members.

19. Telegram, Sidney Kring to W. Lee O'Daniel, May 27, 1940, and telegram, Arthur Wilkerson to W. Lee O'Daniel, May 22, 1940, in O'Daniel Files, box 243; hundreds of other "un-American activities" records are in boxes 207, 219, and 242, O'Daniel Files; *Austin American*, May 21, 23, 1940; telegram, W. Lee O'Daniel to Franklin Roosevelt, May 20, 1940, and Roosevelt to O'Daniel, May 24, 1940, President's Personal File 5938, Franklin D. Roosevelt Library, Hyde Park, New York.

20. McKay, *W. Lee O'Daniel*, pp. 252, 317-319, 327, 333.

21. Ibid., p. 259; Booth Mooney, *Roosevelt and Rayburn* (Philadelphia: Lippincott Company, 1971), pp. 126-127, 141-142 (the Rayburn quote); *El Paso Herald-Post* quoted in "The Congress," *Time* 36 (October 7, 1940): 13-14 (Garner quote); "Garner Finale," *Newsweek* 15 (May 13, 1940): 31-32; Jonathan Daniels, "A Native at Large," *Nation* 151 (November 23, 1940): 506; *Dallas Times Herald*, August 13, 1939; *Houston Post*, May 30, 1940; see letters and telegrams to Tom Connally from five political observers, November 1940, Tom Connally papers, boxes 97, 121, Library of Congress Manuscripts Division, Washington, D.C., plus Connally's correspondence with Germany just after the election, box 121, all relating to Germany's alleged defection; Tom Love, November 1, 1940, and R. E. L. Bobbitt, November 8, 1940, to Tom Connally, Connally Papers, box 97, and Clyde Eustus to Steve Early, August 10, 1940, October 1, 1940, and to Franklin Roosevelt, August 13, 1940, September 6, 1940, President's Official File, 300 E, Roosevelt Library; Gus Taylor to Franklin Roosevelt, April 23, 1941, President's Official File, 300 I-J, Roosevelt Library, and Lillian Collier to Dorothy McAllister, September 29, 1940, October 14, 1940, Democratic National Committee Papers, Women's Division Correspondence, box 260, Roosevelt Library, regarding O'Daniel's stance.

22. David Murph, "Price Daniel: The Life of a Public Man, 1910-1956" (Ph.D. diss., Texas Christian University, 1975), pp. 97-98; McKay, *W. Lee O'Daniel*, pp. 353, 371, 374-376, 387-388; Texas, *House Journal*, 47th Legislature, reg. sess., April 4, 1941, pp. 421, 1747.

23. McKay, *W. Lee O'Daniel*, pp. 367-370. Haley's role in the Jeffersonian Democrats was propagandistic. He went on the radio and into the press charging that the New Deal was fomenting communism, leading Americans to "fascistic green pastures," pandering to the "coloreds," flooding Texas with liquor licenses, and causing the great Panhandle dust storms. See the J. Evetts Haley Correspondence, including the *Jeffersonian Democrat*, September 15, 1936, Barker History Center, University Texas Archives, Austin, and the *Jeffersonian Democrat*, October 1, 22, 1936, J. Evetts Collection, Anti-Defamation League Files, Southwestern Office, Houston.

24. Paul Vickers to W. Lee O'Daniel, March 6, 1939, O'Daniel Files, box 234; V. O. Key, *Southern Politics* (New York: Alfred A. Knopf, 1949), p. 476; *Emancipator*, April-May 1941; McKay, *W. Lee O'Daniel*, p. 400.

25. *Dallas Morning News*, June 18, 28, 1940; *Daily Texan*, January 6, 1941; *Southern Patriot*, February 1944; Goodwyn, *Lone Star Land*, p. 269; *Austin American*,

April 18, 1941, quotes a U.S. Conciliation Service spokesman on the record of Texas labor; Grady Mullennix, "A History of the Texas State Federation of Labor" (Ph.D. diss., University of Texas at Austin, 1955), p. 388.

26. *Houston Post*, March 18, 1941, quotes Garrison; *Texas Industry*, May 1941; W. Lee O'Daniel speech, March 13, 1941, Campaign Material, 2-22/702; John Wortham, "Regulation of Organized Labor in Texas, 1940-1945" (Master's thesis, University of Texas, 1947), pp. 29-32; Goodwyn, *Lone Star Land*, pp. 269-270; McKay, *W. Lee O'Daniel*, p. 403; Mullennix, "History," pp. 390-391; Texas State Federation of Labor Executive Board Minutes, March 6, 1948, Texas AFL-CIO Collection, 110-15-1-1, Texas Labor Archives, University of Texas at Arlington; report of officers for January 1941, and Executive Secretary Harry Acreman to all Texas AFL unions, March 31, 1941, Texas AFL-CIO Collection, 110-15-1-6.

27. John Gunther, *Inside U.S.A.* (New York: Harper and Brothers, 1947), p. 851; *Fort Worth Star-Telegram*, June 30, 1942.

28. U.S., *Congressional Record*, 77th Cong., 1st sess., 1941, 87, pt. 3, 2682, 2905; W. Lee O'Daniel to Hatton Sumners, April 4, 1941, Hatton Sumners Papers, drawer 14, Dallas Historical Society; "Resolution Adopted by the State Democratic Executive Committee in Session at Houston," March 29, 1941, in E. B. Germany to Hatton Sumners, March 31, 1941, Sumners Papers.

29. "Address: Governor W. Lee O'Daniel Appoints General Andrew Jackson Houston to Be United States Senator from Texas," April 21, 1941, W. Lee O'Daniel Clippings, Barker History Center, University of Texas, Austin; untitled address, April 27, 1941, O'Daniel Files, box 235, discusses the visit; Goodwyn, *Lone Star Land*, pp. 272-277; McKay, *W. Lee O'Daniel*, pp. 390-394; Fred Gantt interview with Coke Stevenson, May 13, 1967, and with Bill Lawson, April 19, 1968, North Texas State University Oral History Collection, Denton, on legislative motives.

30. Fred Gantt interview with Claude Gilmer, April 6, 1968, Rocksprings, North Texas State University Oral History Collection, Denton. William Lawson remembers Houston as "completely rational" but concedes that the daughters opposed the appointment and that Houston was physically unable to make the trip to Washington: interview with Lawson and Gantt interview with Lawson.

31. The O'Daniel quotes, in order, came from a speech, May 13, 1941, *W. Lee O'Daniel News*, June 23, 1941, and another speech, June 4, 1941—the speeches are in the Jimmie Allred Papers, box 158, Special Collections, University of Houston, but see also *W. Lee O'Daniel News*, June 19, 1941, and the O'Daniel speeches in the Lyndon Johnson Papers, House Years, box 8, Lyndon B. Johnson Library, Austin; Felix McKnight, column, *Dallas Morning News*, June 25, 1941; "Texas," *Time* 38 (July 7, 1941): 14; Jack Guinn, "Screwball Election in Texas," *American Mercury* 53 (September 1941): 276; on the Patman issue see W. R. Poage to Lyndon Johnson and Ray Roberts to Johnson, both April 28, 1941, Lyndon Johnson Papers, House Years, box 12. See also Joe Frantz interview with Wright Patman, August 11, 1972, Oral History Collection, Johnson Library; Patman, thirty-one years after the event, implied that he voluntarily backed away from the Senate race, in part because Lyndon could get Brown and Root and other corporate money that would be denied to him. The correspondence in the Johnson Papers refutes his assertion that his withdrawal was strictly voluntary.

32. Guinn, "Screwball Election," pp. 275-279; Gunther, *Inside U.S.A.*, p. 850;

McKay, *W. Lee O'Daniel*, pp. 421-422, 472-473; Charles Ashman, *Connally: The Adventures of Big Bad John* (New York: Morrow, 1974), p. 58; on labor, see W. H. Winchester to Texas Legislative Board members, May 16, 1941, and Joe Steadham to John Connally, June 5, 1941, Brotherhood of Locomotive Firemen and Enginemen Files, 38-2-5, plus Austin Building and Construction Trades Council to all Texas councils, April 28, 1941, Sabine Area Trades and Labor Council Collection, Texas Labor Archives, University of Texas at Arlington, plus *Proceedings, Texas State Federation of Labor, 1941* (Austin: n.p., n.d.), pp. 41, 85, 174-175, as well as J. M. Arnold to Lyndon B. Johnson, September 14, 1941, Simeon Hyde and P. F. Kennedy to Johnson, June 24, 1941, Harry Bernhard to Johnson, April 15, 1941, and J. L. M. to Edward Keating, May 3, 1941, Johnson Papers, House Years, boxes 7, 8, 10, 11, respectively; on black support, see Neil Sapper, "A Survey of the History of the Black People of Texas, 1930-1954" (Ph.D. diss., Texas Tech University, 1972), pp. 110-111, Lola Cullom to Franklin Roosevelt, June 17, 1941, President's Personal File 6149, Roosevelt Library & John Connally to Roy Hofheinz, May 9, 1941, Mrs. O. J. Cansler to J. E. Kellum, May 27, 1941, and J. E. Clayton to Lyndon Johnson, May 21, June 11, 24, 1941, Johnson Papers, House Years, box 11; on old-age pension clubs, see Frank Bushick,. Jr., to Lyndon Johnson, September 26, 1941, Johnson Papers, House Years, box 8, and Jan Anderson to John Connally, May 1, 1941, and Connally's reply, May 5, 1941, Johnson Papers, House Years, box 10; on Allred organization, see Jimmie Allred to William O. Douglas, February 9, 1942, Dick Waters to Allred, June 19, 1941, and Grover Burge to Allred, June 13, 1941, Allred Papers, boxes 136, 172 (for latter two); Sid Richardson contribution listed in Raymond Buck Papers, box 141, folder 239-B, Texas Christian University Archives, Fort Worth; Booth Mooney, *The Lyndon Johnson Story* (New York: Farrar, Straus, and Cudahy, 1956), p. 54; Jimmy Banks, *Money, Marbles, and Chalk* (Austin: Texas Publishing Co., 1971), p. 83; "Texas," p. 14; J. Frank Norris speech, 1941, in author's possession; Johnson speeches, 1941, Allred Papers, box 172.

33. George Sessions Perry, *Texas: A World in Itself* (New York: Whittlesey House, 1942), pp. 154-158; Banks, *Money*, pp. 83-84; O'Daniel quotes in O'Daniel speech, June 5, 1941, Allred Papers, box 158; Elliot Roosevelt, ed., *Franklin D. Roosevelt, His Personal Letters* (New York: Duell, Sloan, and Pearce, 1950), pp. 1159-1161, on Jones's alleged role; *Corpus Christi Caller-Times*, July 5, 1941; telegram, Tom Miller to Charles Marsh, June 26, 1941, President's Personal File 6149, Roosevelt Library; R. H. Moodie to Tom Connally, May 5, June 8, 1941, Tom Connally Papers, box 97; Bob McCracken, column, unidentified newspaper, July 25, 1941, O'Daniel Files, box 206; Paul Bolton interview with Gordon Fulcher, November 22, 1968, Oral History Collection, Johnson Library; Dale Odom interview with George Moffett, July 26, 1965, North Texas State University Oral History Collection; Booth Mooney, *Mr. Texas: The Story of Coke Stevenson* (Dallas: Texas Printing House, 1947), p. 32; Gus Hodges to Sam Rayburn, August 4, 1941, Sam Rayburn Papers, series I, reel 10, Sam Rayburn Library, Bonham, Texas, mentions liquor interests scouring the pool halls for O'Daniel—to get him out of Texas.

34. Edgar Shelton, "Political Conditions Among Texas Mexicans Along the Rio Grande" (Master's thesis, University of Texas, 1946), pp. 70-71, on Parr; *Nation* 153 (July 12, 1941): 24; Banks, *Money*, pp. 84-85; *Texas Almanac, 1943-1944*, p. 259; on German vote, see Dr. Louis Bean to Harold Young, August 25, 1941, Johnson

Papers, House Years, box 7, and S. S. McKay, "O'Daniel, Roosevelt, and the Texas Republican Counties," *Southwestern Social Science Quarterly* 26 (June 1945): 12; "Analysis of the 1941 Texas Senatorial Election by Texas Surveys of Public Opinion," confidential poll by Joe Belden, 1941, Johnson Papers, House Years, box 9; according to Robert Sakowitz, "The 1948 Texas Senatorial Campaign and the Crisis in the Democratic Party" (senior paper, Harvard University, 1960), pp. 82-83, an anonymous political speech writer held that the rural east Texas vote was delayed at a time that it seemed to be going to Dies, and that although Johnson's votes were left alone, some of Dies's were switched to O'Daniel. Belden's Angelina survey revealed that it was indeed Dies who lost two-thirds of the votes that switched in such amazing fashion. See also Robert Calvert letter in *Dallas Morning News*, August 27, 1977.

35. Texas Senate, Senate Investigating Committee, *Hearings*, on SR 80, 47th legislature, reg. sess., June 4, 1941.

36. Jimmie Allred to William O. Douglas, August 19, 1941, Allred Papers, box 171; Maston Nixon to Tom Connally, July 8, 1941, and Senator Houghton Brownlee to Connally, July 16, 1941, Connally Papers, box 114; David Welsh, "Building Lyndon Johnson," *Ramparts* 6 (December 1967): 55; Ashman, *Connally*, pp. 58, 60; Drew Pearson, column, *Texas Observer*, March 28, 1956; James Conaway, *The Texans* (New York: Knopf), pp. 98-99; Ed Kilman, column, *Houston Post*, July 3, 1941.

37. U.S., *Congressional Record*, 77th Cong., 1st Sess., 1941, 87, pt. 7, 7530, 7640; McKay, *W. Lee O'Daniel*, pp. 510-512, 570; *Fort Worth Star-Telegram*, July 24, 1942; *Emancipator*, February 1943; Richard Polenberg, *War and Society* (Philadelphia: J. B. Lipincott, 1972), pp. 10-13.

38. McKay, *W. Lee O'Daniel*, pp. 565-580, 611.

39. *Dallas Morning News*, July 18, 1942.

40. McKay, *W. Lee O'Daniel*, pp. 244, 502-504; U.S., *Congressional Record*, 77th Cong., 1st sess., 1941, 87, pt. 7, 6754-6756.

41. McKay, *W. Lee O'Daniel*, pp. 511, 561.

42. Ibid., pp. 589-592; *W. Lee O'Daniel News*, August 14, 1938; strategist quote in *Houston Chronicle*, August 22, 1942; *State Observer*, August 3, 1942; Walter Hornaday, column, *Dallas Morning News*, August 25, 1942; Oscar Dancy to friend, August 1942, Allred Papers, box 146; J. P. Cox to Claude Wild, July 16, 1942, Allred Papers, box 157.

A number of letters written to Allred from around the state indicated that local corporate interests were working for O'Daniel. See, for instance, letters from Dallas attorney Emil Corenbleth, July 27, 1942, and Houston attorney Clarence Lohman, August 11, 1942, Allred Papers, boxes 141, 144. Other such letters are scattered in the Allred Papers, boxes 136-138, 174.

43. William Kittrell, Jr., to Edward Flynn, August 7, 1942, Allred Papers, box 141.

44. Ben Allred, "Report on Kansas Trip," n.d., H. F. Braly to Jimmie Allred, July 4, 1942, unidentified newspaper clipping, n.d., and Tarrant County Tax Assessor-Collector Statement, June 20, 1942, Allred Papers, box 154; Emory Menefee, July 6, 1942, J. Marvin Hunter, July 9, 1942, and J. R. Fleming, July 12, 1942, to Claude Wild, Allred Papers, box 157, and *Proceedings, Texas State Federation of Labor, 1942* (Austin, n.d.), p. 88, on O'Daniel slippage; *Houston Post*, July 16, 1942; *Dallas Morning News*, July 18, 1942; McKay, *W. Lee O'Daniel*, p. 613.

45. D. B. Robertson (president, BLFE) to all members in Texas, August 7, 1942, and Bert Ford (administrator of Texas Liquor Control Board) to Jimmie Allred, August 21, 1942, Allred Papers, box 174; Harry Acreman, March 3, 1942, and W. A. Combs, May 30, 1942, to Jimmie Allred, Allred Papers, box 136; Grover Burge to Sam Low, August 5, 1942, Allred Papers, box 144; *Dallas Morning News*, July 6, 28, 1942; Washington Merry Go Round column in unidentified newspaper, n.d., Allred Papers, box 15.

46. Interviews with Acreman and Crossland; memo from Franklin Roosevelt to Marvin McIntyre, February 4, 1942, Lyndon Johnson to Franklin Roosevelt, March 7, 1942, Roosevelt to Johnson, March 17, 1942, President's Personal File 6149 and President's Official File 300 I-J, Roosevelt Library; Allred speech, August 4, 1942, and Allred brochure, 1942, Allred Papers, box 156; Lewis Nordyke to John McCarthy, July 29, 1942, and telegram, Claude Wild to Jimmie Allred, May 15, 1942, Allred Papers, box 174; W. A. Combs to Sam Low, August 12, 1942, and memo from Low to Allred, August 15, 1942, Allred Papers, box 136; contradictory advice on Roosevelt endorsement scattered throughout Allred Papers, but several letters are in box 144; *Houston Post*, July 29, 1942.

47. Amon Carter's quote in letter to Marvin McIntyre, July 25, 1942, President's Official File 300-C, Roosevelt Library; *Fort Worth Star-Telegram*, August 10, 16, 1942; *Dallas Times-Herald*, July 27-29, August 23, 1942; *Dallas Morning News*, August 16, 1942; *Houston Post*, July 27, 1942; "Politics," *Time* 40 (July 27, 1942): 15-16; list of Allred supporters in Dallas, Allred Papers, box 155; Robert Martindale, "James V. Allred" (Master's thesis, University of Texas, 1958), p. 112; Jimmie Allred to Karl Hoblitzelle, Oveta Culp Hobby, Charles I. Francis, and Tom Gooch, September 2, 3, 1942, and C. K. Quin, October 26, 1942, and J. Frank Norris, June 8, 1942, to Jimmie Allred, Allred Papers, box 174; Roy Coffee to Jimmie Allred, August 26, 1942, and Allred to Ted Dealey, Charles Guy, Bernard Hanks, and Gene Howe, September 3, 1942, Allred Papers, box 136; Jimmie Allred to Sid Richardson, September 3, 1942, and to Ernest Guinn, November 17, 1944 (recalling the River Oaks results), Allred Papers, boxes 137, 171; "Official Returns," 1942, Dallas County Clerk's Office; on Elkins's clout, see Banks, *Money*, p. 85, and George Fuermann, *Houston: Land of the Big Rich* (Garden City, New York: Doubleday, 1951), p. 128.

48. Allred quote in letter to Captain Teller Ammons, September 10, 1942, and banker quote in C. M. Cain to Claude Wild, July 9, 1942, Allred papers, boxes 136, 157; McKay, *W. Lee O'Daniel*, pp. 589-590, 615-618; *Texas Almanac, 1943-1944*, pp. 86-87, 253-255; *Dallas Morning News*, July 6, August 23, 1942; "Minutes of General Labor Meeting," February 22, 1943, Texas AFL-CIO Collection, 110-15-1-6; Polenburg, *War*, p. 189; Mullennix, "History," p. 398; Robert Garson, *The Democratic Party and the Politics of Sectionalism, 1941-1948* (Baton Rouge: Louisiana State University Press, 1974), pp. 28-29, on southern reaction; campaign "postmortem" letters from various Texas officials to Edwin Pauley, November 1942, Democratic National Committee Papers 1156, Franklin D. Roosevelt Library, Hyde Park, New York.

49. McKay, *W. Lee O'Daniel*, pp. 41, 47, 346 (first quote), 348, 483; the other quotes, in order, are in Owen P. White, *Texas* (New York: G. P. Putnam's Sons, 1945), pp. 250-251; Elizabeth Ferguson to Franklin Roosevelt, September 4, 1942,

President's Official File 300 "0," Roosevelt Library; Ledgerwood Sloan and J. B. Krueger, column, *Fort Worth Star-Telegram*, August 27, 1942.

50. Interview with Lawson; quote is in Arthur Holland to Franklin Roosevelt, May 28, 1940, President's Official File 300 "0," Roosevelt Library; Goodwyn, *Lone Star Land*, pp. 281-282; *New York Times*, July 7, 1946; J. P. McEvoy, "I've Got That Million Dollar Smile," *American Mercury* 45 (October 1938): 204; *Washington News*, December 4, 1945.

51. Interviews with Lawson and Calvert; Gantt interviews with Lawson and Stevenson; W. H. Kamp interview with T. Bullock Hyder, May 12, 1966, North Texas State Oral History Collection, Denton; letter to author from Stuart Long, November 11, 1976; *Texas Spectator*, October 18, 1946; Ronnie Dugger, column, *Texas Observer*, March 28, 1956; Fred Gantt, *The Chief Executive in Texas* (Austin: University of Texas Press, 1964), pp. 190-191, on vetoes; McKay, *W. Lee O'Daniel*, p. 182; Raymond Brooks, column, *Austin American-Statesman*, December 11, 1966.

52. Quoted in W. R. Poage, *Politics—Texas Style* (Waco: Texian Press, 1974), p. 117; O'Daniel description came from Senator Joe Hill, quoted in Jimmie Allred to H. M. Baggarly, February 11, 1947, Allred Papers, box 172. Much of this definition of extremism is taken from *The Journal of Social Issues* 19 (April 1963): 1-106, but see also Eric Hoffer, *The True Believer* (New York: New American Library, 1963), pp. 105-106.

CHAPTER 4

1. U.S., House, Special Committee to Investigate Campaign Expenditures, *Hearings: Investigation of Campaign Expenditures*, 78th Cong., 2d sess., 1944, pt. VII, 502, p. VIII, 558, 580, 676, 690-691, 694-695; Stanley Schneider, "The Texas Regular Party of 1944" (Master's thesis, University of Chicago, 1948), pp. 50-53; *Dallas Morning News*, March 1, 17, 22, April 20, 21, 1944; Clyde Eastus to Robert Hannegan, March 23, 24, 1944, Democratic National Committee Papers 1139, Roosevelt Library; see also Robert Garson, *The Democratic Party and the Politics of Sectionalism, 1941-1948* (Baton Rouge: Louisiana State University Press, 1974), pp. 101-104.

2. Harry Seay to Franklin Roosevelt, February 29, 1944, President's Personal File 8699, Roosevelt Library, regarding the fund raiser; *Dallas Morning News*, April 1, 1944, carries poll; V. O. Key, *Southern Politics* (New York: Alfred A. Knopf, 1949), p. 256; Seth Shepard McKay, *Texas Politics, 1906-1944* (Lubbock: Texas Tech Press, 1952), pp. 430-433; E. Roundstream to Homer Rainey, February 22, 1943, Homer Rainey Papers, box 41, Western Historical Manuscripts Collection, University of Missouri, Columbia; Clyde Eastus to Sam Rayburn, March 18, 1944, Rayburn Papers, series I, reel 16; the Roosevelt Library in particular is replete with warnings of increasing unpopularity due to various causes—see Paul Page to Frank Walker, November 23, 1943, and Peter Leyendecker to Walker, November 24, 1943, Democratic National Committee Papers 1157, and Lillian Collier and Margaret Reading to Franklin Roosevelt, January 11, 1943, Clyde Eastus to Robert Hannegan, March 21, 31 and May 4, 15, 1944, Democratic National Committee Papers 1139, and Wright Patman to Franklin Roosevelt, February 21, 1943, and Luther Johnson to Roosevelt, December 29, 1943, President's Personal Files 2488, 7744.

3. Schneider, "Texas Regular Party," pp. 57-59; Alvin Wirtz to Harold Ickes, May 25, 1944, Rayburn Papers, series I, reel 16; Jimmie Allred to D. B. Hardeman,

October 21, 1944, Allred Papers, box 171; W. S. Parker to Robert Hannegan, July 6, 1944, Democratic National Committee Papers 1167, Roosevelt Library; "Report of Officers for the Month of May, 1944," Texas State Federation of Labor report, Texas AFL-CIO Collection, 110-15-1-6; McKay, *Texas Politics*, pp. 430-433; Key, *Southern Politics*, p. 246; Robert Engler, *The Politics of Oil* (Chicago: University of Chicago Press, 1961), p. 354; Frank Goodwyn, *Lone Star 'Land* (New York: Alfred A. Knopf, 1955), pp. 279-280; *Texas Spectator*, June 21, 1946; *Proceedings of the State Democratic Convention*, May 23, 1944 (anti-New Deal convention); "Prominent Lawyers Who Were leaders at the Convention Held in the Senate Chamber, May 23, 1944," Lyndon Johnson Papers, House Years, box 38.

4. McKay, *Texas Politics*, pp. 436-438; Alexander Heard, *A Two-Party South?* (Chapel Hill: University of North Carolina Press, 1952), p. 258; *Proceedings of the State Democratic Convention*, May 23, 1944 (anti-New Deal convention).

5. *Proceedings of the State Democratic Convention*, May 23, 1944 (New Deal convention).

6. "Revolt," *Time* 43 (June 5, 1944): 21-22; "Threat to Fourth Term Move: Growing Revolt of the South," *United States News* 16 (June 9, 1944): 21-22, on "flaming issue"; H. W. Kamp interview with Ed Gossett; Kamp interview with Alla Clary, August 12, 1969, North Texas State University Oral History Collection, Denton; *Dallas Morning News*, May 24, 1944; Margaret Carter, column, *Texas Observer* February 7, 1964; Alfred Steinberg, *Sam Rayburn* (New York: Hawthorn, 1975), pp. 216-220; C. Dwight Dorough, *Mr. Sam* (New York: Random House, 1962), pp. 351-355; McKay, *Texas Politics*, pp. 435, 444; Garson, *Sectionalism*, pp. 108-119; Booth Mooney, *Roosevelt and Rayburn*, (Philadelphia: Lippincott Company, 1971), pp. 196-197; Harry Seay to Sam Rayburn, November 1, 1946, Lewis T. Carpenter to Rayburn, May 25, 1944, Rayburn Papers, series I, reels 21, 16. Three years after this election, Rayburn was still galled by Cullen's efforts. Oilman Jack Porter promised to get Cullen off his back if Rayburn would relax his defense of price controls. Price controls were soon dropped, and the next time Rayburn had an opponent, he received only a telegram from Cullen—Maclyn Burg interview with Joe Ingraham and Jack Porter, November 9, 1972, Oral History 349, Dwight Eisenhower Library, Abilene.

7. Steinberg, *Sam Rayburn*, pp. 218, 223; McKay, *Texas Politics*, pp. 447-449; Carter, *Texas Observer*, February 7, 1964; Pattie Manion to W. H. Winchester, August 4, 1944, Brotherhood of Locomotive Firemen and Enginemen Files, 38-2-6. Manion, who tells the Big Spring story, headed the Ladies' Society of the Texas State Legislative Board (BLFE and others). For another account of a lively county squabble, see Margaret Carter to Don Weaver (editor of the *Fort Worth Press*), September 9, 1944, Margaret Carter Papers, Texas Political History Collection, University of Texas at Arlington.

8. Quoted in William Tolleson, "The Rift in the Texas Democratic Party—1944" (Master's thesis, University of Texas, 1953), pp. 79-80; *Cornered Antis Split on Story on Patronage*, booklet published by Roosevelt-Truman Democrats, September, 1944, Brotherhood of Locomotive Firemen and Enginemen Files, 38-3-1.

9. Interview with Calvert.

10. John Gunther, *Inside U.S.A.* (New York: Harper and Brothers, 1947), pp. 846-847; *State Observer*, May 8, June 26, 1944; Sam Hall, column, *Texas Spectator*, January 18, 1946; Stetson Kennedy, *Southern Exposure* (Garden City, New York: Doubleday and Company, 1946), pp. 156-158; Jesse Jones, *Fifty Billion Dollars:*

My Thirteen Years with the RFC (1932-1945) (New York: Macmillan Company, 1951), pp. 274-275; Engler, *Politics of Oil*, p. 354; *Houston Post*, May 24, 1944; Hart Stilwell, "Civil War in Texas," *Collier's* 115 (January 6, 1945): 30; Schneider, "Texas Regular Party," pp. 97-101, 195; *P.M.*, June 2, 1944; F. Dobney, "The Papers of Will Clayton" (Ph.D. diss., Rice University, 1970), p. 10; Ed Kilman and Theon Wright, *Hugh Roy Cullen* (Englewood Cliffs, N.J.: Prentice-Hall, 1954, pp. 217-218.

According to one authority, Jones could have crushed the Regulars had he really wanted to. See J. B. Shannon, "Presidential Politics in the South," *Journal of Politics* 10 (August 1948): 481. This is denied in another of Bascom Timmons's fawning biographies, *Jesse H. Jones* (New York: Henry Colt and Company, 1956), p. 347.

11. *Austin American*, October 6, 1944.

12. Manning Dauer, "Recent Southern Political Thought," *Journal of Politics* 10 (May 1948): 334-335; William Carleton, "The Southern Politician," *Journal of Politics* 13 (May 1951): 223; *Lubbock Avalanche-Journal*, October 22, 1944; Schneider, "Texas Regular Party," p. 163.

13. Gunther, *Inside U.S.A.*, p. 845.

14. Murray Polakoff, "The Development of the Texas State C.I.O. Council" (Ph.D. diss., Columbia University, 1955), p. 54; quoted in G. D. Gurney to Jimmie Allred, June 13, 1944, Allred Papers, box 171.

15. *State Observer*, June 26, 1944.

16. *Houston Post*, November 3, 4, 1944; *State Observer*, November 6, 13, 1944; first quote in unidentified clipping, 1944, John Lee Smith Papers.

17. U.S., Senate, Committee Investigating Campaign Expenditures, *Investigation of Presidential, Vice-Presidential, and Senatorial Campaign Expenditures*, Report No. 101, 79th Cong., 1st sess., 1944, pp. 19, 47-48; Kennedy, *Southern Exposure*, pp. 137-141; *New York Times*, September 23, 1944; *P.M.*, October 22, 1944; *Houston Press*, March 16, 1945; Walter Hornaday, column, *Dallas Morning News*, October 20, 1944; O'Daniel brochures, 1944, Connally Papers, box 113, and Rayburn Papers, series I, reel 16.

18. Kennedy, *Southern Exposure*, p. 137; Hornaday, October 20, 1944.

19. Committee Investigating Campaign Expenditures, *Investigation*, 1944, pp. 44, 50. Less fanatical was a CCRC-financed full page advertisement in the *Dallas Morning News*, November 3, 1943.

20. Committee to Investigate Campaign Expenditures, *Hearings*, 1944, pt. VIII, 684-687; *Dallas Morning News*, August 15, 1944.

21. Committee to Investigate Campaign Expenditures, *Hearings*, 1944, pt. VII, 377, 400; E. A. Piller, *Time Bomb* (New York: Arco Publishing Company, 1945), pp. 17-18.

22. Committee to Investigate Campaign Expenditures, *Hearings*, 1944, pt. VII, 377, 406, 418, 424; *New York Times*, October 21, 1940.

23. Committee to Investigate Campaign Expenditures, *Hearings*, 1944, pt. VII, 392, 451-453, 491, 494-495, 525-527, 533, 550. One of Ewart's full-page advertisements, a reprint of a typical O'Daniel speech, appeared in the *Dallas Morning News* as early as July 4, 1943; Anti-Defamation League memo listing contributors to the CCG, November 1943, ADL report on the CCG, December 1944, and "Houston Committee for Constitutional Government," April 26, 1945, Committee for Con-

stitutional Government Collection, Anti-Defamation League Files, Southwestern Office, Houston.

24. Committee to Investigate Campaign Expenditures, *Hearings*, 1944, pt. VII, 457, 503-505, and pt. X, 1160-1162, 1166.

25. Ibid., pt. VII, 521; Roland Young, *Congressional Politics in the Second World War* (New York: Columbia University Press, 1956), pp. 262-263, on Patman and Johnson as the only party stalwarts. Rayburn was not rated since he had cast fewer than twenty party votes.

26. Committee to Investigate Campaign Expenditures, *Hearings*, pt. VII, 520, pt. X, 1160-1162, 1164, 1166, 1169, 1198-1199; *Texas Almanac, 1945-1946*, p. 537. In February 1945, the Bureau of Internal Revenue ruled that contributions to the CCG were not tax deductible. See the discussion in the U.S., *Congressional Record*, 79th Cong., 1st sess., 1945, 91, pt. 2, 2157-2163.

27. Committee Investigating Campaign Expenditures, *Investigation* 1944, pp. 52-53; House Committee to Investigate Campaign Expenditures, *Hearings*, 1944, pt. X, 1172.

28. Committee to Investigate Campaign Expenditures, *Hearings*, pt. X, 1157; Schneider, "Texas Regular Party," pp. 107, 111; *Dallas Morning News*, November 4, 1944.

29. Quoted in Margaret Carter, column, *Texas Observer*, February 7, 1964; *Texas Almanac, 1946-1947*, pp. 531-533; Goodwyn, *Lone Star Land*, p. 281; McKay, *Texas Politics*, p. 465.

30. Wayne Gard, "Bringing O'Daniel to Justice," *New Republic* 107 (July 13, 1942): 51; O'Daniel broadcast, quoted in Senate Committee Investigating Campaign Expenditures, *Investigation*, 1944, p. 50; *Dallas Morning News*, September 19, 1947, January 5, 1948.

31. *Dallas Morning News*, February 2, March 17, September 7, 1948; *Austin American*, March 28, 1948; W. Lee O'Daniel to Dear Friend, c. August 1948, Lyndon Johnson Papers, House Years, box 93.

32. Schneider, "Texas Regular Party," pp. 97, 103; *Dallas Morning News*, April 21, 1944; Paul Holcomb, column, *State Observer*, October 19, 1953; Committee to Investigate Campaign Expenditures, *Hearings*, pt. VII, p. 545; Alvin Wirtz to Edwin "Pa" Watson, September 9, 1944, President's Personal File 7562, Roosevelt Library; Tom Connally to E. E. Townes and to D. F. Strickland, June 9, 1944, and to Mrs. Sam Davis, June 26, 1944, Connally Papers, box 103.

33. Quoted in Sam Rayburn to Homer Pharr, November 20, 1944, Rayburn Papers, series I, reel 17; on Kleberg's demise, see Executive Board Minutes, Texas State Joint Social and Legislative Conference, July 30, 1944, Brotherhood of Locomotive Firemen and Enginemen Files, 38-2-6, the *Proceedings of the Ninth Annual Convention of the Texas State Industrial Union Council* (Houston, October 20-21, 1945), p. 43, and Dudley Lynch, *The Duke of Duval: The Life and Times of George B. Parr* (Waco: Texian Press, 1976), p. 52.

34. W. M. Holland, November 3, 1941, September 21, 1944, and J. Cleo Thompson, August 23, 1944, to Hatton Sumners, and Sumners to T. W. Davidson, April 1, 1942, and to R. H. Shuttles, May 8, 1944, Sumners Papers, drawer 17; "Dallas

County United Legislative Committee," 1944 labor leaflet, in author's possession; *Texas Spectator*, October 11, 1946.

35. Mike Carpenter's San Antonio poll, 1945, Rainey Papers, box 40.

CHAPTER 5

1. John Henry Kirby to Joe Bailey, January 16, 1915, and Henry Pope to Kirby, August 25, 1916, John Henry Kirby Paprs, Texas Gulf Coast Historical Association, Houston; Frederick Woltman, column, *Houston Press*, March 29, 1945; George Wolfskill, *Revolt of the Conservatives* (Boston: Houghton Mifflin, 1962), p. 234.

2. Quote and other information in U.S., Senate, Committee to Investigate Lobbying Activities, *Hearings*, 74th Cong., 2d sess., April 15, 1936, pp. 1970-1973, 1994-2014; Austin Callan to J. Evetts Haley, January 13, 1936, J. Evetts Haley Correspondence; T. R. B., "Washington Notes," *New Republic* 86 (February 12, 1936): 17; John Nance Garner to Thomas B. Love, January 11, 1936, Thomas B. Love Papers A50104, Dallas Historical Society.

3. Helen Fuller, "The Christian American Cabal," *New Republic* 108 (January 25, 1943): 116.

4. Walter Davenport, "Savior from Texas," *Collier's* 116 (August 18, 1945): 13, 79-80; E. A. Piller, *Time Bomb* (New York: Arco Publishing Company, 1945), p. 51; *Galveston Daily News*, June 30, 1935, Haley Correspondence, Clippings. One observer found that Ulrey's knowledge of history included the notion that the Spanish Civil War was the fault of Bela Kun, head of the communist government in Hungary in 1918; see Booten Herndon, "Pappy's Dixie Fascists," *New Republic* 107 (July 20, 1942): 79.

5. Lewis Ulrey, *Maco Stewart* (Galveston, 1939), pp. 8, 16-18, 22; Maco Stewart, "Communism," speech to the Galveston Rotary Club (c. 1932), Haley Correspondence.

6. Davenport, "Savior," pp. 79-80.

7. Ibid.; John O. King, "The Early History of the Houston Oil Company of Texas, 1901-1908," *Texas Gulf Coast Historical Association* 3 (April 1959): 92-93; Stetson Kennedy, *Southern Exposure* (Garden City, New York: Doubleday, 1946), pp. 252-253.

8. Davenport, "Savior," p. 80; interview with Ida Darden (Vance Muse's sister), Houston, June 28, 1966.

9. Davenport, "Savior," p. 81; Kennedy, *Southern Exposure*, pp. 250-253; Piller, *Time Bomb*, pp. 48-52; *The Revealer*, 1936, in Haley Correspondence, Clippings; Victor Bernstein, "The Anti-Labor Front," *Antioch Review* 3 (Fall 1943): 336; Texas House of Representatives, Special Committee to Investigate Lobbying, *Hearings: House Lobby Investigating Committee*, 49th legislature, reg. sess., 1945, Exhibit "L" (*Defender*, n.d.), "The Christian American," a newsheet, August 20, 1943, and Muse's testimony, March 22, 1945, p. 103. The Illuminati were the members of a late eighteenth-century rationalist society that flourished briefly and was not involved in any revolution.

10. Interview with William Ruggles, Dallas, April 12, 1967; William Ruggles, column, *Dallas Morning News*, September 1, 1941, March 21, 1967; John Wortham, "Regulation of Organized Labor in Texas, 1940-1945" (Master's thesis, University of Texas, 1947), p. 15; Group Research, Inc., "Special Report #13," December 13, 1962,

pp. 1-2; Robert Garson, *The Democratic Party and the Politics of Sectionalism, 1941-1948* (Baton Rouge: Louisiana State University Press, 1974), pp. 14-15; Harry Millis and Emily Brown, *From the Wagner Act to Taft-Hartley* (Chicago: University of Chicago, 1950), pp. 321-323.

11. Davenport, "Savior," p. 13; organizational bulletin, June 28, 1946, Committee for Constitutional Government Collection; Woltman, *Houston Press*, March 28, 1945; Texas House Committee to Investigate Lobbying, 1945, "Exhibit C" (excerpt from *Congressional Record*, O'Daniel speech, September 25, 1941); letter from William Green to all AFL officers, March 9, 1945, American Federation of Labor Papers, series 3, box 5, Wisconsin State Historical Society, Madison.

Though Tom Connally was a much more effective antilabor spokesman than O'Daniel, Muse was disappointed in Connally's apparent lack of total commitment to the cause—see Muse to Tom Connally, May 7, 1943, Sumners Papers, Drawer 15.

12. Booth Mooney, *Roosevelt and Rayburn* (Philadelphia: J. B. Lippincott, 1971), pp. 178-179. See also Grady Mullennix, "A History of the Texas Federation of Labor" (Ph.D. diss., University of Texas at Austin, 1955), pp. 395-396, and various letters to Sam Rayburn, Rayburn Papers, series I, reels 10, 11.

13. Davenport, "Savior," p. 81; Bernstein, "Anti-Labor Front," p. 337.

14. Piller, *Time Bomb*, pp. 53-54; Texas House Committee to Investigate Lobbying, 1945, "The Christian American," August 1943; Herndon," "Dixie Fascists," pp. 79-80; Bernstein, "Anti-Labor Front," p. 335; Davenport, "Savior," pp. 13, 79.

15. Ibid.; interview with Sam Houston Clinton, Austin, September 17, 1967, on Manford's being the first law mentioning "right to work"; Millis and Brown, *From the Wagner Act*, p. 326; *New York Times*, November 8, 1944; *Texas Industry*, July 1942; *General and Special Laws of the State of Texas* (Austin: State of Texas, 1943), p. 180; for labor beliefs of Christian American influence on the Manford Act, see Victor Riesel, "Let's Look at Labor," *Nation* 157 (July 31, 1943): 125, and *Proceedings of the Sixth Constitutional Convention of the C.I.O.*, November 1-5, 1943 (Philadelphia, 1943), pp. 64-65, 321; for the effectiveness of the Christian Americans in Arkansas, see "Arkansas Travels," Christian American booklet, 1943, and W. C. Mullins to W. H. Winchester, February 11, 1943, in the Brotherhood of Locomotive Firemen and Enginemen Files, 38-4-8; Ray Marshall, *Labor in the South* (Cambridge: Harvard Press, 1967), pp. 241-243.

16. Bernstein, "Anti-Labor Front," p. 336; Marshall, *Labor*, pp. 241-242.

17. Kennedy, *Southern Exposure*, pp. 156-157; Fuller, "The Christian American Cabal," p. 116.

18. Piller, *Time Bomb*, pp. 50, 53; Bernstein, "Anti-Labor Front," pp. 334-335; Davenport, "Savior," pp. 13, 79; Texas House Committee to Investigate Lobbying, 1945, "The Christian American," July 1, 1942, and "Exhibit Q-2" (Christian American receipts and expenditures, 1944). From January 1, 1944, through March 15, 1945, only $4,400 in antilabor money was raised in Texas.

19. Woltman, column, *Houston Press*, March 28, 29, 1945; interview with Milton Muse, Houston, June 29, 1966.

20. Mrs. Mac Strauss to Coke Stevenson, November 20, 1945, Mrs. Jud Collier to Maco Stewart, November 26, 1945, and L. V. Ulrey to Jack Cason, November 25, 1945, to J. K. Noble, November 27, 1945, to Gilbert Denman, May 8, 1946, and another with no date; "The 'Reds' Attack the Educational Setup in Texas," typescript

by L. V. Ulrey, July 1, 1946. All these items are in the Coke Stevenson Files, box 151.

Margaret Carter typescript, March 1946, Margaret Carter Papers; *Texas Spectator*, January 18, 1946, December 1, 1947. See also Ulrey to Beauford Jester, April 25, 1946, Beauford Jester Files, box 58, Texas State Archives, Austin, and *Austin American*, December 8, 11, 1945.

21. U.S., *Congressional Record*, 78th Cong., 2d sess., 1944, 90, pt. 6, 8463, and 79th Cong., 1st. sess., 1945, 91, pt. 2, 2161; State of Texas, *House Journal*, 49th Legislature, reg. sess., June 1, 1945, pp. 2666-2667; Woltman, *Houston Press*, March 29, 1945; *National Union Farmer*, December 15, 1944; Sam Hall, column, *Texas Spectator*, February 15, 1946; "Report of Officers for the Month of May, 1945," Texas State Federation of Labor report, Texas AFL-CIO Collection, 110-15-1-6.

22. See U.S., *Congressional Record*, 78th Cong., 2d sess., 1944, 90, pt. 3, 4328-4329.

23. Ibid., pt. 6, pp. 8462-8463, and pt. 9, pp. A2370-A2371.

24. *Houston Press*, January 16, February 16, 1945.

25. Ibid., March 16, 17, 1945. The bribery is alleged by the man who claims to have given Favors fifty dollars to introduce the bill.

26. Texas House Committee to Investigate Lobbying, 1945, Bell's testimony, pp. 57-64, Taylor's testimony, pp. 45-48, and *Middle-Buster*, n.d. (circa December 1944), and January 9, 1945.

27. Ibid., Acreman's testimony, p. 69, and "Exhibit B" (E. H. Williams to Harry Acreman, March 13, 1945).

28. Ibid., Muse's testimony, pp. 77-78, and "Exhibit P" ("The Christian American," October 25, 1944).

29. Ibid., "Exhibit G" ("Fight for Free Enterprise," leaflet, n.d.) and "Exhibit L" ("Free Enterprise News Bulletin," 1945). See also Kennedy, *Southern Exposure*, p. 236.

One doctor, who was employed by the state, was listed on the FFE letterhead. When unions protested the listing, the doctor claimed that he knew nothing about the organization and that he had never criticized the CIO; he was, he lamented, "a sucker for all kinds of donations." See W. M. Akin and O. A. Knight to Coke Stevenson, August 20, 1945, and Akin press release, September 29, 1945, Texas AFL-CIO Collection, 110-25-3-19, and Dr. L. R. Brown to Weaver Baker, September 15, 1945, Coke Stevenson Files, box 188. Akin was a CIO lobbyist in Austin; Knight was president of the Oil Workers Union.

30. "Proposed Laws Would Banish Imported CIO Goons and End Un-American Teaching in the State," FFE leaflet, n.d., Texas AFL-CIO Collection, 110-25-3-19; *Austin Statesman*, January 15, 1945; *Houston Chronicle*, January 26, 1945.

31. "Confidential Memorandum," FFE booklet, May 12, 1945, Texas AFL-CIO Collection, 110-25-3-19; Kennedy, *Southern Exposure*, pp. 225-258; "Is This a Texas Fascist Front?" CIO pamphlet, Brotherhood of Locomotive Firemen and Enginemen Legislative Board Files, 38-4-4; *Labor News*, August 19, 1945, May 31, 1946; John Gunther, *Inside U.S.A.* (New York: Harper and Brothers, 1947), p. 853; *Dallas Morning News*, November 3, 1945. See also *Southern Patriot*, December 1945.

32. State of Texas, *House Journal*, 49th Legislature, regular session, April 2, 1945, pp. 1037-1038.

33. *Houston Press*, March 21, 1945; Frederick Meyers, *"Right to Work" in Practice* (New York: Fund for the Republic, 1959), p. 3; *Austin Statesman*, March 12, 1945; Woltman, *Houston Press*, March 28, 1945; Murray Polakoff, "The Development of the Texas State C.I.O. Council" (Ph.D. diss., Columbia University, 1955), p. 303; *Proceedings, Texas State Federation of Labor, 1946* (Austin, n.d.), p. 87.

34. Sam Hall, column, *Texas Spectator*, March 8, 1946; predictions of progressive change were also chronicled in *Emancipator*, May 1946, the *Austin American*, February 8, 1945, and in Bruce Bliven, "Texas Is Boiling," *New Republic* 114 (March 25, 1946): 409-410; on labor laws, see Millis and Brown, *From the Wagner Act*, p. 325, Marshall, *Labor*, pp. 243-244, *Austin American*, January 20, April 5, 1945, and Carl Swisher, "The Supreme Court and the South," in Taylor Cole and John Hollowell, eds., *The Southern Political Scene, 1938-1948* (Gainesville: University of Florida Press, 1948), p. 293.

CHAPTER 6

1. William Gellermann, *Martin Dies* (New York: John Day Company, 1944), pp. 17, 18, 23; Harold Ickes, *The Inside Struggle* (New York: Simon and Schuster, 1954), p. 574.

2. Marion Irish, "Recent Political Thought in the South," *American Political Science Review* 46 (March 1952): 132; Ickes, *The Inside Struggle*, pp. 504-505; Martin Dies, *Trojan Horse in America* (New York: Dodd, Mead, 1940), pp. 118-119; *Dallas Morning News*, December 24, 1939; Allen Michie and Frank Ryhlick, *Dixie Demagogues* (New York: Vanguard Press, 1939), p. 67.

3. U.S., *Congressional Record*, 72d Cong., 1st sess., 1931, 75, pt. 1, 736, and 75th Cong., 1st sess., 1937, 81, pt. 5, 5603, 5667; Harold Ickes, *The Secret Diary of Harold Ickes: The 1000 Days, 1933-1936* (New York: Simon and Schuster, 1953), p. 570; Michie and Ryhlick, *Dixie*, p. 63.

4. Gellerman, *Dies*, pp. 33, 47; Dies, *Trojan Horse*, 355; Michie and Ryhlick, *Dixie*, p. 63.

5. U.S., *Congressional Record*, 75th Cong., 3d sess., 1938, 83, pt. 7, 7569; Robert Carr, *The House Committee on Un-American Activities, 1945-1950* (New York: Cornell Press, 1952), 14-15; Nathaniel Weyl, *The Battle Against Disloyalty* (New York: Crowell, 1951), p. 285; Walter Goodman, *The Committee* (New York: Farrar, Straus and Giroux, 1968), pp. 16, 42; Alfred Steinberg, *Sam Rayburn* (New York: Hawthorn, 1975), p. 191; Ray Stephens interview with Martin Dies, April 23, 1966, North Texas State University Oral History Collection, Denton; William Buckley, Jr., *The Committee and Its Critics* (New York: G. P. Putnam's Sons, 1962), p. 96.

6. Michie and Ryhlick, *Dixie*, p. 59; U.S., House of Representatives, Special Committee on Un-American Activities, *Hearings: Investigation of Un-American Propaganda Activities in the U.S.*, 75th Cong., 3d sess., 1938, p. 2857; Robert Stripling, *Red Plot Against America* (Drexel Hill, Pennsylvania: Bell Publishing Company, 1949), p. 57; David Mairowitz, *The Radical Soap Opera* (New York: Avon, 1974), p. 83.

7. *Dallas Morning News*, November 12, 1938, March 5, 1940, October 20, 1941, March 30, 1942, February 5, 1943; Ickes, *Inside Struggle*, p. 529.

8. Michie and Ryhlick, *Dixie*, p. 56; George Seldes, *Witchhunt* (New York: Modern Age Books, 1940), p. 275.

9. Michie and Ryhlick, *Dixie*, pp. 57-58, 65; *Austin American-Statesman*, December 22, 1946.

10. Actually Dies sometimes acted alone without the committee's knowing what he was doing. He published reports of the "committee" that were not even seen by the other members in advance; see Harold Ickes, *The Lowering Clouds* (New York: Simon and Schuster, 1954), p. 380.

11. Joseph Alsop and Robert Kintner, column, *Dallas Morning News*, November 16, 1940; Weyl, *Battle*, p. 286; Ickes, *Lowering Clouds*, p. 381; Gellermann, *Dies*, p. 228; transcript of Dies-Roosevelt conference, November 29, 1940, President's Personal File 3458, Roosevelt Library.

12. *Dallas Morning News*, July 9, 10, 14, 1940. See also Richard Rollins, *I Find Treason* (New York: William Morrow, 1941), p. 215.

13. *Dallas Morning News*, July 12, 13, 19, 1940.

14. Ibid., July 11, 1940; Donald S. Strong, *Organized Anti-Semitism in America* (Washington, D.C.: American Council on Public Affairs, 1941), pp. 31-32.

15. *Fort Worth Star-Telegram*, July 20, 1940; *Dallas Morning News*, July 25, 1940.

16. *Dallas Morning News*, July 31, August 4, 14, 1940; Michie and Ryhlick, *Dixie*, pp. 40-42; *Austin Statesman*, October 2, 14, 1936. Columnist Lorrain Barnes feared that Dr. Henry Harper would have to put away the red neckties he had worn for forty years and that coeds would no longer be permitted to blush at Arthur Dean's anecdotes; see *Austin Statesman*, October 3, 1936.

17. *Dallas Morning News*, April 4, 1941; *Daily Texan*, April 9, 1941; State of Texas, *House Journal*, 47th Legislature, reg. sess., April 4, 1941, pp. 1766-1768.

18. *Dallas Morning News*, January 17, 1941; *Daily Texan*, February 8, April 4, 9, 1941.

19. *Houston Chronicle*, February 11, 1941; *Daily Texan*, March 29, 1941; unidentified paper, February 13, 1941, in Joe Hill Clippings, Texas State Archives, Austin.

20. Interview with former communist who wishes to remain anonymous. A former FBI agent, who also prefers anonymity, recalls that when the few communists in and around the university were finally smoked out in 1954, the legislature played no role in it. Since neither the state nor the federal government prosecuted them, they were evidently not taken very seriously by anyone.

21. *Dallas Morning News*, May 5, 18, June 30, 1941; *Austin American-Statesman*, April 20, 1941; unidentified paper, n.d., 1941, Joe Hill Clippings; Martin Dies press release, June 19, 1941, Lyndon Johnson Papers, House Years, box 8.

22. *Dallas Morning News*, June 30, July 3, 1941; Austin American, July 15, 1941.

23. Goodman, *Committee*, pp. 122-123, 163.

24. Richard Polenberg, *War and Society* (Philadelphia: J. B. Lippincott, 1972), pp. 194-195.

25. *P.M.*, October 22, 1943; *Austin American*, March 30, April 29, May 13, 1944; Mathew Josephson, *Sidney Hillman, Statesman of American Labor* (Garden

City, New York: Doubleday, 1952), p. 610; interview with Morris Akin, Houston, August 19, 1971, University of Texas at Arlington Oral History Project.

26. Josephson, *Hillman*, pp. 608, 610; John Gunther, *Inside U.S.A.* (New York: Harper and Brothers, 1947), pp. 853-854; Michie and Ryhlick, *Dixie*, pp. 59-60; memo to Mrs. Franklin Roosevelt, April 11, 1944, President's Personal File 3458, Roosevelt Library.

27. Interview with Akin. A close friend of Akin's was the group's guide on a hunting or fishing trip.

28. *Austin American*, September 25, 28, October 11, 19, 1944; *Dallas Morning News*, October 1, 1944; Gunther, *Inside U.S.A.*, p. 846; Jimmie Allred to D. B. Hardeman, October 21, 1944, Allred Papers, box 171.

29. *Austin American*, July 29, August 3, 7, 1944; review of *Trojan Horse in America*, *Dallas Morning News*, December 8, 1940; Irving Bernstein, *The Turbulent Years* (Boston: Houghton Mifflin, 1969), pp. 782-783; *Dallas Times-Herald*, July 21, October 1, 1944; Velma Smedley to Hatton Sumners, June 28, July 10, 18, 20, 1944, Sumners to Smedley, July 6, 24, 1944, and Martin Dies to Attorney General Francis Biddle, August 4, 1944, Sumners Papers, drawer 17. The PAC leader, Carl McPeak, did not deny the charge. See his letter to Frank Chappell, July 27, 1944, Carl McPeak Manuscript Vertical File Number 10, Texas Labor Archives, University of Texas at Arlington.

30. Dies attested that he rarely went to conventions; see Ray Stephens interview with Martin Dies.

In regard to the fundamentalism, Dies once noted that the United States has basic rights unknown to all foreign nations because our rights are granted by God; see U.S., *Congressional Record*, 75th Cong., 3d sess., 1938, 83, pt. 7, 7569. See also Clinton Rossiter, *Conservatism in America* (New York: Random House, 1962), pp. 166-173. O'Daniel was an admirer of Dies's book, *Trojan Horse in America*; see *Austin Daily Tribune*, April 1, 1941, Joe Hill Clippings.

31. Walter Lippmann, column, *Washington Post*, January 11, 1940; Frank Donner, "HUAC: the Dossier-Keepers," *Studies on the Left* 2 (1961): 8; Robert Griffith, *The Politics of Fear* (Lexington: University of Kentucky, 1970), pp. 32-33.

32. See Gellerman, *Dies*, p. 6.

CHAPTER 7

1. Dick James, August 18, 1943, Lisle Steel, August 16, 1943, and William Cody, August 16, 1943, to Coke Stevenson, and his replies on September 3, 4, 1943, are in the Coke Stevenson Files, box 136, as are the other letters; Grady Vaughn and Glenn McCarthy, eds., *Shall We Shackle a Texas Heritage?* Statewide Committee of Oil Operators, n.d., Coke Steveson Clippings, Barker History Center, University of Texas Archives, Austin; *Dallas Morning News*, January 9, 1935; Gerald D. Nash, *United States Oil Policy* (Pittsburgh: University of Pittsburgh Press, 1968), p. 177.

The governor of Tennessee estimated the regional freight rate differential at 35 percent; Prentice Cooper to Coke Stevenson, November 28, 1941, Coke Stevenson Files, box 171. A study of discriminatory freight rates at the University of Texas noted that even though Fort Worth was the center of the cattle industry, it was cheaper to send the hides to Boston and manufacture shoes there than to make shoes in Fort Worth; Kendall Cochran interview with Homer Rainey, August 1967, Boulder, Colorado, North Texas State University Oral History Collection, Denton. Freight rate discrimination, however, was vastly overrated; see Dewey Grantham, ed., *The South and the Sectional Image* (New York: Harper and Row, 1967), p. 141.

Stevenson encountered some criticism for accepting thousands of dollars in oil lease money from Magnolia, though the company never drilled on his ranch. Leasing without drilling, however, was common. Other ranches in the neighborhood were leased, and there was some production in the area. Stevenson's views would undoubtedly have been generally the same had the oil connection not existed, though, of course, his proindustry stand may have been unconsciously enhanced by the extra income. An ideal public servant would have avoided this appearance of conflict of interest. Facts, but not opinions, derived from interview with T. Kellis Dibrell, San Antonio, July 28, 1977.

2. The quotes come from the *San Antonio Express*, January 10, 1943, the *Dallas Times-Herald*, August 16, 1943, and *Austin American*, August 31, 1943; Coke Stevenson to H. E. Cutcher, December 2, 1942, Coke Stevenson Files, box 184; Establishment denunciations of gasoline rationing are in Sam Rayburn to Coke Stevenson, May 28, 1942, H. M. Van Auken (general manager of the San Antonio Chamber of Commerce) to Rayburn, May 26, 1942, W. T. White (assistant superintendent of the Dallas schools) to Rayburn, May 26, 1942, Charles I. Frances (of the Jim Elkins law firm in Houston that handled much of the eastern money in Texas) to Rayburn, May 28, 1943, and Fred Sehmann (first vice-president of the North Texas Oil and Gas Association) to Rayburn, September 16, 1942, all in Rayburn Papers, series I, reel 12. Also see John Lee Smith's retort in his letter to Ickes, August 31, 1943, John Lee Smith Papers; Richard Polenberg, *War and Society* (Philadelphia: J. B. Lippincott, 1972), pp. 14-18; Richard Lingeman, *Don't You Know There's a War On?* (New York: Paperback Library, 1970), pp. 285-290.

3. Francis Biddle to Coke Stevenson, July 17, 1942, Stevenson to Biddle, July 27, 1942, Hatton Sumners to Stevenson, August 7, 1942, Mrs. Marilyn Flynn to Stevenson, n.d., 1945, Stevenson to Mrs. Flynn, September 21, 1946, Coke Stevenson Files, boxes 131, 145.

4. James Burran, "The Beaumont Race Riot, 1943" (Master's thesis, Texas Tech University, 1973), pp. 34, 67-68, 88 (the quote), 91, 105, 116, 132, 141-142; Robert Garson, *The Democratic Party and the Politics of Sectionalism, 1941-1948* (Baton Rouge: Louisiana State University Press, 1974), pp. 86-87; interview with A. M. Aikin Jr., Paris, August 4, 1977.

5. Interview with Thomas Sutherland, Arlington, Texas, May 16, 1976; Coke Stevenson to Fco. de P. Jimenez, August 24, 1942, Coke Stevenson Files, box 183; Nellie Ward Kingrea, *History of the First Ten Years of the Good Neighbor Commission* (Fort Worth: Texas Christian University Press, 1954), pp. 32-34, 83, 109-110; Fred Gantt, Jr., *The Chief Executive in Texas* (Austin: University of Texas Press, 1964), p. 148; *The Good Neighbor Policy and Mexicans in Texas* (Mexico City: Department of State for Foreign Affairs, 1943), pp. 8-13.

See also the Interracial Discrimination folder in the Coke Stevenson Files, box 183, and League of Loyal Americans to Coke Stevenson, August 14, 1941, Stevenson Files, box 168.

6. Otey Scruggs, "Texas and the Bracero Program," *Pacific Historical Review* 32 (August 1963): 258-263; George Little, "A Study of the Texas Good Neighbor Commission" (Master's thesis, University of Houston, 1953), p. 14; Hector Perez Martinez to Beauford Jester, September 2, 1947, Beauford Jester Papers, box 122.

The commission never lobbied for a statute against discrimination, in part because of fear of being identified with black desires for civil liberties, which were stirring considerable Anglo resentment: see Kingrea, *History*, p. 47.

7. Wilbourn Benton, *Texas, Its Government and Politics* (Englewood Cliffs, New Jersey: Prentice-Hall, 1966), pp. 522-523; for Smith's handling of the bill, see *Austin Statesman*, March 26, 1943, and unidentified clipping, February 17, 1943, in John Lee Smith Papers; Grady Mullenix, "A History of the Texas State Federation of Labor" (Ph.D. diss., University of Texas at Austin, 1955), p. 394; Ray Marshall, *Labor in the South* (Cambridge Harvard University Press, 1967), p. 243; a copy of the agreement is in the Texas AFL-CIO Collection, 110-15-1-6.

8. Lewis Nordyke, "Calculatin' Coke," *Saturday Evening Post* 217 (October 28, 1944): 15; *Dallas Morning News*, January 21, 1944, July 18, 1963; *State Observer*, April 10, 1944; Coke Stevenson, "To the Members of the Forty-Eighth Legislature," inaugural address, Stevenson Clippings; Neil Sapper, "A Survey of the History of the Black People of Texas, 1930-1954" (Ph.D. diss., Texas Tech University, 1972), pp. 92-93; Garson, *Democratic Party*, pp. 44-45, 51-52; William Thorton, column, *Dallas Morning News*, January 12, 1944. See George B. Tindall, *The Emergence of the New South* (Baton Rouge: Louisiana State University Press, 1967), p. 726.

9. David McComb interview with Walter Hall, June 30, 1969, Oral History Collection, Johnson Library.

10. R. L. Thornton to Coke Stevenson, May 29, 1945, Coke Stevenson Files, box 178; Nordyke, "Calculatin' Coke," p. 15.

11. Preston Smith to Coke Stevenson, March 21, 1946, Ray Leeman to Stevenson, April 12, 1946, and Carl Weaver to Stevenson, January 17, 1946, Coke Stevenson Files, box 175; Coke Stevenson to Richard Roberts, June 21, 1946, Johnson Papers, House Years, box 124; *Texas Spectator*, November 1, 1946; see also Wesley Chumlea, "The Politics of Legislative Reapportionment in Texas, 1921-1957" (Ph.D. diss., University of Texas at Austin, 1959), esp. pp. 143-151. Smith later became senator, lieutenant governor, and governor, 1969-1973. Leeman was executive vice-president of the South Texas Chamber of Commerce. Weaver was Houston's American Legion commander.

F. G. Swanson, column, *The Emancipator*, September 1945, on legislator's quip.

12. Orville Bullington to Carr Collins, November 14, 1938, Carr Collins to Bullington, November 18, 1938, Weaver Moore to W. Lee O'Daniel, January 29, 1940, H. H. Weinert to W. Lee O'Daniel, January 25, 1940, W. Lee O'Daniel Files, boxes 217, 220, 230; Homer Rainey, *The Tower and the Dome* (Boulder: Pruett, 1971), pp. 97-99; *Austin American*, November 29, 1944; Hart Stilwell, "Civil War in Texas," *Collier's* 115 (January 6, 1945): 19; *Dallas Morning News*, August 12, 1936, carries Bullington's opinion of the New Deal; *Daily Texan*, November 2, 1944, and *Austin American*, November 23, 1944, as well as a letter from Gray Twonbly to Homer Rainey, July 11, 1944, Miscellany Concerning the University of Texas Controversy, 48th Legislature, Senate Investigating Committee, Legislative Reference Library, Austin, reveal Dr. Bertner's influence; J. Frank Dobie, "For Your Careful

Consideration," 1943 or 1944 brochure, Margaret Carter Papers; see Texas Senate, Investigation of the University of Texas by Senate Investigating Committee, *Hearings*, 49th Legislature, November 1944, vol. III.

13. *The University of Texas Controversy*, pamphlet from J. R. Parten's statement to the Texas Senate Educational Committee, November 28, 1944, Margaret Carter Papers and in the Homer Rainey Files, Barker History Center, University of Texas Archives, Austin; R. L. Bobbitt statement in Senate Investigating Committee, *Hearings*, Vol. IV, 577-578; see also Ronnie Dugger, *Our Invaded Universities* (New York: W. W. Norton, 1974), pp. 41-42, Dobie, For Your Careful Consideration, Margaret Carter Papers, and Rainey, *Tower*, pp. 6-7, 98.

14. Dugger, *Our Invaded Universities*, pp. 42-43; Rainey, *Tower*, pp. 7-8.

15. *The University of Texas Controversy*, pamphlet from Parten statement, Margaret Carter Papers and Homer Rainey Files.

16. Rainey, *Tower*, pp. 38, 46-47; John Gunther, *Inside U.S.A.* (New York: Harper and Brothers, 1947), p. 856; Frank Goodwyn, *Lone Star Land* (New York: Alfred A. Knopf, 1955), p. 297.

17. *Austin American*, November 23, 25, 1944; Rainey, *Tower*, pp. 50-52.

18. Rainey, *Tower*, pp. 42-43; *Summer Texan*, June 7, 1942; Goodwyn, *Lone Star Land*, pp. 292-295; *State Observer*, October 23, 30, 1944; Kendall Cochran interview with W. N. Peach, June 24, 1966, North Texas State University Oral History Collection, Denton; *Dallas Morning News*, March 17, 1942, contains Hoblitzelle's full-page ad; Clarence Ayres to Bruce Bliven, July 1, 1942, American Civil Liberties Union Papers, vol. 2425, Seeley G. Mudd Manuscripts Library, Princeton, New Jersey; Alice Cox, "The Rainey Affair: A History of the Academic Freedom Controversy at the University of Texas, 1938-1946" (Ph.D. diss., University of Denver, 1960), pp. 41-56; on the dismissal of the instructors, see also the Ralph Himstead-John Bickett correspondence, September-November 1943, Miscellany Concerning the University of Texas Controversy.

Ruth Allen, "War and the Forty Hour Week," April 6, 1942, Allred Papers, box 156, provides a good statement on that topic. Dr. Allen observed that 40 percent of the workers already put in over sixty hours a week in defense plants, that longer work days do not mean greater productivity, and that restricting strikes would not stop labor protests.

19. Homer Rainey to D. F. Strickland, February 10, 1943, and Strickland to Rainey, March 16, 1943, Coke Stevenson Files, box 147; Rainey, *Tower*, pp. 44-45.

20. Rainey, *Tower*, pp. 43, 47-48, 92; Goodwyn, *Lone Star Land*, pp. 296-298; Cox, "Rainey Affair," pp. 68-69; Dugger, *Our Invaded Universities*, pp. 44-45; *State Observer*, October 23, 30, 1944.

Regental reasoning on the various issues is defended in J. Evetts Haley, *The University of Texas and the Issue* (Amarillo: Miller Printing Company, 1945), "Reasons of Dudley K. Woodward, Jr., Chairman of the Board of Regents of the University of Texas, for Voting Against the Election of Dr. Homer P. Rainey as President of the University of Texas," January 26, 1945, and Orville Bullington, "Reasons for Vote," n.d., Miscellany Concerning the University of Texas Controversy.

Veteran regent Lutcher Stark kept his sense of humor about the situation by purchasing innumerable copies of *U.S.A.* from nearby bookstores and distributing autographed copies at the board meeting, as Rainey recalled in his interview with Cochran.

21. Goodwyn, *Lone Star Land*, pp. 299-300; Dugger, *Our Invaded Universities*, p. 46; Raymond Brooks and Margaret Mayer, column, *Austin American*, November 18, 1944; Nina Cunningham to Franklin Roosevelt, November 21, 1944, President's Personal File 3535, Roosevelt Library.

22. Dr. K. H. Aynesworth to Coke Stevenson, March 20, 1943, and Stevenson to Aynesworth, March 23, 1943, Coke Stevenson Files, box 155; Gunther, *Inside U.S.A.*, p. 840; *The Boys Who Fired Rainey*, anonymous leaflet, Margaret Carter Papers; Sam Hall, column, *Texas Spectator*, January 25, 1946; *Austin American*, November 4, 1944.

23. Bernard DeVoto, "The Easy Chair," *Harper's Magazine* 191 (August 1945): 135 (first quote); Henry Nash Smith, *The Controversy at the University of Texas* (Austin: Students' Association, 1946), p. 15; Raymond Brooks and Margaret Mayer, column, *Austin American*, November 18, 1944; Brooks, column, *Austin American*, November 21, 1944; *Austin American*, November 19, 22, 27, 1944; Cox, "Rainey Affair," pp. 111-112, 117; senator's rejoinder in *State Observer*, November 20, 1944; Stark quote in the Senate Investigating Committee, *Hearings*, Vol. II, 571.

24. Goodwyn, *Lone Star Land*, pp. 301-302; *Texas Spectator*, May 31, 1946; *Houston Press*, January 27, 1945. The irreverent *Spectator*, October 12, 1945, declared the board's era of tranquility was actually an "Aeon of Soft Soap." Most of the faculty supported Rainey both before and after his termination, but some prominent ones did not. See William C. Pool, *Eugene C. Barker, Historian* (Austin: Texas State Historical Association, 1971), pp. 187-211.

25. Minnie Fisher Cunningham to the members of the Women's Committee on Educational Freedom, January 9, 1945, Margaret Carter Papers; *Houston Press*, January 20, February 16, 1945; Goodwyn, *Lone Star Land*, p. 302; *Austin American*, January 18, 1945; *Houston Post*, January 20, 1945; Charles Green, ed., *Fellow Texans in Profile* (Austin: Steck, 1948), pp. 136, 140; *Dallas Morning News*, July 19, 1945.

26. *Texas Spectator*, January 18, February 8, 1946.

27. Margaret Carter to Marion Storm, June 29, 1945, and *Religion in Life*, three brochures of Rainey's speeches, April 15-May 9, 1946, Margaret Carter Papers; *San Antonio Express*, January 13, 1946; *Weatherford Democrat Daily*, November 8, 1945; Minnie Fisher Cunningham to Homer Rainey, November 22, 1945, and Rainey to J. C. Granbery, July 12, 1945, and to Senator J. E. Brackert, July 17, 1945, Rainey Papers, box 41; Jimmie Allred to J. A. Clark, July 21, 1945, Allred Papers, box 171; *Texas Spectator*, February 8, 1946.

28. Goodwyn, *Lone Star Land*, pp. 302-303; Stilwell, "Civil War in Texas," p. 31.

29. *Waco Times Herald*, June 2, 1946; *Fort Worth Star-Telegram*, May 11, 1946; *The CIO News*, February 10, 1947; Marshall, *Labor*, pp. 226, 263-264; Garson, *Democratic Party*, pp. 142, 188-189.

30. Hugh Roy Cullen to Coke Stevenson, December 19, 1946, Coke Stevenson Files, box 179; Seth Shepard McKay, *Texas and the Fair Deal, 1945-1952* (San Antonio: The Naylor Company, 1954), pp. 43-45.

31. Ennis Favors to Beauford Jester, February 14, 1946, Beauford Jester Files, box 56.

During the war Stevenson had abolished the Old Age Assistance Special Fund, making it necessary for the legislature to appropriate money from general revenue to pay assistance to the aged, the blind, and dependent children. The Austin representative to the Texas State Pension Association estimated that if the state oil tax had just been raised to Louisiana's lowest tax, that it would finance a special fund for welfare—see *A. B. Rosson Newsletter*, 1946, in Miscellany Concerning the University of Texas Controversy, and A. Hope Wheeler, column, *Texan Citizen*, July 3, 1943.

32. *Houston Post*, March 5, May 9, June 3, 1943; *State Observer*, June 7, 1943; *Dallas Morning News*, Februry 3, 24, 26, 1943; J. Frank Dobie, column, *Dallas Morning News*, February 2, 1943; *Austin American*, February 17, 1943; Alonzo Wasson, column, *Dallas Morning News*, March 17, 1943; unidentified papers, March 17, 1943, June 3, 1943, March 1943; John Lee Smith Papers; *San Angelo Standard-Times*, May 9, 1945; Andy McBride transcript for KTHT, n.d., and "While They Battle on Foreign Fronts There Should be No Strikes on the Home Fronts," 1944 reelection leaflet, John Lee Smith Papers.

33. Paul Bolton, column, *Austin American*, October 29, 1945; D. F. Strickland to Tom Connally, June 30, 1945, and Mrs. John Lee Smith to W. Lee O'Daniel, August 6, 1945, John Lee Smith Papers.

34. Bolton, *Austin American*, October 29, 1945; *Houston Post*, July 21, 1946; *Texas Spectator*, December 21, 1945; *Austin American*, July 18, 1945; D. F. Strickland to John Lee Smith, June 1945, June 27, 1945, and January 17, 1946; John Q. Adams to John Lee Smith, September 27, 1945; Orville Bullington to John Lee Smith, September 6, 1945; W. S. Schreiner to John Lee Smith, August 13, September 6, 1945; D. K. Woodward to John Lee Smith, October 9, 1945, and Smith to Woodward, October 6, 1945; George Armstrong to John Lee Smith, August 6, 1945, and Smith to Armstrong, August 21, 1945. All letters are in the John Lee Smith Papers.

For information on Armstrong see the correspondence of Thomas Freidman and others, George W. Armstrong Collection, Anti-Defamation League Files, Southwestern Office, Houston, as well as Arnold Forster and Benjamin Epstein, *The Troublemakers* (Garden City, New York: Doubleday, 1952), p. 161; George Fuermann, *Reluctant Empire* (Garden City, New York: Doubleday, 1957), pp. 99-100; *Austin American-Statesman*, December 25, 1950; Lynn Landrum, column, *Dallas Morning News*, November 1, 1949.

35. E. J. Price to John Lee Smith, October 10, 1945, March 26, 1946, and Smith to Price, January 30, 1946, John Lee Smith Papers. In 1975 interviews, three politicians noted (anonymously) that they saw nothing wrong with Smith's arrangement with Price or with Price's percentage. "What is unusual," according to one, "is that the fool put it in writing."

36. McKay, *Texas and the Fair Deal*, pp. 79, 96, 99 (Collins quote), 111-112, 116; John Lee Smith speech, n.d., 1946, John Lee Smith Papers; Smith quotes are from speeches, June 16, 1946, and another one with no date, 1946, John Lee Smith Papers.

37. John Lee Smith speech, n.d., 1946, and Smith to D. F. Strickland, July 6, 1945 (noting East Texans's touchiness on race), John Lee Smith Papers.

Smith was not keen on Mexican-Americans either. Sam Smith of Sonora wrote to him, June 4, 1945, that he and his fellow veterans did not fight for "ill-smelling Mexicans," who were overrunning movie houses and would soon probably move into swimming pools, dancing places, schools, and cafés. They were even taking veterans' jobs. "We don't want Mexican relatives," he added. Texas's lieutenant governor replied, June 7, 1945: "I agree with most of your conclusions." Letters in the John Lee Smith Papers.

38. B. C. Utecht, column in unidentified paper, early 1946, the John Lee Smith Papers; *Gainesville Daily Register*, November 11, 1934.

39. *Houston Press*, March 15, 1946; E. M. Pooley, column, *El Paso Herald*, May 15, 1946; *Dallas Morning News*, May 5, July 5, 1946; Anthony Clark, "Politics and Controversy During John Lee Smith's Lieutenant Governorship Years (Master's thesis, Texas Tech, 1971), p. 184; *Texas Spectator*, January 4, July 12, 1946; *Texas Almanac, 1947-1948*, p. 407.

40. Beauford Jester to Virgil Goodman, March 19, April 5, 1946. See also *Texas Spectator*, April 5, 1946. Regarding hints and pledges of backing from Texas Regulars and their ilk, see Beauford Jester to J. R. Allen, April 3, 1946, John Carpenter, March 14, 1946, Jan Anderson, March 5, 1946, and Karl Hoblitzelle, February 11, March 2, 1946, and letters to Beauford Jester from E. B. Germany, May 31, 1946, Maco Stewart, March 6, 1946, J. Frank Norris, March 22, 1946, and Gerald L. K. Smith, February 1, 1947. All are in the Beauford Jester Files, box 56, except for the Smith letter, which is in box 64.

41. Coke Stevenson to Reverend J. S. Newman, June 19, 1946, Coke Stevenson Files, box 154.

42. *Austin American*, August 20, 1946; *Texas Spectator*, November 17, 1947; McKay, *Texas and the Fair Deal*, p. 114; Austin ministers to board of regents, March 23, 1943, Coke Stevenson Files, box 156.

43. Beauford Jester to Byron Utecht, March 7, 1946, and Lloyd Gregory to Beauford Jester, c. May 27, 1946, Beauford Jester Files, boxes 58 and 56, respectively. Jester's blast cost him the support of Frank Erwin, Jr., the powerful regent of the 1960s, who was a student leader for Rainey in 1944, but had backed Jester for governor. He pledged neutrality during the primary. See Frank Erwin, Jr., to Beauford Jester, June 2, 1946, Beauford Jester Files, box 56.

44. Clark, "Politics and Controversy," p. 182; S. S. McKay, "The Rainey-Jester Campaign for the Governorship," *West Texas Historical Association Yearbook* 30 (October 1954): 35; Goodwyn, *Lone Star Land*, p. 307; McKay, *Texas and the Fair Deal*, p. 105.

45. Cochran interview with Rainey; Rainey leaflet, n.d., Margaret Carter Papers; "Let the Record Speak," Rainey leaflet, n.d., and *Dr. Homer P. Rainey and the Negro Question*, pamphlet of UT Students' Anti-Rainey for Governor Club, in author's possession, and George B. Hufford to Homer Rainey, October 23, 1946, Rainey Papers, box 42, plus Mervyn Ramsey to Beauford Jester, July 28, 1946, Beauford Jester Files, box 56—on the race question; G. D. Gurley (oil developer) to Jester, July 6, 1946, and Charles Berry (district judge) to Jester, May 5, 1946, Beauford Jester Files, box 56, and "Does CIO-PAC Plan Communistic Dictatorship Patterned After Russian Soviet System?" full-page advertisement in the *Fort Worth Shopper*, July 14, 1946—on the labor issue; McKay, *Texas and the Fair Deal*, pp. 95, 106, 113; *Texas Almanac, 1947-1948*, p. 407; Cox, "Rainey Affair," pp. 130-132, *Texas Spectator*, December 6, 1946; John Connelly to Homer Rainey, November 15, 1946, Rainey Papers, box 42; affidavit regarding regents' role in Rainey Papers, box 41.

Two weeks before the first primary, one key corporate-political adviser wrote to

Jester that he was getting the Stevenson vote, but that George Parr was "delivering Duval to Sellers": Maston Nixon to Beauford Jester, July 15, 1946, Beauford Jester Files, box 56. Sellers carried Duval with over 96 percent of the vote: *Texas Almanac, 1947-1948*, p. 405.

46. "Let the Record Speak," Rainey leaflet, n.d., in author's possession; Rainey leaflet, n.d., Margaret Carter Papers; *Texas Industry* (August 1946); Cochran interview with Rainey; Gunther, *Inside U.S.A.*; p. 841; Goodwyn, *Lone Star Land*; p. 309; *Texas Spectator*, September 27, 1946, September 1, 1947; V. O. Key, *Southern Politics* (New York: Alfred A. Knopf, 1949), pp. 467-468; McKay, *Texas and the Fair Deal*, pp. 119-130; Allan Duckworth, colum, *Dallas Morning News*, January 18, 1966; Rainey speeches, August 2, 3, 6, 1946, Rainey Papers, box 43; Stuart Long, "The Man Behind the Scenes" (column), *Labor News*, January 22, 1948; Palmer Bradley speech, August 21, 1946, Palmer Bradley Papers, Special Collections, University of Houston; Herbert Parmet, *The Democrats: The Years After FDR* (New York: Oxford, 1976), p. 33.

Among other places, Rainey's full platform was printed in *Emancipator*, September 1946, and in Rainey leaflet, n.d., Miscellany Concerning the University of Texas Controversy. For background on some of the Klan strategy, see J. H. Ridlehuber to Miriam Ferguson, August 19, 1946, and F. H. Leslie to Jimmie Allred, August 19, 1946, Rainey Papers, box 45.

47. "Platform Adopted by the Dallas Committee for Democratic Action," April 17, 1946, Carl Brannin Collection, Texas Political History Collection, University of Texas at Arlington; *Memorandum on U.D.A. Organization for 1946*, n.d., George Lambert Papers, 127-3-1, Texas Labor Archives, University of Texas at Arlington; *A People's Legislative Program*, January 20, 1947, Shivers Papers, 4-15/211; Jack Bass and Walter DeVries, *The Transformation of Southern Politics*, (New York: Basic Books, 1976), p. 310; Chandler Davidson, *Biracial Politics: Conflict and Coalition in the Metropolitan South* (Baton Rouge: Louisiana State University Press, 1972), p. 85; *Texas Spectator*, June 21, 1946; interview with Margaret Carter, Arlington, March 16, 1977; interview with Hank Rabun, Dallas, February 24, 1977, University of Texas at Arlington Oral History Project; Neil Sapper," A Survey of the History of the Black People of Texas, 1930-1954" (Ph.D. diss., Texas Tech University, 1972), pp. 118-120, 142-145, but he overestimates the importance of the back-pedaling activities of the Carter Wesley-Valmo Bellinger black axis as a contributing factor in Rainey's defeat. Rainey would not have won had the black vote been enthusiastically tripled.

48. E. Roundstream to Homer Rainey, March 7, 1946, contains undated clipping from *Dallas Times-Herald; Dallas Times-Herald*, July 28, August 23, 1946; Robert Finklea, column, *Dallas Morning News*, August 25, 1946.

49. Donald Strong, "The Rise of Negro Voting in Texas," *American Political Science Review* 42 (June 1948): 514, 519; David Botter, column , *Dallas Morning News*, August 27, 28, 1946; Garson, *Democratic Party*, p. 169; Sapper, "Survey," p. 126.

50. Gantt interviews with Stevenson, May 13-14, August 2, 1967; Charles Simons, "The American Way," Stevenson campaign brochure, n.d., Brotherhood of Locomotive Firemen and Enginemen Files, 38-2-4; U.S., Department of Commerce, Bureau

of the Census, *United States Census of Population: 1950*, vol. 4: *Special Reports*, pt. 3, chap. C, Persons of Spanish Surname, table 6, 3C-39, and vol. 2, *Detailed Characteristics of the Population, Texas*, pt. 43, chap. C, table 84, 43-590.

51. See *Texas Spectator*, January 10, 27, 1947.

52. Gantt interview with Stevenson, August 2, 1967.

53. George Brown Tindall, *The Disruption of the Solid South* (New York: W. W. Norton, 1962), pp. 34-35.

54. *Texas Spectator*, July 26, 1946.

55. DeVoto, "Easy Chair," p. 137.

CHAPTER 8

1. "Biographical Sketch, "Beauford Jester Files, box 126; on wealth, see Leonard Marks to Jimmie Allred, July 26, 1946, Allred Papers, box 172.

2. Top secret memo, William McGill to Beauford Jester, July 18, 1947, cites Schreiner's feelings; Robert Holliday to Jester, November 21, 1946, refers to board's desire for vindication; letters from R. A. Weinert, December 30, 1946, and J. S. Bridwell, January 7, 1947, display bitterness over Jester's attitude toward reappointment; Jester to W. S. Schreiner, February 27, 1947, and Schreiner to Jester, March 3, 1947, all in Beauford Jester Files, box 54; memo from Schreiner to Allan Shivers, July 16, 1947, Shivers Papers, 4-15/205. See also *State Observer*, January 6 and February 24, 1947.

3. *Summer Texan*, July 24, 1947; W. S. Schreiner to Beauford Jester, October 27, 1947, Beauford Jester Files, box 54.

4. John Bainbridge, *The Super-Americans* (Garden City, New York: Doubleday, 1961), p. 236; Ralph Yarborough, *Frank Dobie: Man and Friend* (Washington, D.C.: The Westerners, 1968), pp. 12-13; Mody Boatright, "A Mustang in the Groves of Academe," in *Three Men in Texas*, ed. Ronnie Dugger (Austin: University of Texas Press, 1967), p. 199. Dobie also displeased some by nailing moose heads to the walls of his office.

5. *State Observer*, April 17, 1947.

6. Ibid.

7. *The CIO News*, February 10, 1947; Tom Brewer, "State Anti-Labor Legislation: Texas—A Case Study," *Labor History* 11 (Winter 1970): 72.

8. Bob Henderson to Beauford Jester, October 14, 1946, and Bob Henderson to Hugh Roy Cullen, August 3, 1945, Beauford Jester Files, boxes 63 and 111, respectively; Paul Holcomb, column, *State Observer*, May 5, 1947; J. Evetts Haley to Allan Shivers, March 13, 1947, Shivers Papers, 4-15/208; *Proceedings of the Tenth Annual Convention of the Texas State Industrial Union Council* (Austin, 1946), pp. 17-18.

9. Milton Gabel and Hortense Gabel, "Texas Newspaper Opinion: 1," *Public Opinion Quarterly*, 10 (Spring 1946): 58-59, 61, 63-66.

10. *Texas Spectator*, January 11, 1946.

11. *The CIO News*, June 2, 1947; Wilbourn Benton, *Texas, Its Government and Politics* (Englewood Cliffs, New Jersey: Prentice-Hall, 1966), p. 523; "Texas CIO Notes," October 1, 1946, Texas AFL-CIO Collection, 110-16-12-1.

12. *The CIO News*, February 10, 1947.

13. Unidentified newspaper clipping, October 1, 1946, enclosed in M. G. Cox to Beauford Jester, October 7, 1946, and *Platform Adopted by the State Democratic Convention*, San Antonio, September 19, 1946, Beauford Jester Files, boxes 118 and 175, respectively.

14. Benton, *Texas*, pp. 523-526; *International Oil Worker*, May 19, 1947; *Newsweek* 29 (June 30, 1947): 60; Frederick Meyers, *"Right-to-Work" in Practice* (New York: Fund for the Republic, 1959), p. 3.

For highlights of legislative action on "right-to-work," see State of Texas, *House Journal*, 50th Legislature, reg. sess., January 16, 1947, pp. 37-40, March 3, 1947, pp. 586-591, March 4, 1947, pp. 610-612, April 2, 1947, pp. 1182-1184, and *Senate Journal*, 50th Legislature, reg. sess., March 20, 1947, pp. 429-431, March 31, 1947, pp. 471-472, April 2, 1947, pp. 495-496.

15. Neville Penrose to Beauford Jester, December 27, 1946, and William McGill to Marshall Bell, May 19, 1947, Beauford Jester Files, box 72; box 51 in the Beauford Jester Files is filled with three files of corporate letters and telegrams on behalf of the antisecondary boycott bills; untitled report to Jester from the Industrial Commission, March 31, 1947, Beauford Jester Files, box 48; also in the Jester Files are his message to the legislature, April 14, 1947 (box 105), letters to house members, May 20, 1947 (box 53), and Jester memoranda to the press, May 30, 1947, June 13, 1947 (box 64); *Labor News*, February 27, 1947, describes the Minnesota bill; memo from Paul Brown to Beauford Jester, May 22, 1947, the William McGill Papers, 2-23/166, Texas State Archives, Austin.

16. Memo from William McGill to Beauford Jester, May 12, 1947, contains quote; unidentified memo to Durwood Manford, May 19, 1947, both in the Beauford Jester Files, box 72; *Texas Spectator*, May 26, 1947.

17. Interview with Milton Muse, June 29, 1966; *State Observer*, February 3, May 19, 1947; Meyers, *"Right-to-Work,"* p. 3; *Austin American*, March 14, 1947; Ruth Koenig to members of the Texas Legislature, March 15, 1947, Beauford Jester Files, box 67; Grady Mullennix, "A History of the Texas State Federation of Labor" (Ph.D. diss., University of Texas at Austin, 1955), p. 420; *Texas Spectator*, March 24, 1947; *Labor News*, August 7, 1947.

18. Harry Acreman agreed with this sentiment in the interview, August 28, 1969. So did Lieutenant Governor John Lee Smith in letters to William Noguess, June 7, 1945, and William Walker, August 4, 1945, John Lee Smith Papers.

Paul Bolton, column, *Austin American*, July 26, 1945; *State Observer*, February 3, 1947; Mullennix, "History," pp. 419-420; on Smith see Hart Stilwell columns in *Texas Spectator*, February 3, 10, 1947; "Yokel" quote in *Texas Spectator*, February 17, 1947.

19. Meyers, *"Right-to-Work,"* p. 3; Benton, *Texas*, p. 539; Mary Bourgeois column, *Texas Industry*, June 1947; Plano Chamber of Commerce to Allan Shivers, February 11, 1947, Shivers Papers, 4-15/208.

20. Hart Stilwell, "Will He Boss Texas?" *Nation* 173 (November 10, 1951): 399; Mullennix, "History," p. 422.

Jester's closeness to Brown is revealed in his letters to the oilman, May 2, 1945, April 14, 1947, August 11, 1948, Beauford Jester Papers, boxes 118, 63, and 11, respectively. On the latter two occasions the governor thanked Brown for the use of his plane and pilot. Oilmen sometimes appeared to fall over themselves in offering Jester their airplanes. After Texas Regular oil millionaire Al Buchanan had lent his plane to Jester, oil millionaire H. H. "Pete" Coffield sent a whining note to the governor, reminding Jester that he had never called for the use of his (Pete's) plane and that it was available any time: Jester to Buchanan, April 27, 1949, and Coffield to Jester, May 7, 1949, Beauford Jester Papers, box 114. See also *Texas Spectator*, June 2, 1947.

21. Meyers, *"Right-to-Work,"* pp. 2-3; *State Observer*, April 7, 1947; *Proceedings, Texas State Federation of Labor, 1947* (Austin, n.d.), pp. 62-67; *Texas Spectator*, February 17, 1947.

22. Meyers, *"Right-to-Work,"* pp. 4-10; Brewer, "State Anti-Labor Legislation," p. 76; Sam Barton, "The Economic Myth of Right-to-Work Laws," *American Federationist* 74 (August 1967): 15-18.

23. Allen Duckworth, "Democratic Dilemma in Texas." *Southwest Review* 32 (Winter 1947): 39-40; Seth Shepard McKay, *Texas and the Fair Deal, 1945-1952* (San Antonio: Naylor Company, 1954), p. 83; *Platform Adopted by the State Democratic Convention*, San Antonio, September 10, 1946, Beauford Jester Files, box 175; *Texas Spectator*, August 16, September 13, 27, October 11, 1946; Stanley Schneider, "The Texas Regular Party of 1944" (Master's thesis, University of Chicago, 1948), p. 116.

24. *Dallas Morning News*, September 12, 1946. Cooperation was so unusual as to be astonishing. In the *Dallas Morning News*, November 12, 1946, Allen Duckworth wrote, "This is news—the Texas Democratic party held a peaceful meeting here Monday." He thought perhaps it was because it was Armistice Day or because children were present, but in any case, no one walked out and no one was publicly branded a communist or a fascist.

25. *Committee Report Made to Southern Governor's Conference*, March 13, 1948 (made public on the day of the meeting, February 7) and memo from William McGill to Beauford Jester, March 11, 1948, shows count of civil-rights letters, Beauford Jester Files, boxes 46 and 93, respectively; McKay, *Texas and the Fair Deal*, pp. 246-247; W. Berman, *The Politics of Civil Rights in the Truman Administration* (Columbus: Ohio State University Press, 1970), pp. 44-51, 76-77, 84; *Dallas Times-Herald*, February 29, 1948, on Calvert; see also Robert Garson, *The Democratic Party and the Politics of Sectionalism, 1941-1948* (Baton Rouge: Louisiana State University Press, 1974), pp. 220-240.

Merritt Gibson to Palmer Bradley, March 6, 7, 1948, and Palmer Bradley to Paul Brown, March 8, 1948, Beauford Jester files, box 93; Hugh Roy Cullen to Jester, April 6, 1948, and memo from Paul Brown to Jester, April 7, 1948, Beauford Jester Files, boxes 63 and 68, respectively; Jester to southern governors, April 26, 27, 1948, Beauford Jester files, box unknown; see also Ross Clarke to Robert Calvert, April 22, 1948, and Mrs. George Starr Hart to Neville Penrose, March 26, 1948, Beauford Jester Files, box 63; *Houston Post*, April 30, 1948, contains Armstrong advertisement.

26. Quote in letter from Merritt Gibson to Arch Rowan, January 14, 1948, Palmer Bradley papers; *St. Louis Post-Dispatch*, August 18, 19, 1948; Garson, *Democratic Party*, p. 250; *Texas Spectator*, July 7, 1947.

27. Interview with Calvert, Paul Holcomb, column, *State Observer*, August

2, 1948, and Dale Odom interview with Weldon Hart, Austin, July 3, 1967, North Texas State University Oral History Collection, Denton, on Jester's personality; Beauford Jester speech, April 28, 1948, Harry S. Truman Papers, Official File 300, box 983, Harry S. Truman Library, Independence, Missouri; Garson, *Democratic Party*, pp. 259-260; Paul Holcomb, column, *State Observer*, May 3, 1948; "The Man Behind the Scenes" (Stuart Long), column in *Labor News*, March 25, 1948.

28. McKay, *Texas and the Fair Deal*, pp. 251, 271; Paul Holcomb, column, *State Observer*, October 19, 1953; Jeff Hickman to all area and local Political Action Councils, June 1948, Beauford Jester Files, box 63; Berman, *Politics*, p. 95; Garson, *Democratic Party*, p. 265; Harvard Sitkoff, "Harry Truman and the Election of 1948: The Coming of Age of Civil Rights in American Politics," *Journal of Southern History* 37 (November 1971): 603; Harry Seay to Harry Truman, June 1, 1948, Truman Papers, Official File 300, box 983; Arch Rowan to Beauford Jester, May 27, 1948, Palmer Bradley Papers.

29. Neville Penrose to Beauford Jester, June 28, 1948, and Jester to SDEC and Others, July 28, 1948, Beauford Jester Files, box 63; M. White, August 9, 1948, William Bates, August 7, 1948, Mart Cole, July 30, 1948, and J. A. Elkins, August 4, 1948, to Jester, Palmer Bradley to R. H. McLeod, August 10, 1948, petition to SDEC, n.d., and roll call vote of SDEC, August 9, 1948, Beauford Jester Files, box 112; Louise Daughtry Barnett (of the DRT) to Jester, August 18, 1948, and Jester to Lamar Fleming, Jr., August 26, 1948, Beauford Jester Files, boxes 97 and 111, respectively; Palmer Bradley to Strom Thurmond, July 20, 23, 1948, and James Elkins to Hugh Roy Cullen, August 4, 1948, Palmer Bradley Papers.

30. R. L. Thornton, August 2, 1948, and Marshall Formby, August 16, 1948, to Beauford Jester, Beauford Jester Files, boxes 112 and 111, respectively; Sitkoff, "Truman and the Election," p. 609; Jules Abels, *Out of the Jaws of Victory* (New York: Holt, 1959), pp. 74-75.

31. McKay, *Texas and the Fair Deal*, pp. 252-270; Beauford Jester to Bob Henderson, June 30, 1948, and Donald Markle to Jester, July 7, 1948, Beauford Jester Files, boxes 68 and 63, respectively.

32. *Minutes of the Three Caucuses of the Texas Delegation to the Democratic National Convention at Philadelphia, 1948*, Beauford Jester Files, box 68; Paul Holcomb, column, *State Observer*, July 19, 1948; Leslie Carpenter and Bascom Timmons, Night Press message, n.d., Bascom Timmons Clippings, 342-5, Texas A&M Archives, Bryan.

33. Mrs. Winston Liles to Allan Shivers, July 23, 1949, on Penrose antics, Allan Shivers Papers, 4-10/58: Ed Kilman, column, *Houston Post*, September 17, 1950; Paul Holcomb, column, *State Observer*, October 19, 1953; *New York Times*, July 14, 15, 1948; J. W. Jackson, "Texas Politics in 1948," *Southwest Social Science Quarterly* 30 (June 1949): 48; "Purge of Dixiecrats," *Newsweek* 32 (September 27, 1948): 19; *1948 Platform of the Democratic Party of Texas* (Austin, 1948); interview with Calvert; Paul Bolton interview with Stuart Long, December 10, 1968, Oral History Collection, Lyndon B. Johnson Library, Austin; T. H. Baker interview with Byron Skelton, October 15, 1968, Oral History Collection, Lyndon B. Johnson Library, Austin.

34. Quote in Palmer Bradley to R. H. McLeod, August 26, 1948, Palmer Bradley Papers; Arch Rowan to Palmer Bradley, September 16, 1948, to Glenn McCarthy, September 23, 1948, and to Curtis Douglass, September 24, 1948, and Curtis Douglass to Palmer Bradley, July 12, 1948, and to John Price, October 28, 1948, and Palmer Bradley to Merritt Gibson, September 17, 1948, to Lloyd Price, October 5, 1948, and to Curtis Douglass, November 11, 1948, and Hugh Roy Cullen to Palmer Bradley and W. B. Bates, May 4, 1949, Palmer Bradley Papers; Robert Engler, *The Politics of Oil* (Chicago: University of Chicago Press, 1961), p. 354; Garson, *Democratic Party*, pp. 260, 302; *St. Louis Post-Dispatch*, August 18, 19, 1948.

35. Alexander Heard, *A Two-Party South?* (Chapel Hill: University of North Carolina Press, 1952), pp. 258-260; V. O. Key, *Southern Politics* (New York: Alfred A. Knopf, 1949), p. 339; James Soukup, Clifton McCleskey, and Harry Holloway, *Party and Factional Division in Texas* (Austin: University of Texas Press, 1964), p. 168; Garson, *Democratic Party*, p. 285; Texas Election Research Project Committee, *Texas Votes: Selected General and Special Election Statistics, 1944-1963* (Austin: University of Texas Press, 1964), p. 8; Emile Ader, *The Dixiecrat Movement: Its Role in Third Party Politics* (Washington, D.C.: Public Affairs Press, 1955), p. 360; *Emancipator*, October 1948, quotes one racist Dixiecratic brochure while another is in the Palmer Bradley Papers.

36. O'Daniel quote reported in McKay, *Texas and the Fair Deal*, p. 178; *Dallas Morning News*, January 2, 1948; *Texas Spectator*, April 5, 1948; W. Lee ODaniel to friend, n.d., Allred Papers, box 172; George Peddy brochure, 1948, Shivers Papers, 4-15/211.

37. Rowland Evans and Robert Novak, *Lyndon B. Johnson: The Exercise of Power* (New York: New American Library, 1966), pp. 18-19, 23-24; *St. Louis Post-Dispatch*, May 23, 1965; *Texas Spectator*, November 24, 1947; Alfred Steinberg, *Sam Johnson's Boy* (New York: Macmillan, 1968), p. 243; June Welch, "The Texas Senatorial Election of 1948" (Master's thesis, Texas Tech University, 1953), pp. 53-58; Voting Record for House Years, list in the Lyndon Johnson Papers, House Years, box 160; Mullennix, "History," p. 436, on labor quote.

38. McKay, *Texas and the Fair Deal*, pp. 187-191, 200-201, 223, 225-230; Allen Duckworth, column, *Dallas Morning News*, January 19, 1966; "Biscuits to Helicopters," *New Republic* 119 (August 9, 1948): 8; Dale Odom interview with Bob Murphey, Nacogdoches, April 19, 1969, North Texas State University Oral History Collection, Denton; Steinberg, *Sam Johnson's Boy*, pp. 244-250; Key, *Southern Politics*, p. 258; Jimmie Allred to Claude Wild, June 26, 1948, Allred Papers, box 172; Lyndon Johnson campaign brochures, 1948, Johnson Papers, House Years, box 94, and in author's possession; Paul Bolton interview with Charles Herring, October 24, 1968, Oral History Collection, Lyndon B. Johnson Library, Austin, on advance men; on minorities, see *Houston Post*, August 31, 1948, *Dallas Morning News*, September 1, 1948, Neil Sapper, "A Survey of the History of the Black People of Texas, 1930-1954" (Ph.D. diss., Texas Tech University, 1972), p. 146, Joe Frantz interviews with Hobart Taylor Sr., January 29, 1972, and with J. C. Looney, October 3, 1968, Oral History Collection, Lyndon B. Johnson Library, Austin. See also Johnson speeches in Raymond Buck Papers, box 141, folders 329-C and 239-D; on labor deal and other points,

T. H. Baker interview with Booth Mooney, April 8, 1969, Oral History Collection, Lyndon B. Johnson Library, Austin.

39. Ted Ryder to Claude Wild, July 12, 1948, Lyndon Johnson Papers, House Years, box 103; interview with Creekmore Fath, Austin, August 26, 1976; J. L. Calbert, "James Edward and Miriam Amanda Ferguson" (Ph.D. diss., Indiana University, 1968), pp. 271-272; for determination of Ferguson counties, see Key, *Southen Politics*, p. 266, and Alexander Heard and Donald Strong, *Southern Primaries and Elections, 1920-1949* (University, Alabama: University of Alabama Press, 1950), pp. 136-148, 182-184. The Ferguson counties were Bell, Cass, Henderson, Lavaca, Leon, Robertson, Sabine, San Augustine, Shelby, and Titus.

40. Jimmy Banks, *Money, Marbles, and Chalk* (Austin: Texas Publishing Company, 1972), pp. 85-90; M. B. Bravo to Lyndon Johnson, August 29, 30, 1948, and Josefa Gutierrez to State Democratic Executive Committee, September 9, 1948, Lyndon Johnson Papers, House Years, boxes 91, 121, 122; Steinberg, *Sam Johnson's Boy*, pp. 258, 261, 263; McKay, *Texas and the Fair Deal*, pp. 238-240; Robert Sherrill, *The Accidental President* (New York: Grossman, 1967), p. 113; Douglass Cater, "The Trouble in Lyndon Johnson's Back Yard," *Reporter* 13 (December 1, 1955): 32; Charles Ashman, *Connally: The Adventures of Big Bad John* (New York: Morrow, 1974), p. 66; interview with anonymous politician, one source of the Duval message; James Mangan, column in the *Dallas Morning News*, July 31, 1977.

41. Banks, *Money*, pp. 87, 93-94; McKay, *Texas and the Fair Deal*, p. 239.

42. Banks, *Money*, pp. 90-92; Ann Fears Crawford and Jack Keever, *John B. Connally: Portrait in Power* (Austin: Jenkins Publishing Company, 1973), pp. 56-57; Jackson, "Texas Politics," p. 46; Steinberg, *Sam Johnson's Boy*, pp. 263-267; interview with Calvert; interview with T. Kellis Dibrell, San Antonio, July 28, 1977; Paul Bolton interview with Stuart Long.

43. Report of the Senate Subcommittee on Privileges and Elections to the Committee on Rules and Administration RE Texas Second Primary, June 21, 1949, Report Concerning Protests of Texas's Primary Election of 1948, n.d., and memo from JEH to AMC, October 28, 1948, Lyndon Johnson Papers, 1948 Campaign, box 3; Supreme Court, Circuit Court, and District Court records and pleadings plus various transcripts of hearings in south Texas, September 27-29, 1948, are in the Johnson Papers, 1948 Campaign, boxes 6 and 8, respectively; more legal proceedings and a letter from Alvin Wirtz to Jimmie Allred, October 19, 1948, are in the Johnson Papers, 1948 Campaign, box 7; Dawson Duncan and Ray Osborne, separate columns in the *Dallas Morning News*, September 30, 1948; *Houston Chronicle*, September 29, 1948; Steinberg, *Sam Johnson's Boy*, pp. 267-272; Banks, *Money*, pp. 92-93; T. Whitfield Davidson, *The Memoirs of Judge T. Whitfield Davidson* (Dallas: T. Whitfield Davidson, 1972), pp. 90-91; Ronnie Dugger, column, *Texas Observer*, September 23, 1977.

44. Lyndon Johnson to Lynn Landrum, October 29, 1948, Lyndon Johnson Papers, House Years, box 94; J. Edward Johnson to Lyndon Johnson, September 11, 1948, and untitled analysis of Brown County returns, n.d., Lyndon Johnson Papers, House Years, box 123; Coke Stevenson press release, November 13, 1948, Johnson Papers, 1948 Campaign, box 7; Paul Holcomb, column, *State Observer*, October 25, 1948.

45. Dave Cheavens eventually described Johnson's statement to his brother Frank, who related it to this writer—interview with Frank Cheavens, Arlington, February 18, 1976; Mangan, *Dallas Morning News*, July 31, 1977, on Allred quote; Hugh Sidey, "The Softer They Fall," *Time* 110 (August 15, 1977): 10, on aide's quote.

There is little doubt that the Johnson camp genuinely thought that Stevenson partisans were tampering with Gregg County returns—see Garland Woodward to Lyndon Johnson, September 1, 1948, and "Ted" to Johnson, September 3, 1948, Johnson Papers, 1948 Campaign, box 1.

46. Merritt Gibson to Curtis Douglass, September 9, 1949, and Palmer Bradley to Curtis Douglass, November 3, 1949, Palmer Bradley Papers; Sam Kinch and Stuart Long, *Allan Shivers: The Pied Piper of Texas Politics* (Austin: Shoal Creek Publishers, 1973), pp. 50-57; McKay, *Texas and the Fair Deal*, p. 278; Stuart Long to author, November 11, 1976, on influence of primary vote on Jester; memo from William McGill to Weldon Hart, April 25, 1949, William McGill Papers, 2-23/163, on amendment's priority; *Austin Report*, November 5, 1949.

47. McKay, *Texas and the Fair Deal*, pp. 284, 291, 294, 305-306; Rae Files Still, *The Gilmer-Aikin Bills* (Austin: Steck Company, 1950), pp. 72-73, 86.

48. Frank Goodwyn, *Lone Star Land* (New York: Alfred A. Knopf, 1955), p. 314.

49. Kinch and Long, *Allan Shivers*, pp. 53-54, 57; Still, *Gilmer-Aikin Bills*, pp. 156, 158; the quote is from Goodwyn, *Lone Star Land*, p. 312.

50. See *Emancipator*, March 1948; Still, *Gilmer-Aikin Bills*, pp. 35, 51, 80; *Texas Spectator*, October 13, 1947; Robert Hayes, column, *Dallas Morning News*, September 1, 1946.

51. Theophilis Painter to D. K. Woodward, May 18, 1949, Woodward to Beauford Jester, May 21, 1949, and Jester to Woodward, May 23, 1949, Allan Shivers Papers, 4-15/332; Alwyn Barr, *Black Texans* (Austin: Jenkins, 1973), p. 215.

52. Memo from Weldon Hart to Beauford Jester, June 9, 1949, Beauford Jester Files, box 88. See also *Austin Report*, June 11, 1949.

53. Dale Odom interview with Weldon Hart, July 3, 1967.

54. Maston Nixon to Beauford Jester, June 13, 1949, and Jester to Nixon, June 25, 1949, box 103; meeting with union leaders—minutes of meeting and Jester typescript, December 1948, describes discussion with union leaders, in box 88; Jester to Hill Hudson (a state senator), June 16, 1949, contains states' rights quote, Shivers Papers, 4-15/329, but see also governor's press memorandum, March 15, 1949, Shivers Papers, 4-9/128; *Wichita Daily Times*, January 1949, clipping enclosed in letter from Mrs. E. T. Duff to Jester, n.d., box 114 (items are from Beauford Jester Files unless otherwise noted); Sapper, "Survey," pp. 155-156; Marian Irish, "The Proletarian South," *Journal of Politics* 2 (August 1940): 241; Beauford Jester speech, April 20, 1948, McGill Papers, 2-23/169, on racial purity; memo from Weldon Hart to Beauford Jester, December 21, 1948, in McGill Papers, 2-23/166, on labor meeting.

CHAPTER 9

1. Quote in Richard Freeland, *The Truman Doctrine and the Origins of McCarthyism* (New York: Knopf, 1972), p. 89; Athan Theoharis, *Seeds of Repression: Harry S. Truman and the Origins of McCarthyism* (Chicago: Quadrangle, 1971), p. 104.

2. Ralph O'Leary, reporter's notes, Ralph O'Leary Papers, box 5, file 10, Special Collections, University of Houston; *Houston Post*, October 11, 1949; David Mc-

Comb, *Houston, the Bayou City* (Austin: University of Texas Press, 1969), pp. 227-228. See Carl Little's columns in the *Houston Press*, April, 1951, regarding hunger in the city and state.

3. Margaret Gibbs, *The DAR* (New York: Holt, Rinehart, and Winston, 1969), pp. 199-200.

4. O'Leary, reporter's notes, O'Leary Papers, box 5, file 10; Don Carleton, "The Minute Women and the George W. Ebey Affair: A Case Study of McCarthyism in Houston" (Master's thesis, University of Houston, 1974), pp. 69-71; *Emancipator*, January 1950; McComb, *Houston*, p. 228; Dugger, column, *Texas Observer*, April 11, 1958.

5. Gordon D. Hall, "Hucksters of Hate," *The Progressive* 17 (August 1953): 5-8; Joe McCarthy to Suzanne Stevenson, May 8, 1952, O'Leary Papers, box 5, file 1; Carleton, "Minute Women," pp. 15-17.

6. Minute Women circular of principles, January 1952, O'Leary Papers, box 5, file 1; Carleton, "Minute Women," p. 10.

7. Ralph O'Leary, column, *Houston Post*, October 11, 1953; *Houston Press*, September 28, 1951.

8. O'Leary, *Houston Post*, October 11, 1953; Hall, "Hucksters of Hate," p. 7; "So They Call It Universal Military Training," Minute Women bulletin, n.d., Minute Women Collection, Anti-Defamation League Files, Southwestern Office, Houston.

9. Minute Women circular of principles; Carleton, "Minute Women," pp. 11-12.

10. O'Leary, *Houston Post*, October 11, 1953.

11. Ibid., October 12, 14, 1953; O'Leary, reporter's notes, O'Leary Papers, box 5, file 10; Carleton, "Minute Women," pp. 13-14, 208.

12. Report of Anti-Defamation League observer at Minute Women meeting, March 10, 1953, Houston, Minute Women Collection.

13. O'Leary, *Houston Post*, October 16, 1953; the *Chronicle* quote is from Don Carleton interview with Mrs. W. N. Allen, Houston, January 20, 1972, quoted in Carleton, "Minute Women," p. 49.

14. O'Leary, *Houston Post*, October 16, 1953.

15. Ibid.

16. Ibid., October 18, 1953.

17. Ibid., October 15, 21, 1953; Mary Raywid, *The Ax-Grinders* (New York: Macmillan, 1962), p. 161. Worthy had a long record of skipping from one broadcasting job to another, always peddling a sensational and flimsy superpatriotism. See Harvey Schechter to Robert Skaife, June 5, 1953, George W. Ebey Papers, box 5, Special Collections, University of Houston, and O'Leary's notes on Worthy in the O'Leary Papers, box 5, file 11.

18. O'Leary, reporter's notes, O'Leary Papers, box 5, file 10; O'Leary, *Houston Post*, October 15, 1953; quote is from "Minute Women of the USA, Inc.," bulletin of the Houston chapter, September 1952, Minute Women Collection.

19. O'Leary, *Houston Post*, October 21, 1953; Carleton, "Minute Women," pp. 108-112.

20. Ibid.

21. Carleton, "Minute Women," pp. 120, 125.

22. Roland Torn and William Storey, *Report on Ebey*, May 18-July 9, 1953, and

the letters from school administrators from Oregon, July-September 1953, Ebey Papers, boxes 2 and 5, respectively. Ebey's stand against the AVC communist is in the *Report on Ebey*, pp. 291-292.

See also O'Leary, *Houston Post*, October 20, 1953; *Texas Observer*, May 16, 1955; Ralph O'Leary, "Minute Women, Daughters of Vigilantism," *Nation* 178 (January 9, 1954): 28; "Fussin' and Fightin,'" *Newsweek* 43 (February 15, 1954): 64; John Letson, "Controversy in Houston," *NEA Journal* 44 (January 1955): 54-56; "The Ebey Story,' *Nation* 177 (September 26, 1953): 242; *Houston Post*, July 19, 1953; Don Carleton, "McCarthyism in Houston: the George Ebey Affair," *Southwestern Historical Quarterly* 80 (October 1976): 163-176.

23. Carleton, "Minute Women," pp. 151-153; John Crossland to James Carey, July 16, 1953, Ebey Papers, box 1.

24. Carleton, "Minute Women," pp. 191-193.

25. *New York Times*, May 10, 1951, quoted in Raywid, *Ax-Grinders*, p. 161; McComb, *Houston*, pp. 229-230; Dugger, column, *Texas Observer*, January 3, 1955, *Houston Post*, July 21, 1953; Carleton, "Minute Women," pp. 227-229.

26. Charles Gallenkamp to author, July 2, 1975; Charles Gallenkamp, "D. H. Lawrence and Subversion," *New Republic* 130 (April 19, 1954): 22; Dugger, column, *Texas Observer*, March 7, 1958; *Houston Post*, April 11, 1954.

27. Carleton "Minute Women," pp. 235-237; *Texas Observer*, February 14, March 21, 1955; grub worm quote in Margaret Bleil to Richard Kennan and Robert Skaife, November 18, 1955, Ebey Papers, box 5. Bleil was subjected to enormous pressure for several years while fighting the Minute Women.

28. O'Leary, *Houston Post*, October 13, 1953; *San Antonio Express*, February 28, 1952.

29. James Rorty, "The Attack on Our Libraries," *Commentary* 19 (June 1955): 545; *Weekly Dispatch*, February 19, 1954; Mike Newberry, *The Yahoos* (New York: Marzani and Munsell, 1964), pp. 63-66; Maury Maverick, "San Antonio—More Fire Fighters Than Fire," *New Republic* 128 (June 29, 1953): 12-13; Richard Henderson, *Maury Maverick* (Austin: University of Texas Press, 1970), pp. 286-287; *New York Times*, June 7, 1953; Stanley Walker, "Book Branding—A Case History," *New York Times Magazine*, July 12, 1953, pp. 11, 20-21.

30. Tomme Call, "Censors and the Library," *Saturday Review* 38 (July 2, 1955): 12; Dugger, column, *Texas Observer*, January 10, 1955.

31. Rorty, "Attack on Our Liberties," p. 545; Call, "Censors," p. 12; Dugger, column, *Texas Observer*, January 24, 1955.

32. *Austin Report*, November 15, 22, 27, 1953; *The Man Behind the Scenes* (Stuart Long), newsletter, October 16, 1953, Texas AFL-CIO Collection, 110-25-8-1.

33. "The Facts," November 1952, and Roy Hofheinz, "Must the Valley be Run According to Hoiles?" speech over radio station KSOX, McAllen, Texas, December 6, 1951, R. C. Hoiles Collection, Anti-Defamation League Files, Southwestern Office, Houston; *Houston Post*, February 6, 1952; Mrs. B. B. McGee to Allan Shivers, December 3, 1951, Shivers Papers, 4-9/80; *Valley Morning Star*, November 28, December 1, 1951; Hank Givens, column, *Pharr Press*, January 25, 1952; Arnold Forster and Benjamin Epstein, *Danger on the Right* (New York: Random House, 1965), p. 169; "According to Hoiles," *Time* 58 (December 31, 1951): 42.

Givens was editor of the *Santa Ana Independent*, an opposition paper to Hoiles's in California.

34. Roy Hofheinz speech over KSOX, and S. Thomas Friedman memo, January 17, 1952, R. C. Hoiles Collection; *Houston Post*, February 7, 1952; Lewis Fay, *Abolish Public Schools*, pamphlet in miscellaneous right-wing materials, Hogg Foundation for Mental Health, University of Texas at Austin; "According to Hoiles," p. 42.

35. "The Facts," November 1952, and Anti-Defamation League memos, November 13, 21, 1952, R. C. Hoiles Collection.

36. George Fuermann, *Reluctant Empire* (New York: Doubleday, 1957), pp. 139-140.

37. Theodore White, "Texas: Land of Wealth and Fear," *Reporter* 10 (June 8, 1954):34.

38. *Austin Report*, February 21, 1954.

39. See Nelson Polsby, "Towards an Explanation of McCarthyism," *Political Studies* 8 (October 1960): 264-268 and Dennis Wrong, "Theories of McCarthyism— A Survey," *Dissent* 1 (Autumn 1954): 388.

CHAPTER 10

1. Quote is from Jacksonville, Texas, newspaper editor, Raymond West, in statement to Jake Pickle, related in Jake Pickle's field notes, late 1949 and early 1950, Shivers Papers, 4-9/141; on jury service for women see Margaret Brand to Allan Shivers, April 18, 1949, and Shivers's reply, April 20, 1949, Shivers Papres, 4-10/30; on poll tax see Shivers to Oscar Dancy, December 22, 1949, Shivers Papers, 4-9/61, and *Valley Morning Star*, December 19, 1941; Shivers biographical sketch, September 25, 1949, and leaflet from lieutenant governor's campaign, 1946, Shivers Papers, 4-15/378 and 4-10/36, respectively; Sam Hall, column, *Texas Spectator*, February 22, 1946; for labor's suspicions, see *State Observer*, August 23, 1954. See also Theodore White, "Texas: Land of Wealth and Fear," *Reporter* 10 (June 8, 1954): 32; D. B. Hardeman, "Shivers of Texas, A Tragedy in Three Acts," *Harper's* 213 (November 1956): 50-51; Sam Kinch and Stuart Long, *Allan Shivers: The Pied Piper of Texas Politics* (Austin: Shoal Creek Publishers, 1973), pp. 37, 40, 46-49, 67-68.

2. Memos from Weldon Hart to Allan Shivers, October 12, 1949, and January 1950, and memo from William McGill to Hart, January 9, 1950, Shivers Papers, 4-9/117, 4-10/33, and 4-9/121, respectively.

Burris, after twenty-six years, does not recollect the Culberson matter or the tax-cutting position, though he affirms that they might have occurred. Usually, he said the TMA just opposed "wasteful increases in taxes." Interview with Ed Burris, July 26, 1976.

3. Pickle's field notes, Shivers Papers, 4-9/141. Former Attorney General Gerald Mann was nicknamed the Little Red Arrow during his football days at Southern Methodist University and was known for his piety, at least in contrast to other Texan politicians.

4. Hardeman, "Shivers," pp. 51-53; Wilbourn Benton, *Texas, Its Government and Politics* (Englewood Cliffs, New Jersey: Prentice-Hall, 1966), p. 174; Lester Velie, "Do You Know Your State's Secret Boss?" *Reader's Digest* 62 (February 1953): 36; Kinch and Long, *Shivers*, pp. 71, 105-107, 128, 147; Seth Shepard McKay, *Texas*

and the Fair Deal, 1945-1952 (San Antonio: Naylor Company, 1954), pp. 309-310, 340-342; interview with Jim Sewell, Corsicana, April 6, 1976; Danny Ingram, column, *Texas Observer*, March 21, 1955; Paul Holcomb, column, *State Observer*, October 19, 1953, mentions Shepperd's lobbying on the floor of the house. Lest anyone over-estimate the 1951 house, keep in mind that it voted to institute impeachment proceedings against Supreme Court Justice William O. Douglas. The vote was not recorded but the house voted against sending it back to committee, 88 to 28. Months later Representative John Barnhart introduced a resolution in favor of freedom of speech, which lost 105 to 17. See *Emancipator*, February and June 1951.

5. J. Webb Howell to Jim Sewell, June 5, 1951, Jim Sewell Papers, Texas Political History Collection, University of Texas at Arlington; Howell's conservatism was evident in his letters to Hatton Sumners, April 4, 21, 30, 1941, in Sumners Papers, drawer 14, 1941; see also *Texas' Natural Gas—Going, Going, Gone*, n.d., Texas AFL-CIO Collection, 110-25-3-16.

6. Kinch and Long, *Shivers*, pp. 127-131.

7. Interview with Tom Sutherland, Arlington, Texas, February 12, 1976; *Texas Spectator*, September 8, 22, 1947, April 5, 1948; Shivers quotes in *Corpus Christi Caller*, September 4, 1947; Ray Osborne, column, *Dallas Morning News*, September 4, 1947; *Port Arthur News*, September 3, 1947; *Austin American*, September 4, 1947; *Annual Report of the Good Neighbor Commission*, 1948, Shivers Papers, 4-15/206; quote on deal in Bob Smith to Allan Shivers, September 22, 1947, and see also Shivers to Smith, October 1, 1947, Shivers Papers, 4-15/206.

8. On the Longoria case see the Three Rivers Case folder in the Beauford Jester Papers, box 82, the Longoria folder in the Good Neighbor Commission Files, Good Neighbor Commission, Austin, especially the Tom Sutherland memo to the press, February 11, 1949, and Representative Oltarf's minority report, and the *Dallas Morning News*, January 30, February 17, March 12, April 8, 1949; Donald McCoy, *Quest and Response: Minority Rights and the Truman Administration* (Lawrence: Kansas University Press, 1973), pp. 307-309.

9. Interview with Sutherland; on Neville Penrose's approach, see his letters to Tom Sutherland, October 18, 1950, to Frank Kelly, April 17, 1952, and to Floyd Dunkerley, April 26, 1952, and see the Good Neighbor Commission's *Weekly Report* in the early 1950s in the Penrose and *Weekly Report* folders in the Good Neighbor Commission Files; memo from Weldon Hart to Allan Shivers, October 24, 1951, Shivers Papers, 4-10/33, on HRC internal difficulties.

10. Memo from John Van Cronkhite to Weldon Hart, n.d., Shivers Papers, 4-10/33.

11. Interview with Sutherland.

12. Ben Kaplan, column, *Houston Press*, September 12, 1950; *Houston Chronicle*, September 13, 1950; *Platform Adopted by the State Democratic Convention, Mineral Wells, Texas*, September 12, 1950, p. 1; for Shivers's original loyalty pledge, see Allen Duckworth and Dave Cheavens columns in the *Dallas Morning News* and *Austin American*, respectively, October 1, 1949; Fred Gantt, *The Chief Executive in Texas* (Austin: University of Texas Press, 1964), p. 315, on the purge.

13. Tom Brewer and Fred Gantt interviews with Allan Shivers, April 8, 1966, and August 13, 1968, respectively; interview with Ralph Yarborough, February 23, 1976; quote is in memo from Maurice Acers to Allan Shivers, April 28, 1952, Shivers Papers, 4-10/33; interview with Hank Brown, January 14, 1971; memo from

Weldon Hart to Allan Shivers, April 28, 1950, Shivers Papers, 4-10/33; Yarborough biographical pamphlet, 1954, in author's possession. See also Caso March leaflet, in author's possession, and in Shivers Papers.

14. Memo from Weldon Hart to Allan Shivers, March 14, 1950, and telegram from Hugh Roy Cullen to Allan Shivers, July 3, 1950, Shivers Papers, 4-9/115; Shivers speech, September 17, 1951, Shivers Papers, 4-10/15; Gerald Nash, *United States Oil Policy* (Pittsburgh: University of Pittsburgh Press, 1968), pp. 190-193; Tom Brewer interviews with Allan Shivers, October 2, 1965, April 8, 1966; transcript of Paul Bolton speech, June 7, 1949, Shivers Papers, 4-10/29; Kinch and Long, *Shivers*, pp. 112-113; for Rowan's power and a rundown on all Shivers leaders in the congressional districts, see Weldon Hart's report to the governor, February 4, 1952, Shivers Papers, 4-10/33; Jimmy Banks, *Money, Marbles and Chalk* (Austin: Texas Publishing Company, 1971), pp. 145-147; describes Daniel's threat to run against Shivers; for a rundown of Texas's oil arguments, see "The Big Grab," brochure of the Texas Property Defense Association, Jim Sewell Papers; Raymond Moley, "Texas Omen," *Newsweek* 38 (July 23, 1951): 88, and "Resistance in Texas," *Newsweek* 39 (February 4, 1952): 84; Winthrop Aldrich to Dwight Eisenhower, November 26, 1951, Dwight D. Eisenhower Presidential Papers, box 2, Dwight D. Eisenhower Library, Abilene, Kansas, on Shivers quote to banker; David Murph, "Price Daniel: The Life of a Public Man, 1910-1956" (Ph.D. diss., Texas Christian University, 1975), pp. 170-174, 178-180; see also Harry S. Truman, *Memoirs: Years of Trial and Hope* (Garden City, New York: Doubleday, 1956), pp. 479-487; on lack of hope for Shivers, see Curtis Douglass to E. E. Townes, July 29, 1949, and Palmer Bradley to Merritt Gibson, September 12, 1949, Palmer Bradley Papers. For other tidelands compromise proposals, see *Austin Report*, May 28, July 16, 1949.

15. Memo from Maurice Acers and Weldon Hart to Allan Shivers, April 11, 1951, and Pickle's Field Notes, Shivers Papers, 4-10/46 and 4-9/141, respectively; Murph, "Price Daniel," pp. 167-168, 190, 201, on Johnson's refusal to help Daniel, on congressional action, and on Truman quote; one stinging editorial appeared in the *Dallas Morning News*, April 1, 1951, a copy of which is in the Rayburn Papers, reel 27. (All Rayburn citations are from series I.)

16. Sam Rayburn to Byron Skelton, July 3, August 11, 1951, and to Walter Hall, October 21, 1951, Rayburn Papers, reel 28; "pauperizing" quote in Shivers speech, April 18, 1952, and LDT memo, October 1951, Texas AFL-CIO Collection, 110-26-7-3; *The Texas Story*, LDT booklet, 1952, in author's possession; Stuart Long, "Democrats for Ike," *Nation* 175 (October 4, 1952): 300-301.

17. On Shivers's commitment to some form of Dixiecratic bolt, see Palmer Bradley to Harry Byrd, January 11, March 3, 17, 1952, Allen Wight to John Van Chronkite, January 17, 1952, Bradley to Curtis Douglass, January 18, and April 1, 1952, Joe Woodward to Bradley, January 21, 1952, and Bradley to Mrs. F. R. Carlton, March 25, 1952, Palmer Bradley Papers; memos from Weldon Hart to Allan Shivers, February 4, April 24, 1952, Shivers Papers, 4-10/33; *Fort Worth Star-Telegram*, May 28, 29, 1952; O. D. Weeks, *Texas Presidential Politics in 1952* (Austin: Institute of Public Affairs, 1953), p. 42.

The *New York Times*, March 15, 1952 observed that the Shivers delegation counted eighteen owners of private businesses out of thirty-seven delegates, while the Maverick delegation had four. The Maverick group also had fewer lawyers, ranchers, and executives, but more intellectuals, labor leaders, minority spokesmen, women, and people under forty.

18. Kenneth Birkhead to Sam Rayburn, October 24, 1952, with extract of transscript of credentials subcommittee, July 18, 1952, Democratic Advisory Council Papers, Texas Political History Collection, University of Texas at Arlington; Maury Maverick to Harry Truman, May 29, 1952, Truman to Maverick, June 2, 1952, Byron Skelton to Truman, May 8, 1952, and Truman to Skelton, May 13, 1952, President's Secretary's File, box 61, Truman Library; John Cofer to Stephen Mitchell, May 31, 1955, on Clements, Stephen Mitchell Papers, box 25, Harry S. Truman Library, Independence, Missouri; "cow chip" quote in William Kimbrough to Harry Truman, August 1, 1952, President's Official File 300, box 983, Truman Library; Weeks, *Texas Presidential Politics*, pp. 78-80; among the prominent Texas Democrats assured by Rayburn that Shivers had pledged not to bolt were Walter Hall, Booth Mooney, and Byron Skelton—David McComb interview with Walter Hall and T. H. Baker interviews with Booth Mooney and Byron Skelton; interview with Ralph Yarborough, Austin, November 24, 1975; Hardeman, "Shivers," pp. 52-53; "Shivers' Democrats," *Newsweek* 40 (September 29, 1952): 26-27; *New York Times*, July 24, 1952; Alfred Steinberg, *Sam Johnson's Boy* (New York: Macmillan, 1968), pp. 326-327.

Alfred Steinberg's 1976 biography, *Sam Rayburn*, glutted with unstinting praise of the Speaker, contradicts his biography of Johnson with the undocumented assertion (p. 273) that Rayburn never agreed to the seating of the Shivers delegation but that Johnson accomplished it by going to the Credentials Committee. Fourteen years after the convention, Shivers recalled that Johnson had been "largely responsible" for the seating of the governor's delegation: Tom Brewer interview with Allan Shivers, August 8, 1966.

19. Kinch and Long, *Shivers*, pp. 120-122; *Dallas Morning News*, August 24, 1952; speech by Allan Shivers, August 27, 1952, Shivers Papers, 4-10/15; Steinberg, *Sam Johnson's Boy*, p. 320; Jeanne Murphy, "Texas—A Toss-Up," *New Republic* 127 (October 20, 1952), 6; Robert Engler, *The Politics of Oil* (Chicago: University of Chicago, 1961), p. 357, for quote on company planes; Weeks, *Texas Presidential Politics*, pp. 83, 88-89; Allen Duckworth and Dawson Duncan, column, *Dallas Morning News*, September 9, 1952; Stuart Long typescript, September 9, 1952, Texas AFL-CIO Collection, 110-26-4-9, and his columns in the *Amarillo Globe-Times*, September 8, 9, 1952; Palmer Bradley to Arch Rowan, May 13, 1952, to Robert Harriss, June 23, 1952 (with equality quote), and to Gene Smith, Curtis Douglass, and Clint Small, all September 2, 1952, and Lamar Fleming, Jr., to Allan Shivers, August 27, 1952, Palmer Bradley Papers.

20. *Austin Report*, November 2, 1952, and *San Antonio Express*, August 28, 1952, on Bentsen; Lloyd Bentsen, Jr., to Sam Rayburn, November 3, 1952, Rayburn Papers, reel 29; Stephen Mitchell to all department heads, September 13, 1952, Stephen 1952, Rayburn Papers, reel 29; Mrs. Jud Collier to Rayburn, November 11, 1952, Rayburn Papers, reel 30; Maury Maverick, Jr., to Jim Sewell, October 4, 1952, Sewell Papers; Steinberg, *Sam Johnson's Boy*, pp. 329-331.

21. Quote in Pat Mayse to Sam Rayburn, November 15, 1952, Sam Rayburn

Papers, reel 29; Stephen Mitchell to all department heads, September 13, 1952, Stephen Mitchell Papers, box 33; Alfred W. Davis to Stevenson headquarters, October 8, 1952, in the Democratic Advisory Council Papers.

22. Margaret Carter to Jim Wright, February 23, 1953, Margaret Carter Papers.

23. Arthur Eisenhower to Edward J. Green, October 1, 1952, and Palmer Bradley to Allan Shivers, October 28, 1952, Palmer Bradley Papers; speeches and statements on the part of Allan Shivers, Claude Gilmer, Galloway Calhoun, and Texas Democrats for Eisenhower, October and November 1952, the Texas AFL-CIO Collection, 110-26-1-4; Wendell Knox, "Democratic Schism in Texas, 1952-1957" (Master's thesis, North Texas State University, 1959), pp. 19, 21; Weeks, *Texas Presidential Politics*, pp. 89-95; Long, "Democrats for Ike," pp. 300-301; Theodore White, "Texas: Land of Wealth and Fear," *Reporter* 10 (June 8, 1954): 35-36; Hardeman, "Shivers," p. 53; Nash, *United States Oil Policy*, pp. 193-194; Democratic campaign brochure, 1952, Democratic Advisory Council Papers.

24. Weeks, *Texas Presidential Politics*, p. 106.

25. Hugh Roy Cullen to Allan Shivers, December 5, 1952, and Wallace Savage to Shivers, November 13, 1953, Shivers Papers, 4-9/86 and 4-9/35, respectively; Fred Gantt interview with Shivers, October 2, 1967; *Austin Report*, November 8, 1953; Weeks, *Texas Presidential Politics*, pp. 99-101, 105-106, 109-111; Donald Strong, "Durable Republicanism in the South," in *Change in the Contemporary South*, ed. Allan Sindler (Durham: Duke University Press, 1963), p. 179; Numan Bartley, *The Rise of Massive Resistance* (Baton Rouge: Louisiana State University Press, 1969), p. 52.

Liberals attempted to make much of the party loyalty issue against Shivers from 1952 through 1956 by accusing the governor of lacking the courage of his Republican convictions. It was a weak reed to lean on, especially since Shivers did what a majority of Texas Democrats wanted him to do. Shivers effectively quoted Adlai Stevenson that the "character of the candidates" and "political ethics" were more important than "party regularity" and "party labels." Liberals did not preach or practice party loyalty themselves in the 1960s when faced with the dismal prospect of putting Bill Blakley and Waggoner Carr in the Senate. For Shivers quotes on Stevenson, see Shivers's speech, October 2, 1952, Shivers Papers, 4-10/15. For liberals' attacks on the governor's concept of party loyalty, see the statements of John White and Jim Sewell in the *Austin Report*, January 10 and June 13, 1954, respectively, the 1953 invitation of Stuart Long's for the Democratic Organizing Committee's convention, in the Shivers Papers, 4-15/395, and Fagan Dickson's letter to J. C. Phillips, in the *Borger News-Herald*, May 20, 1952.

26. Joe Frantz interview with Allan Shivers, May 29, 1970; Tom Brewer interview with Shivers, April 8, 1966; Banks, *Money*, pp. 117-118; Harvey O'Connor, *The Empire of Oil* (New York: Monthly Review Press, 1955), p. 292; Knox, "Democratic Schism," pp. 3-4; E. K. Lindley, "Comparing Candidates," *Newsweek* 40 (October 27, 1952): 30. In the Brewer interview Shivers recalled that Connally, angry at being forced out by Daniel, urged Shivers to run against Daniel for the Senate. Connally, on the other hand, was quoted as accusing Shivers of actively pushing Daniel into the race; see Steinberg, *Sam Johnson's Boy*, p. 325.

27. Robert S. Allen and William V. Shannon, *The Truman Merry-Go-Round* (New York: Vanguard, 1950), pp. 264-265.

28. Engler, *Politics of Oil*, pp. 141, 372; Roland Evans and Robert Novak, *Lyndon B. Johnson: The Exercise of Power* (New York: New American Library, 1966), pp. 17-18; "Texas, Where Everything Is More So," *Time* 60 (September 29, 1952): 16; regarding the potential snag in the Justice Department, see memo from Maurice Acers and Weldon Hart to Allan Shivers, in the Shivers Papers, 4-10/46; Robert Garson, *The Democratic Party and the Politics of Sectionalism, 1941-1948* (Baton Rouge: Louisiana State University Press, 1974), p. 39; John Moore, "The Conservative Coalition in the United States Senate, 1942-1945," *Journal of Southern History* 33 (August 1967): 375.

29. *Behind the Scenes* (Stuart Long), newsletter, March 9, 1956, Texas AFL-CIO Collection, 110-15-4-7; Price Daniel press release, n.d., 1952, Allred Papers, box 172; *Austin Report*, March 11, 1956; Lindley Beckworth to author, July 8, 1977; *Texas Almanac, 1954-1955*, pp. 447, 450-452.

CHAPTER 11

1. Sam Kinch and Stuart Long, *Allan Shivers: The Pied Piper of Texas Politics* (Austin: Shoal Creek Publishers, 1973), pp. 147-150; *State Observer*, March 29, 1954; a list of those in attendance for a "discussion of state problems" is in the Shivers Papers, 4-9/57; *The Man Behind the Scenes* (Stuart Long), newsletter, April 9, 1954, Texas AFL-CIO Collection, 110-15-4-5.

2. *Austin Report*, May 9, 16, 1954; *Austin American*, May 23, July 21, 1954; *State Observer*, May 10, 1954; "Texas: Frauds and Failures," *Time* 63 (May 31, 1954): 64, 66; "Texas Chooses up for a Runoff," *Life* 37 (August 30, 1954): 23; Frank Goodwyn, *Lone Star Land* (New York: Alfred A. Knopf, 1955), p. 315; John Bainbridge, *The Super-Americans* (Garden City, New York: Doubleday, 1961), p. 176; the charge of crookedness against Van Cronkhite is in Jake Pickle's field notes, Shivers Papers, 4-9/141; Yarborough quotes in Yarborough press release, May 29, 1954, Ralph Yarborough File, 47-1-10, Texas Political History Collection, University of Texas at Arlington, and in "Texas Runoff," *New York Times Magazine*, August 28, 1954, pp. 8-9.

3. Speeches by Shivers, July 2, 6, 1954, Shivers Papers, 4-9/153 and 4-10/23, respectively; *Dallas Morning News*, June 25, 27, July 11, 1954; *State Observer*, June 28, 1954; *Austin Report*, June 27, 1954; "Political Notes," *Time* 64 (July 19, 1954): 17; *Austin American*, July 11, 1954; Goodwyn, *Lone Star Land*, pp. 315-316; James Fallows, "Lloyd Bentsen: Can Another Texan Apply?" *Atlantic* 234 (December 1974): 87.

4. "Obiter Dictum," Special Report of the Attorney General's Office, November 25, 1953, and transcript of "Facts Forum State of the Nation," December 1, 1953, Shivers Papers, 4-9/55 and 4-10/14, respectively; *Austin American*, November 28, 1953; *State Observer*, January 11, 1954; *Dallas Morning News*, January 24, 1954; Goodwyn, *Lone Star Land*, pp. 316-317.

5. Press release from governor's office, November 27, 1953, and "Preliminary Report of Industrial Commission of Texas," December 7, 1953, Shivers Papers, 4-9/55 and 4-9/85, respectively; *Austin Report*, January 24, 1954.

6. Theodore White, "Texas: Land of Wealth and Fear," *Reporter* 10 (June 8, 1954): 32-33; *State Observer*, April 5, 1954.

7. A legislative copy of the bill and the vote on it are in the Shivers Papers, 4-9/45; White, "Texas," p. 32; Tomme Call to Allan Shivers, March 9, 1954, and Paul Bolton to Shivers, April 15, 1954, Shivers Papers, 4-15/313 and 4-9/45, respectively. The governor bragged on the passage of the law in a letter to Vice-President Richard Nixon, May 6, 1954, Shivers Papers, 4-15/313.

8. "Preliminary Report of Industrial Commission of Texas," December 7, 1953, Shivers Papers, 4-9/85; Texas Social and Legislative Conference, "Legislative Bulletin No. 1," March 20, 1954, Texas Social and Legislative Conference Files, Texas Political History Collection, University of Texas at Arlington; *Dallas Morning News*, January 24, 1954; *State Observer*, December 7, 1953, January 11, March 22, 1954; Joseph Kushner, "A Survey of the Port Arthur Retail Trades Strike, 1953-1954" (Master's thesis, University of Houston, 1964), p. 97, on wages; *Wichita Falls Record*, December 5, 1953; numerous wage and hour statistics cited in letter from Kilgore oil workers local 207 to Allan Shivers, December 17, 1953, Shivers Papers, 4-9/55 and in *The Strikers' Story*, union pamphlet in the Sabine Area Local Industrial Union 1814 Collection, Texas Labor Archives, University of Texas at Arlington; the request for a fact-finding investigation was in a telegram from Mrs. R. Z. Dutton to Allan Shivers, February 2, 1954, and he replied negatively the same night, Shivers Papers, 4-9/55; "Obiter Dictum," Special Report of the Attorney General's Office, December 10, 1953, Texas AFL-CIO Collection, 110-16-11-7; interviews with Mrs. R. Z. Dutton and Bill Ricks, Port Arthur, November 2, 1970.

9. The Shivers quotes, in order, appeared in the governor's speeches on June 21, January 26, July 15, and July 21, 1954, Shivers Papers, 4-10/23, except that the January quote comes from a panel statement in 4-9/145; speech by L. E. Page to American Legion Post Commanders, January 16, 1954, Shivers Papers, 4-9/45; J. C. Phillips to Texas editors, November 30, 1953, Shivers Papers, 4-9/55; "RMA, The Manager's Confidential Letter to the Members," February 22, 1954, Shivers Papers, 4-9/3; Robert Baskin, columns, *Dallas Morning News*, May 2-7, 1954—the articles were also published as a pamphlet, *The Port Arthur Story*, in the Shivers Papers, 4-10/6, and the Sabine Area Local Industrial Union 1814 Collection; Ann Lanz to other Texas jewelers, July 20, 1954, Shivers Papers, 4-9/3.

10. *Austin Report*, May 23, 30, 1954; *Austin American*, May 25, 1954; D. B. Hardeman, "Shivers of Texas, A Tragedy in Three Acts," *Harper's* 213 (November 1956): 54; Frank Tollman, "Everybody's Friend—Nobody's Leader," *New Republic* 131 (August 9, 1954): 6.

11. Speech by Allan Shivers, June 21, 1954, Shivers Papers, 4-9/145.

12. Speeches by Allan Shivers, July 2, 15, 16, 22, and one with no date, Shivers Papers, 4-9/153, 4-10/23, and 4-10/24.

13. *The Big Lie*, circular in the Shivers Papers, 4-9/101; Jimmy Banks, *Money, Marbles and Chalk* (Austin: Texas Publishing Company, 1971), pp. 20-21.

14. Donald Parker interviews with Mark Adams, Austin, July 22, 1969, and Margaret Carter, Fort Worth, July 19, 1969, quoted in Donald Parker, "The Texas Gubernatorial Campaign of 1954" (Master's thesis, Texas Christian University, 1975), pp. 68-69; Neil Sapper, "A Survey of the History of the Black People of Texas, 1930-1954" (Ph.D. diss., Texas Tech University, 1972), p. 152; Yarborough was quoted as favoring segregation by the *Fort Worth Star-Telegram*, July 18, *Corpus*

Christi Caller July 31, *Austin Report*, August 1, and the *Dallas Morning News*, July 31, August 15, 1954.

15. Hagerty diary, July 20, 1954, Jim Hagerty Papers, box 1, Dwight D. Eisenhower Library, Abilene, Kansas; W. H. Francis Jr., to Charles Willis, President's General File, box 1087, folder 140-B-2, Eisenhower Library; Interior Department press release, July 20, 1954, President's Central File, box 681, folder 134-F-3, Eisenhower Library; *Austin Report*, July 18, 1954; *Houston Chronicle*, July 15, 1954; *Houston Post*, July 20, 1954; see also Sarah McClendon, column, *Austin Statesman*, March 26, 1956.

16. *Austin Report*, July 25, August 1, 1954; *Texas Almanac, 1956-1957*, pp. 524-526; Weldon Hart memo to Allan Shivers, July 31, 1954, Shivers Papers, 4-10/33; information on minor candidates from *Fort Worth Star-Telegram*, March-July, 1954, quoted in Parker, "Texas Gubernatorial Campaign," p. 24; on precincts, see *Behind the Scenes* (Stuart Long), newsletter, July 30, 1954, Texas AFL-CIO Collection, 110-15-4-5, also appendix 6; Doyle Willis to Sam Rayburn, August 1, 1954, Sam Rayburn Papers, reel 33.

17. Hagerty diary, July 25, 1954, Hagerty Papers, box 1; *Public Papers of the Presidents of the United States, Dwight David Eisenhower, 1954* (Washington, D.C.: Government Printing Office, 1960), p. 661; memo from "Lois" to Charles Willis, August 7, 1954, President's General File, box 1087, folder 140-B-1, Eisenhower Library.

18. Joe T. Cook to other editors, July 12, 1954, Shivers Papers, 4-10/3; Dale Odom interview with Allan Shivers, Austin, February 6, 1967; *Dallas Morning News*, August 11, 17, 21, 1954; *Austin Statesman*, August 15, 1954; *Austin Report*, August 15, 1954; *Austin American*, August 13, 1954.

19. "Negro Politicians Solidly Behind Governor Shivers," circular, George Lambert Papers, Texas Labor Archives, University of Texas at Arlington, and Shivers Papers, no box number; Fred Gantt interview with Allan Shivers, Austin, December 18, 1967; *Texas Almanac, 1956-1957*, pp. 532-533.

20. Joe Fisher to Allan Shivers, July 27, 1954, Shivers Papers, 4-9/91; reprint of the *Informer* article, Shivers Papers, 4-10/6; Donald Parker interview with Ben Procter, Fort Worth, September 3, 1969, quoted in Parker, "Texas Gubernatorial Campaign," p. 89.

21, Memo from Weldon Hart to Allan Shivers, August 15, 1954, Shivers Papers, 4-10/33.

22. Speeches by Allan Shivers, August 11, 18, 19, 26, 1954, Shivers Papers, 4-9/2, 4-9/3, and 4-9/145; "The Port Arthur Story," movie housed in the Texas State Archives as part of the Shivers collection; Stuart Long, " 'Scared Money' Wins an Election in Texas," *Reporter* 11 (October 21, 1954): 23, 26; *Dallas Morning News*, August 12, 14, 21, 22, 1954; Hardeman, "Shivers," p. 54; Kinch and Long, *Shivers*, p. 158; *Lubbock Avalanche-Journal*, August 22, 1954; *Texas Observer*, May 2, 16, 1955; Kushner, "Survey," p. 91.

23. Long, " 'Scared Money,' " p. 26; Jerry Holleman, column, *State Observer*, September 6, 1954; Tollman, "Everybody's Friend," p. 6; Eugene Hollon, *The Southwest Old and New* (New York: Knopf, 1961), p. 330; Shivers warned farmers about the CIO in at least two speeches, August 7, 24, 1954, Shivers Papers, 4-9/153 and 4-10/24.

24. Long, " 'Scared Money,' " p. 26; *The Man Behind the Scenes* (Stuart Long), newsletter, August 14, 1954, Texas AFL-CIO Collection, 110-15-4-5. Each of the old Texas paper ballots was numbered, and it was identical to the number placed beside each voter's name on the precinct list. In 1947 the Texas house passed a bill that would have ensured a more nearly private ballot, but it was blocked in the senate by Governor Jester's forces. Robert Calvert, the chairman of the State Democratic Executive Committee, opposed it on the grounds that it would destroy means of checking fraud. Most of the democratic world, however, maintains relatively pure elections without violating the secrecy of the ballot. The outcome of the 1941 and 1948 senatorial elections and the 1956 gubernatorial contest may well have made a mockery of Texas's so-called anti-fraud provisions. See V. O. Key, *Southern Politics* (New York: Alfred A. Knopf, 1949), pp. 458-459, and *Texas Spectator*, March 17 and April 21, 1947.

25. George Lambert typescript, n.d., Lambert Papers; *Texas Almanac, 1956-1957*, p. 532; *Dallas Morning News*, August 8, 14 (quote), 1954.

26. Lillian Collier to members of the Texas Democratic Women's State Committee, early August, August 9, and late August 1954, Texas AFL-CIO Collection, 110-26-7-2; Jon Ford, column, *San Antonio Express*, August 24, 1954.

27. Neal Peirce, *The Great Plains States of Amerca* (New York: Norton, 1973), p. 362; Yarborough brochure, 1954 runoff, Ralph Yarborough File, 47-1-7; *Behind the Scenes* (Stuart Long), newsletter, August 7, 1954, Texas AFL-CIO Collection, 110-15-4-5.

28. Speeches by A. B. Stufflebeme, August 19, 1954, and Jack Dillard, August 20, 1954, Shivers Papers, 4-9/2. Dillard sounded rather rich and aloof himself in a campaign letter he wrote to an Edinburg banker. Dillard sounded incredulous that a particular lawyer was anti-Shivers when "by virtue of background, family affiliations, and previous training [he] should be in our camp. He is the son-in-law of . . . one of the most prominent and well-fixed men in Waco." See letter from Jack Dillard to Sid Hardin, June 16, 1954, Shivers Papers, 4-9/105.

29. Long, " 'Scared Money,' " p. 26; "Texas," *New Republic* 131 (September 31, 1954): 5; *Texas Almanac, 1956-1957*, pp. 117, 141-154, 532-533; H. E. Chiles report to Allan Shivers, August 13, 1954, Shivers Papers, 4-10/33; Fred Gantt interview with Allan Shivers, December 18, 1967; Jon Ford, column, *San Antonio Express*, June 27, August 24, 1954, notes the expenditure discrepancies in the Alamo City. Candidates and even campaign managers do not necessarily know the total costs of a campaign; see Key, *Southern Politics*, p. 464.

30. "Allan Shivers Campaign Contributions," May 19-November 5, 1954, file 11-2265, Office of the Secretary of State of Texas; unlisted financing, May-September 1954, Shivers Papers, 4-15/333 and 4-15/334; "Ralph Yarborough Campaign Contributions," 1954, File 11-2426, Office of the Secretary of State of Texas; *Dallas Morning News*, August 5, 1954; see also Yarborough-Will Clayton correspondence, 1954-1955, Will Clayton Papers, "Politics-State-Texas" folder, Harry S. Truman Library, Independence, Missouri.

31. Larry Goodwyn, *New Shapes in Texas Politics*, 1957 pamphlet, and miscellaneous precinct studies, Lambert Papers, 127-30-7 and 127-30-4, respectively.

32. Long, " 'Scared Money,' " p. 23; Max Skelton, column, *Port Arthur News*,

and in other papers, September 26, 1954; unidentified Beaumont newspaper, January 11, 1955, Sabine Area Local Industrial Union 1814 Collection; Kushner, "Survey," pp. 97-103; Sam Rayburn to J. R. Parten, September 3, 1954, Rayburn Papers, reel 33.

33. The quote is from Hardeman, "Shivers," 54; Kinch and Long, *Shivers*, pp. 158-159; Richard Morehead, column, *Dallas Morning News*, September 24, 1970. See also Bruce Felknor, *Dirty Politics* (New York: Norton, 1966), p. 130, and Emmett Essin interview with Judge R. C. Slagle, Sherman, March 29, 1965, Emmett Essin, "The Democratic Senatorial Primary in Texas: Yarborough vs. Blakley" (Master's thesis, Texas Christian University, 1965), p. 50. The judge, who once served as Yarborough's campaign manager, affirmed that candidates probably do not know half of what is done in their names.

34. On Regan see *El Paso Labor Advocate*, July 30, 1954, and Don Ellinger to Jack Kroll, July 27, 1954; on Lucas, see Ellinger to Kroll, June 14, 1954, Les Carpenter, column, *Houston Post*, August 2, 1953, and Peirce, *Great Plains States*, p. 355; on Savage, see interview with Hank Rabun, Ellinger to Kroll, November 4, 1954; on Fox advice, John Luter interview with Alvin Lane, Dallas, December 22, 1969, Oral History 217, Columbia Oral History Project, Eisenhower Library; Bernard Cosman, "The Republican Congressman from Dallas" (Master's thesis, University of Alabama, 1958), pp. 20-108, 113; Alger's plight was illustrated in a letter he wrote to Sherman Adams and others, May 13, 1955, in which he confessed he was chagrined over his inability to deliver patronage, President's General File, box 536, Eisenhower Library. The Ellinger-Kroll letters are in the Texas AFL-CIO Collection, 110-9-1-3.

35. Larry Goodwyn, column, *Texas Observer*, December 27, 1974.

36. Allan Shivers to John Young, October 7, 1952, Shivers Papers, 4-9/125; *Austin Report*, November 8, 22, 1953, June 6, July 18, 1954; *Austin American*, August 4, 1956.

Ralph Yarborough confirmed that the drought was a big help to his campaigns against Shivers in 1952 and 1954 and against Daniel in 1956: interview with Yarborough, Austin, November 24, 1975.

37. William McGill memos to Allan Shivers, February 16, August 15, October 9, 1954, Shivers Papers, 4-10/33; *Austin Report*, November 22, 1953, August 22, 1954, January 6, 1957; Daniel quote in *Austin American*, August 4, 1956.

38. "One for the Record," *Time* 65 (March 7, 1955): 84-85; *Dallas Morning News*, November 18, December 12, 1954.

39. *Chaparral*, Adams's occasional newsletter, dealt with the land issue in vol. 4, no. 1, 1946; "Texas," *Time* 66 (August 8, 1955): 15; *New York Times*, April 3, 1955; Kinch and Long, *Shivers*, pp. 172-173; Fred Gantt interview with Allan Shivers, April 18, 1968; W. L. Dorries, "An Appraisal of the Texas Veterans' Land Program" *Southwestern Social Science Quarterly* 36 (September 1955): 182.

40. "Keep the Rascal In," *Time* 68 (July 2, 1956): 65; *Austin Statesman*, November 1, 1955; Ronnie Dugger, "What Corrupted Texas?" *Harper's* 214 (March 1957): 74.

41. State of Texas, *House Journal*, 54th Legislature, regular session, March 16, 1955, pp. 898-902, and June 7, 1955, pp. 3525-3528; "Texas: Bonus for the Boys," *Time* 66 (August 8, 1955): 15; *Texas Observer*, May 9, 1955; *New York Times*, April 3, 1955; Craig Thompson, "Those Texas Scandals," *Saturday Evening Post* 228 (November 12, 1955): 89.

42. *Dallas Morning News*, May 6, June 19, 1955.

43. Edward H. Austin to John Osorio, December 16, 1955, February 6, 1956, Shivers Papers, 4-9/43.

44. *Dallas Morning News*, January 1, 21, 22, 27, 29, 31, 1956; *Texas Observer*, December 21, 1955, January 4, 11, February 22, 1956; Kinch and Long, *Shivers*, p. 174.

45. State of Texas, *House Journal*, 55th Legislature, regular session, April 1, 1957, pp. 1258-1259; *Dallas Morning News*, November 23, 1975.

46. Excerpt from *Texas Observer*, February 22, 1956, and memo from Governor Shivers regarding (Secretary of State) Tom Reavley, March 1, 1956; Theodore Miller to Allan Shivers, May 1, 1956, and Shivers memo, n.d.; memo from Howard Carney to Allan Shivers, June 26, 1956. All items are in the Shivers Papers, 4-10/34, 4-10/48, and 4-10/33, respectively.

Ironically, among all Texas governors only Shivers himself was victimized slightly by the red scare. On August 25, 1953, the governor charged that the FBI was snooping in Texas on civil-rights matters without consulting local authorities. The charge prompted a long retort from J. Edgar Hoover and a number of protests from Texans accusing Shivers of helping the communist cause, including letters from prominent oilman D. H. "Dry Hole" Byrd (September 4, 1953) and Fort Worth department store magnate R. E. Cox (September 4, 1953). See the Shivers Papers 4-9/84.

47. Dale Odom interview with Allan Shivers, February 6, 1967; *Austin Report*, November 4, 1956; Hardeman, "Shivers," p. 52; *Texas Observer*, March 7, 1956; quote in Allen Duckworth, column, *Dallas Morning News*, January 20, 1966.

CHAPTER 12

1. Press memorandum, March 29, 1956, Shivers Papers, 4-15/311; George Lambert to Edward Hollender, January 5, 1954, Lambert Papers, 127-2-8; T. H. Baker interview with Byron Skelton; interview with Creekmore Fath, Austin, July 28, 1976; Alfred Steinberg, *Sam Johnson's Boy* (New York: Macmillan, 1968), pp. 425-426; Walter Mansell, column, *Houston Chronicle*, March 29, 1956; Sam Kinch, column, *Fort Worth Star-Telegram*, March 27, 1956; Raymond Brooks, column, *Waco News-Tribune*, March 28, 1956; on Rayburn's actions, see Byron Skelton to Sam Rayburn, March 9, 1956, Rayburn Papers, series I, reel 35, Margaret Carter to Stephen Mitchell, February 17, 1953, Margaret Carter Papers, and D. B. Hardeman to Stephen Mitchell, April 4, 1956, Mitchell Papers, box 40, plus unidentified clipping, March 1956, anonymous analysis of Texas presidential politics, 1956, and Don Ellinger to Jack Kroll and Jim McDevitt, March 13, 29, 1956, Texas AFL-CIO Collection, 110-26-5-1, 110-26-2-1, and 110-9-1-4, respectively. Useful background on the 1956 maneuvering is in the Mitchell Papers, boxes 25, 33, 35, and 40, while a lucid secondary account is Charles Stephenson, "The Democrats of Texas and Texas Liberalism, 1944-1960: A Study in Political Frustration" (Master's thesis, Southwest Texas State University, 1967).

2. Memo from Weldon Hart to Allan Shivers, April 5, 1956, Shivers Papers, 4-10/33.

3. Press memorandum, April 6, 1956, Shivers Papers, 4-15/311; Frantz interview with Shivers.

4. Interview with Kathleen Voigt, San Antonio, July 26, 1976; *Texas Observer*, March 28, 1956; anonymous analysis of Texas presidential politics, 1956, letter from

Don Ellinger to Jack Kroll and Jim McDevitt, April 13, 1956, and "Texas Report," DAC newsletter, March 26, 1956, Texas AFL-CIO Collection, 110-26-2-1, 110-9-1-4, and 110-26-8-1, respectively; Sam Rayburn to Mrs. Homer Thornberry, May 23, 1956, Rayburn Papers, series I, reel 35. On liberal in-fighting see especially the Democratic Advisory Council Papers, notably the 1954-1955 correspondence between Bob Sawtelle and T. Lawrence Jones.

5. Allan Shivers speeches, April 20, 1956, in 4-15/218, and May 1, 4, and 5, 1956, in 4-15/311, and press memorandum, May 2 and 3, 1956, in 4-9/57 and 4-15/311, respectively, Shivers Papers; Rayburn press release, n.d., Raymond Buck Papers, box 141, folder 239F; "Trip to the Woodshed," *Newsweek* 47 (April 9, 1956): 36; *Dallas Morning News*, April 11, May 1, 22, 23, 1956; *Fort Worth Star-Telegram*, May 4, 1956; *Texas Observer*, February 29, April 18, May 2, 9, 23, 1956; Sam Kinch, Sr., and Stuart Long, *Allan Shivers: The Pied Piper of Texas Politics* (Austin: Shoal Creek Publishers, 1973), p. 190. See also Jerry Hendrix, "A Comparative Analysis of Selected Public Addresses by Allan Shivers and Lyndon B. Johnson in the Texas Pre-Convention Campaign of 1956" (Master's thesis, University of Oklahoma, 1957), pp. 77-95. Shivers's reference of Johnson's having benefited from doctored ballots in 1948 brings to mind such returns as Shivers's 1947 margin over five opponents in Starr County, 2,206 to 182, or over three opponents in 1954 in Zapata, 541 to 30, see *Texas Almanac, 1947-1948*, p. 410, and *Texas Almanac, 1956-1957*, p. 526.

6. Allan Shivers to Bill Blakley, May 28, 1956, and Blakley to Shivers, June 8, 1956, Shivers Papers, 4-15/215; Shivers speech, April 30, 1956, Shivers Papers, 4-15/311.

7. Interview with Voigt; George Lambert to Violet Gunther, April 10, 1956 (on Connally) and April 26, 1956 ("strange world"), Lambert Papers. Lambert was a veteran labor organizer who was serving temporarily as Texas representative of the Americans for Democratic Action in 1956; "Vi" Gunther was political secretary of the ADA.

8. *Texas Observer*, May 23, 1956; *Dallas Morning News*, May 23, 1956; Ronnie Dugger, "Texas Liberals Revolt," *Nation* 182 (June 2, 1956): 463; Steinberg, *Sam Rayburn*, pp. 302-303; Frantz interview with Shivers; Edward McMillan, "Texas and the Eisenhower Campaigns" (Ph.D. diss., Texas Tech University, 1960), pp. 365-370. Mrs. Bentsen's own testimony indicated that she had never done much for the party. See David McComb interview with Mrs. Lloyd Bentsen, Jr., Houston, December 23, 1968, Oral History Collection, LBJ Library, University of Texas at Austin.

9. The O'Daniel quotes are in the *Dallas Morning News*, May 14 and July 4, 1956, and in "Texas," *Time* 68 (August 6, 1956): 18. Regarding Haley, see the *Dallas Morning News*, June 8, 15, 21, 1956; *Fort Worth Star-Telegram*, July 27, 1956; unidentified clipping, 1956, Haley Correspondence.

10. *Texas Observer*, May 16, June 6, July 4, 11, 18, 25, August 1, 8, 1956; Jimmy Banks, *Money, Marbles and Chalk* (Austin: Texas Publishing Company, 1971), p. 141; *Lubbock Morning Avalanche*, July 19, 25, 1956; *Texas Almanac, 1958-1959*, pp. 461-463; George Fuermann, *Reluctant Empire*, (Garden City, New York: Doubleday, 1957), pp. 59-61; *Austin American*, July 22, 1956; Daniel campaign leaflet, 1956, Raymond Buck Papers, box 138, folder 209-A; J. C. Martin, "The First Administration of Governor Price Daniel" (Master's thesis, University of Texas at Austin, 1967), pp. 41, 51, on press support.

11. *Texas Observer*, August 15, 22, 29, 1956; *Austin American*, September 7,

1956; Robert Hayes, column, *Dallas Morning News*, August 11, 1956; Don Ellinger to Jack Kroll and Jim McDevitt, July 28, August 4, 1956, Texas AFL-CIO Collection, 110-9-1-4; *Texas Almanac, 1958-1959*, pp. 468-469.

12. Price Daniel to Raymond Buck, December 8, 1955, and Buck to Daniel, December 16, 1955, Buck Papers, box 138, folder 209-A; Banks, *Money*, pp. 139-142.

13. *Texas Observer*, August 22, 1956; Robert Sherrill, *The Accidental President* (New York: Grossman, 1967), pp. 103-104.

14. Douglass Cater, "The Trouble in Lyndon Johnson's Back Yard," *Reporter* 13 (December 1, 1955): 34; Dawson Duncan, column, *Dallas Morning News*, September 6, 1956; *Behind the Scenes* (Stuart Long), newsletter, September 14, 1956, Texas AFL-CIO Collection, 110-15-4-7; *Austin American*, September 7, 10, 1956; on the rumors, Sam Kinch, column, *Fort Worth Star-Telegram*, September 9, 1956, and Allen Duckworth, column, *Dallas Morning News*, September 10, 1956; various letters and telegrams to Raymond Buck urging him to reconvene the May state convention and elect a genuinely Democratic SDEC are in the Buck Papers, box 140, folder 236 F; *Texas Observer*, August 1, 8, 15, 1956; *Dallas Morning News*, August 1, 5, 1956; Banks, *Money*, p. 150; Kinch and Long, *Shivers*, p. 187; Larry King, "My Hero LBJ," *Harper's* 233 (October 1966): 57-58; interviews with Yarborough and Fath; interview with Luther Hagard, Arlington, August 31, 1976.

15. David McComb interview with Walter Hall; William Gardner, column, *Houston Post*, May 10, 1956; *Dallas Morning News*, June 27, 1956; Sam Kinch, column, *Fort Worth Star-Telegram*, September 11-13, 1956; *San Antonio Light*, September 13, 1956.

16. Interview with Hagard; "Harris County Story," August 30, 1956, brochure, Shivers Papers, 4-9/57; King, "My Hero LBJ," p. 58; "Texas: What Price Daniel?" *New Republic* 135 (September 24, 1956): 6; McComb interview with Walter Hall; *Texas Observer*, September 12, 1956; Dan Bus, column, *Ennis Daily News*, September 13, 1956; *The Big Steal of the Texas Democratic Party*, 1956 pamphlet, Lambert Papers, 127-23-6.

17. *Houston Chronicle*, July 31, 1956; *Proceedings of the Sub-Committee on Credentials of the State Democratic Executive Committee of Texas on Contests of County Delegations*, September 10, 1956, Texas State Democratic Executive Committee Papers, 4-22/152, Texas State Archives, Austin—see especially pp. 213-255; Jon Ford, column, *San Antonio Express*, September 16, 1956.

18. "Texas: What Price Daniel?" p. 6.

19. *Texas Observer*, October 24, 31, November 14, 1956; *Dallas Morning News*, October 8, 9, 26, November 3, 1956; Ronnie Dugger, "What Corrupted Texas?" *Harper's* 214 (March 1957): 74; Shivers quote in *Lubbock Evening Journal*, October 23, 1956; Kathleen Voigt to Adlai Stevenson, September 23, 1956, Mitchell Papers, box 40.

20. See *Dallas Morning News*, March 2, May 20, 1950; Stuart Long, "Never Say Dies," *Nation* 175 (August 23, 1952): 140.

21. *Dallas Morning News*, July 30, November 25, 1952, July 4, 29, 1956; form letter to constituents, 1954, Martin Dies Clippings, Barker History Center, University of Texas Archives, Austin; *Southern Conservative*, February 1953, May 1954.

22. "Confidential Interview, 1964," and "Closed Manuscript," in possession of

Ben Procter, Texas Christian University, quoted in Emmett Essin, "The Democratic Senatorial Primary in Texas: Yarborough vs. Blakley" (Master's thesis, Texas Christian University, 1965), p. 13; *Texas Observer*, February 5, 12, 19, 26, 1957; *Dallas Morning News*, January 16, February 1, 3, 1957; *Austin Report*, February 3 and 9, 1957; Walter Goodman, *The Committee* (New York: Farrar, Straus & Giroux, 1968), p. 55, notes Mr. Sam's opinion of Dies; *San Angelo Evening Standard*, February 15, 1957; "Harris County Democrat," newsletter, March 1957, and Don Ellinger to Jack Kroll and Jim McDevitt, March 15, 1957, Texas AFL-CIO Collection, 110-9-1-4, and 110-9-1-4, respectively.

23. "Tumult over Texas," *Newsweek* 49 (March 25, 1957): 35; *Texas Observer*, February 26, 1957; Larry King, "Joe Pool of HUAC," *Harper's* 133 (November 1966): 62; Lewis Nordyke, *The Truth About Texas* (New York York: Thomas Y. Crowell Co., 1957), p. 238; *Austin Report*, February 3, 9, 1957; *Houston Press*, April 4, 1957; *San Angelo Evening Standard*, February 15, 1957; on Rayburn motives and on his ultimate unannounced backing for Yarborough over Dies, see Don Ellinger to Jack Kroll and Jim McDevitt, March 15, 1957, Texas AFL-CIO Collection, 110-9-1-4, and Rayburn to Rhea Howard, February 8, 1957 (and others that month), and Yarborough to Rayburn, April 22, 1957, Rayburn Papers, series I, reel 38.

24. *Texas Observer*, February 25, March 6, 1957; *Dallas Morning News*, February 16, 19, 1957; interview with Yarborough, November 24, 1975; Allen Duckworth, column, *Dallas Morning News*, February 16, 1957. Hart was actually lobbying for the Herring bill, a substitute measure that would have retained the appointee, William A. Blakley, in office until the 1958 elections.

25. Ben Bock to Jim Lindsey, March 25, 1957, Texas AFL-CIO Collection, 110-26-6-5.

26. Ibid.; *San Angelo Evening Standard*, February 15, 1957; *Houston Press*, April 4, 1957.

27. *Dallas Morning News*, January 20, February 3, March 31, 1957; *Texas Observer*, January 2, March 12, 26, 1957; "Texans for Martin Dies," three leaflets, 1957, Dies Clippings; "Texas: Senate Anyone?" *Time* 69 (March 11, 1957): 20; memo from Yarborough headquarters staff, March 6, 1957, Yarborough File, 47-1-16; Hutcheson leaflet, n.d., President's Official File 697, Eisenhower Library.

28. *Texas Almanac, 1958-1959*, pp. 457-458; *Texas Observer*, April 9, 1957; *Dallas Morning News*, April 3, 4, 1957; James Soukup, Clifton McCleskey, and Harry Holloway, *Party and Factional Division in Texas* (Austin: University of Texas Press, 1964), pp. 31, 69, 130; "After the Free-for-All," *Newsweek* 49 (April 15, 1957): 35.

29. Interview with Jim Yancy, Austin, December 23, 1977; interview with Roy Evans, Corpus Christi, January 30, 1978.

30. Memos from William McGill to Allan Shivers, February 28, 1951, July 28, 1954, Shivers Papers, 4-10/34; *Austin Report*, July 11, 1954. These items refer to Chancellor Hart.

State Observer, December 21, 1953, and March 8, 1954; Frank Goodwyn, *Lone Star Land* (New York: Alred A. Knopf, 1955), pp. 305-306; Zeke Zbranek, column, *Texas Observer*, October 16, 1959; quote is from *Texas Businessman*, September 4, 1959.

31. Willie Morris, *North Toward Home* (New York: Dell, 1967), pp. 186-192; Willie Morris, "Mississippi Rebel on a Texas Campus," *Nation* 182 (March 24, 1957):

232-233; Dugger, "What Corrupted Texas?" p. 73; Ronnie Dugger, *Our Invaded Universities* (New York; W. W. Norton, 1974), p. 64; Willie Morris, column, *Texas Observer*, May 16, 1956.

32. List of recommendations for Texas Tech board of regents in Shivers Papers, 4-9/137; *Dallas Morning News*, July 15, 1957; George Fuermann, *Reluctant Empire* (Garden City, New York: Doubleday, 1957), pp. 71-72; James Mathis, column, *Houston Post*, October 13, 1964; Ronnie Dugger, column, *Texas Observer*, September 20, 1957; interview with Byron Abernethy, May 26, 1976; Margaret Carter to Price Daniel, July 16, 1957, Buck Papers, 236-G. Carter, Mathis, and Fuermann blame all the terminations on Haley, but Dr. Abernethy believes that Haley took the initiative only in the Stensland case.

33. *Texas Observer*, June 26, 1970; Morris, *North Toward Home*, p. 192.

34. Donald Strong, "The Rise of Negro Voting in Texas," *American Political Science Review* 42 (June 1948): 516-522; Newsletter, Texas Commission on Interracial Cooperation, September 1949, Shivers Papers, 4-9/114; V. O. Key, *Southern Politics* (New York: Alfred A. Knopf, 1949), pp. 590-591; *Race Relations* 1 (November 1943), p. 13; Alwyn Barr, *Black Texans* (Austin: Jenkins, 1973), p. 175; *Texas Spectator*, April 19, 1948; see also Neil Sapper, "A Survey of the History of the Black People of Texas, 1930-1954" (Ph.D. diss., Texas Tech University, 1972), pp. 130-140, 167.

35. Clifton Carter to Weldon Hart, January 28, 1950, 4-10/33; memos from William McGill to Allan Shivers, January 22, 24, 1950, 4-9/121; Democratic Progressive Voters League of Texas to Allan Shivers, March 3, 1950, 4-9/127—all in the Shivers Papers.

Carter was owner of the 7-Up Bottling Company in Bryan. The DPVL was a statewide black organization.

36. Numan Bartley, *The Rise of Massive Resistance* (Baton Rouge: Louisiana State University Press, 1969), p. 138; press memoranda from the governor's office, July 27, August 21, 1955, in 4-9/56, and Wallace Savage to Allan Shivers, October 21, 1955, in 4-9/35, Shivers Papers; *McKinney* v. *Blankenship* 282 S.W. 2d 691.

In regard to the factors considered for appointees to the committee, see D. M. Pollard to Allan Shivers, June 29, 1955, and the memo from Maurice Acers to Shivers, n.d., 4-9/56, Shivers Papers, recommending Beaumont attorney Charles Howell. They noted in so many words that Howell was a bitter-end segregationist. He got the appointment.

37. *Texas Almanac, 1958-1959*, pp. 455-456; *Texas Observer*, April 11, August 17, September 17, 1955; Bartley, *Rise of Massive Resistance*, p. 138; quote in letter from J. R. Parten to Sam Rayburn, March 28, 1956, Rayburn Papers, series I, reel 35; Alan Scott, "Twenty-Five Years of Opinion on Integration in Texas," *Southwestern Social Science Quarterly* 48 (September 1967): 158-161.

38. Weldon Hart memo to Allan Shivers, August 27, 1956, Shivers Papers, 4-10/33; Report of the Legal and Legislative Subcommittee on the Texas Advisory Committee on Segregation in the Public Schools, September 1, 1956.

39. *Texas Observer*, September 5, 12, 1956; press memorandum from the governor's office, August 31, 1956, Shivers Papers, 4-15/n.n.; Fuermann, *Reluctant Empire*, pp. 203-205; John Howard Griffin and Theodore Freedman, *Mansfield, Texas: A Report of the Crisis Situation Resulting from Efforts to Desegregate the School*

System, Anti-Defamation League pamphlet, n.d., in author's possession; Robert Sherrill, *Gothic Politics in the Deep South* (New York: Ballentine, 1968), pp. 94-95; F. Ross Peterson, "Prelude to Little Rock: The Eisenhower Administration and Mansfield, Texas," unpublished article in author's possession.

40. *Austin Report*, January 6, 1957.

41. State of Texas, *Senate Journal*, 55th Legislature, regular session, May 15, 1957, pp. 1331-1333; *Austin Report*, December 9, 1956, and January 27, and February 13, 1957; Ronnie Dugger, "Texas Christians Stem the Tide," *Christian Century* 74 (July 31, 1957): 912-915; Hart Stilwell, "Texas Rebel with a Cause," *Coronet* 44 (August 1958): 44; Robert Cuellar, "A Social and Political History of the Mexican-American Population of Texas, 1929-1963" (Master's thesis, North Texas State University, 1969), p. 49; J. C. Martin, "Price Daniel," pp. 107-108, 121; Stuart Long, "White Supremacy and the 'Filibusteros,'" *Reporter* 16 (June 27, 1957): 15.

For other segregationist bills that passed see State of Texas *House Journal*, 55th Legislature, first called session October 31, 1957, pp. 186-190, 464-471, and second called session, November 12, 1957, pp. 2-4, and *Senate Journal*, first called session, November 11, 1957, p. 208.

42. Lyndon Johnson to Valmo and Harry Bellinger, J. B. Sutton, and Archie Johnson, August 26, 1957, to Mrs. Walter Dyer, July 11, 1957, and to Mrs. T. B. Stroud, July 15, 1957—among proponents—and letters to Jack Ferrill, September 5, 1957, and to Luther Finley and Webb Joiner, both August 30, 1957—among opponents— in the Lyndon B. Johnson Papers, Senatorial Years, Civil Rights Folder, box 2, Lyndon B. Johnson Library, Austin; Fuermann, *Reluctant Empire*, p. 197; Bartley, *Rise of Massive Resistance*, pp. 139-141, 157; T. Harry Williams, "Huey, Lyndon and Southern Radicalism," *Journal of American History* 60 (September 1973): 283.

Texas still has more than its share of racial problems—see Texas Advisory Committee to the U.S. Commission on Civil Rights, *Civil Rights in Texas*, February 1970.

43. Robert Hilburn, column, *Fort Worth Star-Telegram*, April 7, 1957.

CHAPTER 13

1. Herbert Jacob and Kenneth Vines, *Politics in the American States* (Boston: Little, Brown, 1965), pp. 297, 308; "Legislative Bulletin #2," March 27, 1954, Texas Social and Legislative Conference Files, 120-1-1; Paul Carrington to Beauford Jester, June 8, 1949, Beauford Jester Files. TMA lobbyist Ed Burris argued that all taxes are paid by the same people—letter to Allan Shivers, December 29, 1949, Shivers Papers, 4-9/73.

2. These ideas have been bandied about in Texas at least since the Establishment took over—see Wallace Jenkins, column, *Emancipator*, July 1939; Byron Utecht, "The Power to Tax Is the Power to Destroy," article in Byron Utecht Scrapbook, 1949, Texas State Archives, Austin, 2-1/374. On levels of oil taxation, see *Oil and Gas Occupation Tax Laws* (Austin: Texas Comptroller's Office, 1977), p. 2.

3. Hart Stilwell, *Texas* (Austin: Texas Social and Legislative Conference, 1949), p. 4; *Texas Observer*, May 3, 1963; John Bainbridge, *The Super-Americans* (Garden City, New York: Doubleday, 1961), pp. 175-176; Sam Hall, column, *Texas Spectator*,

January 11, 1947; A. G. Mezerik, "Dixie in Black and White," *Nation* 164 (May 3, 1947): 511.

4. Geologist quote in A. Hope Wheeler, column, *Texas Citizen*, January 4, 1941; Culberson quote in *Texas Spectator*, September 1, 1947. Also illustrative of Establishment policy was Ernest Thompson's assurance to President Truman in 1950 that foreign oil imports were too heavy and Jack Porter's identical claim to President Eisenhower in 1954—see Thompson to Truman, May 19, 1950, President's General File, Texas A-B, Truman Library, and Porter to Eisenhower, August 5, 1954, Administration Series, box 32, Eisenhower Library.

5. Richard Fish, column, *Houston Chronicle*, December 26, 1976; Mody Boatright interview with E. I. Thompson, September 3, 1952, University of Texas Oral History on Oil, Number 66, Barker History Center, University of Texas Archives, Austin.

6. Jacob and Vines, *Politics*, pp. 325-327, 391, 398-400, 405-406; *Book of the States, 1948-1949* (Chicago: Council of State Governments, 1948), pp. 375-377; *Book of the States, 1956-1957*, pp. 324-328; Mezerik, "Dixie," p. 509; Ronnie Dugger, "What Corrupted Texas?" *Harper's* 214 (March 1957): 74; all education statistics from *The Book of the States, 1943-1944*, pp. 266-267, *1948-1949*, pp. 400-401, *1952-1953*, p. 250, *1954-1955*, p. 245, and *1960-1961*, p. 297. Regarding the political studies, see Dan Nimmo and William Oden, *The Texas Political System* (Englewood Cliffs, N.J.: Prentice-Hall, 1971), and Jack Walker, "The Diffusion of Innovations among the American States," *American Political Science Review* 63 (September 1969): 880-899.

7. C. Wright Mills, *The Power Elite* (New York: Oxford University Press, 1956), pp. 342, 346.

8. Lawrence Peter and Raymond Hull, *The Peter Principle* (New York: Bantam, 1969), pp. 56-57, 121-122.

9. "Surprise in Texas," *Fortune* 51 (March 1955): 50, 52.

10. See Neal Peirce, *The Great Plains States* (New York: Norton, 1973), pp. 209-210; on Eisenhower's dealings with Democrats to the disadvantage of the state's Republicans, see Bruce Alger to Sherman Adams and others, May 13, 1955, General File 536, Jack Porter to Eisenhower, May 1, 1956, Central File 696, folder 138, and Texas Republican Newsletter, number 17, n.d., General File 530, all in the Eisenhower Library.

11. V. O. Key, *Public Opinion and American Democracy* (New York: Alfred A. Knopf, 1961), pp. 103-105; James Soukup, Clifton McCleskey, and Harry Holloway, *Party and Factional Division in Texas* (Austin: University of Texas Press, 1964), pp. 123, 137, 176.

12. Martha Dickenson, "Electoral Behavior in Texas, 1944 through 1972" (Master's thesis, North Texas State University, 1973), pp. 126-132, 141. Other aggregate data analysis of the same years concur with many of these findings but do not agree that factionalism was related to socioeconomic variables either before or after 1956—see John Todd and Kay Ellis, "Analyzing Factional Patterns in State Politics: Texas 1944-1972," *Social Science Quarterly* 55 (December 1974): 718-731.

13. Dickenson, "Electoral Behavior," pp. 59, 126.

14. Goodwyn, "New Shapes in Texas Politics," Lambert Papers, 127-30-7; Soukup, McCleskey, and Holloway, *Division in Texas*, pp. 88-89, 148-149, 176-177.

15. Goodwyn, "New Shapes in Texas Politics," Lambert Papers, 127-30-7; Soukup, McClesky, and Holloway, *Division in Texas*, p. 173; Tarrant County *Official Returns*, 1948 and 1956; Bernard Cosman, "The Republican Congressman from Dallas" (Master's thesis, University of Alabama, 1958), pp. 20-108; Harris County returns, 1956, pamphlet, Texas AFL-CIO Collection, 110-26-11-2.

16. Kathleen Voigt, "Texas Politicans, Political Philosophies, and Constituencies" (Master's thesis, St. Mary's University, 1968), pp. 43-44, 121, 126; C. D. Dorough, *Mr. Sam* (New York: Random House, 1962), pp. 83-84, 238, 399-401, 503-504, 554-559; Soukup, McCleskey, and Holloway, *Division in Texas*, p. 6.

17. *Texas Observer*, December 1 and 15, 1961, January 5, 1962, and January 20, 1967; Jimmy Banks, *Money, Marbles and Chalk* (Austin: Texas Publishing Company, 1971), p. 152; Soukup, McCleskey, and Holloway, *Division in Texas*, p. 7; Willie Morris, "Legislating in Texas," *Commentary* 38 (November 1964): 38, 41.

18. Ronnie Dugger, "Texas' New Junior Senator," *New Republic* 136 (April 22, 1957):8.

19. William G. Phillips, *Yarborough of Texas* (Washington, D.C.: Acropolis Books, 1969), pp. 102-104, 130; Soukup, McCleskey, and Holloway, *Division in Texas*, pp. 6-7; Dickenson, "Electoral Behavior," pp. 125, 140-141.

20. Emmett Essin interviews with Charles M. Johnston, Austin, December 29, 1964, with William Blakley, Dallas, February 22, 1965, and with Ralph Yarborough, Austin, December 30, 1964, in Emmett Essin, "The Democratic Senatorial Primary in Texas: Yarborough vs. Blakely" (Master's thesis, Texas Christian University, 1965), pp. 27, 36, and 48-49, respectively; *Austin Statesman*, June 4, 1958, quoted in Essin, "Senatorial Primary," pp. 36-37; "Political Notes," *Time* 69 (April 15, 1957): 33-34; "Yarborough's Opponent," *New Republic* 138 (April 21, 1958): 4-5; on Republican hopes for 1958, see letters from Jack Porter to Sherman Adams, April 16, 1957, and William Burrow to Max Rabb, April 4, 1957, in President's General File 531, folder 109-A-2, Eisenhower Library.

21. Roland Evans and Robert Novak, *Lyndon B. Johnson: The Exercise of Power* (New York: New American Library, 1966), pp. 351-354; Banks, *Money*, p. 55; Ann Crawford and Jack Keever, *John B. Connally: Portrait in Power* (Austin: Jenkins, 1973), p. 100; Sam Kinch, Sr., and Stuart Long, *Allan Shivers: The Pied Piper of Texas Politics* (Austin: Shoal Creek, 1973), p. 220; Baker interview with Mooney.

22. Quote is from Nimmo and Oden, *Texas Political System*, p. 63; *Texas Observer*, May 30, 1963, April 16, 1965, October 4, 1968; *Dallas Morning News*, April 2, 1968; Crawford and Keever, *Connally*, p. 237.

23. Crawford and Keever, *Connally*, pp. 94, 158-164, 168-179.

24. Ibid., p. 123; Harvey Pershing, column, *Fort Worth Star-Telegram*, October 10, 1967.

25. See Jimmy Banks, column, *Dallas Morning News*, August 30, 1969; Earl Golz, column, *Dallas Morning News*, September 8, 1969.

26. The best account is Sam Kinch, Jr., and Ben Procter, *Texas Under a Cloud* (Austin: Jenkins Publishing Co., 1972).

27. Ibid., p. 99; Sam Kinch, Jr., column, *Dallas Morning News*, June 5, 1973. The TMA opposed new taxes and thought the state should cancel teacher pay raises and quadruple college tuition—*Dallas Morning News*, February 18, 1971—but it went along with the consumer tax.

28. Eva Galambos, *State and Local Taxes in the South, 1973* (Atlanta: Southern Regional Council, 1973), pp. 8-9, 20-21.

29. *Dallas Morning News*, November 3, 14, December 12, 1976, April 3, 1977; Stuart Davis, column, *Dallas Morning News*, November 20, 1976.

A survey of *The Book of the States* over the years indicates that during the past generation Texas's average ranking among the states in payments per pupil in the public schools and aid to the blind has sunk several notches below its performance during the primitive years.

30. Sam Kinch, Jr., column, *Dallas Morning News*, February 12, 1978, on Briscoe's unfortunate appointments; Soukup, McCleskey, and Holloway, *Division in Texas*, pp. 24, 69.

31. Tom Johnson, Dave McNeeley, Carolyn Barta, and Dick West, columns in the *Dallas Morning News*, February 13, 1972, November 25, 1972, March 19, 1973, and March 30, 1975, respectively; Molly Ivins, column, *Texas Observer*, February 14, 1975; "Dallas: Up the Establishment," *Newsweek* 77 (May 3, 1971): 32.

For historical background on the Dallas Establishment, see Carol Thometz, *The Decision Makers: The Power Structure of Dallas* (Dallas: Southern Methodist University Press, 1963), pp. 30-37, 63-66, 83; Warren Leslie, *Dallas Public and Private* (New York: Avon Books, 1964), pp. 49-67; "The Dydamic Men of Dallas," *Fortune* 39 (February 1949): 98-103, 162-166; Richard Smith, "How Business Failed Dallas," *Fortune* 70 (July 1964): 157-163, 211-216.

32. *Dallas Morning News*, September 3, 1975; Al Altwegg, column, *Dallas Morning News*, January 19, 1975; *Journal of Commerce*, February 5, 1974; *Beaumont Enterprise*, January 29, 1974; untitled script for slide program, Bob Armstrong's office, 1975; Fred Bonavita, column, *Houston Post*, May 4, 1975; interview with John Rogers, Austin, August 13, 1975; Sam Kinch, Jr., column, *Dallas Morning News*, January 16, 1975; telephoned statement from comptroller's office, January 10, 1978; interview with Jim Yancy.

Essay
on Sources

MANUSCRIPT COLLECTIONS

The most indispensable records for any examination of recent Texas political history are the governors' papers in the State Archives, even though the papers of W. Lee O'Daniel, Coke Stevenson, Beauford Jester, and Allan Shivers have not yet been processed by archivists. These files are, in fact, subject to occasional reshelving, which may eventually invalidate some of the row, shelf, and box numbers that are cited in the notes. The most revealing of the four is the Shivers collection; the O'Daniel files are the least useful, since they are relatively scanty and do not contain much intra-office correspondence. Filling in many of the gaps in the O'Daniel and Stevenson records, especially for elections in the 1940s, are the papers of Jimmie Allred in the Special Collections department at the University of Houston Library.

Useful for the entire period are the papers of Sam Rayburn at the Rayburn Library in Bonham, Lyndon Johnson at the presidential library in Austin, Tom Connally at the Library of Congress, and the Texas AFL-CIO Collection in the Labor Archives at the University of Texas at Arlington. The Rayburn and Connally papers, however, are a bit thin, especially Connally's, and many of the Johnson papers are still closed to researchers.

The presidential papers in the Franklin Roosevelt Library in Hyde Park, New York, Harry Truman Library in Independence, Missouri, and Dwight Eisenhower Library in Abilene, Kansas, offer the necessary national perspectives on Texas political events and were valuable for most election years. Valuable associated papers are those of the Democratic National Committee at the Roosevelt Library, Stephen Mitchell and Will Clayton at the Truman Library, and Jim Hagerty at the Eisenhower Library.

Very revealing on more narrow topics are the Palmer Bradley papers at the University of Houston (on Dixiecrats), the George Ebey and Ralph O'Leary papers at the University of Houston (on Minute Women), the Hatton Sumners Papers at the Dallas Historical Society (on the congressman's career in the 1940s), the John Lee Smith Papers at the Southwest Collection at Texas Tech University (on Smith's activities in the 1940s), and the Homer Rainey Papers in the Manuscript Collection at the University of Missouri (on the 1946 primary).

The thoughts and deeds of the liberal opposition to the Establishment are covered quite adequately in the Brotherhood of Locomotive Firemen and Enginemen Files, the Texas Social and Legislative Conference Files, and the papers of the Democratic Advisory Council, Margaret Carter, George Lambert, Jim Sewell, and John C. Granbery. All but the latter are in the political or labor archives at UT Arlington, while Granbery's are in the Barker Center archives at UT Austin. The files of the governors and the Texas AFL-CIO also shed considerable light on the liberals.

Right-wing activities were best chronicled by the Anti-Defamation League in its Houston office, which once housed collections on George Armstrong, the Committee for Constitutional Government, J. Evetts Haley, R. C. Hoiles, the Minute Women, and Edwin A. Walker. These records have since been moved to the New York office of the Anti-Defamation League. The AFL-CIO Collection also contains much on the right wing.

Other collections that were consulted and cited from the political and labor archives at UT Arlington were the files on Ralph Yarborough, Carl Brannin, Carl McPeak, Sabine Area Local Industrial Union 1814, and the Sabine Area Trades and Labor Council. From the Barker Center at UT Austin, the Homer Rainey file and the correspondence of J. Evetts Haley and the Jeffersonian Democrats were used. At Texas Christian University the William Blakley Scrapbook and the Raymond Buck Papers were used. The Texas State Archives in Austin provided the papers of William McGill and the Texas State Democratic Executive Committee as well as the Byron Utecht Scrapbook. Also useful were the John Henry Kirby Papers at the Gulf Coast Historical Association at the University of Houston, the Tom Love Papers at the Dallas Historical Society, the Miscellany Concerning the UT Controversy at the Legislative Reference Library in Austin, and Miscellaneous Right Wing Materials at the Hogg Foundation for Mental Health at UT Austin. Out-of-state collections that were used include the American Civil Liberties Union papers at the Seeley Mudd Library at Princeton and the American Federation of Labor papers at the Wisconsin State Historical Society in Madison.

INTERVIEWS

The oral history programs at the Lyndon Johnson Library and at North Texas State University are important sources. Interviewers for the two projects held some forty sessions with twenty-five political figures whose recollections I used. The North Texas State project in particular recorded the memories of some of the principal politicians, notably Stevenson, Dies, and Shivers. I interviewed Ralph Yarborough plus some thirty-nine others who were embroiled with Texas politics, and all were useful on particular topics. (Three were part of the UT Arlington Oral History Project.) Also useful were transcripts of interviews with three Texas Republicans at the Eisenhower Library. Interview statements, of course, cannot necessarily be taken at face value, and no single interview is crucial to the conclusions in any chapter. Probably the most useful are the Shivers interviews and my own session with William Lawson.

GOVERNMENT DOCUMENTS

Texas legislative hearings were vital regarding the investigation of the 1941 Democratic senatorial primary, the probe into the Rainey case in 1944, and the investigation of lobbying in 1945. Texas House and Senate *Journals* were also useful on labor and civil-rights issues. Congressional hearings were crucial to the discussion of extreme anti-Roosevelt sentiment in the 1944 election, and the *Congressional Record* was of some use in describing Martin Dies's beliefs.

NEWSPAPERS

Many of the newspaper citations came from collections of clippings, especially the files kept on individuals and events by the Barker Center at UT Austin. Virtually all the manuscript collections contained many clippings, and the Bascom Timmons Clippings at the Texas A&M Archives were also useful.

I consulted most of the big urban corporation publications that comprise the Establishment press, especially the dailies in Dallas, Houston, Austin, and Fort Worth. The essence of conservative thinking was represented in the newspaper cited most often, the *Dallas Morning News*. Anti-Establishment thinking in the 1940s and 1950s was gleaned from a clutch of small but spritely organs: the *Texas Spectator, Austin Report, State Observer, Texas Observer*, and the *Emancipator*. From the late 1940s through the late 1950s, Stuart Long, who wrote the *Austin Report* and secretly wrote the "Behind-the-Scenes" column and newsletter, seemed to be the most successful reporter in digging up and revealing inside political information.

BOOKS

S. S. McKay's books— *W. Lee O'Daniel and Texas Politics, 1938-1942* (Lubbock, 1944), *Texas Politics, 1906-1944* (Lubbock, 1952), and *Texas and the Fair Deal, 1945-1952* (San Antonio, 1954)—are very useful reference works and are thorough summaries of the newspaper coverage of the day. McKay offered few interpretations of political events, and, of course, had no access to primary resource materials. Jimmy Banks's *Money, Marbles, and Chalk* (Austin, 1971) offers tidbits and the insights of a veteran conservative reporter in a rather disorganized fashion, but most of the book concerns 1960s politics. Banks made no attempt to research primary resources. Frank Goodwyn's *Lone Star Land* (New York, 1955) and George Fuermann's *Reluctant Empire* (New York, 1957) offer cogent and perceptive glimpses into Texas politics in the 1940s and 1950s, though neither work is strictly about politics. They had no access to most of the files that are open today.

A number of biographies were serviceable. Among the more judicious ones were Richard Henderson's *Maury Maverick* (Austin, 1970), William Gellerman's *Martin Dies* (New York, 1944), Roland Evans and Robert Novak's *Lyndon B. Johnson: The Exercise of Power* (New York, 1966), and Ann Fears Crawford and Jack Keever's *John B. Connally: Portrait in Power* (Austin, 1973). Less critical, but still worthy of mention, are C. D. Dorough, *Mr. Sam* (New York, 1962), Sam Kinch, Sr., and Stuart Long, *Allan Shivers: The Pied Piper of Texas Politics* (Austin, 1973), and the Alfred Steinberg books, *Sam Rayburn* (New York, 1975), *Sam Johnson's Boy* (New York, 1968), and the one he coauthored with Senator Connally, *My Name Is Tom Connally* (New York, 1954).

Among the best books on particular Texas topics are Robert Engler, *The Politics of Oil* (Chicago, 1961), Gerald Nash, *United States Oil Policy* (Pittsburgh, 1968)—neither is strictly about Texas—and Homer Rainey, *The Tower and the Dome* (Boulder, 1971), Alwyn Barr, *Black Texans* (Austin, 1973), Paul Casdorph, *A History of the Republican Party in Texas* (Austin, 1965), Nellie Kingrea, *History of the First Ten Years of the Texas Good Neighbor Commission* (Fort Worth, 1954), Frederick Meyers, *"Right-to-Work" in Practice* (New York, 1959), Rae Files Still, *The Gilmer-Aiken Bills* (Austin, 1950), O. D. Weeks, *Texas Presidential Politics in 1952* (Austin, 1953), and *Texas One-Party Politics in 1956* (Austin, 1957), and David Nevin, *The Texans* (New York, 1968), on the Texas character.

Innumerable books were beneficial in relating Texas politics to the regional and national scene, including George Tindall's *The Emergence of the New South, 1913-1945* (Baton Rouge, 1967), Samuel Lubell's *Revolt of the Moderates* (New York, 1956), and Robert Garson's *The Democratic Party and the Politics of Sectionalism, 1941-1948* (Baton Rouge, 1974). Those with separate essays on Texas, all very perceptive, are V. O. Key's *Southern Politics* (New York, 1949), John Gunther's *Inside U.S.A.* (New York, 1947), Hart Stilwell's "Texas," in Robert Allen's *Our Sovereign State* (New York, 1949), Willie Morris's *North Toward Home* (New York, 1967), and Neal Peirce's *The Great Plains States of America* (New York, 1973).

Concepts of the Establishment depended in part on William Domhoff, *Who Rules America?* (Englewood Cliffs, New Jersey, 1967), Daniel Elazar, *American Federalism* (New York, 1956), and Dan Nimmo and William Oden, *The Texas Political System* (Englewood Cliffs, 1971).

PERIODICALS

Scores of articles are excellent on particular topics. Among the best ones are Theodore White, "Texas: Land of Wealth and Fear," *Reporter* 10 (May 25, 1954): 10-17, and (June 8, 1954): 30-37, on the Establishment; Stuart Long, " 'Scared Money' Wins an Election in Texas," *Reporter* 11 (October 21, 1954): 23, 26, on the 1954 primary; Walter Davenport, "Savior from Texas," *Collier's* 116 (August 18, 1945): 13, 79-81, on Vance Muse and the Christian Americans; Don Carleton, "McCarthyism in Houston: The George Ebey Affair," *Southwestern Historical Quarterly* 80 (October 1976): 163-176, on the Minute Women; Donald Strong, "The Rise of Negro Voting in Texas," *American Political Science Review* 62 (June 1948): 510-522.

Individuals were the focal point for other useful articles, notably on Lyndon Johnson and Allan Shivers. On Johnson, see Douglass Cater. "The Trouble in Lyndon Johnson's Back Yard," *Reporter* 13 (December 1, 1955): 31-35; Selig Harrison, "Lyndon Johnson's World," *New Republic* 142 (June 13, 1960): 15-23; Larry King, "My Hero LBJ," *Harper's* 233 (October 1966): 51-61. On Shivers and his administration, consult Ronnie Dugger, "What Corrupted Texas?" *Harper's* 214 (March 1957): 68-74, and D. B. Hardeman, "Shivers of Texas, A Tragedy in Three Acts," *Harper's* 213 (November 1956): 50-56. Coke Stevenson was portrayed usefully in Lewis Nordyke, "Calculatin' Coke," *Saturday Evening Post* 217 (October 28, 1944): 14-15, 37-41, and information on the power wielded by Herman Brown is in Hart Stilwell, "Will He Boss Texas?" *Nation* 173 (November 10, 1951): 398-400.

UNPUBLISHED SOURCES

Some three dozen theses and dissertations are efficacious on various political topics of the period. Among the best are Don Carleton, "The Minute Women and the George W. Ebey Affair: A Case Study of McCarthyism in Houston" (Master's thesis, University of Houston, 1974); Alice Cox, "The Rainey Affair: A History of the Academic Freedom Controversy at the University of Texas, 1938-1946" (Ph.D. dissertation, University of Denver, 1970); Martha Kay Dickenson, "Electoral Behavior in Texas from 1944 through 1972" (Master's thesis, North Texas State University, 1973); Neil Sapper, "A Survey of the History of the Black People of Texas" (Ph.D. dissertation, Texas Tech University, 1972); and Stanley Schneider, "The Texas Regular Party of 1944" (Master's thesis, University of Chicago, 1948).

Index

ABOUT THE AUTHOR

George Norris Green is Associate Professor of History at the University of Texas at Arlington. His articles have appeared in such
journals as *Labor History*, *Florida Historical Quarterly*, and the
Journal of Mexican-American History.